AEPA 36
Early Childhood Education
Teacher Certification Exam

By: Sharon Wynne, M.S
Southern Connecticut State University

"And, while there's no reason yet to panic, I think it's only prudent that we make preparations to panic."

XAMonline, INC.
Boston

Copyright © 2007 XAMonline, Inc.

All rights reserved. No part of the material protected by this copyright notice may be reproduced or utilized in any form or by any means, electronic or mechanical, including photocopying, recording or by any information storage and retrievable system, without written permission from the copyright holder.

To obtain permission(s) to use the material from this work for any purpose including workshops or seminars, please submit a written request to:

XAMonline, Inc.
21 Orient Ave.
Melrose, MA 02176
Toll Free 1-800-509-4128
Email: info@xamonline.com
Web www.xamonline.com
Fax: 1-781-662-9268

Library of Congress Cataloging-in-Publication Data

Wynne, Sharon A.
    Early Childhood Education 36: Teacher Certification / Sharon A. Wynne. -2nd ed.
    ISBN 978-1-58197-747-9
    1. Early Childhood Education 36.   2. Study Guides.   3. AEPA
    4. Teachers' Certification & Licensure.   5. Careers

Disclaimer:

The opinions expressed in this publication are the sole works of XAMonline and were created independently from the National Education Association, Educational Testing Service, or any State Department of Education, National Evaluation Systems or other testing affiliates.

Between the time of publication and printing, state specific standards as well as testing formats and website information may change that is not included in part or in whole within this product. Sample test questions are developed by XAMonline and reflect similar content as on real tests; however, they are not former tests. XAMonline assembles content that aligns with state standards but makes no claims nor guarantees teacher candidates a passing score. Numerical scores are determined by testing companies such as NES or ETS and then are compared with individual state standards. A passing score varies from state to state.

Printed in the United States of America

AEPA: Early Childhood Education 36
ISBN: 978-1-58197-747-9

TEACHER CERTIFICATION STUDY GUIDE

Project Manager: Sharon Wynne, MS

Project Coordinator: Victoria Anderson, MS

Content Coordinators/Authors:
Fran Stanford, MS
Victoria Anderson, MS
Christina Godard, BS
Kimberly Putney, BS
Vickie Pittard, MS
Deborah Suber. BS
Kelley Eldredge, MS

Sample test:
Shelley Wake, MS
Deborah Harbin, MS
Christina Godard, BS
Kim Putney, BS
Carol Moore, BS
Vickie Pittard, MS

Editors:
Proof reader — Janis Mercer, MS
Copy editor — Janis Mercer, MS
Sample test — Shelley Wake, MS
Production — David Aronson

Graphic Artist Jenna Hamilton

EARLY CHILDHOOD EDUCATION

Table of Contents

DOMAIN I – CHILD DEVELOPMENT AND LEARNING 1

COMPETENCY 1.0 UNDERSTAND HUMAN GROWTH AND DEVELOPMENT AND HOW TO USE THIS UNDERSTANDING TO PROMOTE LEARNING AND DEVELOPMENT IN ALL DOMAINS 1

Skill 1.1 Identifying characteristics, processes, and progressions of typical and atypical cognitive, physical, motor, social, emotional, and language/communicative development 1

Skill 1.2 Recognizing ways in which development in any domain (e.g., cognitive, social, language/communicative) may affect development and performance in other domains 6

Skill 1.3 Demonstrating knowledge of how specific factors may affect development and understanding that developmental variations among children may affect learning in given situations 7

Skill 1.4 Demonstrating knowledge of the importance of considering children's ages and developmental characteristics when designing and evaluating learning opportunities 9

Skill 1.5 Recognizing the role of play in children's development 11

Skill 1.6 Recognizing learning opportunities and environments for promoting developmental progress 13

Skill 1.7 Recognizing behaviors and factors that affect individual, family, and community health and safety 14

Skill 1.8 Demonstrating familiarity with the principles of nutrition 18

TEACHER CERTIFICATION STUDY GUIDE

COMPETENCY 2.0 **UNDERSTAND FACTORS THAT MAY AFFECT CHILDREN'S DEVELOPMENT AND LEARNING AND USE THIS KNOWLEDGE TO CREATE LEARNING ENVIRONMENTS THAT SUPPORT CHILDREN'S PROGRESS** 21

Skill 2.1 Recognizing factors (e.g., biological, social, emotional, cognitive, behavioral, physiological, gender, linguistic, environmental, familial, cultural, economic) that may affect children's development and learning 21

Skill 2.2 Recognizing the effects of the home environment (e.g., nature of the expectations of parents/guardians, degree of their involvement in a child's education) on children's learning 27

Skill 2.3 Recognizing how current and prior learning experiences outside the home (e.g., interactions with caregivers and teachers, prior successes and challenges, peer interactions) may affect children's self-concepts, perceptions, motivation, and attitudes about learning 29

Skill 2.4 Recognizing cultural, linguistic, and socioeconomic diversity and their significance for child development and learning 31

Skill 2.5 Demonstrating awareness of types of exceptionalities and their implications for learning 39

Skill 2.6 Understanding how community characteristics (e.g., socioeconomic profile, opportunities for out-of-school educational experiences, availability of community resources) may affect children 52

EARLY CHILDHOOD EDUCATION

COMPETENCY 3.0 UNDERSTAND INTEGRATED CURRICULUM DESIGN THAT REFLECTS THE WAYS CHILDREN CONSTRUCT KNOWLEDGE 54

Skill 3.1 Demonstrating understanding of the holistic nature of children's learning 54

Skill 3.2 Demonstrating knowledge of the benefits of integrated curriculum and its role in promoting children's learning 55

Skill 3.3 Knowing how to use children's interests and experiences to generate ideas and concepts for investigation and study 58

Skill 3.4 Demonstrating knowledge of how to construct integrated learning experiences that reflect learning standards across the curriculum and support children's progress 59

Skill 3.5 Applying knowledge of strategies for integrating curriculum in literacy, mathematics, science, social studies, and the arts to promote children's learning 61

TEACHER CERTIFICATION STUDY GUIDE

DOMAIN II – COMMUNICATION, LANGUAGE, AND LITERACY DEVELOPMENT 66

COMPETENCY 4.0 UNDERSTAND COMMUNICATION AND LANGUAGE DEVELOPMENT IN YOUNG CHILDREN 66

Skill 4.1 Demonstrating knowledge of characteristics, processes, and progressions in the development of receptive and expressive language and speech 66

Skill 4.2 Demonstrating knowledge of factors that influence children's communication and language development 69

Skill 4.3 Demonstrating knowledge of how children convey meaning through nonverbal and verbal communication 72

Skill 4.4 Identifying ways to promote children's communication and language development 74

Skill 4.5 Identifying ways to promote vocabulary development and the use of vocabulary knowledge in new contexts 75

Skill 4.6 Recognizing ways for developing increasingly complex language and vocabulary to express thoughts and feelings, describe experiences, interact with others, and communicate needs 77

Skill 4.7 Demonstrating knowledge of methods for motivating children to use oral language to communicate (e.g., telling and retelling stories through play, pictures, illustrations, props, and other materials) 79

EARLY CHILDHOOD EDUCATION

COMPETENCY 5.0 UNDERSTAND SECOND-LANGUAGE ACQUISITION AND HOW TO FACILITATE THE ENGLISH LANGUAGE DEVELOPMENT OF YOUNG CHILDREN WITH DIVERSE LINGUISTIC BACKGROUND 80

Skill 5.1 Recognizing characteristics, processes, and progressions of second-language acquisition in young children; analyzing factors and issues affecting the learning experiences of children with a home language other than English (e.g., age, prior experiences) 80

Skill 5.2 Identifying strategies and techniques for promoting the English language development of children with diverse linguistic backgrounds 83

Skill 5.3 Demonstrating knowledge of methods for ensuring that the home language of each child is respected and the natural propensity of all children for acquiring language is fostered 85

Skill 5.4 Understanding the importance of collaborating with families to set and accomplish language learning goals 86

Skill 5.5 Recognizing ways to create a language-rich environment that encourages all children to learn to communicate effectively 89

TEACHER CERTIFICATION STUDY GUIDE

COMPETENCY 6.0 UNDERSTAND THE DEVELOPMENT OF CONCEPTS ABOUT PRINT AND HOW TO CREATE A LEARNING ENVIRONMENT TO PROMOTE EMERGENT LITERACY 91

Skill 6.1   Recognizing characteristics, processes, and progressions of the development of concepts about print (e.g., interest in print, awareness that print carries meaning, book-handling skills, letter recognition) 91

Skill 6.2   Understanding the importance of collaborating with families to promote literacy development 92

Skill 6.3   Recognizing relationships between young children's emergent literacy and factors such as enjoyment of stories and awareness of environmental print 94

Skill 6.4   Identifying strategies and techniques for promoting children's emergent literacy and development of concepts about print 95

Skill 6.5   Recognizing methods for promoting children's interaction with print in varied and meaningful contexts 97

Skill 6.6   Recognizing the importance of and strategies for creating a print-rich environment 97

Skill 6.7   Demonstrating knowledge of strategies for encouraging children's enjoyment of and positive attitudes toward literacy 98

Skill 6.8   Demonstrating knowledge of high-quality children's literature (e.g., genres of children's literature, elements of story, equity issues) 100

TEACHER CERTIFICATION STUDY GUIDE

COMPETENCY 7.0 UNDERSTAND FOUNDATIONS OF READING DEVELOPMENT 108

Skill 7.1 Demonstrating knowledge of factors affecting children's reading development (e.g., teacher modeling, read-alouds, reading practices in the home, enjoyment of reading) 108

Skill 7.2 Recognizing strategies for promoting phonological awareness (hearing and discriminating the rhythm and sounds of speech) and phonemic awareness (manipulating the smallest units of speech) 111

Skill 7.3 Demonstrating knowledge of phonics skills (association between sounds and written letters), orthographic awareness, semantic and syntactic cueing systems, and other word identification skills (e.g., sight words, high-frequency words) 114

Skill 7.4 Identifying ways for promoting vocabulary development and the use of vocabulary knowledge in new contexts 117

Skill 7.5 Identifying appropriate strategies for promoting reading fluency 118

Skill 7.6 Demonstrating knowledge of literal, inferential, interpretive, and evaluative comprehension skills and strategies for promoting children's development of these skills 126

Skill 7.7 Recognizing strategies for facilitating comprehension before, during, and after reading (e.g., predicting, self-monitoring, questioning, rereading, engaging in dialogue, reflecting) 127

COMPETENCY 8.0 UNDERSTAND WRITING PROCESSES AND HOW TO CREATE EFFECTIVE LEARNING OPPORTUNITIES FOR PROMOTING YOUNG CHILDREN'S WRITING SKILLS 132

Skill 8.1 Recognizing the characteristics, processes, and progressions of writing development 132

Skill 8.2 Analyzing factors that affect young children's development of writing skills (e.g., access to writing materials, opportunities to write, fine-motor development) 139

Skill 8.3 Demonstrating knowledge of strategies for helping children develop and apply writing skills and for promoting children's interest and engagement in writing for different purposes and audiences 142

Skill 8.4 Recognizing the reciprocal relationships between children's writing and reading experiences 144

Skill 8.5 Understanding factors affecting spelling development (e.g., visual processing, recognizing patterns of speech sounds, word knowledge) 145

Skill 8.6 Demonstrating knowledge of methods for supporting children at each stage of writing development... 152

TEACHER CERTIFICATION STUDY GUIDE

DOMAIN III – LEARNING IN THE CONTENT AREAS 155

COMPETENCY 9.0 UNDERSTAND MATHEMATICS CONCEPTS AND SKILLS 155

Skill 9.1　Recognizing, interpreting, and using mathematical terminology, symbols, and representations (e.g., cardinal and ordinal numbers; properties of real numbers; base number systems; fractions, decimals, and percents) 155

Skill 9.2　Demonstrating knowledge of number sense and numerical operations 165

Skill 9.3　Demonstrating understanding of fundamental concepts of algebra and geometry 172

Skill 9.4　Demonstrating understanding of patterns, relations, and functions (e.g., recognizing and analyzing patterns in numbers, shapes, and data; the translation of problem-solving situations into expressions and equations involving variables and unknowns) 177

Skill 9.5　Recognizing standard and nonstandard measurement instruments and units 179

Skill 9.6　Demonstrating knowledge of procedures for solving problems involving length, area, angles, volume, mass, and temperature 183

Skill 9.7　Identifying methods for collection, organization, and analysis of data 188

Skill 9.8　Applying mathematical logic and reasoning to analyze and solve problems in real-world contexts 191

EARLY CHILDHOOD EDUCATION　　x

TEACHER CERTIFICATION STUDY GUIDE

COMPETENCY 10.0	**UNDERSTAND HOW TO FACILITATE LEARNING FOR YOUNG CHILDREN IN THE AREA OF MATHEMATICS**	**194**
Skill 10.1	Recognizing characteristics, processes, and progressions in children's mathematical development, including intuitive and emergent numeracy	194
Skill 10.2	Demonstrating knowledge of factors that affect young children's mathematical development	195
Skill 10.3	Understanding the importance of collaborating with families to promote children's mathematical development	196
Skill 10.4	Recognizing the roles of exploration, active engagement, inquiry, and questioning in building knowledge, language, and concepts related to mathematics	197
Skill 10.5	Demonstrating knowledge of learning experiences for promoting understanding of mathematics concepts and acquisition of mathematics skills	200
Skill 10.6	Demonstrating knowledge of strategies for encouraging children to develop positive attitudes toward mathematics	202
Skill 10.7	Demonstrating knowledge of strategies for encouraging the use of mathematical concepts and skills in everyday life	203

COMPETENCY 11.0	UNDERSTAND SCIENCE CONTENT AND INQUIRY PROCESSES AND HOW TO FACILITATE SCIENCE LEARNING FOR YOUNG CHILDREN 205
Skill 11.1	Demonstrating knowledge of basic concepts in physical, life, and earth science 205
Skill 11.2	Applying knowledge of scientific processes (e.g., observing, hypothesizing, experimenting) 218
Skill 11.3	Recognizing the roles of exploration, active engagement, inquiry, and questioning in building knowledge, language, and concepts related to science 219
Skill 11.4	Demonstrating knowledge of learning experiences for promoting understanding of science concepts and acquisition of science skills 222
Skill 11.5	Demonstrating knowledge of strategies for encouraging children to develop positive attitudes toward science 223
Skill 11.6	Demonstrating knowledge of strategies for encouraging the use of science concepts and skills in everyday life 224

TEACHER CERTIFICATION STUDY GUIDE

COMPETENCY 12.0 UNDERSTAND SOCIAL STUDIES CONTENT AND SKILLS AND HOW TO FACILITATE SOCIAL STUDIES LEARNING 225

Skill 12.1 Demonstrating knowledge of basic concepts in geography, history, civics, and economics 225

Skill 12.2 Demonstrating knowledge of social studies skills (e.g., mapping, research) 239

Skill 12.3 Recognizing the roles of exploration, active engagement, inquiry, and questioning in building knowledge, language, and concepts related to social studies 247

Skill 12.4 Demonstrating knowledge of learning experiences for promoting understanding of social studies concepts and acquisition of social studies skills 249

Skill 12.5 Demonstrating knowledge of strategies for encouraging children to develop positive attitudes toward social studies 250

Skill 12.6 Identifying strategies for using everyday and current events to promote understanding of social studies concepts 252

Skill 12.7 Demonstrating knowledge of how to promote children's use of social studies skills (e.g., conflict resolution, community building) in a variety of settings 255

COMPETENCY 13.0 UNDERSTAND THE VISUAL AND PERFORMING ARTS AND HOW TO FACILITATE YOUNG CHILDREN'S LEARNING IN AND APPRECIATION OF THE ARTS 257

Skill 13.1 Demonstrating knowledge of basic concepts and skills (e.g., creating, appreciating) in visual arts, music, movement, and drama 257

Skill 13.2 Recognizing the roles of exploration, active engagement, inquiry, and questioning in building knowledge, language, and concepts related to the arts 261

Skill 13.3 Demonstrating knowledge of learning experiences for promoting arts concepts and skills 264

Skill 13.4 Demonstrating knowledge of strategies for supporting children's creativity and for encouraging children to develop positive attitudes toward the arts 266

Skill 13.5 Demonstrating knowledge of activities and resources for promoting aesthetic appreciation 268

Skill 13.6 Recognizing the role of the arts in promoting self expression, creative thinking, and a healthy self-concept 269

Skill 13.7 Recognizing the role of the arts as a way for children to express and understand knowledge and ideas in other curricular areas 269

AEPA Pre test 271

Pre test Answer Key 294

Pre Test Rigor Table 295

Pre Test Answer key Rationale 296

AEPA Post Test 339

Post Test Answer Key 362

Post Test Rigor Table 363

Post Test Answer Key Rationale 364

TEACHER CERTIFICATION STUDY GUIDE

Great Study and Testing Tips!

What to study in order to prepare for the subject assessments is the focus of this study guide but equally important is *how* you study.

You can increase your chances of truly mastering the information by taking some simple, but effective, steps.

Study Tips:

1. <u>Some foods aid the learning process</u>. Foods such as milk, nuts, seeds, rice, and oats help your study efforts by releasing natural memory enhancers called CCKs (*cholecystokinin*) composed of *tryptophan*, *choline*, and *phenylalanine*. All of these chemicals enhance the neurotransmitters associated with memory. Before studying, try a light, protein-rich meal of eggs, turkey, and fish. All of these foods release the memory-enhancing chemicals. The better the connections, the more you comprehend.

Likewise, before you take a test, stick to a light snack of energy boosting and relaxing foods. A glass of milk, a piece of fruit, or some peanuts all release various memory-boosting chemicals and help you to relax and focus on the subject at hand.

2. <u>Learn to take great notes</u>. A by-product of our modern culture is that we have grown accustomed to getting our information in short doses (i.e. TV news sound bites or *USA Today*-style newspaper articles.)

Consequently, we've subconsciously trained ourselves to assimilate information better in <u>neat little packages</u>. If your notes are scrawled all over the paper, it fragments the flow of the information. Strive for clarity. Newspapers use a standard format to achieve clarity. Your notes can be much clearer through use of proper formatting. A very effective format is called the *"Cornell Method."*

> Take a sheet of loose-leaf lined notebook paper and draw a line all the way down the paper about 1-2" from the left-hand edge.

Draw another line across the width of the paper about 1-2" up from the bottom. Repeat this process on the reverse side of the page.

Look at the highly effective result. You have ample room for notes, a left-hand margin for special emphasis items or inserting supplementary data from the textbook, a large area at the bottom for a brief summary, and a little rectangular space for just about anything you want.

3. Get the concept then the details. Too often we focus on the details and don't gather an understanding of the concept. However, if you simply memorize only dates, places, or names, you may well miss the whole point of the subject.

A key way to understand things is to put them in your own words. If you are working from a textbook, automatically summarize each paragraph in your mind. If you are outlining text, don't simply copy the author's words.

Rephrase them in your own words. You remember your own thoughts and words much better than someone else's, and subconsciously tend to associate the important details to the core concepts.

4. Ask Why? Pull apart written material paragraph by paragraph and don't forget the captions under the illustrations.

Example: If the heading is "Stream Erosion," flip it around to read, "Why do streams erode?" Then answer the questions.

If you train your mind to think in a series of questions and answers, not only will you learn more, but it also helps to lessen the test anxiety because you are used to answering questions.

5. Read for reinforcement and future needs. Even if you only have ten minutes, put your notes or a book in your hand. Your mind is similar to a computer; you have to input data in order to have it processed. *By reading, you are creating the neural connections for future retrieval.* The more times you read something, the more you reinforce the learning of ideas.

Even if you don't fully understand something on the first pass, *your mind stores much of the material for later recall.*

6. Relax to learn so go into exile. Our bodies respond to an inner clock called biorhythms. Burning the midnight oil works well for some people, but not everyone.

If possible, set aside a particular place to study that is free of distractions. Shut off the television, cell phone, and pager and exile your friends and family during your study period.

If you really are bothered by silence, try background music. Light classical music at a low volume has been shown to aid in concentration over other types. Music that evokes pleasant emotions without lyrics is highly suggested. Try just about anything by Mozart. It relaxes you.

7. **Use arrows not highlighters**. At best, it's difficult to read a page full of yellow, pink, blue, and green streaks. Try staring at a neon sign for a while and you'll soon see that the horde of colors obscure the message.

A quick note, a brief dash of color, an underline, and an arrow pointing to a particular passage is much clearer than a horde of highlighted words.

8. **Budget your study time**. Although you shouldn't ignore any of the material, *allocate your available study time in the same ratio that topics may appear on the test.*

TEACHER CERTIFICATION STUDY GUIDE

Testing Tips:

1. Get smart, play dumb. **Don't read anything into the question.** Don't make an assumption that the test writer is looking for something else than what is asked. Stick to the question as written and don't read extra things into it.

2. Read the question and all the choices *twice* before answering the question. You may miss something by not carefully reading, and then re-reading, both the question and the answers.

If you really don't have a clue as to the right answer, leave it blank on the first time through. Go on to the other questions, as they may provide a clue as to how to answer the skipped questions.

If later on, you still can't answer the skipped ones . . . ***Guess.*** The only penalty for guessing is that you *might* get it wrong. Only one thing is certain; if you don't put anything down, you will get it wrong!

3. Turn the question into a statement. Look at the way the questions are worded. The syntax of the question usually provides a clue. Does it seem more familiar as a statement rather than as a question? Does it sound strange?

By turning a question into a statement, you may be able to spot if an answer sounds right, and it may also trigger memories of material you have read.

4. Look for hidden clues. It's actually very difficult to compose multiple-foil (choice) questions without giving away part of the answer in the options presented.

In most multiple-choice questions you can often readily eliminate one or two of the potential answers. This leaves you with only two real possibilities, and automatically your odds go to fifty-fifty for very little work.

5. Trust your instincts. For every fact that you have read, you subconsciously retain something of that knowledge. On questions that you aren't really certain about, go with your basic instincts. **Your first impression on how to answer a question is usually correct.**

6. Mark your answers directly on the test booklet. Don't bother trying to fill in the optical scan sheet on the first pass through the test.

Just be very careful not to miss-mark your answers when you eventually transcribe them to the scan sheet.

7. Watch the clock! You have a set amount of time to answer the questions. Don't get bogged down trying to answer a single question at the expense of 10 questions you can more readily answer.

DOMAIN I. CHILD DEVELOPMENT AND LEARNING

Competency 001 UNDERSTAND HUMAN GROWTH AND DEVELOPMENT AND HOW TO USE THIS UNDERSTANDING TO PROMOTE LEARNING AND DEVELOPMENT IN ALL DOMAINS

Skill 1.1 Identifying characteristics, processes, and progressions of typical and atypical cognitive, physical, motor, social, emotional, and language/communicative development

The teacher of students in early childhood should have a broad knowledge and understanding of the phases of development that typically occur during this stage of life. The teacher must also be aware of how receptive children are to specific methods of instruction and learning during each period of development. A significant premise in the study of child development holds that all domains of development (physical, social, and academic) are integrated. Development in each dimension is influenced by and influences the others. Equally important to the teacher's understanding of the process is the knowledge that developmental advances within the domains occur neither simultaneously nor parallel to one another, necessarily.

Physical Development

It is important for the teacher to be aware of the physical stages of development and how changes to the child's physical attributes (which include internal developments, increased muscle capacity, improved coordination and other attributes as well as obvious growth) affect the child's ability to learn. Factors determined by the physical stage of development include: the ability to sit and attend, the need for activity, the relationship between physical coordination and self-esteem, and the degree to which physical involvement in an activity (as opposed to being able to understand an abstract concept) affects learning and the child's sense of achievement.

By the time children reach school age there are certain physical activities they should be able to do. Careful observation of children when they first start school with regard to these activities should alert the teacher that there may be a problem with the child's physical development. These include:
- Being able to ride a tricycle
- Throwing, catching and holding a ball
- Being able to dress oneself, but still needing help with zippers and buttons
- Being able to walk on tiptoe
- Being able to use scissors to cut paper
- Being active at play outdoors and in the classroom

In addition, children with physical disabilities are not able to move as quickly as other children of the same age.

Cognitive (Academic) Development

Children go through patterns of learning beginning with pre-operational thought processes and move to concrete operational thoughts. Eventually, they begin to acquire the intellectual ability to contemplate and solve problems independently, when they mature enough to manipulate objects symbolically. Students in early childhood can use symbols such as words and numbers to represent objects and relations, but they need concrete reference points. Successful acquisition of the skills taught in early childhood, through the fourth grade, will progressively prepare the student for more advanced problem solving and abstract thinking in the later grades. The content of curriculum for younger students must be relevant for their stage of development (accessible and comprised of acquirable skills), engaging, and meaningful to the students.

It is important for teachers of the early childhood grades to be aware of the warning signs of cognitive delay in children, although most of these are apparent before the children come to school. In order for a child to be diagnosed as having an impairment in cognitive development, there must be a deficiency in at least two of the following:
- Speech and communication
- Self-care
- Social and Interpersonal skills
- Functional academic skills for the grade level

Social Development

Children progress through a variety of social stages beginning with an awareness of self and self-concern. They soon develop an awareness of peers, but demonstrate a lack of concern for their presence. For a time, young children engage in "parallel" activities, playing alongside their peers without directly interacting with one another.

During the primary years, children develop an intense interest in peers. They establish productive, positive, social and working relationships with one another. This area of social growth will continue to increase in significance throughout the child's academic career. The foundation for the students' successful development in this area is established through the efforts of the classroom teacher to plan and develop positive peer group relationships and to provide opportunities and support for cooperative small group projects that not only develop cognitive ability, but promote peer interaction. The ability to work and relate effectively with peers contributes greatly to the child's sense of competence. In order to develop this sense of competence, children need to be successful in acquiring the information base and social skill sets which promote cooperative effort to achieve academic and social objectives.

High expectations for student achievement, which are age-appropriate and focused, provide the foundation for a teacher's positive relationship with young students and are consistent with effective instructional strategies. It is equally important to determine what is appropriate for specific individuals in the classroom, and approach classroom groups and individual students with an understanding and respect for their emerging capabilities. Those who study childhood development recognize that young students grow and mature in common, recognizable patterns, but at different rates, which cannot be effectively accelerated. This can result in variance in the academic performance of different children in the same classroom. With the establishment of inclusion as a standard in the classroom, it is necessary for all teachers to understand that variation in development among the student population is another aspect of diversity within the classroom. This has implications for the ways in which instruction is planned and delivered and the ways in which students learn and are evaluated.

Children may exhibit behaviors that alert the teacher to a problem involving a delay in social development. Before children enter school, they may not be in the presence of children their own age for long periods of time and so these behaviors may not be noticed. Children who fight with the other children or hit them for no reason show signs of not having the proper social skills for the age or grade level. This may be the result of being the only child or one that is pampered at home. It can also be a warning sign that the child is emulating the behavior of the parents.

> **For more information on the identification of typical and atypical development in early childhood and intervention strategies:**
>
> www.ldao.ca/documents/LearningDisabilities**andYoungChildren**.pdf

Language Development

Learning approach
Early theories of language development were formulated from learning theory research. The assumption was that language development evolved from learning the rules of language structures and applying them through imitation and reinforcement. This approach also assumed that language, cognitive, and social developments were independent of each other. Thus, children were expected to learn language from patterning after adults who spoke and wrote Standard English. No allowance was made for communication through child jargon, idiomatic expressions, or grammatical and mechanical errors resulting from too strict adherence to the rules of inflection (childs instead of children) or conjugation (runned instead of ran). No association was made between physical and operational development and language mastery.

Linguistic approach
Studies spearheaded by Noam Chomsky in the 1950s formulated the theory that language ability is innate and develops through natural human maturation as environmental stimuli trigger acquisition of syntactical structures appropriate to each exposure level. The assumption of a hierarchy of syntax downplayed the significance of semantics. Because of the complexity of syntax and the relative speed with which children acquire language, linguists attributed language development to biological rather than cognitive or social influences.

Cognitive approach
Researchers in the 1970s proposed that language knowledge derives from both syntactic and semantic structures. Drawing on the studies of Piaget and other cognitive learning theorists, supporters of the cognitive approach maintained that children acquire knowledge of linguistic structures after they have acquired the cognitive structures necessary to process language. For example, joining words for specific meaning necessitates sensory motor intelligence. The child must be able to coordinate movement and recognize objects before being able to identify words that name the objects or word groups to describe the actions performed with those objects. Children must have developed the mental abilities for organizing concepts as well as concrete operations, predicting outcomes, and theorizing before they can assimilate and verbalize complex sentence structures, choose vocabulary for particular nuances of meaning, and examine semantic structures for tone and manipulative effect.

Socio-cognitive approach
Other theorists in the 1970s proposed that language development results from sociolinguistic competence. Language, cognitive, and social knowledge are interactive elements of total human development. Emphasis on verbal communication as the medium for language expression resulted in the inclusion of speech activities in most language arts curricula.

Unlike previous approaches, the socio-cognitive allowed that determining the appropriateness of language in given situations for specific listeners is as important as understanding semantic and syntactic structures. By engaging in conversation, children at all stages of development have opportunities to test their language skills, receive feedback, and make modifications. As a social activity, conversation is as structured by social order as grammar is structured by the rules of syntax. Conversation satisfies the learner's need to be heard and understood and to influence others. Thus, his choices of vocabulary, tone, and content are dictated by his ability to assess the language knowledge of his listeners. He is constantly applying his cognitive skills to using language in a social interaction. If the capacity to acquire language is inborn, without an environment in which to practice language, a child would not pass beyond grunts and gestures as did primitive man.

Of course, the varying degrees of environmental stimuli to which children are exposed at all age levels create a slower or faster development of language. Some children are prepared to articulate concepts and recognize symbolism by the time they enter fifth grade because they have been exposed to challenging reading and conversations with well-spoken adults at home or in their social groups. Others are still trying to master the sight recognition skills and are not yet ready to combine words in complex patterns.

Skill 1.2   Recognizing ways in which development in any domain (e.g., cognitive, social, language/communicative) may affect development and performance in other domains

Child development does not occur in a vacuum. Each element of child development impacts the other elements. For example, as cognitive development progresses, social development often follows. The reason for this is that all areas of development are fairly inter-related. People laugh about how adolescents often develop slower in the physical domain than they do in the social or cognitive domain (e.g., they may think like teenagers, but they still look like children).. However, the truth is that even in such cases, physical development is under progress—just not as evident on the surface. As children develop physically, they develop the dexterity to demonstrate cognitive development, such as writing something on a piece of paper (in this case, this is cognitive development that only can be demonstrated by physical development). Or, as they develop emotionally, they learn to be more sensitive to others and therefore enhance social development.

What does this mean for teachers? The concept of latent development is particularly important. While teachers may not see some aspects of development present in their students, other areas of development may give clues as to a child's current or near-future capabilities. For example, as students' linguistic development increases, observable ability may not be present (i.e., a student may know a word, but cannot quite use it yet). As the student develops emotionally and socially, the ability to use more advanced words and sentence structures develops because the student will have a greater need to communicate in an expressive way.

In general, by understanding that developmental domains are not exclusive, teachers can identify current needs of students better, and they can plan for future instructional activities meant to assist students as they develop into adults.

Skill 1.3 Demonstrating knowledge of how specific factors may affect development and understanding that developmental variations among children may affect learning in given situations

Beginning teachers must be cognizant of the profound effect that they will have as an authority figure, instructor and behavior model for students in the early formative years. At this stage of life, children are not only continually developing physically, emotionally and intellectually, acquiring new skills in all of these areas. They are also beginning to retain basic concepts, modes of thinking and behavioral models, which will continue to develop and will serve them—for better or for worse—throughout life.

The influences on all aspects of a child's development come from the home and family and the community, as well as the school. However, the most directed, purposeful and productive time in the average child's day is the time spent in the classroom and the school environment, generally. This is why teachers plan, schedule, monitor and measure to such high standards. The adult into whom the child will develop is (to a considerable extent) the product of what the educational system provides. That is why—at various stages of the process—we incorporate instruction on life skills, independent thinking, social values and social interaction, at-risk behaviors, and many other non-traditional topics intended to equip our students to make appropriate choices and improve their lives, now and in the future.

For the beginning teacher, this process will often start with affirming the teacher's high expectations for the success of each student and the teacher's confidence in each student's ability to perform up to this expectation. Unfortunately, in some school systems, there are very high expectations placed on certain students and little expectation placed on others. Often, the result is predictable: you get exactly what you expect to get and you seldom get more out of a situation or person than you are willing to put in. A teacher is expected to provide the same standards of excellence in education for all students. This standard cannot be upheld or met unless the teacher has (and conveys) high expectations for all students.

Considerable research has been done, over several decades, regarding student performance. Time and again, a direct correlation has been demonstrated between the teacher's expectations for a particular student and that student's academic performance. This may be unintended and subtle, but the effects are manifest and measurable.

Another early issue for the beginning teacher to address is discipline. Appropriate discipline from authority will become acceptable to the child and certain values may be instilled which will promote the eventual development of self-discipline within the individual. While early childhood and elementary students are generally more easily controlled—often appearing better behaved and more responsive to authority—than older students, they still have a tendency to socialize and play just for the sake of play. This can quickly allow the classroom situation to deteriorate, replacing the learning environment with chaos. When the teacher is implementing a well-structured plan, with measurable milestones and specific objectives, it may be necessary to quickly identify and redirect conversation and activity that is not relevant or supportive of the instructional objectives. A teacher may allow younger students a greater degree of latitude, but their longitude needs to be restricted.

Allowing for the differing needs of younger students does not mean abandoning classroom discipline and organized instruction. At this level, students need the reassurance of structure, organization and discipline. If the appropriate attitudes and responses to structure and discipline are internalized at an early age, they will serve the students throughout their educational experience and provide a solid foundation upon which the individual can develop the self-discipline necessary in later life. The teacher who can instill these values in a young student will have earned the gratitude and respect of all the teachers who instruct this student in the future.

The time to implement organization and classroom discipline is not at a moment of crisis or chaos. This is an issue that will significantly affect the teacher's ability to teach and the student's ability to learn, day after day. A good deal of thought and preparation, on the part of the classroom teacher, should be devoted to this aspect of the educational experience. There are volumes of text available to the novice teacher, providing criteria and examples for structuring an organized, disciplined, classroom environment. Specific recommendations for discipline and organization in normal and in unusual classroom situations are available from experienced teachers in journals and on the Internet. Guidelines and structure may be made flexible to allow for certain contingencies, but they must be put into practice with specific limits provided In addition, the students must be made fully aware of the structure, the guidelines, their responsibilities and the consequences of their actions should they fail to observe these guidelines.

For more information on how developmental variations affect learning, **SEE** Skill 1.4

Skill 1.4   Demonstrating knowledge of the importance of considering children's ages and developmental characteristics when designing and evaluating learning opportunities

Child Development

Jean Piaget, a European scientist who died in the late 20th Century, developed many theories about the way humans learn. The most famous of these theories deals with the stages of the development of human minds. The first stage is the "sensory-motor" stage that lasts until a child is in the toddler years. In this stage, children begin to understand their senses.

The next stage, called the "pre-operational" stage, is where children begin to understand symbols. For example, as they learn language, they begin to realize that words are symbols of thoughts, actions, items, and other elements in the world. This stage lasts into early elementary school.

The third stage is referred to as the "concrete operations" stage. This lasts until late elementary school. In this stage, children go one step beyond learning what a symbol is. They learn how to manipulate symbols, objects, and other elements. A common example of this stage is the displacement of water. In this stage, they can reason that a wide and short cup of water poured into a tall and thin cup of water can actually have the same amount of water.

The next stage is called the "formal operations" stage. It usually starts in adolescence or early teen years and it continues on into adulthood. During this stage critical thinking, hypothesis, systematic organization of knowledge, etc. develops.

Generally, when we say that children move from a stage of concrete thinking to logical and abstract thinking, we mean that they are moving from the "pre-operational" and "concrete" stage TO the "formal operations" stage. But as anyone who spends time with children knows, there are many bumps in the way to a person's ability to be a strong critical thinker. Just because children move into a particular stage does not mean that they will be able to complete function at the specified level. For example, adolescents may be able to think critically, but they need plenty of instruction and assistance to do so at an adequate level. This does not necessarily mean that critical thinking skills should be taught out of context. Rather, through all lessons, teachers should work to instill components that help develop the thinking of children.

Developmental Variations and Learning

Effective teachers of reading should provide scaffolded instruction in comprehension strategies (predicting, thinking aloud, attending to text structure, constructing visual representations, generating questions and summarizing). Students are better able to comprehend texts and perform research when they are taught to make connections between what they know and what they are reading.

> Read more about scaffolded instruction:
>
> http://www.vtaide.com/png/ERIC/Scaffolding.htm

It is important for teachers to consider students' development and readiness when making instructional decisions. If an educational program is child-centered, then it will surely address the developmental abilities and needs of the students because it will take its cues from students' interests, concerns, and questions. Making an educational program child-centered involves building on the natural curiosity children bring to school, and asking them what they want to learn.

Teachers help students to identify their own questions, puzzles, and goals, and then structure widening circles of experience and investigation of those topics for them. Teachers manage to infuse all the skills, knowledge, and concepts that society mandates into a child-driven curriculum. This does not involve passive teachers who respond only to students' explicit cues. Teachers also draw on their understanding of children's developmental characteristic needs and enthusiasms to design experiences that lead them into areas they might not otherwise choose, but that they do enjoy and engage them. Teachers also bring their own interests and enthusiasms into the classroom to share and act as a motivational means of guiding children.

It is the role of the teacher to ensure that the activities and lessons they plan for the delivery of the curriculum are appropriate for the age and developmental characteristics of the students. The language used in class should be such that the students can understand it at their level and the activities should be ones the students can complete without being expected to use skills beyond their scope of understanding. By using a variety of instructional techniques and assessments, teachers are able to observe children as they complete the assigned tasks and determine whether the child is having difficulty with them, whether the tasks are appropriate for the child or whether they are too easy. Students should also have frequent opportunities to practice and refine new learning in order to further develop their skills.

When teachers assign activities that require higher-order thinking skills they are encouraging the young children to develop their thoughts in order to communicate with the teacher and with each other in a better way.

Skill 1.5   Recognizing the role of play in children's development

Too often, recess and play is considered peripheral or unimportant to a child's development. It's sometimes seen as a way to allow kids to just get physical energy out or a "tradition" of childhood. The truth is, though, that play is very important to human development. First, an obvious point, in this country, even though we are very industrious, we believe strongly that all individuals deserve time to relax and enjoy the "fruits of our labors."

But even more importantly, for the full development of children (who will soon be active citizens of our democracy, parents, spouses, friends, colleagues, and neighbors), play is an activity that helps teach basic values such as sharing and cooperation. It also teaches that taking care of oneself (as opposed to constantly working) is good for human beings and further creates a more enjoyable society.

The stages of play development do indeed move from solitary (particularly in infancy stages) to cooperative (in early childhood), but even in early childhood, children should be able to play on their own and entertain themselves from time to time. Children who do not know what to do with themselves when they are bored should be encouraged to think about particular activities that might be of interest.

But it is also extremely important that children play with peers. While the emerging stages of cooperative play may be awkward (as children will at first not want to share toys, for example), with some guidance and experience, children will learn how to be good peers and friends.

Play—both cooperative and solitary—helps to develop very important attributes in children. For example, children learn and develop personal interests and practice particular skills. The play that children engage in may even develop future professional interests.

Finally, playing with objects helps to develop motor skills. The objects that children play with should be varied and age appropriate. For example, playing with a doll can actually help to develop hand-eye coordination. Sports, for both boys and girls, can be equally valuable. Parents and teachers, though, need to remember that sports at young ages should only be for the purpose of development of interests and motor skills—not competition. Many children will learn that they do not enjoy sports, and parents and teachers should be respectful of these decisions.

In general, play is an appropriate place of children to learn many things about themselves, their world, and their interests. Children should be encouraged to participate in different types of play, and they should be watched over as they encounter new types of play.

For information on the stages of play development and appropriate toys: http://www.fisher-price.com/us/playstages/	Read About the stages of play development in children with delays: http://www.braintraining.com/PlayStages.htm

Skill 1.6 Recognizing learning opportunities and environments for promoting developmental progress

The effective teacher is aware of students' individual learning styles and human growth and development theory and applies these principles in the selection and implementation of appropriate instructional activities. With regards to the identification and implementation of appropriate learning activities, effective teachers select and implement instructional activities consistent with principles of human growth and development theory.

Learning activities selected for younger students (below age eight) should focus on short time frames in highly simplified form. The nature of the activity and the content in which the activity is presented affects the approach that the students will take in processing the information. Younger children tend to process information at a slower rate than older children (age eight and older).

It is important for teachers to create learning environments that enable children to feel safe and at the same time encourage them to take risks with their learning. Children who are fearful when they first enter school do need time to get to know the teacher and the other students. In order for this to take place, it is important for the teacher to create a classroom routine. Then children know what will be happening next and won't be surprised or taken off guard.

In classrooms where the activities are closely aligned with the state standards and objectives, teachers can easily determine when students are making progress or when they are experiencing developmental delays. Formative assessment during each class will give the teacher the information needed to make an informed decision about whether or not another professional within or outside the school needs to be called in.

Information about any delays that the teacher notices should also be relayed to the parents. Sometimes, parents may not be permitting the child to do an activity at home for fear of getting hurt without realizing that this is a component of the school program. An example of this could be allowing the child to use scissors for cutting paper. Many parents don't want their children handling scissors for fear they may cut themselves. They may not realize that the scissors used in school are safety oriented. Once the teacher explains the observations, parents are usually more than willing to work with the school to help their children at home.

Skill 1.7   Recognizing behaviors and factors that affect individual, family, and community health and safety

Factors that Affect Family Health

The primary factors that affect family health include environmental conditions such as pollution and proximity to industrial areas, smoking and drinking habits of family members, economic conditions that affect nutritional factors, and general levels of education among family members as related to an understanding of healthy living habits.

The relative levels of pollution in the family's area can significantly contribute to family health. For example, proximity to industrial areas, which may be releasing carcinogenic emissions, can be dangerous. Similarly, a smoking habit within the home environment is highly detrimental, as it will negatively affect the respiratory and circulatory systems of all members of the household. A drinking habit can also pose a risk both to the individual and to those in proximity to him or her.

Economic conditions can affect family health in that lower economic means can lead to neglect of some nutritional factors (which are critical to healthy living and proper physical and cognitive development). Similarly, families with two working parents may not have as much time to spend with children to monitor their eating habits. Education levels among family members as related to an understanding of healthy living habits are also significant. Even with all of the required financial means, parents/caregivers may not have the requisite knowledge to direct them to habits for healthy living.

Strategies for Promoting Environmental Health

Environmental health demonstrates concern about environmental issues. Examples of environmental issues include outdoor air pollution, indoor air pollution, noise pollution, water contamination, radiation exposure, disposal of hazardous wastes, and recycling.

Air pollution is a primary environmental health hazard. Various air pollutants are highly dangerous. Examples of air pollutants include motor vehicle emissions such as carbon monoxide, sulfur oxide, nitrogen oxide, hydrocarbons, and airborne lead. The Clean Air Act of 1979 reduced some motor vehicle emissions; however, the levels remain dangerously high due to large numbers of vehicles on the road, long commutes, and oversized vehicles. Carpooling and the use of smaller vehicles could significantly decrease the amount of motor vehicle emissions.

> **Time Line of the Clean Air Act:**
>
> http://www.environmentaldefense.org/documents/2695_cleanairact.htm

Another type of pollution is indoor air pollution. The most dangerous types of indoor pollution are tobacco smoke, carbon monoxide, asbestos, radon, and lead. To prevent indoor air pollution, avoid tobacco smoking indoors and ensure that indoor areas have adequate ventilation with fresh outdoor air. Remove the sources of any pollutants. Keep appliances and heating systems in good condition and follow the regular maintenance schedule. Homes should have at least one carbon monoxide detector located near the sleeping area. Check homes for asbestos, lead, and radon. When detected, safely remove them.

Noise is an additional environmental concern. To protect the ears, keep headphones at a low level, sit at a safe distance from the speakers at concerts, and wear earplugs when exposed to loud sounds.

Yet another major environmental hazard is water pollution. Water pollution can cause dysentery (a severe intestinal infection), increases in hypertension (due to increased sodium content), and chemical poisoning (such as mercury poisoning). The Safe Water Drinking Act passed in 1974 requires water treatment facilities to notify consumers when they violate safe drinking water requirements. However, this regulation is not strictly enforced. To ensure safe drinking water, consumers should not assume that their facility is following the regulations. They should contact their individual facility to determine the contaminant levels in the drinking water. Additionally, consumers should avoid dumping garbage or chemicals in lakes, rivers, on the ground, or down the drain. Instead, take chemicals to a hazardous waste disposal center. Finally, everyone should practice water conservation. Methods of water conservation include installing a low-flow showerhead, running the dishwasher and washing machine only when completely full, turning off the water while brushing teeth and washing hands, taking quick showers, and watering the lawn at the coolest time of the day. Radiation exposure is also an environmental concern. Application of a thirty SPF sunscreen every hour and the use of ultraviolet-ray-blocking sunglasses can minimize the effects of ultraviolet radiation exposure.

> **Information about the Safe Water Drinking Act**:
>
> http://www.mvwa.us/Water%20Quality/Safe%20Water%20Drinking%20Act.htm

One final environmental concern is the proper disposal of hazardous wastes. Consumers should always read and follow label information regarding the proper disposal of household products. Recycling is the process of breaking down products to their fundamental elements for use in another product. Recycling can help reduce air, water, and soil contaminants. Consumers should buy recycled products and recycle their own household materials. Additionally, consumers should avoid one-use products, especially disposable products made of plastic, paper, and foam.

Technology

The technology market is rapidly changing. Consumers are progressively turning to technology for a healthier life. Consumer-focused healthcare information technology helps patients handle the significant demands of healthcare management.

Healthcare information technology is a term describing the broad digital resources that are available to promote community health and proper health care for consumers. Healthcare information technology empowers patients to direct their healthcare and to advocate for themselves and their families as they use health care services. Healthcare information technology enables consumers, patients, and informal caregivers to gather facts, make choices, communicate with healthcare providers, control chronic disease, and participate in other health-related activities. Consumers should take caution when reviewing healthcare information on the Internet, as much information is invalid. Consumers need to be educated in regards to website evaluation before using information from the Internet in making healthcare decisions.

Healthcare information technology functions in numerous ways. The functions include providing general health information, supporting behavior change, providing tools to self-manage health, providing access to online groups, providing decision-making assistance, aiding in disease control, and providing access to healthcare tools. Information technology has the power to bring patients into full partnership with their healthcare providers. Specifically, instead of waiting for a return phone call, patients can simply e-mail the physician regarding his or her non-urgent condition. Healthcare providers can then respond to patient e-mails.

Many healthcare facilities are also moving towards complying with the executive order mandating electronic personal healthcare records. At some point in the near future, all healthcare facilities will link personal healthcare records. Consumers can also utilize computerized re-ordering systems for prescription refills. Many pharmacies and physicians are also moving towards electronic prescriptions. The increasingly widespread use of electronic personal healthcare records and computerized prescriptions will decrease the number of medical errors.

Peer Pressure

Peer pressure can cause children to make decisions, both positive and negative. For example, a child that interacts with other children that practice poor health behaviors, such as drug use, are more likely to mimic such behaviors. On the other hand, interacting with children that are committed to exercise may encourage a previously inactive child to become physically active.

Media

Media-based expectations influence the development of self-concept by setting media-based role models as the benchmarks against which students will measure their traits. Self-concept is a set of statements describing the child's own cognitive, physical, emotional, and social self-assessment. These statements will usually tend to be fairly objective ("good at baseball" or "has red hair"), media-based expectations can change the statements to be measurements against role models ("athletic like this actor" or "tall like that pop star").

Skill 1.8 Demonstrating familiarity with the principles of nutrition

Young children need ample time to exercise to help them develop as they should. Along with providing time in the classroom for children to move about, they should also experience dance and exercises as part of the Physical Education classes. During these classes, they will be exposed to rules of age appropriate sports and safety when running about. Outside activities with the children playing on the playground and engaging in physical exercise also gives them the fresh air that they need instead of keeping all play indoors.

It is important for children to get at least 10 hours of sleep a night. Children who are sleepy in school may not be getting the sleep they need and this should be a cause of concern for the teacher. A meeting may need to be called with the parents who do not have a regular bedtime for their children explaining to them that during sleep the child's brain and body becomes revitalized for the next day. Children who are tired and sleepy in class cannot learn at the correct rate and therefore may lag behind their peers.

There are also environmental conditions that can affect young children. Air pollution can cause respiratory problems and this will affect how children learn and how much school they miss due to illness. The air pollution could be the result of factories in the town, but it could also be the result of secondhand smoke in the home.

The temperature of the classroom has to be closely monitored to ensure that it is neither too hot nor too cold for the children. During warmer weather, an air conditioner or fan in the classroom can help keep temperature to the correct level.

The Components of Nutrition

The components of nutrition are **carbohydrates, proteins, fats, vitamins, minerals, and water.**

Carbohydrates – the main source of energy (glucose) in the human diet. The two types of carbohydrates are simple and complex. Complex carbohydrates have greater nutritional value because they take longer to digest, contain dietary fiber, and do not excessively elevate blood sugar levels. Common sources of carbohydrates are fruits, vegetables, grains, dairy products, and legumes.

Proteins – are necessary for growth, development, and cellular function. The body breaks down consumed protein into component amino acids for future use. Major sources of protein are meat, poultry, fish, legumes, eggs, dairy products, grains, and legumes.

Fats – a concentrated energy source and important component of the human body. The different types of fats are saturated, monounsaturated, and polyunsaturated. Polyunsaturated fats are the healthiest because they may lower cholesterol levels, while saturated fats increase cholesterol levels. Common sources of saturated fats include dairy products, meat, coconut oil, and palm oil. Common sources of unsaturated fats include nuts, most vegetable oils, and fish.

Vitamins and minerals – organic substances that the body requires in small quantities for proper functioning. People acquire vitamins and minerals in their diets and in supplements. Important vitamins include A, B, C, D, E, and K. Important minerals include calcium, phosphorus, magnesium, potassium, sodium, chlorine, and sulfur.

Water – makes up 55 – 75% of the human body. It is essential for most bodily functions and can be attained through foods and liquids.

Determine the adequacy of diets in meeting the nutritional needs of students

Nutritional requirements vary from person to person. General guidelines for meeting adequate nutritional needs are: no more than 30% total caloric intake from fats (preferably 10% from saturated fats, 10% from monounsaturated fats, 10% from polyunsaturated fats), no more than 15% total caloric intake from protein (complete), and at least 55% of caloric intake from carbohydrates (mainly complex carbohydrates).

Exercise and diet help maintain proper body weight by equalizing caloric intake and caloric output.

Body Composition Management

It is vital to analyze procedures, activities, resources, and benefits involved in developing and maintaining healthy levels of body composition. Maintaining a healthy body composition allows an individual to move freely and to obtain a certain pattern that is necessary for a specific activity. Furthermore, maintaining a healthy body composition is positively related with long-term health and resistance to disease and sickness.

The total weight of an individual is a combination of bones, ligaments, tendons, organs, fluids, muscles and fat. Because muscle weighs three times more than fat per unit of volume, a person who exercises often gains muscle. This could cause individuals to be smaller physically, but weigh more than they appear to weigh.

The only proven method for maintaining a healthy body composition is following a healthy diet and engaging in regular exercise. A healthy diet emphasizes fruits, vegetables, whole grains, unsaturated fats, and lean protein, and minimizes saturated fat and sugar consumption. Such a program of nutrition and exercise helps balance caloric intake and output, thus preventing excessive body fat production.

For extensive information about the principles of nutrition:

http://www.anyvitamins.com/dietary.htm

Competency 002   **UNDERSTAND FACTORS THAT MAY AFFECT CHILDREN'S DEVELOPMENT AND LEARNING AND USE THIS KNOWLEDGE TO CREATE LEARNING ENVIRONMENTS THAT SUPPORT CHILDREN'S PROGRESS**

Skill 2.1   **Recognizing factors (e.g., biological, social, emotional, cognitive, behavioral, physiological, gender, linguistic, environmental, familial, cultural, economic) that may affect children's development and learning**

Generally, teachers and parents should know what specific attributes develop over time in children. There is usually no cause for alarm, as many children do develop later in childhood (and certain domains may be developed later than others). Concern regarding intervention might arise when teachers notice that certain functions or attributes seem abnormally absent. In such a case, certain tasks may be very difficult for a child. Later in childhood, a large concern of teasing and bullying may arise, and the teacher may want to ensure that the child is fully protected.

When in doubt, though, the teacher should privately discuss the concern with a special education teacher or school psychologist first. That professional may be able to assist the teacher in determining whether it would be important to evaluate the child, or whether it would be important to contact the parent to ask questions, seek clarification, or point out a potential delay.

Very often, though, parents will be aware of the delay, and the child will be able to receive special accomodations in the classroom. Teachers should be forewarned about this by the special education personnel prior to the beginning of the schoolyear.

Emotional Factors

In early elementary school, children are particularly affected by emotional upsets in family structure, and they are particularly susceptible to emotional harm when they are not cared for in an appropriate manner at home.

While it would be too easy to say that teachers should look out for children who show signs of emotional abuse or emotional neglect, whenever a teacher does notice something unusual in a child's behavior, it might be a good idea to look into it. A note of caution, though: teachers should remember that a student's privacy is extremely important.

Furthermore, teachers should remember that all schools, districts, and states have very specific procedures and laws about the reporting of concerns. Yet, it goes without saying that teachers who see problems should figure out procedures for dealing with them.

Environmental Factors

Environmental factors that can cause delays in the development of some children could include:
- Lead poisoning
- Exposure to contaminants in water, food and air

Because children are smaller, exposure to contaminants can be more harmful for them that it is for adults. The body's systems and organs are still developing and the fact that children often out foreign objects in their mouths only adds to the amount of exposure for them.

When children are emotionally neglected or have recently endured family upsets, what sorts of things would this impact in a child? Well, first, the level of attention toward school will be greatly reduced. While children may actually think about these things, they may also show signs of jealousy of other children, or they may feel a sense of anger toward other children, the teacher, or their parents. Aggression is a very common behavior of emotionally neglected children.

When a child has had little verbal interaction, the symptoms can be rather similar to the symptoms of abuse or neglect. The child might have a "deer in the headlights" look and maintain a very socially awkward set of behaviors. In general, such a child will have a drastically reduced ability to communicate through words, and often, aggression can be a better tool for the child to get the thoughts across.

Cognitive Factors

Although cognitive ability is not lost due to such circumstances (abuse, neglect, emotional upset, lack of verbal interaction), the child will most likely not be able to provide as much intellectual energy as the child would if none of these things were present. But, also, note that a child can see the classroom as a "safe" place, so it is imperative that teachers be attentive to the needs and emotions of their students.

Behavioral Factors

The home environment and even the neighborhood can have an affect on the development of children and cause them to come to school with behavior problems. Recent studies indicate that children from neighborhoods where there are few affluent families tend to exhibit more behavioral issues in school than those who do, such as not paying attention, fighting and in general causing disturbances in the class.

There are also issues that do cause children to have behavior problems, such as the mother consuming alcohol while pregnant and an exposure to violence in the home. The teacher has to be very observant of how children behave towards one another in the classroom to rule out any possibilities that some children may be bringing their frustrations with the home environment into the school setting.

Biological Factors

Children develop at rapidly different rates. However, there are certain impairments and delays that should cause concern. Generally, one might divide delays into cognitive delays (which could delays in verbal communication, mathematical reasoning, logical reasoning, visual processing, auditoring processing, memorization, etc.), physical delays (which could include a lack of motor skills, the inability to stand up straight, walk normally, play simple sport-like activities, hold a pencil; in very young children, it could include not being able to walk or sit up, for example), and social delays (which could include a child's inability to relate to other children). The potential delays or impairments are endless.

They might relate to specific disabilities that can stay with a child for life (everything from problems with eyesight to autism) or learning disabilities (everything from attention deficit disorder to dyslexia). They might also be things that fade as a child gets older (such as problems with motor skills).

Social Factors

A positive self-concept for a child or adolescent is a very important element in terms of the student's ability to learn and to be an integral member of society. If students think poorly of themselves or have sustained feelings of inferiority, they probably will not be able to optimize their potentials for learning. It is therefore part of the teacher's task to ensure that each student develops a positive self-concept.

A positive self-concept does not imply feelings of superiority, perfection, or competence/efficacy. Instead, a positive self-concept involves self-acceptance as a person, liking and having a proper respect for oneself. The teacher who encourages these factors contributes to the development of a positive self-concept in students.

Teachers may take a number of approaches to enhancement of self-concept among students. One such scheme is the **process approach**, which proposes a three-phase model for teaching. This model includes a sensing function, a transforming function, and an acting function. These three factors can be simplified into the words by which the model is usually given: reach, touch, and teach. The sensing, or perceptual, function incorporates information or stimuli in an intuitive manner. The transforming function conceptualizes, abstracts, evaluates, and provides meaning and value to perceived information. The acting function chooses actions from several different alternatives to be set forth overtly. The process model may be applied to almost any curricular field.

An approach that aims directly at the enhancement of self-concept is called **Invitational Education**. According to this approach, teachers and their behaviors may be inviting or they may be disinviting. Inviting behaviors enhance self-concept among students, while disinviting behaviors diminish self-concept.

Disinviting behaviors include those that demean students, as well as those that may be chauvinistic, sexist, condescending, thoughtless, or insensitive to student feelings. Inviting behaviors are the opposite of these behaviors, and characterize teachers who act with consistency and sensitivity. Inviting teacher behaviors reflect an attitude of "doing with" rather than "doing to." Students are "invited" or "disinvited" depending on the teacher behaviors.

Invitational teachers exhibit the following skills (Biehler and Snowman, 394):

    a) reaching each student (e.g., learning names, having one-to-one contact)
    b) listening with care (e.g., picking up subtle cues)
    c) being real with students (e.g., providing only realistic praise, "coming on straight")
    d) being real with oneself (e.g., honestly appraising your own feelings and disappointments)
    e) inviting good discipline (e.g., showing students you have respect in personal ways)
    f) handling rejection (e.g., not taking lack of student response in personal ways)
    g) inviting oneself (e.g., thinking positively about oneself)

Physiological Factors

Anyone who has been in a Kindergarten to grade four classroom knows that students do not sit still and focus on one thing for too long. Some people joke that the age of a person equals the amount of time the person is willing to sit and listen for any one time. So, a kindergartener, under this premise, would only be able to sit and concentrate on one thing for 5 to 6 minutes. Many kindergarten teachers would agree with this. But think about someone at age 30 to 50: most adults don't want to sit and listen for longer than one hour. So, there may be some truth to this, unscientific as it is!

The bottom line is this: young children do not concentrate for long periods of time, and good teachers know how to capitalize on the need of children to move and change topics. Generally, young children should be changing academic activities every 15-20 minutes. This means that if a teacher wants to fill a block of two hours for literacy learning in the morning, the teacher should have about 6-8 activities planned. Here's an example:

1. Teacher has students write something to access background knowledge. In kindergarten, this might include just a picture. In grade four, this might include a paragraph.
2. Teacher might spend a few minutes asking students what they wrote about in a large group.
3. Teacher might introduce a new book by doing a "book walk"—looking at the title, the pictures, etc.
4. Teacher reads book aloud as students follow along.
5. Students do a pair-share where they turn to their neighbors to discuss a question.
6. Students return to desks to do a comprehension activity on their own.
7. The teacher leads a whole class discussion of what they wrote.
8. Students go to centers to practice specific skills as teacher works with small groups of students.
9. Teacher conducts a vocabulary activity with the whole class.

This list could go on and on. Hopefully, you'll see that the activity changes rapidly, but the same skills are being hit upon over and over in different ways. Teachers who switch things around like this are more likely to keep their students' attention, engage their students more, and have a more behaved classroom. When children get bored, they obviously will start to not pay attention, and many will become disruptive. The key is to keep them interested in what they are learning.

Familal Factors

SEE Skill 2.2

Linguistic Factors

SEE Skill 1.1

Gender Factors

Research has proven that boys are more likely to be autistic than girls, as well as other developmental delays such as Attention Deficit Disorder. Experts claim that boys seem to be more vulnerable to brain dysfunction although the reasons for it are not clear.

Cultural Factors

In early childhood classrooms, the teacher must be sensitive to the culture that each child comes from. Culture is individual and the teacher may need to assess the child indivudally to identify cultural factors that may affect the child's development. Some of the cultural factors that may have an impact on the child's learning in school include:
- Race
- Religion
- Ethnic background
- Socio-economic status
- Gender
- Place of birth
- Language

The beliefs of the parents come through in the child's reactions to experiences in school. The teacher has to be able to determine if there is a cultural problem that may be causing the child to experience a delay in some aspect of development.

Economic Factors

The socio-economic status of the family has a direct bearing on the development of some children. For example a child that comes to school wiuth no knowledge of books or writing could come from a home where there is no extra money for books. It could also be a cultural factor in that the parenst are new immigrants and cannot read any of the books published in a different language. Children raised in poverty may not have the proper nutrition they need to develop normally and this could cause medical problems as well. In addition, parents of children with disabilities may not not have the monetary means to provide medical care for the children or may not be aware of any social programs available to them within the community.

Skill 2.2 Recognizing the effects of the home environment (e.g., nature of the expectations of parents/guardians, degree of their involvement in a child's education) on children's learning

The student's capacity and potential for academic success within the overall educational experience are products of the total environment: classroom and school system; home and family; neighborhood and community in general. All of these segments are interrelated and can be supportive, one of the other, or divisive, one against the other.

As a matter of course, the teacher will become familiar with all aspects of the system, the school and the classroom pertinent to the students' educational experience. This would include not only process and protocols, but also the availability of resources provided to meet the academic, health and welfare needs of students. However, it is incumbent upon the teacher to look beyond the boundaries of the school system to identify additional resources, as well as issues and situations that will affect (directly or indirectly) a student's ability to succeed in the classroom.

Examples of Resources

- Libraries, museums, zoos, planetariums, etc.
- Clubs, societies and civic organizations, community outreach programs of private businesses and corporations and of government agencies
  These can provide a variety of materials and media as well as possible speakers and presenters
- Departments of social services operating within the local community
  These can provide background and program information relevant to social issues, which may be impacting individual students. This can also be a resource for classroom instruction regarding life skills, at-risk behaviors, etc.

Initial contacts for resources outside of the school system will usually come from within the system itself: from administration, teacher organizations, department heads, and other colleagues.

Examples of Issues/Situations

- Students from multicultural backgrounds:

Curriculum objectives and instructional strategies may be inappropriate and unsuccessful when presented in a single format that relies on the students' understanding and acceptance of the values and common attributes of a specific culture which is not their own.

- Parental/family influences: Attitude, resources and encouragement available in the home environment may be attributes for success or failure.

Families with higher incomes are able to provide increased opportunities for students. Students from lower income families will need to depend on the resources available from the school system and the community. The classroom teacher should orchestrate this in cooperation with school administrators and educational advocates in the community.

Family members with higher levels of education often serve as models for students, and have high expectations for academic success. Families with specific aspirations for children (often, regardless of their own educational background) encourage students to achieve academic success, and are most often active participants in the process.

A family in crisis (caused by economic difficulties, divorce, substance abuse, physical abuse, etc.) creates a negative environment, which may profoundly impact all aspects of a student's life, and particularly the ability to function academically. The situation may require professional intervention. It is often the classroom teacher who will recognize a family in crisis situation and instigate an intervention by reporting on this to school or civil authorities.

Regardless of the positive or negative impacts on the students' education from outside sources, it is the teacher's responsibility to ensure that all students in the classroom have an equal opportunity for academic success. This begins with the teacher's statement of high expectations for every student, and develops through planning, delivery and evaluation of instruction which provides for inclusion and ensures that all students have equal access to the resources necessary for successful acquisition of the academic skills being taught and measured in the classroom.

Skill 2.3 **Recognizing how current and prior learning experiences outside the home (e.g., interactions with caregivers and teachers, prior successes and challenges, peer interactions) may affect children's self-concepts, perceptions, motivation, and attitudes about learning**

SEE Skill 2.2

Importance of Background Knowledge

All children bring some level of background knowledge (e.g., how to hold a book, awareness of directionality of print) to beginning reading. Teachers can utilize children's background knowledge to help children link their personal literacy experiences to beginning reading instruction, while also closing the gap between students with rich and students with impoverished literacy experiences. Activities that draw upon background knowledge include incorporating oral language activities (which discriminate between printed letters and words) into daily read-alouds, as well as frequent opportunities to retell stories, look at books with predictable patterns, write messages with invented spellings, and respond to literature through drawing.

Many children with diverse literacy experiences have difficulty making connections between old and new information. Strategic integration can be applied to help link old and new learning. For example, in the classroom, strategic integration can be accomplished by providing access to literacy materials in classroom writing centers and libraries. Students should also have opportunities to integrate and extend their literacy knowledge by reading aloud, listening to other students read aloud, and listening to tape recordings and videotapes in reading corners.

Interactions With Caregivers and Teachers

Prior experiences that children have with caregivers and/or teachers can directly impact their attitude towards learning in school. Caregivers/Parents who lead the child to believe that education is not important can deeply impact this attitude, especially if the child has a feeling of attachment to that person. A child that comes to school not being familiar with books may have come from a home where reading is not considered important and may not display an active interest in reading.

Teachers who tended to be strict with the child in the past or did not show a lot of caring in helping the child to understand how to correct mistakes could leave the child with the thought that all teachers act in this way. This is especially true if the child is experiencing problems with learning or the tasks assigned and does not get the needed help and support.

It is a fact of life that everyone does not get along in a classroom. However, a teacher that gives a child the impression of not being liked or wanted in the classroom could be seriously impeding that child's attitude for future school years. Teachers do need to take an impartial approach when dealing with students who do not get along, yet it is important to demonstrate caring to each and every one of them.

Prior Successes and Challenges

Whether a child has been successful at a task in the past will affect the attitude of tasks assigned in the present. Take for example, child who experienced failure with addition in a previous grade. When faced with addition in the next grade, the child is likely to exhibit an attitude of acceptance of failure assuming that it will be a challenge that cannot be mastered. Similarly, a child who has experienced great success with math in one grade may approach all future Math experiences with an attitude that it will be easy to master.

Peer Interactions

Teachers need to be very cognizant about how the children in the class interact with one another. This extends to their interactions on the playground as well. Children can be very cruel to one another and single out a child they perceive to be different. At the same time, children can be very helpful towards one another when the need arises.

Children who are teased in school or feel threatened by one or more students may not want to go to school at all or want to contribute to class discussions. The interaction that causes this may occur outside the school setting, so it may be necessary for the teacher to talk to the child in private to determine the cause of the attitude towards school. On the other hand, an only child or one that is outgoing may have a healthy attitude towards school because of the wide range of friends that exist in the classroom.

Peers can influence how children conduct themselves in the classroom and the amount of time they spend attending to their assigned tasks. For example, students who do well on school assignments may be ridiculed by other students who find these same assignments more difficult. In order to be accepted by this group of peers, a child may deliberately do poorly in the schoolwork.

Skill 2.4 **Recognizing cultural, linguistic, and socioeconomic diversity and their significance for child development and learning**

The educational experience for most students is a complicated and complex experience with a diversity of interlocking meanings and inferences. If one aspect of the complexity is altered, it affects other aspects, which may impact how a student or teacher views an instructional or learning experience. With the current demographic profile of today's school communities, the complexity of understanding, interpreting, synthesizing the nuances from the diversity of cultural lineages can provide many communication and learning blockages that could impede the acquisition of learning for students.

Oftentimes, students absorb the culture and social environment around them without deciphering contextual meaning of the experiences. When provided with a diversity of cultural contexts, students are able to adapt and incorporate multiple meanings from cultural cues vastly different from their own socioeconomic backgrounds. Socio-cultural factors provide a definitive impact on a students' psychological, emotional, affective, and physiological development, along with a students' academic learning and future opportunities.

Establishing a Community of Learners in the Classroom

Teachers must create personalized learning communities where every student is a valued member and contributor of the classroom experiences. In classrooms where socio-cultural attributes of the student population are incorporated into the fabric of the learning process, dynamic interrelationships are created that enhance the learning experience and the personalization of learning. When students are provided with numerous academic and social opportunities to share cultural incorporations into the learning, everyone in the classroom benefits from bonding through shared experiences and having an expanded viewpoint of a world experience and culture that vastly differs from their own.

Researchers continue to show that personalized learning environments increase the learning affect for students; decrease drop-out rates among marginalized students, and decrease unproductive student behavior, which can result from constant cultural misunderstandings or miscues between students. Promoting diversity of learning and cultural competency in the classroom for students and teachers creates a world of multicultural opportunities and learning. When students are able to step outside their comfort zones and share the world of a homeless student or empathize with an English Language Learner (ELL) who has just immigrated to the United States, is learning English for the first time and is still trying to keep up with the academic learning in an unfamiliar language, then students grow exponentially in social understanding and cultural connectedness.

Personalized learning communities provide supportive learning environments that address the academic and emotional needs of students. As socio-cultural knowledge is conveyed continuously in the interrelated experiences shared cooperatively and collaboratively in student groupings and individualized learning, the current and future benefits will continue to present the case and importance of understanding the "whole" child, inclusive of the social and the cultural context.

In personalized learning communities, relationships and connections between students, staff, parents and community members promote lifelong learning for all students. School communities that promote an inclusion of diversity in the classroom, community, curriculum and connections enable students to maximize their academic capabilities and educational opportunities. Setting school climates that are inclusive of the multicultural demographic student population create positive and proactive mission and vision themes that align student and staff expectations.

Integrating Diversity into Learning

The following factors enable students and staff to emphasize and integrate diversity in student learning:
- Inclusion of multicultural themes in curriculum and assessments
- Creation of a learning environment that promotes multicultural research, learning, collaboration, and social construction of knowledge and application.
- Provision of learning tasks that emphasize student cognitive, critical thinking and problem-solving skills.
- Learning tasks that personalize the cultural aspects of diversity and celebrate diversity in the subject matter and student projects.
- Promotion of intercultural positive social peer interrelationships and connections.

Teachers can communicate diversity through instructional practices and experiential learning activities that create curiosity in students who want to understand the interrelationship of cultural experiences. This helps students become self-directed in discovering the global world in and outside the classroom. When teachers understand that when diversity becomes an integral part of the classroom environment, students become global thinkers and doers.

Communicating Among Cultures

In the intercultural communication model, students are able to learn how different cultures engage in both verbal and nonverbal modes of communicating meaning. Students who become multilingual in understanding the stereotypes that have defined other cultures are able to create new bonding experiences that will typify a more integrated global culture. When students understand how to effectively communicate with diverse cultural groups they are able to maximize their own learning experiences by being able to transmit both verbally and non-verbally cues and expectations in project collaborations and in performance based activities.

The learning curve for teachers in intercultural understanding is exponential in that they are able to engage all learners in the academic process and learning engagement. Teaching students how to incorporate learning techniques from a cultural aspect enriches the cognitive expansion experience, since students are able to expand their cultural knowledge bases.

Diversity in classroom makeup may not be as distinctive as race and ethnicity, gender and so forth. Students who are physically or intellectually challenged may also add diversity within a general student population. A student population including members from varying socioeconomic situations also provides diversity. All students must be included in the learning process. Acceptance of this diversity, by students, and any specific requirements necessary to aid individual students to accomplish on a par with classmates, must be incorporated in lesson planning, teacher presentation and classroom activities. For example, access to technology and media, generally, may vary greatly within the student population. In planning classroom work, homework assignments and other projects, the teacher must take this into account. First, the teacher must be knowledgeable about the resources available to the students, directly, within the school, the library system and the community. The teacher must also be sure that any issues that might restrict a student's access (physical impediments, language difficulties, expenses, etc.) are addressed. Secondly, never plan for work or assignments where every student would not have equal access to information and technology. As in all aspects of education, each student must have an equal opportunity to succeed.

Benefits of Cultural Diversity in the Classroom

When diversity is promoted in learning environments and curriculum, both students and teachers are the beneficiaries of increased academic success. Using classrooms as vital resources for cultural and ethnic inclusion can assist students in contributing cultural norms and artifacts to the acquisition of learning. Teachers are able to create global thinkers by helping students identify cultural assumptions and biases that may direct the type of social and academic groupings that occur in the classroom and influence the type of thinking and construction of learning that happens within a classroom. For example, if a student is struggling in math, a teacher can examine the cultural aspect of learning math. For some students, math is insignificant when socioeconomic issues of poverty and survival are the daily reality of existence. When students see parents juggling finances, the only math that becomes important for them is that less is never enough to keep the lights on and mortgage paid.

When there is equity pedagogy, teachers can use a variety of instructional styles to facilitate diversity in cooperative learning and individualized instruction that will provide more opportunities for positive student experiences and academic success. Empowering the school culture and climate by establishing an anti-bias learning environment and promoting multicultural learning inclusion will discourage disproportionality and unfair labeling of certain students.

Features of a Culturally Diverse Classroom

A culturally diverse classroom should display a positive environment, where open, discussion-oriented, non-threatening communication among all students can occur, is a critical factor in creating an effective learning culture. The teacher must take the lead and model appropriate actions and speech, and intervene quickly when a student makes a misstep and offends (often inadvertently) another.

Communication issues that the teacher in a diverse classroom should be aware of include:

- Be sensitive to terminology and language patterns that may exclude or demean students. Regularly switch between the use of "he" and "she" in speech and writing. Know and use the current terms that ethnic and cultural groups use to identify themselves (e.g., "Latinos" (favored) vs. "Hispanics").
- Be aware of body language that is intimidating or offensive to some cultures, such as direct eye contact, and adjust accordingly.
- Monitor your own reactions to students to ensure equal responses to males and females, as well as students who perform differently

- Don't "protect" students from criticism because of their ethnicity or gender. Likewise, acknowledge and praise all meritorious work without singling out any one student. Both actions can make all students hyper-aware of ethnic and gender differences and cause anxiety or resentment throughout the class.
- Emphasize the importance of discussing and considering different viewpoints and opinions. Demonstrate and express value for all opinions and comments and lead students to do the same

SEE Skill 3.5 for more information about a culturally diverse classroom.

Instructional techniques for Cultural Diversity

Most class rosters will consist of students from a variety of cultures. Teachers should get to know their students (of all cultures) so that they may incorporate elements of their cultures into classroom activities and planning. Also, getting to know about a student's background/cultural traditions helps to build a rapport with each student, as well as further educate the teacher about the world. For example, it is important to know the correct spelling and pronunciation of each student's name, and any preference in how the student would like to be addressed. The teacher should plan time for interaction in the classroom, when the teacher and the class can become familiar with each student's interests and experiences. This will help the teacher and the students avoid making assumptions based on any individual's background or appearance.

Teachers can use various toolkits of assessing integration and incorporation of ethnic and cultural inclusion in classroom. Effective promotion should translate into increased academic success and opportunities for all students. Looking at diverse or homogenous groupings in the classroom can provide teachers with opportunities to restructure cooperative learning groupings and increase diverse student interactions, which can provide increased improvements for school communities.

CultureGrams are representations that provide information about various cultures beyond just the basic facts that simpler graphs display. CultureGrams help students understand different cultures and research cultural diversity are a useful tool teachers can use in profiling student learning styles and engagement in the classroom. Students can use technology to learn how students learn in other cultures and in other states. Observing students, as they communicate with other learners, is another way teachers can compile and categorize cultural profiles that may help identify learning styles and the ways students acquire learning. An interesting aspect of using CultureGrams is the manner in which it helps students connect to other cultures and their perceptions of students who identify with different cultures.

For students still learning English, teachers must make every attempt to communicate with that student daily. Whether it's with another student who speaks the same language, word cards, computer programs, drawings or other methods, teachers must find ways to encourage each student's participation. Of course, the teacher must also be sure the appropriate language services begin for the student in a timely manner, as well.

Teachers must also consider students from various socioeconomic backgrounds. These students are just as likely as anyone else to work well in a classroom. Unfortunately, difficulties sometimes occur with these children when it comes to completing homework consistently. These students may need help deriving a homework system or perhaps need more attention on study or test-taking skills. Teachers should encourage these students as much as possible and offer positive reinforcements when they meet or exceed classroom expectations. Teachers should also watch these students carefully for signs of malnutrition, fatigue and possible learning disorders.

The primary responsibility of the classroom teacher is to ensure that all aspects of the educational process, and all information necessary to master specified skills, are readily accessible by all students in the classroom. In the classroom, the teacher must actively promote inclusion and devise presentations, which address commonalities among heterogeneous groups. In the development of lesson plans and presentation formats, this should be evident in the concept and in the language used (e.g., incorporating ideas and phrases which suggest "we" rather than "they" whenever possible). Initially, the teacher must take the time to know each student as an individual, and demonstrate a sincere interest in each student.

Encourage all students to respond to each other's questions and statements in the classroom. Be prepared to respond, appropriately, should any issue or question regarding diversity arise during classroom discussions or activities. If necessary to promote or control discussion in the classroom, the teacher should provide the students with specific guidelines (which are easy to understand and to follow, at their level) defining the intended objectives and any restrictions. Inclusion means involving everyone in classroom discussions. The teacher should allow the students to volunteer, and then call on the more reluctant students to provide additional information or opinions. All opinions (which are not derogatory in case or by nature) are valid and should be reinforced as such by the teacher's approval.

The prescribed teaching material in a given subject area will usually provide an adequate format appropriate to the grade level and the diversity of a general, student population. By assuring that any additional content or instructional aids used in classroom presentation are thematically the same as the prescribed material, the teacher can usually assume these will also be appropriate. Since teachers are the final arbiters regarding content, format and presentation in the classroom, they must exercise judgment when reviewing all classroom materials, lesson plans, presentations and activities against set criteria. For example, they should be cognizant of material that is:

Offensive: Anything that might be considered derogatory regarding any individual or group. Any comment or material that is insensitive to any nationality, religion, culture, race, family structure, etc. Regardless of the composition of a particular classroom, negativism about any group harbors an acceptance of such negativism and contributes to a "them" versus "us" attitude.

Exclusive: Anything that ignores or nullifies the needs, rights or value of an individual or any group. Anything that stratifies society, placing some group or groups above others in significance.

Inappropriate: Below or beyond the suitable comprehension level. Imprecise, inadequate for mastery of specific skills within the subject matter. Fails to provide for accurately measurable skill acquisition.

The teacher should actively work to broaden the students' sense of "we," even beyond the classroom and the local community, to foster a sense of all people as "we." For example, while avoiding the use of colloquialisms or local slang within lesson presentation, the teacher would demonstrate an understanding and acceptance of the richness and variety of ways in which people communicate.

Effective teaching and learning for students begins with teachers who can demonstrate sensitivity for diversity in teaching and relationships within school communities. Student portfolios include work that has a multicultural perspective and inclusion where students share cultural and ethnic life experiences in their learning. Teachers are responsive to including cultural and diverse resources in their curriculum and instructional practices. Exposing students to culturally sensitive room decorations and posters that show positive and inclusive messages is one way to demonstrate inclusion of multiple cultures.

Teachers should also continuously make cultural connections that are relevant and empowering for all students and communicate academic and behavioral expectations. Cultural sensitivity is communicated beyond the classroom with parents and community members to establish and maintain relationships.

Teachers must establish a classroom climate that is culturally respectful and engaging for students. In a culturally sensitive classroom, teachers maintain equity and fairness in student interactions and curriculum implementation. Assessments include cultural responses and perspectives that become further learning opportunities for students.

Other artifacts that could reflect teacher/student sensitivity to diversity might consist of the following:

- Student portfolios reflecting multicultural/multiethnic perspectives
- Journals and reflections from field trips/ guest speakers from diverse cultural backgrounds
- Printed materials and wall displays from multicultural perspectives
- Parent/guardian letters in a variety of languages reflecting cultural diversity
- Projects that include cultural history and diverse inclusions
- Disaggregated student data reflecting cultural groups
- Classroom climate of professionalism that fosters diversity and cultural inclusion

When planning instruction for a diverse group (or teaching about diversity, for that matter) incorporate teaching through the use of perspective. There is always more than one way to "see" or approach a problem, an example, a process, fact or event, or any learning situation. Varying approaches for instruction helps to maintain the students' interest in the material and enables the teacher to address the diverse needs of individuals to comprehend the material.

The requirement for students within a diverse classroom to acquire the same academic skills (at the same levels) can sometimes be achieved with programmed learning, instructional materials. While not widely available for every subject, at every level, a good deal of useful material is in publication. In addition, professional teachers familiar with the format have often created their own modules for student use, to be incorporated within their lesson planning.

For more resources on addressing literacy in a culturally diverse classroom:	Extensive information about teaching culture:
http://www.ncrel.org/sdrs/areas/issues/content/cntareas/reading/li400.htm	http://nadabs.tripod.com/culture/

Skill 2.5 Demonstrating awareness of types of exceptionalities and their implications for learning

Identify the Characteristics of Emotionally Disturbed Children

Children with emotional disturbances or behavioral disorders are not always easy to identify. It is, of course, easy to identify the acting-out child who is constantly fighting, who cannot stay on task for more than a few minutes, or who shouts obscenities when angry. It is not always easy to identify the child who internalizes his or her problems, on the other hand, or may appear to be the "model" student, but suffers from depression, shyness, or fears. Unless the problem becomes severe enough to impact school performance, the internalizing child may go for long periods without being identified or served.

Studies of children with behavioral and emotional disorders indicate that children with these disorders share some general characteristics:

Lower academic performance: While it is true that some emotionally disturbed children have above average IQ scores, the majority of these children are behind their peers in measures of intelligence and school achievement. Most score in the "slow learner" or "mildly mentally retarded" range on IQ tests, averaging about 90. Many have learning problems that exacerbate their acting out or "giving-up" behavior. As these children enter secondary school, the gap between them and their non-disabled peers widens until they may be as many as 2 to 4 years behind in reading and/or math skills by high school. Children with severe degrees of impairment may be difficult to evaluate.

Social skills deficits: Students with deficits may be uncooperative, selfish in dealing with others, unaware of what to do in social situations, or ignorant of the consequences of their actions. This may be a combination of lack of prior training, lack of opportunities to interact, and dysfunctional value systems and beliefs learned from their family.

Classroom behaviors: Often, emotionally disturbed children display classroom behavior that is highly disruptive to the classroom setting. Emotionally disturbed children are often out of their seat or running around the room, hitting, fighting, or disturbing their classmates, stealing or destroying property, defiant and noncompliant, and/or verbally disruptive. They do not follow directions and often do not complete assignments.

Aggressive behaviors: Aggressive children often fight or instigate their peers to strike back at them. Aggressiveness may also take the form of vandalism or destruction of property. Aggressive children also engage in verbal abuse.

Delinquency: As emotionally disturbed, acting-out children enter adolescence, they may become involved in socialized aggression (i.e., gang membership) and delinquency. Delinquency is a legal term, rather than medical, and describes truancy and actions that would be criminal if adults committed them. Not every delinquent is classified as emotionally disturbed, but children with behavioral and emotional disorders are especially at risk for becoming delinquent because of their problems at school (the primary place for socializing with peers), deficits in social skills that may make them unpopular at school, and/or dysfunctional homes.

Withdrawn behaviors: Children who manifest withdrawn behaviors may consistently act in an immature fashion or prefer to play with younger children. They may daydream or complain of being sick in order to "escape". They may also cry often, cling to the teacher, ignore those who attempt to interact, or suffer from fears or depression.

Schizophrenia and psychotic behaviors: Children may have bizarre delusions, hallucinations, incoherent thoughts, and disconnected thinking. Schizophrenia typically manifests itself between the ages of 15 and 45, and the younger the onset, the more severe the disorder. These behaviors usually require intensive treatment beyond the scope of the regular classroom setting.

Gender: Many more boys than girls are identified as having emotional and behavioral problems, especially hyperactivity and attention deficit disorder, autism, childhood psychosis, and problems with undercontrol (aggression, socialized aggression). Girls, on the other hand, have more problems with overcontrol (i.e., withdrawal and phobias). Boys are much more prevalent than girls in problems with mental retardation and language and learning disabilities.

Age Characteristics: When they enter adolescence, girls tend to experience affective or emotional disorders such as anorexia, depression, bulimia, and anxiety at twice the rate of boys, which mirrors the adult prevalence pattern.

Family Characteristics: Having a child with an emotional or behavioral disorder does not automatically mean that the family is dysfunctional. However, there are family factors that create or contribute to the development of behavior disorders and emotional disturbance.
- Abuse and neglect
- Lack of appropriate supervision
- Lax, punitive, and/or lack of discipline
- High rates of negative types of interaction among family members
- Lack of parental concern and interest
- Negative adult role models
- Lack of proper health care and/or nutrition
- Disruption in the family

Children with mild learning, intellectual, and behavioral disabilities

Children with mild learning, intellectual and behavioral difficulties do not display any one characteristic in their behavior in the classroom. In order to determine whether or not a disability may exist, it is imperative that teachers observe the children over time and in varied situations. These children may display some or all of the following characteristics:

- A lack of interest in schoolwork
- Preference for concrete rather than abstract lessons
- Weak listening skills
- Low achievement, limited verbal and/or listening skills
- Respond better to active rather than passive learning tasks
- Possess areas of talent or abilities often overlooked by teachers
- Preference for special help in the regular classroom
- A higher dropout rate than regular education students
- Achieve in accordance with teacher expectations
- Require modification in classroom instruction and are easily distracted

Identify characteristic of students who have a learning disability

Characteristics that students with a learning disability may display in the classroom include:

- hyperactivity: a rate of motor activity higher than normal
- perceptual difficulties: visual, auditory, and perceptual problems
- perceptual-motor impairments: poor integration of visual and motor systems, often affecting fine motor coordination
- disorders of memory and thinking: memory deficits, trouble with problem-solving, concept formation and association, poor awareness of own metacognitive skills (learning strategies)
- impulsiveness: act before considering consequences, poor impulse control, often followed by remorselessness
- academic problems in reading, math, writing or spelling; significant discrepancies in ability levels

Identify characteristics of individuals with mental retardation or intellectual disabilities

Students with mental retardation or intellectual disabilities may have:

- an IQ of 70 or below
- limited cognitive ability; delayed academic achievement, particularly in language-related subjects
- deficits in memory that often relate to poor initial perception or inability to apply stored information to relevant situations
- impaired formulation of learning strategies
- difficulty in attending to relevant aspects of stimuli; slowness in reaction time or in employing alternate strategies

Identify characteristics of individuals with autism

This exceptionality appears very early in childhood. Six common features of autism are:

- **Apparent sensory deficit** –The child may appear not to see, hear or react to a stimulus and then react in an extreme fashion to a seemingly insignificant stimulus.
- **Severe affect isolation**—The child does not respond to the usual signs of affection such as smiles and hugs.
- **Self-stimulation** – Stereotyped behavior takes the form of repeated or ritualistic actions that make no sense to others, such as hand flapping, rocking, staring at objects, or humming the same sounds for hours at a time.
- **Tantrums and self-injurious behavior (SIB)** – Autistic children may bite themselves, pull their hair, bang their heads, or hit themselves. They can throw severe tantrums and direct aggression and destructive behavior toward others.
- **Echolalia** (also known as "parrot talk")—The autistic child may repeat what is played on television, for example, or respond to others by repeating what was said to him. Alternatively, he may simply not speak at all.
- **Severe deficits in behavior and self-care skills**—Autistic children may behave like children much younger than themselves.

IDEA 2004 defines *a child with a disability. . . as having mental retardation, a hearing impairment (including deafness), a speech or language impairment, a visual impairment (including blindness), a serious emotional disturbance (referred to in this part as emotional disturbance), an orthopedic impairment, autism, traumatic brain injury, an other health impairment, a specific learning disability, deaf-blindness, or multiple disabilities, and who, by reason thereof, needs special education and related services.*

Eligibility for special education services is based on a student having one of the above disabilities (or a combination thereof) and demonstration of educational need through professional evaluation.

Seldom does a student with a disability fall into only one of the characteristics listed in IDEA 2004. For example, a student with a hearing impairment may also have a specific learning disability, or a student on the autism spectrum may also demonstrate language impairment. In fact, language impairment is inherent in autism. Sometimes the eligibility is defined as multiple disabilities (with one listed as a primary eligibility on the IEP and the others listed as secondary). Sometimes there are overlapping needs that are not necessarily listed as a secondary disability.

Teachers of special education students should be aware of the similarities between areas of disabilities, as well as the differences.

Students with disabilities (in all areas) may demonstrate difficulty in social skills. For a student with a hearing impairment, social skills may be difficult because of not hearing social language. However, the emotionally disturbed student may have difficulty because of a special type of psychological disturbance. An autistic student, as a third example, would be unaware of the social cues given with voice, facial expression, and body language. Each of these students would need social skill instruction, but in a different way.

Students with disabilities (in all areas) may demonstrate difficulty in academic skills. A student with mental retardation will need special instruction across all areas of academics, while a student with a learning disability may need assistance in only one or two subject areas.

Students with disabilities may demonstrate difficulty with independence or self-help skills. A student with a visual impairment may need specific mobility training while a student with a specific learning disability may need a checklist to help in managing materials and assignments.

Special education teachers should be aware that although students across disabilities may demonstrate difficulty in similar ways, the causes may be very different. For example, some disabilities are due to specific sensory impairments (hearing or vision), some due to cognitive ability (mental retardation), and some due to neurological impairment (autism or some learning disabilities). The reason for the difficulty should be a consideration when planning the program of special education intervention.

Additionally, special education teachers should be aware that each area of disability has a range of involvement. Some students may have minimal disability and require no services. Others may need only a few accommodations and have a 504 plan. Some may need an IEP that outlines a specific special education program that might be implemented in an inclusion/resource program, self-contained program, or in a residential setting.

A student with ADD may be able to participate in the regular education program with a 504 plan that outlines a checklist system to keep the student organized and additional communication between school and home. Other students with ADD may need instruction in a smaller group with fewer distractions and would be better served in a resource room.

Special educators should be knowledgeable of the cause and severity of the disability and its manifestations in the specific student when planning an appropriate special education program. Because of the unique needs of the child, such programs are documented in the child's IEP – Individualized Education Program.

Normality in child behavior is influenced by society's attitudes and cultural beliefs about what is normal for children (e.g., the motto for the Victorian era was "Children should be seen and not heard"). However, criteria for what is "normal" involves consideration of these questions:

- **Is the behavior age appropriate?** An occasional tantrum may be expected for a toddler, but is not typical for a high school student.
- **Is the behavior pathological in itself?** Drug or alcohol use would be harmful to children, regardless of how many engage in it.
- **How persistent is the problem?** A kindergarten student initially may be afraid to go to school. However, if the fear persisted into first or second grade, then the problem would be considered persistent.
- **How severe is the behavior?** Self-injurious, cruel, and extremely destructive behaviors would be examples of behaviors that require intervention.
- **How often does the behavior occur?** An occasional tantrum in a young child or a brief mood of depression in an adolescent would not be considered problematic. However, if the behaviors occur frequently, that behavior would not be characteristic of normal child development.
- **Do several problem behaviors occur as a group?** Clusters of behaviors, especially severe behaviors that occur together, may be indicative of a serious problem, such as schizophrenia.
- **Is the behavior sex-appropriate?** Cultural and societal attitudes towards gender change over time. While attitudes towards younger boys playing with dolls or girls preferring sports to dolls have relaxed, children eventually are expected as adults to conform to the expected behaviors for males and females.

Certain stages of child development have their own sets of problems, and it should be kept in mind that short-term undesirable behaviors can and will occur over these stages. Child development is also a continuum, and children may manifest these problem behaviors somewhat earlier or later than their peers.

About 15-20% of the school-aged population between 6 and 17 years old receive special education services. The categories of learning disabilities and emotional disturbance are the most prevalent. Exceptional students are very much like their peers without disabilities. The main difference is that they have an intellectual, emotional, behavioral, or physical deficit that significantly interferes with their ability to benefit from education.

For more information about IDEA 2004:

http://www.ldonline.org/features/idea2004

http://idea.ed.gov/

Explore a sample 504 checklist:

http://www.schools.utah.gov/equity/Section%20504/section_504_checklist.htm

---

For comprehensive information about developing an IEP:

http://www.ed.gov/parents/needs/speced/iepguide/index.html

Differentiating Instruction: Children with Disabilities and Second Language Learners

No two students are alike. It follows, then, that no students *learn* alike. To apply a one-dimensional instructional approach and a strict tunnel vision perspective of testing is to impose learning limits on students. All students have the right to an education, but there cannot be a singular path to that education. A teacher must acknowledge the variety of learning styles and abilities among students within a class (and, indeed, the varieties from class to class) and apply multiple instructional and assessment processes to ensure that every child has appropriate opportunities to master the subject matter, demonstrate such mastery, and improve and enhance learning skills with each lesson.

Students' attitudes and perceptions about learning are the most powerful factors influencing academic focus and success. When instructional objectives center on students' interests and are relevant to their lives, effective learning occurs. Learners must believe that the tasks that they are asked to perform have some value and that they have the ability and resources to perform them. If a student thinks a task is unimportant, he/she will not put much effort into it.

When a student feels lacking in the ability or resources to successfully complete a task, even attempting the task becomes too great a risk. Not only must the teacher understand the students' abilities and interests, it is also necessary to help students develop positive attitudes and perceptions about tasks and learning.

Differentiated Instruction

The effective teacher will seek to connect all students to the subject matter through multiple techniques, with the goal that each student, through their own abilities, will relate to one or more techniques and excel in the learning process.

Differentiated instruction encompasses several areas:
- **Content**: What is the teacher going to teach? Or, perhaps better put, what does the teacher want the students to learn? Differentiating content means that students will have access to content that piques their interest about a topic, with a complexity that provides an appropriate challenge to their intellectual development.
- **Process**: A classroom management technique where instructional organization and delivery is maximized for the diverse student group. These techniques should include dynamic, flexible grouping activities, where instruction and learning occurs both as whole-class, teacher-led activities, as well as peer learning and teaching (while teacher observes and coaches) within small groups or pairs.
- **Product**: The expectations and requirements placed on students to demonstrate their knowledge or understanding. The type of product expected from each student should reflect each student's own capabilities.

> **Learn more about Differentiated Instruction:**
>
> http://members.shaw.ca/priscillatheroux/differentiating.html

Alternative Assessments

Alternative assessment is an assessment where students create an answer or a response to a question or task, as opposed to traditional, inflexible assessments where students choose a prepared response from among a selection of responses, such as matching, multiple-choice or true/false.

When implemented effectively, an alternative assessment approach will exhibit these characteristics, among others:
- Requires higher-order thinking and problem-solving
- Provides opportunities for student self-reflection and self-assessment
- Uses real world applications to connect students to the subject
- Provides opportunities for students to learn and examine subjects on their own, as well as to collaborate with their peers.
- Encourages students to continuing learning beyond the requirements of the assignment
- Clearly defines objective and performance goals

> **For more information on Alternative Assessment:**
>
> http://www.nclrc.org/essentials/assessing/alternative.htm

Testing Modifications

The intent of testing modifications is to minimize the effect of a student's disability or learning challenge and to provide an equal opportunity to participate in assessments to demonstrate and express knowledge and ability.

Testing modifications should be identified in the student's IEP, be consistently implemented, and should be used to the least extent possible. Types of testing modifications include:
- Flexible scheduling: providing time extensions or altering testing duration (e.g., by inserting appropriate breaks)
- Flexible setting: Using special lighting or acoustics, minimizing distractions (e.g., testing the student in a separate location), using adaptive equipment.
- Alternate test format: Using large print or Braille, increasing the space allocated for student response, realigning the format of question and answer selections (e.g., vertically rather than horizontally).
- Use of mechanical aids: tape recorders, word processors, visual and auditory magnification devices, calculators, spell check and grammar check software (where spelling and grammar are not the focus of assessment).

Most classrooms contain a mixture of the following:
- Differences among learners, classroom settings and academic outcomes
- Biological, sociological, ethnicity, socioeconomic status psychological needs, learning modalities and styles among learners
- Differences in classroom settings that promote learning opportunities such as collaborative, participatory, and individualized learning groupings
- Expected learning outcomes that are theoretical, affective and cognitive for students

Students generally do not realize their own abilities and frequently lack self-confidence. Teachers can instill positive self-concepts in children and thereby enhance their innate abilities by providing certain types of feedback. Such feedback includes attributing students' successes to their effort and specifying what the student did that produced the success. Qualitative comments influence attitudes more than quantitative feedback such as grades.

Teachers must avoid teaching tasks that fit their own interests and goals and design activities that address the students' concerns. In order to do this, it is necessary to find out about students and to have a sense of their interests and goals. Teachers can do this by conducting student surveys and simply by questioning and listening to students. Once this information is obtained the teacher can link students' interests with classroom tasks.

Teachers should recognize the value of giving assignments that meet the individual abilities and needs of students. After instruction, discussion, questioning, and practice have been provided, rather than assigning one task to all students—teachers ask students to generate tasks that will show their knowledge of the information presented. Through choices in the types of tasks they complete, to demonstrate learning, students have the opportunity to demonstrate more effectively the skills, concepts, or topics that they as individuals have learned.

A diverse classroom should also address children who are learning English, as well as those with disabilities and exceptionalities. The types of disabilities in children are very numerous. Some disabilities are entirely physical, while others are entirely related to learning and the mind or background. Some involve a combination of both. While it would be a disservice to say that all kids should display the same types of characteristics to be considered "normal," when abnormalities are noticed, such as a student's incredible ability to solve a math problem without working it out (a potential attribute of giftedness) or another student's extreme trouble with spelling (a potential attribute of dyslexia), a teacher may assume that a disability or exceptional ability is present.

Common learning disabilities include attention deficit hyperactivity disorder (where concentration can be very tough), auditory processing disorders (where listening comprehension is very difficult), visual processing disorders (where reading can be tough and visual memory may be impaired), dyslexia (where reading can be confusing), and many others. Physical disabilities include Down's Syndrome, where mental retardation may be a factor; cerebral palsy, where physical movement is impaired; and many others. Developmental disabilities might include the lack of ability to use fine motor skills.

When giftedness is observed, teachers should also concern themselves with ensuring that such children get the attention they need and deserve so that they can continue to learn and grow.

ELL Approaches for the Classroom

This section will provide you with information about some of the more common approaches used in today's K-12 classrooms for children still acquiring English. **Cognitive approaches** to language learning focus on concepts. While words and grammar are important, when teachers use the cognitive approach, they focus on using language for conceptual purposes—rather than learning words and grammar for the sake of simply learning new words and grammatical structures. This approach focuses heavily on students' learning styles, and it cannot necessarily be pinned down as having specific techniques. Rather, it is more of a philosophy of instruction.

Another very common motivational approach is **Total Physical Response**. This is a kinesthetic approach that combines language learning and physical movement. In essence, students learn new vocabulary and grammar by responding with physical motion to verbal commands. Some people say it is particularly effective because the physical actions create good brain connections with the words.

In general, the best methods do not treat students as if they have a language deficit. Rather, the best methods build upon what students already know, and they help to instill the target language as a communicative process rather than a list of vocabulary words that have to be memorized.

To ensure the maximum education for all diverse learners, teachers must plan accordingly to meet the needs of all their students. The target of diversity allows teachers a variety of opportunities to expand their experiences with students, staff, community members and parents from culturally diverse backgrounds, so that their experiences can be proactively applied in promoting cultural diversity inclusion in the classroom. Teachers are able to engage and challenge students to develop and incorporate their own diversity skills in building character and relationships with cultures beyond their own. In changing the thinking patterns of students to become more cultural inclusive in the 21st century, teachers are addressing the globalization of our world.

First, teachers should realize that historically, there are two broad sides regarding the construction of meaning, the application of strategies, etc. One is **behavioral learning**. Behavioral learning theory suggests that people learn socially or through some sort of stimulation or repetition. For example, when we touch a hot stove, we learn not to do that again. When we make a social error, and are made fun of for it, we learn proper social conventions, or, we learn to produce something by watching someone do the same thing.

The other broad theory is cognitive. **Cognitive learning theories** suggest that learning takes place in the mind, and that the mind processes ideas through brain mapping and connections with other material and experiences. In other words, with behaviorism, learning is somewhat external. We see something, for example, and then we copy it. With cognitive theories, learning is internal. For example, we see something, analyze it in our minds, and make sense of it for ourselves. Then, if we choose to copy it, we do, but we do so having internalized (or thought about) the process.

Today, even though behavioral theories exist, most educators believe that children learn cognitively. So, for example, when teachers introduce new topics by relating those topics to information students are already familiar with or exposed to, they are expecting that students will be able to better integrate new information into their memories by attaching it to something that is already there. When teachers apply new learning to real-world situations, they are expecting that the information will make more sense when it is applied to a real situation. In all of the examples given in this standard, the importance is the application of new learning to something concrete. In essence, what is going on with these examples is that the teacher is slowing building on knowledge or adding knowledge to what students already know. Cognitively, this makes a great deal of sense. Think of a file cabinet. When we already have files for certain things, it's easy for us to find a file and throw new information into it. When we're given something that doesn't fit into one of the pre-existing files, we struggle to know what to do with it. The same is true with human minds.

Skill 2.6 Understanding how community characteristics (e.g., socioeconomic profile, opportunities for out-of-school educational experiences, availability of community resources) may affect children

Socio-economic characteristics

It is a proven fact that the socio-economic profile of a child can affect how the child develops and the school experience. Those children born to parents who have money available for health and education definitely have an advantage over those who don't. Even before birth, the socio-economic status of the mother can have a direct affect on the child. For example, a mother who does not have access to the proper medical care, smokes, drinks or takes drugs during pregnancy could give birth to a baby with developmental or brain injury conditions.

During the period of development between birth and attending school, children need to have opportunities for activity and the proper medical attention. In families where money is tight, there may not be enough attention paid to these issues and not necessarily because the family doesn't think they are important. Children may not have access to books or be read to before they reach school age, may not have proper training in socializing with other children and may not be fully developed in mind and body.

At school, children from low socio-economic backgrounds will easily see that they are not the same as other children in the class and this can affect their self-esteem. They may not be dressed properly for the weather and may not have all the school tools that they need.

Opportunities for out-of-school educational experiences

Children who do not have educational experiences outside of the school environment may be lacking in the prior knowledge they need to comprehend some of the school content. Visiting a library, a zoo or even a shopping mall may seriously impact how these children can relate to materials and content about these subjects because they don't have any experiences which they can relate to when encountering reading or learning about them.

Fieldtrips are important as part of the regular school year. Through field trips students do gain educational experiences to which they might otherwise not have access. Some of the benefits of providing out of school experiences for young children include:

- Opportunities to enrich the curriculum
- Different cultural experiences that are not available in the immediate community
- Provides a broadened sense of historical heritage
- Provides opportunities for children to interact with their peers in a supervised setting away from the school
- Opportunities for children to experience more leisure activities
- Opportunities for children to have life skill experiences

Availability of community resources

Community resources are as important to the development of young children as teachers and schools. Before they enter school, children who attend pre-school or daycares, where there is a structured program, are much more ready for Kindergarten than those children who do not have this opportunity. Quite often stay-at-home moms put their children in daycare for a portion of the week just for the educational experience. In areas where this resource is not available, it does have an affect on the children entering school.

Children who have problems need the aid of community resources. Living in a rural area that is quite a distance form the city often makes this very difficult if the parents have to travel long distances to get the support they need for the child and themselves.

When children enter school, if there are no paraprofessionals on staff, such as a speech therapist, the school has to avail of the community resources to get the help the children need. Other resources of this nature that are an important part of the school include nurses, police officers and business people. In the case of ESL students, the school may need the help of a translator to communicate with the child and the family.

Community businesses can support the children in the school by helping arrange field trips, providing assistance to the school and by providing money for resources when necessary.

Competency 003 **UNDERSTAND INTEGRATED CURRICULUM DESIGN THAT REFLECTS THE WAYS CHILDREN CONSTRUCT KNOWLEDGE**

Skill 3.1 **Demonstrating understanding of the holistic nature of children's learning**

Young children look at the world as being their own personal space. It is often very difficult for them to make connections between individual concepts. Therefore, it is necessary for teachers to approach their instruction in a holistic manner. What this means is that the teachers should view themselves as facilitators of learning rather than instructors who impart knowledge to the children. This means beginning with the whole concept and then moving to the parts. Teachers should allow the students to observe the parts carefully and give them a chance to experiment on their own. This is usually done through play or learning centers in the classroom. When children internalize the small parts of the whole, they can then grasp the whole concept. Visual displays are particularly important so that the children can see the modeling of the tasks.

Children learn within a social context. If you look at how children learn to speak within the family setting, experimenting with language and gradually making the proper sounds of communication, this will give you an idea of how they learn in the classroom. The learning has to be authentic and relevant to their lives and prior learning experiences. By using big books and shared reading, for example, the teacher models how readers behave. In the beginning, you may notice a young child attempting to read, but holding the book upside down.

Children have a desire to make sense of their environment. They do this in various ways and in various stages. No two children learn exactly in the same way or at the same rate. When you have an integrated curriculum in the early years, children get a better idea of how all the subjects are interrelated.

Teachers should also recognize that children need the support of many people in their lives – caregivers, teachers and support staff in a school. All of these people should be part of an early child hood educational program.

Skill 3.2 Demonstrating knowledge of the benefits of integrated curriculum and its role in promoting children's learning

An integrated curriculum is one in which lessons are taught in several different subject areas according to the outcomes that deal with the same concepts. It may also be known as thematic teaching or interdisciplinary teaching.

When the teacher actively and frequently models viewing from multiple perspectives as an approach to learning in the classroom, the students not only benefit through improved academic skill development, they also begin to adopt this approach for learning and contemplating as a personal skill. The ability to consider a situation, issue, problem or event from multiple viewpoints is a skill that will serve the individual well, throughout one's academic career and beyond.

- Internalizing the concept of teaching from perspective starts by posing a simple challenge for oneself. You intend to introduce one fact or skill from your subject area to a student. You do so in the prescribed format—giving the standard explanation and ancillary examples of application. The student doesn't get it: doesn't acquire the skill—can't internalize the information. As the teacher, what do you do? Repeat the instruction, verbatim, until it sinks in? Chastise or cajole the student into acknowledging an understanding? Since you are genuinely concerned about the student's acquisition of skills and academic success, you will immediately realize that the dilemma is yours, not the student's, and you will seek different ways to communicate an understanding of the information so that the student will completely comprehend and acquire a meaningful skill. After all, if the student does not succeed, it is the teacher who has failed.

Integrating the curriculum can save time by teaching the same concepts while reaching the content of more than one subject area of the curriculum. There are various levels of curriculum integration, such as:
- Teaching the objectives of more than one subject area in a single unit
- Developing lessons that incorporate more than one subject area and assessments
- Developing enhancement or enrichment activities that will cause the students to apply what they have learned in other subject areas
- Using cross-curricular assessments

Basic skills, such as reading and math, can be integrated into Social Studies, Science, the arts, and Physical Education classes. Some teachers think in terms of themes in early childhood education and integrate the objectives they wish to accomplish within the theme. Thus students can learn the concepts of the theme in different ways.

Technology can be integrated in all subject areas. Students can write paragraphs using a word processor, use the Internet to conduct research, or display reports through Power Point presentations. These are just a few ways to utilize technology within subject areas..

SEE Skill 3.5 for specific ways to integrate subject areas.

Interdisciplinary and thematic instruction, by definition and design, provide for teaching from perspective. Examples of effective, readily available instructional units are displayed, below.

Discovering Your World by Anita Yeoman
This integrated unit introduces students to various countries as they plan a trip around the world. The unit is very flexible and can be adapted for any middle-level grade and time period. It consists of detailed suggestions for planning a "journey" according to the needs of each class. Worksheets for planning an itinerary, making passports and calculating distances are included, together with peer and self evaluation sheets and tracking sheets. Students will utilize research skills as they learn about language, history, geography and culture of the countries they "visit" on their world trip.

Let's Create An Island by Philip Richards
In this unit students will create an island, following a set of suggestions, deciding on such things as its location, topography, climate, population, employment, form of government, leisure activities, education etc. It enables students to learn important geographic, scientific and civic concepts in a manner that is enjoyable and imaginative. For each activity a concept is taught as a class activity, followed by independent exercises to reinforce what has been taught. The students then this use this knowledge when creating their own island. Includes tracking sheets, suggestions for teaching the unit, a rubric for evaluation and an answer key. Grades 6 – 9

COOL CHARACTER by Charlotte Wilcox, Sharon, Toothman, Linda Hatfield
The objective of this unit is to teach character education through the integration of different subject areas, primarily Health, English/Language Arts, Science, and Social Studies. Intended level: Grade 6.

National Standards
Language Arts:
Gathers and uses information for research purposes.
Demonstrates competence in the general skills and strategies of the writing process.
Demonstrates competence in speaking and listening as tools for learning.

Social Studies:
Understands the importance of Americans sharing and supporting certain values, beliefs, and principles of American constitutional democracy.
Understands economic, social and cultural developments in the contemporary United States.

Health:
Knows how to maintain mental and emotional health.
Understands the fundamental concepts of growth and development.

Career Clusters

Fine Arts and Humanities

Health and Human Services

Keywords

Character Education
Self-Knowledge
Positive Attitude
Leadership
Character Traits

> **Lesson Plans on Cool Characters:**
>
> http://www.thesolutionsite.com/lesson/857/overview.html

Teaching from multiple perspectives opens the door to a world of ideas teachers can use to make education an interesting, fun and effective learning experience where every student can be included in the process and be successful in attaining the objectives. The possibilities may only be limited by the teacher's imagination. Should that limit actually be reached, the teacher has only to look to his or her colleagues to expand the horizon of teaching possibilities.

A philosophy of teaching from perspective: It is less important which path we take, than that we all arrive at the same destination.

Skill 3.3   Knowing how to use children's interests and experiences to generate ideas and concepts for investigation and study

It has been established that student choice increases student originality, intrinsic motivation, and higher mental processes. By listening to children talk and play with one another, through classroom discussions and by asking direct questions, teachers can learn about the topics students are interested in. By designing lessons centered around these topics and ensuring that the lessons are aligned with the specific objectives in the state standards, the teacher can keep the children interested and motivated to learn.

Children in the early grades are naturally curious about the world and want to investigate and explore. Activities that let them learn about concepts through inquiry can help the teacher get to know more about what the children like and don't like to do. For example, in a lesson where the children are learning about spiders, teachers can observe what they are doing and use this information to deliver more lessons that reteach or challenge the children.

At the beginning of the year, teachers should ask students to fill out a survey of their likes and dislikes. For early grades, the teacher can ask the students the questions to complete the survey or send the survey home for completion with the help of the parents. Then the teacher can go through the surveys to find common lists of likes. This will help determine the curriculum for certain subjects and maybe areas where the unit objectives for two or more subjects can be combined. It will also give the teacher an idea of where differentiated instruction would be helpful with a group of students or even an independent study.

Using a K-W-L chart at the beginning of the unit helps the teacher find out how much students already know about the topic so that the lessons don't duplicate any of that information and thus cause them to become bored. The three sections of this type of chart are: What do you know?; What do you want to learn?; and What have you learned?. By completing the second section of what the students want to learn about the topic teachers then have the direction that the students want the teaching and learning to take.

The first month of any school year is one in which the teachers get to know the students and how they learn. This is also a time to determine which students would benefit from certain types of learning experiences, such as by experimenting, visualizing, working in groups or working alone. All this information is as important as knowing the curriculum because it, too, will determine the children's interest and motivation.

Skill 3.4 Demonstrating knowledge of how to construct integrated learning experiences that reflect learning standards across the curriculum and support children's progress

An integrated curriculum is a program of study that describes a movement toward integrated lessons that enables students to make connections across curricula. This curriculum links among the humanities, art. natural sciences, mathematics, music, and social studies.

The integrated curriculum is a method that teaches students to break down barriers between subjects. Lessons are planned around broad themes that students can identify with, such as "The Environment." Major concepts are pulled from this broad concept, and teachers then plan activities that teach these concepts.

Characteristics of an Integrated Curriculum

- A combination of subjects
- An emphasis on projects
- Sources that go beyond textbooks
- Relationships among concepts
- Thematic units as organizing principles
- Flexible schedules
- Flexible student groupings.

Integrated curriculum is an education that is organized in such a way that it cuts across subject-matter lines, bringing together various aspects of the curriculum into meaningful association to focus upon broad areas of study. It views learning and teaching in a holistic way and reflects the real world, which is interactive. (Humphreys, Post, and Ellis)

Involvement between families, teachers, libraries, principals, and other school professionals should be viewed as a partnership, where each actively strives to create and promote an enriching environment for children to have the opportunity to develop their research and comprehension skills. Many schools are instituting school-wide computer programs and other technology to aid in the ongoing research skills of their students. Schools can collaborate with local libraries to create summer reading programs that encourage comprehension and research skills for students. Teachers can also form literacy programs to involve the community and families in the students' reading curriculum.

Implementing such a child-centered curriculum is the result of very careful and deliberate planning. Planning serves as a means of organizing instruction and influences classroom teaching. Well thought-out planning includes: specifying behavioral objectives, specifying students' entry behavior (knowledge and skills), selecting and sequencing learning activities so as to move students from entry behavior to objective, and evaluating the outcomes of instruction in order to improve planning.

SEE also Skill 3.2

Links to further reading on Integrating the Curriculum:

http://www.nwrel.org/scpd/sirs/8/c016.html

http://vocserve.berkeley.edu/ST2.1/TowardanIntegrated.html

http://vocserve.berkeley.edu/ST2.1/TowardanIntegrated.html

TEACHER CERTIFICATION STUDY GUIDE

Skill 3.5   **Applying knowledge of strategies for integrating curriculum in literacy, mathematics, science, social studies, and the arts to promote children's learning**

SEE Skill 3.4 for a general discussion of integrating curriculum

Language Arts

Most people think of Language Arts when they think of literacy. Literacy applies to all areas of the curriculum, as children need to read and write in order to succeed in all subject areas. All of the areas of literacy, mathematics, science, social studies and the arts are integral parts that make up the whole curriculum. Integrating the curriculum does require an amount of preparatory work on the part of teachers, as they have to be aware of the skills and objectives of all areas and be able to bring them together when necessary. Once they do this, it does make the delivery of the curriculum much easier as they can spend longer amounts of time on one area and accomplish several goals or objectives at the same time.

Once the teacher has aligned the objectives that can fit together, then lessons can be designed that meet the objectives of two or three areas of study.

Literacy refers to the child's ability to read and write effectively. This is one of the easiest areas to integrate with all other subject areas. Literacy and Social Studies (which refers to the combination of history, geography and civics) have many areas in common. A teacher can teach a unit on government, for example, within the context of a Language Arts class. The reading materials are all related to government and students achieve the literacy objectives through the reading and writing they do for this unit. Class discussions, formal and informal writing assignments, art projects and reading fiction and non-fiction will all help the student to learn the content for the grade with regards to government and the Language Arts standards for the grade level. Mathematics can be part of this in having the students create different kinds of maps and diagrams to demonstrate their understanding.

Mathematics can be integrated with Literacy in several ways. In order to introduce a new concept, the teacher can start off reading a picture book to the class about that concept. In teaching about large numbers, the picture book *How Much is a Million?* is one of the best ways to introduce the topic because it gets children thinking about numbers. When students learn how to add, subtract, multiple or divide, a good way to get them to demonstrate what they have learned is to have them write out the process they went through to get the correct answer. They could also prepare a poster demonstrating the steps in solving the problem. In fact, problem solving in Math in the early grades focuses on having students create drawings to help them find the solution. Diagrams are a common part of Language Arts in story maps, for example.

EARLY CHILDHOOD EDUCATION

Physical science is a term for the branches of science that study non-living systems. However, the term "physical" creates an unintended, arbitrary distinction, since many branches of physical science also study biological phenomena. Topics in physical science, such as movement of an object through space and the effect of gravity on moving objects, are of great relevance to physical education. Physical sciences allow us to determine the limits of physical activities.

Math, science, and technology have common themes in how they are applied and understood. All three use models, diagrams, and graphs to simplify a concept for analysis and interpretation. Patterns observed in these systems lead to predictions based on these observations. Another common theme among these three systems is equilibrium. Equilibrium is a state in which forces are balanced, resulting in stability. Static equilibrium is stability due to a lack of changes and dynamic equilibrium is stability due to a balance between opposite forces.

The fundamental relationship between the natural and social sciences is the use of the scientific method and the rigorous standards of proof that both disciplines require. This emphasis on organization and evidence separates the sciences from the arts and humanities. Natural science, particularly biology, is closely related to social science, the study of human behavior. Biological and environmental factors often dictate human behavior and accurate assessment of behavior requires a sound understanding of biological factors.

Science, too, can be integrated with both Mathematics and Language Arts. Students learn how to use the scientific process in the early grade and for the most part, the teacher writes out the steps for the experiments on the chalkboard for them. Teachers can prepare a sheet that students have to fill in to show the steps in their experiment and report their results. It is not as detailed as in the later grades, but it does integrate Literacy. For some Science inquiries, students have to do Math computations to find a result. This helps to integrate this subject and if the teacher aligns the computations or problem solving with the math objectives, it serves two purposes.

Physical Education can also be part of other subject areas. Teachers may already be doing this without even realizing it. Asking the students to divide into teams, for example, means that they have to apply Math skills to have even numbers. Keeping score in a game is another example. If you ask students to explain the rules of a game to another group of students, this is an example of integrating Literacy into Physical Education classes. Teachers can also have students make up a new game for which they have to write the rules and explain them to the class and then play the game.

The arts can be part of just about all classes in having students prepare a response to their reading or showing that they understand the concept by asking them to respond by means of a piece of art work, a song or dance. When students have the opportunity to demonstrate what they have learned in this way, teachers can tap into their talents and individual ways of learning.

At the end of the day, it is helpful to ask the students to write in a Learning Log. In this journal, they must explain one or two things that they learned that day and how it helped them. They can also list other things they would like to learn about that or another topic.

Mathematics

Mathematics is the search for fundamental truths in pattern, quantity, and change. Examples of mathematical applications in sport include measuring speed, momentum, and height of objects; measuring distances and weights; scorekeeping; and statistical computations.

Teachers can increase student interest in math and promote learning and understanding by relating mathematical concepts to the lives of students. Instead of using only abstract presentations and examples, teachers should relate concepts to real-world situations to shift the emphasis from memorization and abstract application to understanding and applied problem solving. In addition, relating math to careers and professions helps illustrate the relevance of math and aids in the career exploration process.

For example, when teaching a unit on the geometry of certain shapes, teachers can ask students to design a structure of interest to the student using the shapes in question. This exercise serves the dual purpose of teaching students to learn and apply the properties (e.g. area, volume) of shapes while demonstrating the relevance of geometry to architectural and engineering professions.

Science

Social Science

The social sciences are a group of academic disciplines that study the human aspects of the world. Social scientists engage in research and theorize about both aggregate and individual behaviors. For example, a basic understanding of psychology is essential to the discussion of human patterns of nutrition and attitudes toward exercise and fitness. In addition, sport psychology is a specialized social science that explores the mental aspects of athletic performance.

Physical Studies

Kinesiology encompasses human anatomy, physiology, neuroscience, biochemistry, biomechanics, exercise psychology, and sociology of sport. Kinesiologists also study the relationship between the quality of movement and overall human health. Kinesiology is an important part of physical therapy, occupational therapy, chiropractics, osteopathy, exercise physiology, kinesiotherapy, massage therapy, ergonomics, physical education, and athletic coaching. The purpose of these applications may be therapeutic, preventive, or high-performance. The application of kinesiology can also incorporate knowledge from other academic disciplines such as psychology, sociology, cultural studies, ecology, evolutionary biology, and anthropology. The study of kinesiology is often part of the physical education curriculum and illustrates the truly interdisciplinary nature of physical education.

Physical education is a key component of an interdisciplinary learning approach because it draws from many other curriculum areas. Instructors can relate concepts from the physical sciences, mathematics, natural sciences, social sciences, and kinesiology to physical education activities.

Creative Arts

Artists, musicians, scientists, social scientists, and business people use mathematical modeling to solve problems in their disciplines. These disciplines rely on the tools and symbology of mathematics to model natural events and manipulate data.

Mathematics is a key aspect of visual art. Artists use the geometric properties of shapes, ratios, and proportions in creating paintings and sculptures. For example, mathematics is essential to the concept of perspective. Artists must determine the appropriate lengths and heights of objects to portray three-dimensional distance in two dimensions.

Mathematics is also an important part of music. Many musical terms have mathematical connections. For example, the musical octave contains twelve notes and spans a factor of two in frequency. In other words, the frequency, the speed of vibration that determines tone and sound quality, doubles from the first note in an octave to the last. Thus, starting from any note we can determine the frequency of any other note with the following formula.

$$\text{Freq} = \text{note} \times 2^{N/12}$$

Where N is the number of notes from the starting point and note is the frequency of the starting note. Mathematical understanding of frequency plays an important role in the tuning of musical instruments.

In addition to the visual and auditory arts, mathematics is an integral part of most scientific disciplines. The uses of mathematics in science are almost endless. The following are but a few examples of how scientists use mathematics. Physical scientists use vectors, functions, derivatives, and integrals to describe and model the movement of objects. Biologists and ecologists use mathematics to model ecosystems and study DNA. Finally, chemists use mathematics to study the interaction of molecules and to determine proper amounts and proportions of reactants.

Many social science disciplines use mathematics to model and solve problems. Economists, for example, use functions, graphs, and matrices to model the activities of producers, consumers, and firms.

Sample lesson plan for Integrating the Curriculum:

http://members.tripod.com/arturo_lopez_1/id68.htm

Template for an Integrated Lesson:

http://pt3.cl.uh.edu/lessonplan/lessonplan2.cfm

Lesson Plans for Early Childhood classrooms:

http://www.childrensresources.org/toc810.html

DOMAIN II. COMMUNICATION, LANGUAGE, AND LITERACY DEVELOPMENT

Competency 004   **UNDERSTAND COMMUNICATION AND LANGUAGE DEVELOPMENT IN YOUNG CHILDREN**

Skill 4.1   Demonstrating knowledge of characteristics, processes, and progressions in the development of receptive and expressive language and speech

Phonemes

In everyday language, we attach affective meanings to words unconsciously; we exercise more conscious control of informative connotations. In the process of language development, the student must come not only to grasp the definitions of words but also to become more conscious of the affective connotations and how listeners process these connotations. Gaining this conscious control over language makes it possible to use language appropriately in various situations and to evaluate its uses in literature and other forms of communication.

The manipulation of language for a variety of purposes is the goal of language instruction. Advertisers and satirists are especially conscious of the effect word choice has on their audiences. By evoking the proper responses from readers/listeners, we can prompt them to take action.

A phoneme is the smallest contrastive unit in a language system, and the representation of a sound. The phoneme has been described as the smallest meaningful psychological unit of sound. The phoneme is said to have mental, physiological, and physical substance. Our brains process the sounds, which are produced by the human speech organs and are physical entities that can be recorded and measured. Consider the English words "pat" and "sat," which appear to differ only in their initial consonants. This difference, known as contrastiveness or opposition, is adequate to distinguish these words, and therefore the P and S sounds are said to be different phonemes in English. A pair of words, identical except for such a sound, is known as a minimal pair, and the two sounds are separate phonemes.

Phonemic Awareness

Phonemic awareness is the acknowledgement of sounds and words, such as a child's realization that some words rhyme. Onset and rhyme, for example, are skills that might help students learn that the sound of the first letter "b" in the word "bad" can be changed with the sound "d" to make it "dad." The key in phonemic awareness is that when you teach it to children, it can be taught with the students' eyes closed. In other words, it's all about sounds, not about ascribing written letters to sounds.

To be phonemically aware means that the reader and listener can recognize and manipulate specific sounds in spoken words. Phonemic awareness deals with sounds in spoken words. The majority of phonemic awareness tasks, activities, and exercises are ORAL.

Since the ability to distinguish between individual sounds, or phonemes, within words is a prerequisite to association of sounds with letters and manipulating sounds to blend words (a fancy way of saying "reading") the teaching of phonemic awareness is crucial to emergent literacy. Children need a strong background in phonemic awareness in order for phonics instruction to be effective.

Phonics

As opposed to phonemic awareness, the study of phonics must be done with the eyes open. It's the connection between the sounds and letters on a page. In other words, students learning phonics might see the word "bad" and sound each letter out slowly until they recognize that they just said the word.

Phonological awareness means the ability of the reader to recognize the sound of spoken language. This recognition includes how these sounds can be blended together, segmented (divided up), and manipulated (switched around). This awareness then leads to phonics - a method for teaching children to read. It helps them "sound out words."

Development of phonological skills may begin during pre-K years. Indeed by the age of 5, a child who has been exposed to rhyme can recognize a rhyme. Such a child can demonstrate phonological awareness by filling in the missing rhyming word in a familiar rhyme or rhymed picture book.

You teach children phonological awareness when you teach them the sounds made by the letters, the sounds made by various combinations of letters and to recognize individual sounds in words.

Phonological awareness skills include:
1. Rhyming and syllabification
2. Blending sounds into words—such as pic-tur-bo-k
3. Identifying the beginning or starting sounds of words and the ending or closing sounds of words
4. Breaking words down into sounds—also called "segmenting" words
5. Recognizing other smaller words in the big word, by removing starting sounds, "hear" to ear

Morphology, Syntax, Semantics and Pragmatics

Morphology is the study of word structure. When readers develop morphemic skills, they are developing an understanding of patterns they see in words. For example, English speakers realize that cat, cats, and caterpillar share some similarities in structure. This understanding helps readers to recognize words at a faster and easier rate, since each word doesn't need individual decoding.

Syntax refers to the rules or patterned relationships that correctly create phrases and sentences from words. When readers develop an understanding of syntax, they begin to understand the structure of how sentences are built, and eventually the beginning of grammar.

Example:
   "I am going to the movies"

This statement is syntactically and grammatically correct

Example:
   "They am going to the movies"

This statement is syntactically correct since all the words are in their correct place, but it is grammatically incorrect with the use of the word "They" rather than "I."

Semantics refers to the meaning expressed when words are arranged in a specific way. This is where connotation and denotation of words eventually will have a role with readers.

All of these skill sets are important to developing effective word recognition skills, which help emerging readers develop fluency.

Pragmatics

Pragmatics is concerned with the difference between the writer's meaning and the sentence meaning (the literal meaning of the sentence) based on social context. When students are competent in pragmatics, they are able to understand the writer's intended meaning or what the writer is trying to convey. In a simpler sense, pragmatics can be considered the social rules of language.

For example, a little girl sitting beside her mother at a fancy restaurant after her great-grandmother's funeral looks over to the table next to them. She sees a very elderly woman eating her dessert. "Mom?" she asks, patiently waiting for response. When her mother addresses her, she states loudly, "That woman is old like Grandma. Is she going to die soon too?" Of course embarrassed, the mother hushes her child. However, this is a simple example of immature pragmatics. The child has the vocabulary, the patience to wait her turn, and some knowledge of conversational rules. However, she is not aware that certain topics are socially inappropriate and therefore fails to adapt her language to the situation.

Skill 4.2   Demonstrating knowledge of factors that influence children's communication and language development

Factors that Affect Student Learning

There are many factors that affect student learning. There are several educational learning theories that can be applied to classroom practices. Some of the most prominent learning theories in education today include **brain-based learning** and the Multiple Intelligence Theory. Supported by recent brain research, brain-based learning suggests that knowledge about the way the brain retains information enables educators to design the most effective learning environments. As a result, researchers have developed twelve principles that relate knowledge about the brain to teaching practices. These twelve principles are:

- The brain is a complex adaptive system
- The brain is social
- The search for meaning is innate
- We use patterns to learn more effectively
- Emotions are crucial to developing patterns
- Each brain perceives and creates parts and whole simultaneously
- Learning involves focused and peripheral attention
- Learning involves conscious and unconscious processes
- We have at least two ways of organizing memory
- Learning is developmental
- Complex learning is enhanced by challenged (and inhibited by threat)
- Every brain is unique (Caine & Caine, 1994, Mind/Brain Learning Principles)

Educators can use these principles to help design methods and environments in their classrooms to maximize student learning.

> **Brain-based Learning**:
>
> http://www.brainconnection.com/topics/?main=fa/brain-based

The **Multiple Intelligence Theory**, developed by Howard Gardner, suggests that students learn in (at least) seven different ways. These include visually/spatially, musically, verbally, logically/mathematically, interpersonally, interpersonally, and bodily/kinesthetically.

> **Learn more about the Multiple Intelligence Theory:**
>
> http://www.thomasarmstrong.com/multiple_intelligences.htm

The most current learning theory of **constructivist learning** allows students to construct learning opportunities. For constructivist teachers, the belief is that students create their own reality of knowledge and understanding of how to process and observe the world around them. Students are constantly constructing new ideas, which serve as frameworks for learning and teaching. Researchers have shown that the constructivist model is comprised of the four components:

1. Learner creates knowledge
2. Learner constructs and makes meaningful new knowledge from existing knowledge
3. Learner shapes and constructs knowledge by life experiences and social interactions
4. In constructivist learning communities, the student, teacher and classmates establish knowledge cooperatively on a daily basis.

Kelly (1969) states, "human beings that construct knowledge systems based on their observations parallel Piaget's theory that individuals construct knowledge systems as they work with others who share a common background of thought and processes." Constructivist learning for students is dynamic and ongoing. For constructivist teachers, the classroom becomes a place where students are encouraged to interact with the instructional process by asking questions and posing new ideas to old theories. The use of cooperative learning that encourages students to work in supportive learning environments using their own ideas to stimulate questions and propose outcomes is a major aspect of a constructivist classroom.

> For further reading on the Constructivist Learning Theory:
>
> http://www.stemnet.nf.ca/~elmurphy/emurphy/cle2b.html

The **metacognition learning theory** deals with "the study of how to help the learner gain understanding about how knowledge is constructed and about the conscious tools for constructing that knowledge" (Joyce and Weil 1996). The cognitive approach to learning involves the teacher's understanding that teaching the student to process his/her own learning and mastery of skill provides the greatest learning and retention opportunities in the classroom. Students are taught to develop concepts and teach themselves skills in problem solving and critical thinking. The student becomes an active participant in the learning process and the teacher facilitates that conceptual and cognitive learning process.

> **Find out more about the Metacognition Learning Theory:**
>
> http://coe.sdsu.edu/eet/Articles/metacognition/start.htm

Social and behavioral theories look at the social interactions of students in the classroom that instruct or impact learning opportunities in the classroom. The psychological approaches behind both theories are subject to individual variables that are learned and applied either proactively or negatively in the classroom. The stimulus of the classroom can be conducive to learning or evoke behavior that is counterproductive for both students and teachers. Students are social beings that normally gravitate to action in the classroom, so teachers must be cognizant in planning classroom environments that provide both focus and engagement to maximize learning opportunities.

Learn more about Social and Behavioral theories: Social Learning Theory: http://teachnet.edb.utexas.edu/~lynda_abbott/Social.html	For more information about Learning Theories: http://www.funderstanding.com/about_learning.cfm

Skill 4.3 Demonstrating knowledge of how children convey meaning through nonverbal and verbal communication

Only a small part of the brain is devoted to verbal communication. Non-verbal communication is the core of language development. Language is best learned through the combination of verbal and nonverbal communication. It is best learned when synchronizing the two forms of communication, in other words, when combining words and matching action. If the action doesn't match the words, it confuses the language development of the young child. For example, saying a child is doing a great job on an art project, then throwing the drawing or other product away, confuses the child and delays language development.

Nonverbal communication has several components. They are: 1) Kinesics–body movement, facial expression, gesture; 2) tactilism–touching behavior; 3) paralanguage- pitch, stress, intonation, and voice quality; 4) proxemics–distance or space; 5) artifacts–clothing, cosmetic aids; 6) environmental factors–getting on the floor with the child, getting down on child's level.

Young children enter school with varying degrees of experiences and development. This is true of communication more than anything else.

Communication skills follow sequential development levels. A child may be using more that one level at any one time, perfecting one level while using a prior level.

Stages of Nonverbal and Verbal Development

Nonverbal
During this stage, children use gestures and materials to communicate ideas. They are developing a special, 'school' language. Using gestures and manipulative materials to communicate an idea does this. Body movement and drawing are other avenues they may use. For example, to explain/define a square the child may draw it, use yarn to form one, walk off a square shape, or select square shapes from a pile of attribute blocks.

Oral Language
The next stage of language development involves developing an oral language. The child may use rudimentary vocabulary skills to describe something. For example, in explaining the square, the child may say, "It looks like ..." or "It is squarish." Children move toward standard oral language in different stages. For example, one student may use the term above, while another may say it is shaped like this: it has four sides, the sides are the same (equal), and use other vocabulary terms to which they have been introduced.

One aspect of oral language is listening. The child learns to listen to other students and to the teacher and/or other adults. Listening includes questioning and answering.

Interplay of oral and written language
During this stage, children begin to use written language along with the oral language skills. They will use symbols, at first invented symbols, then standard symbols, while using oral language in congruence with their writing.

Written language
The final stage of language development is written language. Though it is a separate developmental stage, the child will continue to use the interplay of oral and written language.

> For more information on the stages of verbal and nonverbal development:
>
> www.mnstate.edu/pccp/

EARLY CHILDHOOD EDUCATION

Teacher's Role in Language Development

The teacher can help the child move through these stages by allowing challenging tasks, encouraging group work on them, encouraging the group to talk about the task, and then requiring a written product.

The teacher also must note the difficulties individual students and groups have with a task and then ask leading questions that encourage further exploration by the students.

Help with written products can be in the form of the above type questioning, as well as giving written models of vocabulary words and key terms, and written questions for the child to explore.

Skill 4.4 Identifying ways to promote children's communication and language development

In order to stimulate the development of their oral language skills, children should be exposed to a challenging environment that is rich in opportunities. The following activities encourage students to develop oral language skills in the early stages of oral language development.

Activities

Encourage meaningful conversation
Let students "read" a favorite book to you. Ask them why it is their favorite book. Ask questions prompting a purposeful discussion that allows the students to develop and demonstrate their speaking skills.

Allow dramatic playtime
Make sure children have time for "pretend play" to develop. Provide props that associate play to favorite books.

Let children share personal stories.
Support their efforts to communicate complex thoughts by waiting patiently, suggesting words as needed, and encouraging their efforts to vocalize new words, while they compare their own experiences with other students.

Sing Alphabet Songs
Sing the alphabet song in order to teach students to enjoy and identify the different musical sounds of the alphabet.

Teach the art of questioning
Read a book to the students. Allow them to ask curiosity questions (who, what, why, when and where). This encourages the students to develop higher cognitive skills through questions.

Read Rhyming books
By listening to a favorite book of rhymes, students can identify the rhyming words and sound them out.

Play listening games
Let students pretend they are talking on the phone to each other. Have them repeat the conversation. This encourages students to hear the words and then repeat them.

Encourage sharing of information
By encouraging each student to share information about an idea, the student is able to vocalize words and thoughts in a logical sequence

Skill 4.5 Identifying ways to promote vocabulary development and the use of vocabulary knowledge in new contexts

The explicit teaching of word analysis requires that the teacher pre-select words from a given text for vocabulary learning. These words should be chosen based on the storyline and main ideas of the text. The teacher may even want to create a story map for a narrative text or develop a graphic organizer for an expository text. Once the story mapping and/or graphic organizing have been done, the teacher can compile a list of words that relate to the storyline and/or main ideas. Next, the teacher should decide which key words are already well defined in the text. Obviously, these will not need explicit class review.

Identify the words that the child can determine through use of prefixes, suffixes or base words. Again these words will not require direct teaching. Then reflect on the words in relation to the children's background, prior knowledge base and language experiences (including native language/dialect words). Based on the above steps, decide which words need to be taught.

The number of words that require explicit teaching should only be two or three. If the number is higher than that, the children need guided reading and the text needs to be broken down into smaller sections for teaching. When broken down into smaller sections, each text section should only have two to three words that need explicit teaching. Some researchers, including Tierney and Cunningham, believe that a few words should be taught as a means of improving comprehension. It is up to the teacher whether the vocabulary selected for teaching needs review before reading, during reading, or after reading.

Introduce vocabulary BEFORE READING if. . .

- Children are having difficulty constructing meaning on their own. Children themselves have previewed the text and indicated words they want to know.
- The teacher has seen that there are words within the text, which are definitely keys necessary for reading comprehension
- The text, itself, in the judgment of the teacher, contains difficult concepts for the children to grasp.

Introduce vocabulary DURING READING if . . .

- Children are already doing guided reading.
- The text has words that are crucial to its comprehension and the children will have trouble comprehending it, if they are not helped with the text.

Introduce vocabulary AFTER READING if. . .

- The children themselves have shared words that they found difficult or interesting
- The children need to expand their vocabulary
- The text itself is one that is particularly suited for vocabulary building.

Strategies, which can be used to support word analysis, and as a vehicle for enhancing and enriching reading comprehension, include:

- Use of a graphic organizer, such as a word map
- Semantic mapping
- Semantic feature analysis
- Hierarchical and linear arrays
- Preview in context
- Contextual redefinition
- Vocabulary self-collection

Some ways to encourage a child's vocabulary development include:

- Using "rare" and new words when speaking to children
- Identifying words in context for children. In other words, using new words and defining them in the same sentence when speaking
- Creating word walls on the classroom wall. Children can be encouraged to add new words to the wall when they come across unfamiliar words
- Encouraging the use or creation of a glossary to identify unknown words in reading assignments
- Using flash cards to remember and study unfamiliar vocabulary
- Systematically teaching basic roots, prefixes, and suffixes

- Exposing children to foreign languages and encouraging them to notice similarities between foreign words and English ones
- Vocabulary lessons incorporated with spelling tests
- Teaching vocabulary lessons "across the curriculum"—not just in English class
- Direct instruction in vocabulary and "cluster words" that go together
- Encouraging wide reading of quality literature
- Promoting the regular use of dictionaries, thesauruses, and glossaries

To encourage the use of vocabulary knowledge in new contexts, teachers in different subject areas could share their vocabulary lists with one another. The incorporation of words learned in one class in another will reinforce the knowledge gained. Modeling is another important way in which teachers promote the use of newly acquired vocabulary in different contexts. Teachers should continually expand their own vocabularies, and as they learn new words, they may want to share them with students or add them to the word wall. Teachers could also promote a "word of the day" or "word of the week" and reward students for working it into their written or spoken communication.

Skill 4.6 Recognizing ways for developing increasingly complex language and vocabulary to express thoughts and feelings, describe experiences, interact with others, and communicate needs

An excellent way to increase language and vocabulary is simply reading to children and talking to them about what was read. Since the language used in books is more complex than that used in speaking, the child is exposed to more complex language and vocabulary.

Developing listening skills will increase complex language. Ways to develop listening skills include modeling listening skills, directly teaching listening skills, and playing listening games.

Strategies for increasing vocabulary include:
- reading books with new and unusual words
- building on the child's interest to learn new words
- taking field trips to places the child may not have been, utilizing pre- and post-activities for those field trips
- exposing the child to a varied curricula including science, math and social studies
- introducing a child to new words and using them in conversations
- introduce new and expanding vocabulary and grammar, including:
    1. **positional** and **directional** words (e.g., in, on, out, under, off, beside, behind)
    2. **temporal words** (e.g., before-after)
    3. **comparative words** (e.g., faster-slower, heavier-lighter)

Strategies for enhancing complex language include:
- engaging the child in one-on-one conversations
- expanding on conversations by asking open-ended questions requiring the child to expand on their ideas
- providing dramatic play opportunities with props, guided scripts, and teacher-initiated conversation
- direct teaching of descriptive words and phrases for describing familiar objects, people, events, and their attributes
- direct teaching of multiple word sentences with grammatical complexity to describe ideas, feelings, activities, and experiences

Encouraging children to share their personal thoughts, feelings, experiences, and opinions creates confidence in using complex language and new vocabulary. Accepting the child's developmental level and expanding on it helps the child become a risk-taker and expand on existing language and vocabulary skills.

Part of teaching complex language skills to express thoughts and feelings, describe experiences, interact with others, and communicate needs is to teach the child to recognize when a listener doesn't understand and to use techniques to clarify the message.

A teacher should be able to recognize when a child is competent in using complex language and vocabulary. Some milestones for a teacher to look for include when the child:
- develops abstract thoughts and understands abstract vocabulary, such as freedom, friendship, and honesty
- develops non-literal meaning and humor
- develops social perspective, such as feelings of others and the effects of their own utterances
- develops interest-specific vocabulary, such as dinosaurs, collector cards, sports
- communicates needs, wants, and thoughts, through non-verbal gestures, actions, or expressions
- makes relevant responses to questions and comments from others
- initiates conversations
- uses appropriate **tone** and **inflection** to express ideas, feelings, and needs
- sustains or expands conversations

Learning complex language and vocabulary occurs more quickly when both the teacher and the student have fun with language and language activities.

Skill 4.7 **Demonstrating knowledge of methods for motivating children to use oral language to communicate (e.g., telling and retelling stories through play, pictures, illustrations, props, and other materials)**

SEE Skill 4.4

Competency 005 **UNDERSTAND SECOND-LANGUAGE ACQUISITION AND HOW TO FACILITATE THE ENGLISH LANGUAGE DEVELOPMENT OF YOUNG CHILDREN WITH DIVERSE LINGUISTIC BACKGROUND**

Skill 5.1 Recognizing characteristics, processes, and progressions of second-language acquisition in young children; analyzing factors and issues affecting the learning experiences of children with a home language other than English (e.g., age, prior experiences)

One of the most important things to know about the differences between L1 (first language) and L2 (second language) acquisition is that people usually will master L1, but they will almost never be fully proficient in L2. However, if children can be trained in L2 before about the age of seven, their chances at full mastery will be much higher. Children learn language with so little effort, which is why they can be babbling one year and speaking with complete, complex ideas just a few years later. It is important to know that language is innate, meaning that our brains are ready to learn a language from birth. Yet, a lot of language learning is behavioral, meaning that children imitate adults' speech.

Stages of Language Acquisition

There is wide agreement that there are generally five stages of second language development. The first stage is "pre-production." While students in this stage may actually understand what someone says to them (for the most part), they have a much harder time talking back in the target language. Teachers must realize that if a student cannot "produce" the target language, it does not mean that they aren't learning. Most likely, they are. They are taking it in, and their brains are trying to figure out what to do with all the new language.

The second phase is early production. , In this stage, the student can actually start to produce the target language. It is quite limited, and teachers most likely should not expect students to produce eloquent speeches during this time.

The third phase is emergent speech or speech emergence. Longer, more complex sentences are used, particularly in speech—and in social situations. It is important to remember that students aren't fully fluent in this stage, and they cannot handle complex academic language tasks.

The fourth phase is intermediate fluency. This is the stage in which more complex language is produced. Grammatical errors are common.

The fifth stage is advanced fluency. While students may appear to be completely fluent, they will still need academic and language support from teachers.

Many people say that there are prescribed amounts of time by which students should reach each stage. However, keep in mind that it depends on the level at which students are exposed to the language. For example, students who get opportunities to practice with the target language outside of school may have greater ease in reaching the fifth stage. In general, though, it does take years to reach the fifth stage, and students should never be expected to have complete mastery within one school year.

> **For more information on the stages of language acquisition:**
>
> http://www.everythingesl.net/inservices/language_stages.php

Theories of Language Acquisition

L2 acquisition is much harder for adults. Multiple theories of L2 acquisition have emerged. Some of the more notable ones come from Jim Cummins who argues that there are two types of language that usually need to be acquired by students learning English as a second language: Basic Interpersonal Communication Skills (BICS) Cognitive Academic Language Proficiency (CALP). BICS is general, everyday language used to communicate simple thoughts, whereas CALP is the more complex, academic language used in school. It is harder for students to acquire CALP, and many teachers mistakenly assume that students can learn complex academic concepts in English if they have already mastered BICS. The truth is that CALP takes much longer to master, and in some cases, particularly with little exposure in certain subjects, it may never be mastered.

> **Read more about Jim Cummins:**
>
> http://iteachilearn.com/cummins/

Another set of theories is based on Stephen Krashen's research in L2 acquisition. Most people understand his theories based on five principles:

1. The acquisition-learning hypothesis: This states that there is a difference between learning a language and acquiring it. Children "acquire" a first language easily—it's natural. However, adults often have to "learn" a language through coursework, studying, and memorizing. One can acquire a second language, but often it requires more deliberate and natural interaction within that language.
2. The monitor hypothesis: This is when the learned language "monitors" the acquired language. In other words, this is when a person's "grammar check" kicks in and keeps awkward, incorrect language out of a person's L2 communication.
3. The natural order hypothesis: This suggests that the learning of grammatical structures is predictable and follows a "natural order."
4. The input hypothesis: Some people call this "comprehensible input." This means that a language learner will learn best when the instruction or conversation is just above the learner's ability. That way, the learner has the foundation to understand most of the language, but still will have to figure out, often in context, what that extra, more difficult element means.
5. The affective filter hypothesis: This suggests that people will learn a second language when they are relaxed, have high levels of motivation, and have a decent level of self-confidence.

SEE also Skill 5.2 and Skill 5.3

> **For further reading about Second Language Learning:**
>
> http://www.ualberta.ca/~gkoble/project/overview_main.htm

Skill 5.2 Identifying strategies and techniques for promoting the English language development of children with diverse linguistic backgrounds

Teaching students who are learning English as a second language poses some unique challenges, particularly in a standards-based environment. The key is realizing that no matter how little English a student knows, the teacher should teach with the student's developmental level in mind. This means that instruction should not be "dumbed-down" for ESOL (English to Speakers of Other Languages) students. Different approaches should be used, however, to ensure that these students (a) get multiple opportunities to learn and practice English and (b) still learn content.

Many ESOL approaches are based on social learning methods. By being placed in mixed level groups or by being paired with a student of another ability level, students will get a chance to practice English in a natural, non-threatening environment. While in these groups, students should not be pushed to use complex language or to experiment with words that are too difficult. They should simply get a chance to practice with simple words and phrases.

In teacher-directed instructional situations, visual aids, such as pictures, objects, and video are particularly effective at helping students make connections between words and items with which they are already familiar.

ESOL students may need additional accommodations with assessments, assignments, and projects. For example, teachers may find that written tests provide little or no information about a student's understanding of the content. Therefore, an oral test may be better suited for ESOL students. When students are somewhat comfortable and capable with written tests, a shortened test may actually be preferable provided they have the extra time needed to translate.

The most important concept to remember regarding the difference between learning a first language and a second one is that if the learner is approximately age seven or older, learning a second language will occur very differently in the learner's brain than it will had the learner been younger. The reason for this is that there is a language-learning function that exists in young children that appears to go away as they mature. Learning a language prior to age seven is almost guaranteed, with relatively little effort. The mind is like a sponge, and it soaks up language very readily.

Some theorists, including the famous linguist Noam Chomsky, argue that the brain has a "universal grammar" and that only vocabulary and very particular grammatical structures, related to specific languages, need to be introduced in order for a child to learn a language. What this really means is that, in essence, there are slots into which language gets filled in a child's mind. This is definitely not the case with learning a second language after about seven years old.

Learning a second language as a pre-adolescent, adolescent or adult requires quite a bit of translation from the first language to the second. Vocabulary and grammar particulars are memorized, not necessarily internalized (at least, as readily as a first language). In fact, many (though not all) people who are immersed in a second language never fully function totally fluent in the language. They may appear to be totally fluent, but often there will be small traits that are hard to pick up and internalize.

It is fairly clear that learning a second language successfully does require fluency in the first language. This is because, as stated above, the second language is translated from the first in the learner's mind. First language literacy is also a crucial factor in second language learning, particularly second language literacy.

When helping second language learners make the "cross-over" in language fluency or literacy from first language to second language, it is important to help them identify strategies they use in the first language and apply those to the second language. It is also important to note similarities and differences in phonetic principles in the two languages. Sometimes it is helpful to encourage students to translate; other times, it is helpful for them to practice production in the target language. In either case, teachers must realize that learning a second language is a slow and complicated process.

Skill 5.3 Demonstrating knowledge of methods for ensuring that the home language of each child is respected and the natural propensity of all children for acquiring language is fostered

It is important for teachers to consider students' development and readiness when making instructional decisions. If an educational program is child-centered, then it will surely address the developmental abilities and needs of the students because it will take its cues from students' interests, concerns, and questions. Making an educational program child-centered involves building on the natural curiosity children bring to school, and asking children what they want to learn.

Teachers help students to identify their own questions, puzzles, and goals, and then structure widening circles of experience and investigation of those topics. Teachers manage to infuse all the skills, knowledge, and concepts that society mandates into a child-driven curriculum. Teachers of such programs are not passive in that they do far more than merely respond to the explicit cues of the students. . Teachers also draw on their understanding of children's developmentally characteristic needs and enthusiasms to design experiences that lead children into areas they might not choose, but that they do enjoy and that engage them. Teachers also bring their own interests and enthusiasms into the classroom to share and to act as a motivational means of guiding children.

Implementing such a child-centered curriculum is the result of very careful and deliberate planning. Planning serves as a means of organizing instruction and influences classroom teaching. Well thought-out planning includes specifying behavioral objectives, specifying students' entry behavior (knowledge and skills), selecting and sequencing learning activities to move students from entry behavior to objective, and evaluating the outcomes of instruction in order to improve planning.

English Language Learners

While there is a continuous effort to establish a "Standard English" for teaching English Language Learners (ELLs), in reality English learning and acquisition is dependent on both the cultural and linguistic background of the ELL as well as preconceived perceptions of English Language cultural influences. These preconceived notions can act as a filter, causing confusion. Since language by definition is an attempt to share knowledge, individuals must deal with the cultural, ethnic and linguistic diversity both in their own history as well as within the English language.

The teacher needs to assess the ELL to determine how cultural, ethnic and linguistic experience can impact the student's learning. This evaluation should take into account many factors, including:

- *The cultural background and educational sophistication of the ELL*
- *The exposure of the ELL to various English language variants and cultural beliefs.*

The reality is that no single approach, program or set of practices fits all students' needs, backgrounds and experiences. What works for a U.S.-born child whose first language is English may *not* work for a recent Chinese immigrant. The ideal program for a Native American teenager attending an isolated tribal school may fail to reach a Hispanic youth enrolled in an inner city or suburban district.

The individual teacher is best placed to determine the type and focus of resource material to supplement the learning of the ELL. Additional resources can be of assistance in the prevention of cross cultural misunderstanding and persecution within schools and communities, as well as the promotion of healing and respect for differences. Broken down into three categories, methods include:

- **Promote Cross-Cultural Understanding:** By providing personal communication with another person from a different cultural environment.

- **Challenge Stereotypes, Intolerance and Racism:** Many expressions and behaviors normal or common in the ELL's home culture may be considered abhorrent in an English Language culture.

- **Explain and clarify typical English Language cultural views, morals and societal norms**: To give context to ELL beliefs in English Language culture

---

For more information on how to promote English language development:

http://www.ncrel.org/sdrs/areas/issues/students/earlycld/ea400.htm

Skill 5.4 Understanding the importance of collaborating with families to set and accomplish language learning goals

Teachers and evaluators of children's language development must work effectively with families to create a continuum of language procurement and enhancement. Fostering collaborative efforts to provide a community approach to promoting children's oral development is both pragmatic and necessary if children are given a diversity of tools to become effective communicators.

Children are eager to fit in with peers and acquire language to communicate with families and friends. As children develop speech patterns, parents and teachers can nurture their language development. Teachers and parents can provide natural language environments that include technological opportunities that enrich and enhance children's oral language development.

When parents and teachers understand that children have individualized language foundations that for them are valid communication systems, a child can develop beginning speech patterns without the stereotype of an adult's perception of language delay or differences. Children are reflective of the environment of origin and will reflect their cultural and familial identifications.

Engaging children in conversations with teachers and parents can provide the nonverbal and verbal clues on how conversations work and what visual cues or body cues can be used to express non-verbal meaning. Teachers and other specialists involved in a child's educational development can provide families with information about speech and language developmental milestones to ensure a team approach to developing the whole child.

When children are provided with effective language and speech tools to share, communicate, and exchange information and feedback, language development is the key to that toolbox. In oral language development, there are critical milestones or periods where children are able to absorb and develop mechanics of simulating language. If those periods from infant to 3 years old (when a child's brain is increasing neural pathways in response to external stimuli) are not being fostered by adult collaboration, the outcome can translate into language and oral development concerns.

Teachers and caregivers of children developing oral language proficiency can provide effective instructional cultural, linguistic and language development tools that enhance and increase language acquisition. Teachers and parents must remember that language development in children develops in an efficient manner, so the focus should be on allowing the child to create his/her own language scenarios in constructing language repertoires.

Children develop a diversity of language patterns and speech of intelligible clarity as they produce foundational basis for language simulation. The act of simulating the sounds and words in their environment provides the child with language enhancement and acquisition. The promotion of language development should include repetition and language engagement. Children can be presented with a question that helps them process object and meaning association, such as when pointing to the color blue in the sky "What color is that?" or to the sky, "What is that?"

The concentration for selecting instructional strategies for enhancing children's language development should including the following methodologies:

- Sustenance of the child's natural language development by providing cultural, linguistic and home environments that nurture and support oral language development opportunities.
- Incorporating a diversity of language enrichment activities, technological inclusion, community resources, and individualized engagement.

Additional strategies could include child-centered learning activities that provide a diversity of learning opportunities and stimuli for constructive learning. Engaging a child's interest is crucial during the language acquisition years when the practice of speech is forming intelligible language patterns for the child in communicating and for the parent or teacher interpreting the child's conversation.

Children's toys, games and books can be used to further language development. Providing language simulation activities that model for children how to ask questions or put words into sentences are effective instructional strategies that can provide children with proper guidance through the maze of language acquisition and oral communication.

Providing children with instructional language cues can facilitate learning and language development. Using strategic tools such as rephrasing sentences into questions (example: "dada goed" into "Is daddy going?") can provide children with sentence formats and other ways of looking at oral meaning. When children are given labels for objects, they can use word association in developing language acquisition. Personalizing interactions with children during the formative years of oral and language development can become effective tools and strategies to create life long learners.

Skill 5.5 Recognizing ways to create a language-rich environment that encourages all children to learn to communicate effectively

A child's concept of print develops through repeated exposure to literature. Children quickly learn that stories and other texts are written from left to right, that the spaces between words matter and words on a page correspond with the words the reader is speaking.

Components of a Print-Rich Environment

Classroom Libraries
Students need many opportunities to read and comprehend a wide assortment of books and other texts. Classroom libraries should offer students a variety of reading materials, and the teacher should attempt to build a collection with various genres of children's literature. The reading difficulty should vary to include multiple levels of reading. That is, a number of the books are easy to read, while others are more challenging and of increasing difficulty and complexity. Libraries should include a variety of topics to interest all students, and a diversity of books and their themes should also be considered.

Word Walls
A word wall is an organized collection of words displayed on a classroom wall to support students in correctly spelling high frequency words. The words should include the words students encounter in their daily reading and writing, and also words they frequently misspell. Word-wall words can be arranged alphabetically, by spelling patterns, or by themes. Activities with a word wall could include clapping out the letters in a word, solving mystery words, making word cards, and organizing them (i.e., by parts of speech, by letters, or subjects/themes).

The use of a word wall is a great teaching tool for words in isolation and with writing. Each of the letters of the alphabet is displayed with words under each one that begin with that letter. Students are able to find the letter on the wall and read the words under each one.

Labeling
Labeling items in the classroom takes word walls to another level. They provide students with another everyday visual of additional words that are commonly encountered in a classroom. Labeling can also be done in multiple languages to promote diversity in the classroom.

Displays

Teachers should display the students' work throughout the room. Children can be encouraged to dictate their title for their own artwork and "stories". The students' work should be placed at the children's eye level for the other students to read, recognize, and enjoy each other's handiwork.

Experiences with print (through writing and reading) facilitate young children in developing a better appreciation and understanding of the purposes and functions of print. A print-rich environment contributes to the students' learning of phonological awareness and letter recognition. Children can then begin to acquire early reading proficiency by developing word-recognition skills.

Encouraging Effective Communication

While it is important to expose children to numerous opportunities throughout the day to read and interact with print, it is equally important for students to have the opportunity to express themselves and communicate with each other. *Teacher-talk*, is often one sided and limited. Instead, teachers should provide opportunities for students to develop and expand their vocabularies.

Encouraging more than single word answers, inviting descriptive language, and modeling more descriptive phrases are all strategies teachers can utilize to help students become more effective communicators. Tying these skills into how students interact with print and the types and quality of literature to which they are exposed will also help to develop this area.

For students for whom English is not the native language, it is important for teachers to encourage and provide significant examples of descriptive language. It is through these descriptions that these students can build a foundation upon which they can build comprehension. In the case of second language learners, the cliché of a picture being worth a thousand words cannot be truer. Anytime the teacher can tie a picture with descriptive language, it is more powerful for all learners.

Additionally, it is also important to sometimes limit language required for those students learning English. Students may have understanding of complex concepts well beyond their understanding of English. Limiting the language they need to use in a response, allows them to become more active participants within the classroom, builds their self-confidence, and demonstrates to peers the wealth of knowledge they have to share with the classroom

Competency 006 Understand the development of concepts about print and how to create a learning environment to promote emergent literacy

Skill 6.1 Recognizing characteristics, processes, and progressions of the development of concepts about print (e.g., interest in print, awareness that print carries meaning, book-handling skills, letter recognition)

Areas of Emerging Evidence

1. **Experiences with print (through reading and writing) help preschool children develop an understanding of the conventions, purpose, and functions of print.** Children learn about print from a variety of sources and in the process come to realize that print carries the story. They also learn how text is structured visually (i.e., text begins at the top of the page, moves from left to right, and carries over to the next page when it is turned). While knowledge about the conventions of print enables children to understand the physical structure of language, the conceptual knowledge that printed words convey a message also helps children bridge the gap between oral and written language.
2. **Phonological awareness and letter recognition** contribute to initial reading acquisition by helping children develop efficient word recognition strategies (e.g., detecting pronunciations and storing associations in memory.) Phonological awareness and knowledge of print-speech relations play an important role in facilitating reading acquisition. Therefore, phonological awareness instruction should be an integral component of early reading programs. Within the emergent literacy research, viewpoints diverged on whether acquisition of phonological awareness and letter recognition are preconditions of literacy acquisition or whether they develop interdependently with literacy activities such as story reading and writing.
3. **Storybook reading affects children's knowledge about, strategies for, and attitudes towards reading.** Of all the strategies intended to promote growth in literacy acquisition, none is as commonly practiced, nor as strongly supported across the emergent literacy literature as storybook reading. Children in different social and cultural groups have differing degrees of access to storybook reading. For example, it is not unusual for a teacher to have students who have experienced thousands of hours of story reading time, along with other students who have had little or no such exposure.

> **For more information about the stages of emergent literacy:**
>
> http://www.bankstreet.edu/literacyguide/early.html

SEE also Skill 6.4

Skill 6.2 Understanding the importance of collaborating with families to promote literacy development

The student's capacity and potential for academic success within the overall educational experience are products of the total environment: classroom and school system; home and family; neighborhood and community in general. All of these segments are interrelated and can be supportive, one of the other, or divisive, one against the other. As a matter of course, the teacher will become familiar with all aspects of the system of the school and the classroom pertinent to the students' educational experience. This would include not only process and protocols, but also the availability of resources provided to meet the academic, health and welfare needs of students. It is important that the teacher look beyond the boundaries of the school system to identify additional resources as well as issues and situations, which will affect (directly or indirectly) a student's ability to succeed in the classroom.

Examples of Resources
- Libraries, museums, zoos, planetariums, etc.
- Clubs, societies and civic organizations, community outreach programs of private businesses and corporations and of government agencies. These can provide a variety of materials and media as well as possible speakers and presenters.
- Departments of social services operating within the local community. These can provide background and program information relevant to social issues that may be impacting individual students. This can also be a resource for classroom instruction regarding life skills, at-risk behaviors, etc.

Initial contacts for resources outside of the school system will usually come from within the system itself: from administration; teacher organizations; department heads; and other colleagues.

Examples of Issues/Situations

- <u>Students from multicultural backgrounds</u>:

Curriculum objectives and instructional strategies may be inappropriate and unsuccessful when presented in a single format that relies on the student's understanding and acceptance of the values and common attributes of a specific culture which is not his or her own.

- <u>Parental/family influences</u>: Attitude, resources and encouragement available in the home environment may be attributes for success or failure.

Families with higher incomes are able to provide increased opportunities for students. Students from lower income families will need to depend on the resources available from the school system and the community. The classroom teacher should orchestrate this in cooperation with school administrators and educational advocates in the community.

Family members with higher levels of education often serve as models for students, and have high expectations for academic success. In addition, families with specific aspirations for children (often, regardless of their own educational background) encourage students to achieve academic success, and are most often active participants in the process.

A family in crisis (caused by economic difficulties, divorce, substance abuse, physical abuse, etc.) creates a negative environment, which may profoundly impact all aspects of a student's life, and particularly the ability to function academically. The situation may require professional intervention. It is often the classroom teacher who recognizes a family in crisis situation and instigates an intervention by reporting this to school or civil authorities.

Regardless of the positive or negative impacts on the students' education from outside sources, it is the teacher's responsibility to ensure that all students in the classroom have an equal opportunity for academic success. This begins with the teacher's statement of high expectations for every student, and develops through planning, delivery and evaluation of instruction, which provides for inclusion and ensures that all students have equal access to the resources necessary for successful acquisition of the academic skills being taught and measured in the classroom.

Skill 6.3 Recognizing relationships between young children's emergent literacy and factors such as enjoyment of stories and awareness of environmental print

Metalinguistics is a term used to describe a theory or model that helps to explain the interaction between a written text and language, especially for young children and English language learners. Reid (1988, p. 165) describes four metalinguistic abilities that young children acquire through early involvement in reading activities:

1. Word consciousness. Children who have access to books first can tell the story through the pictures. Gradually, they begin to realize the connection between the spoken words and the printed words. The beginning of letter and word discrimination begins in the early years.

2. Language and conventions of print. During this stage, children learn the way to hold a book, where to begin to read, the left to right motion, and how to continue from one line to another.

3. Functions of print. Children discover that print can be used for a variety of purposes and functions, including entertainment and information.

4. Phonemic, syntactic and pragmatic awareness. Children learn phonics and the sounds of letters to form words.

In metalinguistics, the alphabetic principle and phonics are deemed as being the most important factor in teaching young children to read.

During the preschool years, children acquire cognitive skills in oral language that they apply later on to reading comprehension. Reading aloud to young children is one of the most important things that an adult can do because they are teaching children how to monitor, question, predict, and confirm what they hear in the stories. Young children are aware of print before they can read, As such they will often read the pictures in a story with which they are familiar and make up their own story based on what they can remember or create an entirely new story based solely on the pictures in the book.

SEE also Skill 6.7

Skill 6.4 Identifying strategies and techniques for promoting children's emergent literacy and development of concepts about print

Understanding that print carries meaning is demonstrated every day in the elementary classroom as the teacher holds up a selected book to read it aloud to the class. The teachers explicitly and deliberately think aloud about how to hold the book, how to focus the class on looking at its cover, where to start reading, and in what direction to begin. Even in writing the morning message on the board, the teacher targets the children on the placement of the message and its proper place at the top of the board to be followed by additional activities and a schedule for the rest of the day.

When the teacher challenges children to make letter posters of a single letter and the items that start with that letter, in the classroom, their home, or their knowledge base the children are making concrete the understanding that print carries meaning.

Teachers need to look for five basic behaviors in students:

- Do students know how to hold the book?
- Can students match speech to print?
- Do students know the difference between letters and words?
- Do students know that print conveys meaning?
- Can students track print from left to right?

In order for students to understand concepts of print, they must be able to recognize text and understand the various mechanics that text contains. This includes:

- All text contains a message
- The English language has a specific structure
- In order to decode words and read text, students must be able to understand that structure.

The structure of the English language consists of rules of grammar, capitalization and punctuation. For younger children, this means being able to recognize letters and form words. For older children, it means being able to recognize different types of text, such as lists, stories and signs, and knowing the purpose of each one.

When reading to children, teachers point to words as they read them. Illustrations and pictures also contribute to the students' understanding of the meaning of the text. Therefore, teachers should also discuss illustrations related to the text.

When reading to students, teachers also discuss the common characteristics of books (author, title page, table of contents, etc.) Asking students to predict what the story might be about is a good strategy to help teach students about the cover and its importance to the story. Pocket charts, big books and song charts provide ample opportunity for teachers to point to words as they read.

Instructional Strategies

Using big books in the classroom
Gather the children around you in a group with the big book placed on a stand. This allows all children to see the words and pictures. As you read point to each word. It is best to use a pointer so that you are not covering any other words or part of the page. When students read from the big book on their own, have them also use the pointer for each word.

When students begin reading from smaller books, have them transfer what they have learned about pointing to the words by using their finger to track the reading. Observation is a key point in assessing students' ability to track words and speech.

A classroom rich in print
Having words from a familiar rhyme or poem in a pocket chart lends itself to an activity where the students arrange the words in the correct order and then read the rhyme. This is an instructional strategy that reinforces directionality of print. It also reinforces punctuation, capitalization and matching print to speech.

Using highlighters or sticky tabs to locate upper and lower case letters or specific words can help students isolate words and learn about the structure of language they need to have for reading.

There should be plenty of books in the classroom for children to read on their own or in small groups. As you observe each of these groups, take note of how the child holds the book in addition to the tracking and reading of the words.

Word Wall
The use of a word wall is a great teaching tool for words in isolation and with writing. Each of the letters of the alphabet is displayed with words under each one that begin with that letter. Students are able to find the letter on the wall and read the words under each one.

Sounds of the letters

In addition to teaching the letter names, students should learn the corresponding sound of each letter. This is a key feature of decoding when beginning to read. The use of rhyming words is an effective way to teach letter sounds so that children have a solid background.

Students should be exposed to daily opportunities for viewing and reading texts. Teachers can do this by engaging the students in discussions about books during shared, guided and independent reading times. The teacher should draw the students' attention to the conventions of print and discuss with them the reasons for choosing different books. For example, teachers should let the students know that it is perfectly acceptable to return a book and select another if they think it is too hard for them.

Predictable books help engage the students in reading. Once the students realize what words are repeated in the text, they will eagerly chime in to repeat the words at the appropriate time during the reading. Rereading of texts helps the students learn the words and helps them to read these lines fluently.

Some things for teachers to observe during reading:

- Students' responses during reading conferences, such as pointing to letters or words.
- Ask students where they should begin reading and how they know to stop or pause depending on the punctuation.
- Student behavior when holding a book (e.g., holding the book right side up or upside down, reading from left to right, stopping to look at the pictures to confirm meaning)

Skill 6.5 **Recognizing methods for promoting children's interaction with print in varied and meaningful contexts**

SEE Skills 6.4, 6.7 and 7.1

Skill 6.6 **Recognizing the importance of and strategies for creating a print-rich environment**

SEE Skill 6.4

Skill 6.7 Demonstrating knowledge of strategies for encouraging children's enjoyment of and positive attitudes toward literacy

Teachers can encourage positive attitudes towards literacy by incorporating some of the following activities:

Reading aloud

Create a positive read aloud atmosphere
Allow time for students to settle as you make yourself comfortable. Whether you are sitting in a low chair or on the floor, be sure that each child can see the book.

- As you read, move the book around so that each student can see the illustrations.
- Allow time for the student listeners to think about what they are hearing.
- Develop open-ended questions to stimulate your student's imaginations.
- Plan related activities to precede or follow the read aloud.

Instructional Strategies

Reading aloud effectively
- Set a purpose for listening by sharing the reason you selected the book
- Discuss the title, author and illustrator
- Read with expression; create a mood
- Modulate your voice to reflect emotions and emphasize key points
- Ask the students to imagine what he or she might do in a situation similar to that faced by a character

Discuss the story
Through discussion, students can synthesize and extend their understanding of the reading. They can connect their prior knowledge to the new information presented in the reading. After reading the story, ask children to draw pictures of the setting, the main characters, or their favorite parts of the story.

To learn some tips for reading aloud:	For an alphabetical list of instructional strategies see:
http://www.rif.org/parents/tips/tip.mspx?View=31	http://olc.spsd.sk.ca/DE/PD/instr/alpha.html

Reading Activities

- *Reading campout:* Set up a tent in the classroom. Students can bring in their pillows and read by flashlight.
- *Pajama party:* Students can wear their slippers. They can bring in a blanket and favorite stuffed animal.
- *Hats off to a "reading" party:* Students create fun hats to wear or wear their favorite hats.

Read alouds promote language acquisition and correlate with literacy development, achieving better reading comprehension and overall success in school.

As with any learning experience, it is important for students to connect learning with real world experiences. Therefore with reading, students should be given opportunities to experience reading outside the classroom or traditional classroom methods. They can also refer to their own experiences to help them make connections with the text. Questions teachers can ask to help children make these connections include:
- Have you read another book like this?
- Where have you seen a building like this before?
- Have you seen a show on television with a story something like this one?
- Do you know someone that is like the main character?
- Who is your favorite character in the story> Why?

Literature circles involve a group discussion about a book. The group should consist of no more than six children, but usually fewer than four, who have read the same work of literature (narrative or expository text). They talk about key parts of the work, relate it to their own experience, listen to the responses of others, and discuss how parts of the text relate to the whole. Literature circles are excellent for the classroom setting because they mimic book clubs while providing a format for the discussion meeting for students who are learning to discuss literature.

Book clubs are another excellent opportunity for students to discuss reading in an open setting. Whether it be at a local library, school library group, recess group, or parent-child evening reading program, book clubs promote reading in an enjoyable setting not attached to traditional homework assignments and book reports.

TEACHER CERTIFICATION STUDY GUIDE

Skill 6.8 Demonstrating knowledge of high-quality children's literature (e.g., genres of children's literature, elements of story, equity issues)

Types of Literature Appropriate at Different Developmental Stages

Note: Books marked with an asterisk (*) have won the Caldecott medal, which is explained in the section on picture books.

Fine children's literature opens children up to vicarious experiences that enrich their world. From being read to by parents and caregivers from the earliest ages, children duringthe toddler years can handle **board books** with sturdy pages such as Kit Allen's *Sweater*, Donald Crews's *Freight Train,* and Margaret Wise Brown's *Goodnight, Moon.*

Children ages two and three enjoy what are called "**toy books**," i.e. those that have flaps to lift up, textures to touch, or holes to peek through. Examples include Dorothy Kunhardt's *Pat the Bunny* and Eric Hill's *Where's Spot?*

From ages three to seven, children enjoy a variety of nonfiction **concept books**. These books combine language and pictures to show concrete examples of abstract concepts. Hundreds of beautiful books comprise this genre, such as Lois Ehlert's *Color Zoo* (animals, shapes, and colors), counting books such as Eric Carle's *10 Little Rubber Ducks* (directions, numbers, and up and down) Tana Hoban's *Count and See* (numbers and sets of l0 up to l00), and Molly Bang's *Ten, Nine, Eight* (a gentle lullaby as an African-American father readies his daughter for bed).

Another category of concept books is **alphabet books**, popular with children from preschool through grade 2. Outstanding examples include the Lobels's *On Market Street* (every item purchased from the market is in alphabetical order); Ehlert's *Eating the Alphabet: Fruits and Vegetables From A to Z*; Bowen's *Antler, Bear, Canoe: A Northwoods Alphabet Year*; Musgrove's *Ashanti to Zulu: African Traditions*; and Lara Rankin's *The Handmade Alphabet* (this gives the American Sign Language signal for each alphabet letter in sequence).

In grades K, 1, and 2 when children are becoming early readers, two other genres of literature become salient: **wordless picture books** and **easy-to-read books**. The first of these, the wordless picture book, is excellent for children just breaking into reading. The books accommodate readers and nonreaders alike, for there is no text. Children must be capable of "reading" the pictures and creative enough to supply the dialogue and descriptive language to accompany them. Many children have enjoyed Mercer Mayer's *Frog Goes to Dinner*, Emily Arnold McCully's *Picnic*, Peter Sis's *Dinosaur!* and Mitsumasa Anno's *Anno's Journey*. The teacher should be discriminating about easy-to-read books because some are of questionable literary quality. Among the best are such familiars as Arnold Lobel's *Frog and Toad Are Friends*, Cynthia Rylant's *Henry and Mudge* books, and Else Minarik's *Little Bear* books illustrated by Maurice Sendak.

From the preschool years onward, the **picture book**, characterized by illustrations and a plot that are closely interrelated (one usually cannot exist independently of the other) are suitable for children. With the explosion of picture books in the last fifteen years, there are some that may even be used with children in grade 6 and above. Each year the Caldecott committee awards a medal in the U.S. to the best-illustrated picture book. This committee also chooses one or two honor books. Teachers of children ages 4-8 should be intimately familiar with the Caldecott list, which can be found in any children's library or on the Internet, as these books are exemplary reading choices. In this discussion, those books which are Caldecott winners have been marked with an asterisk (*). Well-illustrated children's books show sensitivity to line, color, shape, texture, and overall composition.

Illustrators use various artistic media from watercolor (David Wiesner's *Tuesday*), to oil painting (Paul Zelinsky's *Rapunzel* and Lane Smith's illustrations of Jon Scieszka's *The True Story of the 3 Little Pigs!*), collage (used extensively by Eric Carle in *The Very Hungry Caterpillar*) and Ezra Jack Keats in *The Snowy Day* and *Goggles!*), to pastels (Ed Young's *Lon Po Po: A Red-Riding Hood Story from China*). Other outstanding picture books include Morris Sendak's *Where the Wild Things Are*, Vera B. Williams's *More More More Said the Baby*, Barbara Joosse's *Mama, Do You Love Me?* Jane Yolen's *Owl Moon* and Leo Lionni's *Swimmy*.

Chapter books are appropriate for readers in grades 2, 3, and 4 and beyond. They are characterized by occasional illustrations, relatively short chapters to begin with, and interesting plots that appeal to children ages 8 and up. High quality chapter books include the following for children ages 8-10: Patricia McKissack's, *Porch Lies: Tales of Slicksters, Tricksters, and Other Wily Characters*; Kate DiCamillo's *Because of Winn-Dixie*, and E.B. White's *Charlotte's Web*.

It seems that in every generation, there is one writer or one book that tends to dominate children's literature—the most recent one being the *Harry Potter* books. There is always a lot of discussion about what is appropriate for children and at what age. The criticism about the themes in the Harry Potter books is that it revolves around witchery and witchcraft, which has upset some communities enough that the books have been abolished in the curricula and libraries of the schools.

Another theme that is extremely controversial is violence. Some parents go so far as to condemn the traditional and time-tested fairy tales because of the amount of violence in them. Themes that are adult in nature have also been the source of controversy. For example, *And Tango Makes Three*, a book based on a true story of two obviously homosexual male penguins in New York City's Central Park Zoo who adopted a fertilized egg and raised the chick as their own stirred up a controversy when it began to appear on elementary school library shelves. Many parents felt that their children were not ready for such an adult theme.

What actually constitutes "children's literature"? It is usually defined as literature that is selected and read by children rather than those that the powers-that-be such as teachers, reviewers, parents, etc., deem appropriate. However, sometimes it is defined as literature written especially for children, but that definition tends to fall by the wayside when we look at some of the major books that are read primarily by children such as Mark Twain's *The Prince and the Pauper* and *Huckleberry Finn* that were written specifically for adults. There is great ambiguity in the publishing world as to whether a book will be categorized and marketed as children's literature or adult literature or even young adult literature, and many books cross the line in all directions.

Of course, much of what has been traditionally regarded as children's literature has multiple levels of meaning and adults who read *Alice in Wonderland*, for example, as a child, will read it again as an adult and will derive meanings they did not see and could not understand as a child.

Following are some authors who are making significant contributions to children's literature and some examples of their works:

Enid Blyton, British author, *The Famous Five, The Secret Seven* series.

J.K. Rowling, British author, *Harry Potter* series.

Jacqueline Wilson, British author, *Tracy Beaker* series.

Jane Yolen, American author, *Owl Moon*, *Devil's Arithmetic*.

Betsy Byars, American author, *Summer of the Swans*.

To view the Lists of Children's Book Awards:	For further reading about Children's Literature:
http://www.acs.ucalgary.ca/~dkbrown/awards.html	http://www.scils.rutgers.edu/~kvander/ChildrenLit/index.html

Genres of Literature

The major literary genres include allegory, ballad, drama, epic, epistle, essay, fable, novel, poem, romance, and the short story.

Allegory: A story in verse or prose with characters representing virtues and vices. There are two meanings, symbolic and literal. John Bunyan's *The Pilgrim's Progress* is the most renowned of this genre.

Ballad: A story told or sung, usually in verse and accompanied by music. Literary devices found in ballads include the refrain, or repeated section, and incremental repetition, or anaphora, for effect. Earliest forms were anonymous folk ballads. Later forms include Coleridge's Romantic masterpiece, "The Rime of the Ancient Mariner."

Drama: Plays – comedy, modern, or tragedy - typically in five acts. Traditionalists and neoclassicists adhere to Aristotle's unities of time, place and action. Plot development is advanced via dialogue. Literary devices include asides, soliloquies and the chorus representing public opinion. Greatest of all dramatists/playwrights is William Shakespeare. Other dramaturges include Ibsen, Williams, Miller, Shaw, Stoppard, Racine, Moliére, Sophocles, Aeschylus, Euripides, and Aristophanes.

Epic: A long poem usually of book length reflecting values inherent in the generative society. Epic devices include an invocation to a Muse for inspiration, purpose for writing, universal setting, protagonist and antagonist who possess supernatural strength and acumen, and interventions of a God or the gods. Understandably, there are very few epics: Homer's *Iliad* and *Odyssey*, Virgil's *Aeneid*, Milton's *Paradise Lost*, Spenser's *The Fairie Queene*, Barrett Browning's *Aurora Leigh*, and Pope's mock-epic, *The Rape of the Lock*.

Epistle: A letter that is not always originally intended for public distribution, but due to the fame of the sender and/or recipient, it becomes public domain. Paul wrote epistles that were later placed in the Bible.

Essay: Typically a limited length prose work focusing on a topic and propounding a definite point of view and authoritative tone. Great essayists include Carlyle, Lamb, DeQuincy, Emerson and Montaigne, who is credited with defining this genre.

Fable: Terse tale offering up a moral or exemplum. Chaucer's "The Nun's Priest's Tale" is a fine example of a bête fabliau or beast fable in which animals speak and act characteristically human, illustrating human foibles.

Legend: A traditional narrative or collection of related narratives, popularly regarded as historically factual, but which are actually a mixture of fact and fiction.

Myth: Stories that are more or less universally shared within a culture to explain its history and traditions.

Novel: The longest form of fictional prose containing a variety of characterizations, settings, local color and regionalism. Most have complex plots, expanded description, and attention to detail. Some of the great novelists include Austin, the Brontes, Twain, Tolstoy, Hugo, Hardy, Dickens, Hawthorne, Forster, and Flaubert.

Poem: The only requirement is rhythm. Sub-genres include fixed types of literature such as the sonnet, elegy, ode, pastoral, and villanelle. Unfixed types of literature include blank verse and dramatic monologue.

Romance: A highly imaginative tale set in a fantastical realm dealing with the conflicts between heroes, villains and/or monsters. "The Knight's Tale" from Chaucer's Canterbury Tales, Sir Gawain and the Green Knight and Keats' "The Eve of St. Agnes" are prime representatives.

Short Story: Typically a terse narrative, with less developmental background about characters. May include description, author's point of view, and tone. Poe emphasized that a successful short story should create one focused impact. Hemingway, Faulkner, Twain, Joyce, Shirley Jackson, Flannery O'Connor, de Maupassant, Saki, Edgar Allen Poe, and Pushkin are considered to be some of the great short story writers

Children's literature is a genre of its own and emerged as a distinct and independent form in the second half of the 18th century. *The Visible World in Pictures* by John Amos Comenius, a Czech educator, was one of the first printed works and the first picture book. For the first time, educators acknowledged that children are different from adults in many respects. Modern educators acknowledge that introducing elementary students to a wide range of reading experiences plays an important role in their mental/social/psychological development. Some of the most common forms of literature specifically for children include:

- **Traditional Literature:** Traditional literature opens up a world where right wins out over wrong, where hard work and perseverance are rewarded, and where helpless victims find vindication—all worthwhile values that children identify with even as early as kindergarten. In traditional literature, children are introduced to fanciful beings, humans with exaggerated powers, talking animals, and heroes that will inspire them. For younger elementary children, these stories in Big Book format are ideal for providing predictable and repetitive elements that can be grasped by these children.

  - **Folktales/Fairy Tales:**

    Adventures of animals or humans and the supernatural characterize these stories. The hero is usually on a quest and is aided by other-worldly helpers. More often than not, the story focuses on good and evil and reward and punishment. Some examples: The Three Bears, Little Red Riding Hood, Snow White, Sleeping Beauty, Puss-in-Boots, Rapunzel and Rumpelstiltskin.

  - **Fables:** Animals that act like humans are featured in these stories and usually reveal human foibles or sometimes teach a lesson. Example: Aesop's Fables.

  - **Myths:** These stories about events from the earliest times, such as the origin of the world, are considered true in their own societies.

- **Legends:** These are similar to myths except that they tend to deal with events that happened more recently. Example: Arthurian legends.

- **Tall tales:** These are purposely exaggerated accounts of individuals with superhuman strength. Examples: Paul Bunyan, John Henry, and Pecos Bill.

- **Modern Fantasy:** Many of the themes found in these stories are similar to those in traditional literature. The stories start out based in reality, which makes it easier for the reader to suspend disbelief and enter worlds of unreality. For example, little people live in the walls in *The Borrowers* and time travel is possible in *The Trolley to Yesterday*. Including some fantasy tales in the curriculum helps elementary-grade children develop their sense of imagination. These often appeal to ideals of justice and issues having to do with good and evil and because children tend to identify with the characters, the message is more likely to be retained.

- **Science Fiction:** Robots, spacecraft, mystery, and civilizations from other ages often appear in these stories. Most presume advances in science on other planets or in a future time. Most children like these stories because of their interest in space and the "what if" aspect of the stories.
  Examples: *Outer Space and All That Junk* and *A Wrinkle in Time*.

- **Modern Realistic Fiction:** These stories are about real problems that real children face. By finding that others share their hopes and fears, young children can find insight into their own problems. Young readers also tend to experience a broadening of interests as the result of this kind of reading. It's good for them to know that a child can be brave and intelligent and can solve difficult problems. Examples: Are You There God? It's Me, Margaret, Sunmmer of the Swans, Dear Mr. Henshaw

- **Historical Fiction:** *Rifles for Watie* is an example of this kind of story. Presented in a historically accurate setting, it's about a young boy (16 years) who serves in the Union army. He experiences great hardship but discovers that his enemy is an admirable human being. It provides a good opportunity to introduce younger children to history in a beneficial way. Other examples of historical fiction: *Underground to Canada* (slavery), *The Ballad of Lucy Whipple* (the Gold Rush) and *Journey to the River Sea* (Titanic)

- **Biography:** Reading about inventors, explorers, scientists, political and religious leaders, social reformers, artists, sports figures, doctors, teachers, writers, and war heroes help children to see that one person can make a difference. They also open new vistas for children to think about when they choose an occupation to fantasize about.

> **For a list of biographies suitable for children see:**
>
> www.ualr.edu/giftedctr/slufy/Biographies_for_Children.pdf

- **Informational Books:** These are ways to learn more about something you are interested in or something that you know nothing about. Encyclopedias are good resources, of course, but a book like *Polar Wildlife* by Kamini Khanduri shows pictures and facts that will capture the imaginations of young children.

Competency 007   **UNDERSTAND FOUNDATIONS OF READING DEVELOPMENT**

Skill 7.1   Demonstrating knowledge of factors affecting children's reading development (e.g., teacher modeling, read-alouds, reading practices in the home, enjoyment of reading)

Teacher Modeling

Teacher modeling occurs whenever a teacher reads a book to a group of children. All of the teacher's actions should serve as a model for the children of what good readers do. For example, as a teacher reads to the children from a big book, the use of a pointer to follow the words shows the children that the teacher is actually reading and that these words carry a message – the storyline.

Other factors of teacher modeling that will affect children's reading development include:
- Think Alouds – In this technique the teacher stops at a point in the story and asks a question, such as "I wonder why (a character) did that?" This helps the students to learn how to reflect on their own reading.
- Rereading – When the teacher rereads a part of the text when it doesn't seem to make sense, children learn that this is important for understanding the text.
- Holding the book – The children see the way the teacher holds the book when reading and therefore will do the same thing when they are reading.
- Picture Walk – By taking a picture walk before reading the story, the teacher can model how to predict what the story may be about by looking at the pictures

Read Alouds

Research "confirms that reading aloud positively impacts overall academic achievement as well as reading skills and interest in reading" (Routmann, 2000). Here are several tips related to read alouds in the classroom:

- Do read the book silently to yourself first! Be well prepared.

- Ham it up. Be expressive, using pauses, dynamic volume, and different voices for characters.

- Bring in an item that relates to the book as an attention-getter, such as a rock for Marcia Brown's *Stone Soup*, a piece of spaghetti for Tomie de Paola's *Stega Nona* or a pair of glasses for Marc Brown's *Arthur's Eyes*.

- Give stretch breaks to the youngest children.

- Have your audience participate by repeating refrains with you, as in Doreen Cronin's *Cows That Type: Click Clack Moo*, or have children provide sound effects throughout the story.

Among some of the favorite books to read aloud are Lynne Reid Banks' *The Indian in the Cupboard*, Bernard Waber's *Ira Sleeps Over*, Roald Dahl's *James and the Giant Peach*, Barbara Park's *Junie B. Jones* Series, Beverly Cleary's *Ramona* Series, Kate DiCamillo's *Because of Winn-Dixie*.

Classroom Activities that Respond to Literature

Responding to literature through art, writing, and drama helps children to reflect on the books they have read and make them a part of their lives. The following list suggests just a few of the extending activities teachers can facilitate using children's books to make them come alive.

- Have younger children make puppets to retell the story.
- Allow children to act out the story with the teacher as the first narrator. Books like John Burningham's *Mr. Gumpy's Outing* work well for this.
- Do an art project using the same artistic medium as was in the book, such as a collage after reading Ezra Jack Keats or Eric Carle.
- Have children create a tableau (a montage of still figures) that captures a critical scene from a book.
- Use the interlocking structure of Bill Martin's *Brown Bear, Brown Bear* as the template for a new story in which the children draw new characters. This can be made into a classroom Big Book.
- After reading a book like *The Village of Round and Square Houses*, have the children create a village of box sculptures.
- Have children create a story map to show critical places in the setting.
- Ask students to write telegraphs or emails to characters explaining how to handle a problem.
- Encourage older children to retell a story from another character's point of view, as in Jon Scieszka's *The True Story of the Three Little Pigs* which is told from the point of view of the wolf.
- Children can create a newspaper based on a book, such as the multiple perspectives in Anthony Browne's *Voices in the Park*.
- In writing, have children connect a book to their own lives. For example, after reading *Jamaica's Friend*, write about something you and your best friend do together.

Reading Practices in the Home

Reading practices in the home before and after children come to school have a direct impact on the children's reading development. Children who are exposed to books and have been read to already have the prerequisite knowledge about books and stories. They are eager to listen to stories and may have favorite books they like to read over and over.

Children who have not had previous exposure to books will need instruction and modeling in how to hold a book and how to interpret the pictures in the book. The teacher can encourage reading in the home by meeting with the parents and explaining the importance of this activity. By sending home books with the child that the parents can read with or to them will enhance their reading development. There are also book clubs from which the parents can purchase quality literature to read to their children, but in the case of families where finances don't permit this, the school or class library or even the public library is an excellent source of reading material.

Reading practices in the home can also include such simple things as reading grocery lists or looking at magazines. When children see their parents reading, they realize that it is a worthwhile activity and is something that adults do.

Enjoyment of Reading

Reading for enjoyment in the classroom is essential as it helps the children develop a lifelong love of reading, which in essence is the object of the reading program. Teachers choose stories and books with topics of interest to the students and choose a time during the day when they read aloud to the class. There should also be a time for silent reading, where the students can read their own books, reread ones that the teacher has read or read material on the walls of the classroom. After a while students will develop a love of a particular genre or a particular author.

Teachers should display books in the classroom that relate to the theme they are teaching. A classroom library can include different genres of books as well as bins of books that are on the children's reading levels. Following the Fountas and Pinell Guided Reading strategy, the bins can be color-coded or letter coded, so that children can choose books from their level that they can read independently.

For more information on leveled book lists:

http://home.comcast.net/~ngiansante/

TEACHER CERTIFICATION STUDY GUIDE

Skill 7.2   Recognizing strategies for promoting phonological awareness (hearing and discriminating the rhythm and sounds of speech) and phonemic awareness (manipulating the smallest units of speech)

SEE also Skills 4.1 and 7.3

Theorist Marilyn Jager Adams who researches early reading has outlined five basic types of phonemic awareness tasks.

Task 1- Ability to hear rhymes and alliteration.
Children would listen to a poem, rhyming picture book or song and identify the rhyming words hear, while the teacher records or lists them on an experiential chart.

Task 2- Ability to do oddity tasks (recognize the member of a set that is different [odd] among the group.)
The children would look at the pictures of (a blade of) **g**rass, a **g**arden and a **r**ose and be able to tell which starts with a different sound.

Task 3 –The ability to orally blend words and split syllables.
The children can say the first sound of a word and then the rest of the word and put it together as a single word.

Task 4 –The ability to orally segment words.
This is the ability to count sounds. The children would be asked as a group to count the sounds in "hamburger."

Task 5- The ability to do phonics manipulation tasks.
The children would replace the "r" sound in rose with a "p" sound to get the word "pose."

Instructional Methods

Since the ability to distinguish between individual sounds, or phonemes, within words is a prerequisite to association of sounds with letters and manipulating sounds to blend words, i.e. reading, the teaching of phonemic awareness is crucial to emergent literacy (early childhood K-2nd reading instruction). Children need a strong background in phonemic awareness in order for phonics instruction (sound/spelling relationships in printed materials) to be effective.

Instructional methods that may be effective for teaching phonemic awareness can include:
- Clapping syllables in words
- Distinguishing between a word and a sound
- Using visual cues and movements to help children understand when the speaker goes from one sound to another
- Oral segmentation activities that focus on easily distinguished syllables rather than sounds
- Singing familiar songs (e.g. Happy Birthday, Knick Knack Paddy Wack) and replacing key words in the song with words having a different ending or middle sound (oral segmentation)
- Dealing children a deck of picture cards and having them sound out the words for the pictures on their cards or calling for a picture by asking for its first and second sound.

EXAMPLES OF COMMON PHONEMES APPLIED

Phoneme	Uses
/A/	a (table), a_e (bake), ai (train), ay (say)
/a/	a (flat)
/b/	b (ball)
/k/	c (cake), k (Key), ck (back)
/d/	d (door)
/E/	e (me), ee (feet), ea (leap), y (baby)
/e/	e (pet), ea (head)
/f/	f (fix), ph (phone)
/g/	g (gas)
/h/	h (hot)
/I/	i (I), i_e (bite), igh (light), y (sky)
/i/	i (sit)
/j/	j (jet), dge (edge), g (gem)
/l/	l (lamp)
/m/	m (map)
/n/	n (no), kn (knock)
/O/	o (okay), o_e (bone), oa (soap), ow (low)
/o/	o (hot)
/p/	p (pie)
/kw/	qu (quick)
/r/	r (road), wr (wrong), er (her), ir (sir), ur (fur)
/s/	s (say), c (cent)
/t/	t (time)
/U/	u (future), u_e (use), ew (few)
/u/	u (thumb), a (about)
/v/	v (voice)
/w/	w (wash)
/gz/	x (exam)
/ks/	x (box)

/y/	y (yes)
/z/	z (zoo), s (nose)
/OO/	oo (boot), u (truth), u_e (rude), ew (chew)
/oo/	oo (book), u (put)
/oi/	oi (soil), oy (toy)
/ou/	ou (out), ow (cow)
/aw/	aw (saw), au (caught), al (tall)
/ar/	ar (car)
/sh/	sh (ship), ti (nation), ci (special)
/hw/	wh (white)
/ch/	ch (chest), tch (catch)
/th/	th (thick)
/th/	th (this)
/ng/	ng (sing)
/zh/	s (measure)

Choice of the medium through which the message is delivered to the receiver is a significant factor in controlling language. Spoken language relies as much on the gestures, facial expression, and tone of voice of the speaker as on the spoken words. Slapstick comics can evoke laughter without speaking a word. Young children use body language overtly and older children more subtly to convey messages. These refinings of body language are paralleled by an ability to recognize and apply the nuances of spoken language. To work strictly with written work, the writer must use words to imply the body language.

By the time children begin to speak, they have begun to acquire the ability to use language to inform and manipulate. They have already used kinesthetic and verbal cues to attract attention when they seek some physical or emotional gratification. Children learn to apply names to objects and actions. They learn to use language to describe the persons and events in their lives and to express their feelings about the world around them.

> **For further information on teaching phonemic awareness:**
>
> http://www.ldonline.org/article/6254

Skill 7.3 Demonstrating knowledge of phonics skills (association between sounds and written letters), orthographic awareness, semantic and syntactic cueing systems, and other word identification skills (e.g., sight words, high-frequency words)

Phonics is a widely used method for teaching students to read. This method includes studying the rules and patterns found in language. By age 5 or 6, children can typically begin to use phonics to begin to understand the connections between letters, their patterns, vowel sounds (i.e., short vowels, long vowels) and the collective sounds they all make.

Phonemic awareness is the ability to break down and hear separate and/or different sounds and distinguish between the sounds one hears. Although these terms are different; they are interdependent. Phonemic awareness is required to begin studying phonics, where students will require the ability to break down words into the smalls units of sound, or phonemes, to later identify syllables, blends, and patterns.

Children who have problems with phonics generally have not acquired or been exposed to phonemic awareness activities usually fostered at home and in preschool-2nd grade. This includes extensive songs, rhymes and read alouds.

Word analysis (a.k.a. phonics or decoding) is the process readers use to figure out unfamiliar words based on written patterns. Word recognition is the process of automatically determining the pronunciation and some degree of the meaning of an unknown word. In other words, fluent readers recognize most written words easily and correctly, without consciously decoding or breaking them down. These elements of literacy are skills readers need for word recognition.

To decode means to change communication signals into messages. Reading comprehension requires that the reader learn the code within which a message is written and be able to decode it to get the message. Encoding involves changing a message into symbols: for example, to encode oral language into writing (spelling) or to encode an idea into words or to encode a mathematical or physical idea into appropriate mathematical symbols.

Although effective reading comprehension requires identifying words automatically (Adams, 1990, Perfetti, 1985), children do not have to be able to identify every single word or know the exact meaning of every word in a text to understand it. Indeed, Nagy (1988) says that, children can read a book with a high level of comprehension even if they do not fully know as many as 15 percent of the words within a given text.

Reading fluency and comprehension involve three cueing methods-orthographic awareness, semantic cueing and syntactic cueing. Also, sight word and high frequency word skills contribute to reading fluency. Teachers need to be aware of how to assess and teach those skills to enhance reading fluency.

Orthographic awareness is the ability to perceive and recall letter strings and word forms, as well as the retrieval of letters and words. Sight word vocabulary for both reading and spelling depends on this skill.

A weakness in orthographic awareness results in slow reading rates and problems with spelling. This, in turn, affects reading comprehension and writing fluency.

Syntactic cueing involves evaluating a word for its part of speech and its place in the sentence. For example, the reader determines if it is a noun, verb, adjective, etc. If it is an adjective, the reader determines which word it modifies. If it is a pronoun, the reader must decide which noun it takes the place of. Syntactic cueing directly affects reading comprehension.

Semantic cueing requires determining the meaning of the word, phrase or sentence. It involves determining what the passage is about.

> **Learn more about these three cueing systems:**
>
> http://www.sedl.org/reading/topics/cueing.html

Reading develops in sequential skills levels.

These are:
- **Schema Stage**– pre-reading level, page turning and telling story from memory
- **Early Semantic/Syntactic Stage**– begins to match story recall to random words, cannot read known word in all contexts
- **Later Semantic/Syntactic Stage**– using meaning clues, not tied to orthographic , i.e. horse for pony
- **Orthographic Stage**– begins to match word to what is actually printed, struggles to sound out words using orthographic awareness skills
- **Simultaneous Stage**– uses all three cueing methods, predicts meaning using semantics/syntactics, tries orthographic cues to match word to prediction

When assessing reading errors or miscues, there are nine categories to use when classifying the errors. Categorizing the errors helps the teacher determine the appropriate intervention.

The categories are:
- **Dialect variation** – pronunciation difference due to dialect, i.e. caw for car
- **Intonation shift or prosody**—stress or emphasis changes meaning, i.e. The girl WAS in the house vs. The GIRL was in the house
- **Graphic similarity**—word looks similar to correct one, i.e. horse for house
- **Sound similarity**—i.e. cook, look
- **Grammatical similarity**—i.e. the blue book is read as the red book
- **Syntactic acceptability**—same as grammatical similarity
- **Semantic acceptability**—meaning is the same, i.e. child is read as baby
- **Meaning change**—i.e. he rode the horse read as he wrote the horse
- **Self-correction with semantic acceptability**—self-corrects based on meaning, i.e. as in example above, reader would change wrote to rode because it doesn't make sense otherwise

If the miscues are due to orthographic mistakes, the teacher should stress phonics instruction. If miscues are due to semantic mistakes, the teacher should teach the child to read for meaning. Syntactic miscues means the teacher needs to address grammar, such as parts of speech and sentence structure.

High frequency words are the words most often used in the English language. Depending on the list used, these range from 100 to 300 words. It has been estimated that 100 words make up 50% of all words used in reading. Other lists, such as Dolch and Fry, use the most frequently encountered words in early childhood reading texts.

Sight words are words that the reader learns to read spontaneously either because of frequency or lack of conformity to orthographic rules. For example, words like 'the', 'what', and 'there' because they don't conform to rules, and words like 'boy', 'girl', and 'book' because they are seen very frequently in early reading texts.

For further discussion of orthographic awareness, **SEE** Skill 7.5.

Skill 7.4 **Identifying ways for promoting vocabulary development and the use of vocabulary knowledge in new contexts**

The National Reading Panel has put forth the following conclusions about vocabulary instruction.

1. There is a need for direct instruction of vocabulary items required for a specific text.
2. Repetition and multiple exposures to vocabulary items are important. Students should be given items that will be likely to appear in many contexts.
3. Learning in rich contexts is valuable for vocabulary learning. Vocabulary words should be those that the learner will find useful in many contexts. When vocabulary items are derived from content learning materials, the learner will be better equipped to deal with specific reading matter in content areas.
4. Vocabulary tasks should be restructured as necessary. It is important to be certain that students fully understand what is asked of them in the context of reading rather than focusing only on the words to be learned.
5. Vocabulary learning is effective when it entails active engagement in learning tasks.
6. Computer technology can be used effectively to help teach vocabulary.
7. Vocabulary can be acquired through incidental learning. Much of a student's vocabulary will have to be learned in the course of doing things other than explicit vocabulary learning. Repetition, richness of context, and motivation may also add to the efficacy of incidental learning of vocabulary.
8. Dependence on a single vocabulary instruction method will not result in optimal learning. A variety of methods were used effectively with emphasis on multimedia aspects of learning, richness of context in which words are to be learned, and the number of exposures to words that learners receive.

The Panel found that a critical feature of effective classrooms is the instruction of specific words that includes lessons and activities where students apply their vocabulary knowledge and strategies to reading and writing. Included in the activities were discussions where teachers and students talked about words, their features, and strategies for understanding unfamiliar words.

There are many methods for directly and explicitly teaching words. In fact, the Panel identified twenty-one methods that have been found effective in research projects. Many emphasize the underlying concept of a word and its connections to other words such as semantic mapping and diagrams that use graphics. The keyword method uses words and illustrations that highlight salient features of meaning. Visualizing or drawing a picture either by the student or by the teacher was found to be effective. Many words cannot be learned in this way, of course, so it should be used as only one method among others. Effective classrooms provide multiple ways for students to learn and interact with words. The Panel also found that computer-assisted activities can have a very positive role in the development of vocabulary.

> **For more information on how to incorporate these findings into the classroom:**
>
> http://www.nationalreadingpanel.org/Publications/researchread.htm

Skill 7.5 Identifying appropriate strategies for promoting reading fluency

Accuracy

One way to evaluate reading fluency is to look at student accuracy, and one way to do this is to record running records of students during oral reading. Calculating the reading level lets you know if the book is at the level from which the child can read it independently or comfortably with guidance or if the book is at a level where reading it frustrates the child.

As part of the informal assessment of primary grade reading, it is important to record the child's word insertions, omissions, requests for help, and attempts to get the word. In informal assessment the rate of accuracy can be estimated from the ratio of errors to total words read.

Results of Running Record Informal Assessment can be used for teaching based on Text Accuracy. If a child reads from 95%-100% correct, the child is ready for independent reading. If the child reads from 92% to 97% right, the child is ready for guided reading. Below 92% the child needs a read-aloud or shared reading activity.

Automacity

Fluency in reading is dependent on automatic word identification, which assists the student in achieving comprehension of the material. Even slight difficulties in word identification can significantly increase the time it takes a student to read material, may require rereading parts or passages of the material and reduce the level of comprehension expected. If the student experiences reading as a constant struggle or an arduous chore, then the student will avoid reading whenever possible and consider it a negative experience when necessary. Obviously, the ability to read for comprehension, and learning in general, will suffer if all aspects of reading fluency are not presented to the student as acquirable skills, which will be readily accomplished with the appropriate effort.

Automatic reading involves the development of strong orthographic representations, which allows fast and accurate identification of whole words made up of specific letter patterns. Most young students move easily from the use of alphabetic strategies to the use of orthographic representations, which can be accessed automatically. Initially, word identification is based on the application of phonic word-accessibility strategies (letter-sound associations). These strategies are, in turn, based on the development of phonemic awareness, which is necessary to learn how to relate speech to print.

One of the most useful devices for developing automaticity in young students is through the visual pattern provided in the six syllable types.

EXAMPLES OF THE SIX SYLLABLE TYPES

1. **NOT** (CLOSED)
   Closed in by a consonant—vowel makes its **short** sound
- **NO** (OPEN)
   Ends in a vowel—vowel makes its **long** sound
1) **NOTE** (SILENT "E")
   Ends in vowel consonant "e"--vowel makes its **long** sound
- **NAIL** (VOWEL COMBINATION)
   Two vowels together make the sound
5. **BIRD** ("R" CONTROLLED)
   Contains a vowel plus 4—vowel sound is changed
6. **TABLE** (CONSONANT "L"-"E")
   Applied at the end of a word

These orthographic (letter) patterns signal vowel pronunciation to the reader. Students must become able to apply their knowledge of these patterns to recognize the syllable types and to see these patterns automatically, and ultimately, to read words as wholes. The move from decoding letter symbols to identifying recognizable terms, to automatic word recognition is a substantial move toward fluency. A significant aid for helping students move through this phase was developed by Anna Gillingham when she incorporated the Phonetic Word Cards activity into the Orton-Gillingham lesson plan (Gillingham and Stillman, 1997). This activity involves having the students practice reading words (and some non words) on cards as wholes, beginning with simple syllables and moving systematically through the syllable types to complex syllables and two-syllable words. The words are divided into groups that correspond to the specific sequence of skills being taught.

The student's development of the elements necessary for automaticity continually moves through stages. Another important stage involves the automatic recognition of single graphemes as a critical first step to the development of the letter patterns that make up words or word parts. English orthography is made up of four basic word types:

1. Regular, for reading and spelling (e.g., cat, print)
2. Regular, for reading but not for spelling (e.g. float, brain - could be spelled "flote" or "brane," respectively)
3. Rule based (e.g., canning - doubling rule, faking - drop e rule)
4. Irregular (e.g., beauty).

Students must be taught to recognize all four types of words automatically in order to be effective readers. Repeated practice in pattern recognition is often necessary. Practice techniques for student development can include speed drills in which they read lists of isolated words with contrasting vowel sounds that are signaled by the syllable type. For example, several closed syllable and vowel-consonant-"e" words containing the vowel *a* are arranged randomly on pages containing about 12 lines and read for one minute. Individual goals are established and charts are kept of the number of words read correctly in successive sessions. The same word lists are repeated in sessions until the goal has been achieved for several succeeding sessions. When selecting words for these lists, the use of high-frequency words within a syllable category increases the likelihood of generalization to text reading.

True automaticity should be linked with prosody and anticipation to acquire full fluency. Such things as which syllable is accented and how word structure can be predictive are necessary to true automaticity and essential to complete fluency.

A student whose reading rate is slow, or halting and inconsistent, is exhibiting a lack of reading fluency. According to an article by Mastropieri, Leinart, & Scruggs (1999), some students have developed accurate word pronunciation skills, but read at a slow rate. They have not moved to the phase where decoding is automatic, and their limited fluency may affect performance in the following ways:

1. They read less text than peers and have less time to remember, review, or comprehend the text
2. They expend more cognitive energy than peers trying to identify individual words
3. They may be less able to retain text in their memories and less likely to integrate those segments with other parts of the text

The simplest means of determining a student's reading rate is to have the student read aloud from a prescribed passage, which is at the appropriate reading level for age and grade and contains a specified number of words. The passage should not be too familiar for the student (some will try to memorize or "work out" difficult bits ahead of time), and should not contain more words than can be read comfortably and accurately by a normal reader in one or two minutes. Count only the words <u>correctly</u> pronounced on first reading, and divide this word count into elapsed time to determine the student's reading rate. To determine the student's standing and progress, compare this rate with the norm for the class and the average for all students who read fluently at that specific age/grade level.

The following general guidelines can be applied for reading lists of words with a speed drill and a 1-minute timing: 30 correct wpm for first- and second-grade children; 40 correct wpm for third- grade children; 60 correct wpm for mid-third-grade; and 80 wpm for students in fourth grade and higher.

Various techniques are useful with students who have acquired some proficiency in decoding skill but whose levels of skill are lower than their oral language abilities. Such techniques have certain, common features:

1. Students listen to text as they follow along with the book
2. Students follow the print using their fingers as guides
3. Reading materials are used that students would be unable to read independently.

Experts recommend that a beginning reading program should incorporate partner reading, practice reading difficult words prior to reading the text, timings for accuracy and rate, opportunities to hear books read, and opportunities to read to others.

Prosody

Prosody concerns versification of text and involves such matters as which syllable of a word is accented. It is that aspect which translates reading into the same experience as listening, within the reader's mind. It involves intonation and rhythm through such devices as syllable accent and punctuation.

In their article for *Perspectives* (Winter, 2002), Pamela Hook and Sandra Jones proposed that teachers can begin to develop awareness of the prosodic features of language by introducing a short three-word sentence with each of the three different words underlined for stress (e.g., *He is sick. He is sick. He is sick*.) The teacher can then model the three sentences while discussing the possible meaning for each variation. The students can practice reading them with different stress until they are fluent. These simple three-word sentences can be modified and expanded to include various verbs, pronouns, and tenses. (e.g., *You are sick. I am sick. They are sick.*) This strategy can also be used while increasing the length of phrases and emphasizing the different meanings (e.g., *Get out of bed. Get out of bed. Get out of bed now.*) Teachers can also practice fluency with common phrases that frequently occur in text. Prepositional phrases are good syntactic structures for this type of work (e.g., *on the _____, in the _____, over the _____ etc.*). Teachers can pair these printed phrases to oral intonation patterns that include variations of rate, intensity, and pitch. Students can infer the intended meaning as the teacher presents different prosodic variations of a sentence. For example, when speakers want to stress a concept they often slow their rate of speech and may speak in a louder voice (e.g., *Joshua, get-out-of-bed-**NOW!**)*. Often, the only text marker for this sentence will be the exclamation point (!) but the speaker's intent will affect the manner in which it is delivered.

> **Read the full article about Prosody and automaticity:**
>
> http://dyslexia.mtsu.edu/modules/articles/displayarticle.jsp?id=30

Practicing oral variations and then mapping the prosodic features onto the text will assist students in making the connection when reading. This strategy can also be used to alert students to the prosodic features present in punctuation marks. In the early stages, using the alphabet helps to focus a student on the punctuation marks without having to deal with meaning. The teacher models for the students and then has them practice the combinations using the correct intonation patterns to fit the punctuation mark (e.g., ABC. DE? FGH! IJKL? or ABCD! EFGHI? KL.) Teachers can then move to simple two-word or three-word sentences. The sentences are punctuated with a period, question mark and exclamation point and the differences in meaning that occur with each different punctuation mark (e.g., *Chris hops. Chris hops? Chris hops!*) are discussed.

It may help students to point out that the printed words convey the fact that someone named Chris is engaged in the physical activity of hopping, but the intonation patterns get their cue from the punctuation mark. The meaning extracted from an encounter with a punctuation mark is dependent upon a reader's prior experiences or background knowledge in order to project an appropriate intonation pattern onto the printed text. Keeping the text static while changing the punctuation marks helps students to attend to prosodic patterns.

Students who read word-for-word may benefit initially from practicing phrasing with the alphabet rather than words since letters do not tax the meaning system. The letters are grouped, an arc is drawn underneath, and students recite the alphabet in chunks (e.g., ABC DE FGH IJK LM NOP QRS TU VW XYZ). Once students understand the concept of phrasing, it is recommended that teachers help students chunk text into syntactic (noun phrases, verb phrases, prepositional phrases) or meaning units until they are proficient themselves. There are no hard and fast rules for chunking but syntactic units are most commonly used.

For better readers, teachers can mark the phrasal boundaries with slashes for short passages. Eventually, the slashes are used only at the beginning of long passages and then students are asked to continue "phrase reading" even after the marks end. Marking phrases can be done together with students or those on an independent level may divide passages into phrases themselves. Comparisons can be made to clarify reasons for differences in phrasing. Another way to encourage students to focus on phrase meaning and prosody in addition to word identification is to provide tasks that require them to identify or supply a paraphrase of an original statement.

Benchmarks are readily available for every level of reading. These are texts with words on grade level the teacher can use for miscue analysis. The teacher takes a running record of the student reading a text and makes notes on the strategies the student uses as well as whether or not the student reads word by word or fluently.

These assessments can help the teacher decide whether or not the student is reading at grade level and whether the student needs instruction in one or more reading strategies to help him/her read fluently.

There are some students who can read fluently and yet not have adequate comprehension skills. Just because some students readily recognizes every word in the text does not make them fluent readers. Therefore, the assessment must include asking comprehension questions that test the students' literal, inferential and critical levels of comprehension.

Strategies that teachers can use to help students develop fluency in reading include modeling fluent reading and explaining to students what fluent reading sounds like as opposed to reading word by word.

Strategies that teachers can use to teach students sound to letter correspondence include:
- recognizing and producing rhyming words
- modeling the correct pronunciation of words
- orally breaking the words into syllables
- identifying where a sound occurs in a word
- identifying the number of phonemes in a word
- deleting initial, middle and final phonemes from a word
- substituting phonemes in a word

Once students know these strategies, teachers can ensure success in reading by making sure that students choose texts at their instructional level for use in independent reading. The Guided Reading model of Fountas and Pinnell has texts leveled according to difficulty. Teachers can assess students' reading abilities and assign: leveled text for students.

Repeated readings of the same text ensure that students recognize the words readily and can read at a normal pace. Some might argue that the students have memorized the text, but the teacher can easily check this by choosing pages at random for the student to read.

Paired reading means pairing a good reader with a struggling reader to read together. One student can read a page and then the other student can read a page. The struggling reader will then be able to see what fluent reading looks and sounds like.

There should be periods in the Language Arts class where students engage in silent reading. During this time, the teacher can select students and ask them to read aloud quietly from where they are. This will give the teacher information on whether or not the student is reading texts at his/her appropriate level. The silent reading period should start off for short periods of time and lengthen gradually throughout the year. Thus, if students are not reading at home, time is provided for them to do so in school.

> **For a summary of reading difficulties children may have:**
>
> http://www.pbs.org/wgbh/misunderstoodminds/readingdiffs.html

Skill 7.6 Demonstrating knowledge of literal, inferential, interpretive, and evaluative comprehension skills and strategies for promoting children's development of these skills

Reading comprehension skills such as generating and answering literal, inferential, and interpretive questions to demonstrate understanding about what is read in complex text are often found in the differing levels of Bloom's Taxonomy. These levels, in ascending order of sophistication, are: (1) knowledge, (2) comprehension, (3) application, (4) analysis, (5) synthesis, and (6) evaluation.

> **Learn more about Bloom's Taxonomy:**
>
> http://faculty.washington.edu/krumme/guides/bloom1.html

These higher cognitive questions are defined as those which ask the student to mentally manipulate bits of information previously learned to support an answer with logically reasoned evidence. Higher cognitive questions are also called open-ended, interpretive, evaluative, and inferential questions. Lower cognitive questions are those that ask the student merely to recall verbatim or literally the material previously read or taught by the teacher.

Beginning readers must learn to recognize the conventions that create meaning and expectations in the text. For beginning readers, these literal skills include deciphering the words, punctuation, and grammar in a text. When readers ascertain comprehension, they create meaning from a text. Comprehension occurs when readers are able to make predictions, select main ideas, and establish significant and supporting details of the story.

A successful program of comprehension instruction should include four components:

- large amounts of time for actual text reading,
- teacher-directed instruction in comprehension strategies
- opportunities for peer and collaborative learning
- occasions for students to talk to a teacher and one another about their responses to reading.

Teachers can improve comprehension skills by providing children with opportunities and guidance in making text selections. Student choice is related to interest and motivation, both of which are related directly to learning. Teachers can encourage re-reading of texts, which research suggests leads to greater fluency and comprehension. Teachers can also allow time for students to read in pairs, including students of different abilities. This provides regular opportunities for readers to discuss their reading with the teacher and with one another. Teachers can also employ guided practice strategies in which feedback is given back to the students' attempts, gradually giving students more and more responsibility for evaluating their own performances.

Skill 7.7   Recognizing strategies for facilitating comprehension before, during, and after reading (e.g., predicting, self-monitoring, questioning, rereading, engaging in dialogue, reflecting)

Making Predictions

One theory or approach to the teaching of reading that gained currency in the late sixties and the early seventies was the importance of asking inferential and critical thinking questions of the reader - questions that would challenge and engage the children in the text. This approach to reading went beyond the literal level of what was stated in the text to an inferential level of using text clues to make predictions and to a critical level of involving the child in evaluating the text. While asking engaging and thought-provoking questions is still viewed as part of the teaching of reading, it is currently viewed as just one of several components of the teaching of reading.

Prior Knowledge

Prior knowledge can be defined as all of an individual's prior experiences, learning, and development that precede one's entering a specific learning situation or attempting to comprehend a specific text. Sometimes prior knowledge can be erroneous or incomplete. Obviously, if there are misconceptions in a child's prior knowledge, these must be corrected so that the child's overall comprehension skills can continue to progress.

Even the prior knowledge of kindergarteners includes their accumulated positive and negative experiences, both in and out of school. These might range from family travels, watching television, visiting museums and libraries, to visiting hospitals, prisons and surviving poverty. Whatever the prior knowledge that the child brings to the school setting, the independent reading and writing the child does in school immeasurably expands the prior knowledge base and hence broadens the child's reading comprehension capabilities.

Literary response skills are dependent on prior knowledge, schemata and background. Schemata (the plural of schema) are those structures that represent generic concepts stored in our memory. Readers who effectively comprehend text, whether they are adults or children, use both their schemata and prior knowledge PLUS the ideas from the printed text for reading comprehension, and graphic organizers help organize this information.

Graphic Organizers

Graphic organizers solidify, in a chart or diagram format, a visual relationship among various reading and writing ideas including: sequence, timelines, character traits, fact and opinion, main idea and details, differences and likenesses (generally done using a VENN DIAGRAM of interlocking circles, KWL Chart, etc). These charts and diagrams are essential for providing scaffolding for instruction through activating pertinent prior knowledge.

KWL charts are exceptionally useful for reading comprehension by outlining what readers KNOW, what they WANT to know, and what they've LEARNED after reading. Students are asked to activate prior knowledge about a topic and further develop their knowledge about a topic using this organizer. Teachers often opt to display and maintain KWL charts throughout a text to continually record pertinent information about students' reading.

When the teacher first introduces the K-W-L strategy, the children should be allowed sufficient time to brainstorm in response to the first question, listing what each student the class or small group actually knows about the topic. The children should have a three-columned K-W-L worksheet template for their journals and there should be a chart to record the responses from class or group discussion. The children can write under each column in their own journal, and should also help the teacher with notations on the chart. This strategy allows the children to gain experience in note taking and in creating a concrete record of new data and information they have gleaned from the passage about the topic.

Depending on the grade level of the participating children, the teacher may also want to ask them to consider categories of information they hope to find out from the expository passage. For instance, they may be reading a book on animals to find out more about the animal's habitats during the winter or about the animal's mating habits.

When children are working on the middle section of their K-W-L strategy sheet—What I want to know the teacher may want to give them a chance to share what they would like to learn further about the topic and help them to express it in question format.

K-W-L is useful and can even be introduced as early as grade 2 with extensive teacher discussion support. It not only serves to support the child's comprehension of a particular expository text, but also models for children a format for note taking. Beyond note taking, when the teacher wants to introduce report writing, the K-W-L format provides excellent outlines and question introductions for at least three paragraphs of a report.

Cooper (2004) recommends this strategy for use with thematic units and with reading chapters in required science, social studies, or health text books. In addition to its usefulness with thematic unit study, K-W-L is wonderful for providing the teacher with a concrete format to assess how well children have absorbed pertinent new knowledge within the passage by looking at the third section—What I learned. Ultimately, it is hoped that students will learn to use this strategy, not only under explicit teacher direction with templates of K-W-L sheets, but also on their own by informally writing questions they want to find out about in their journals and then going back to their own questions and answering them after the reading.

> **For more examples of graphic organizers:**
>
> http://www.eduplace.com/graphicorganizer/

Sample Venn Diagram:

Mr. Jones 3rd Grade class

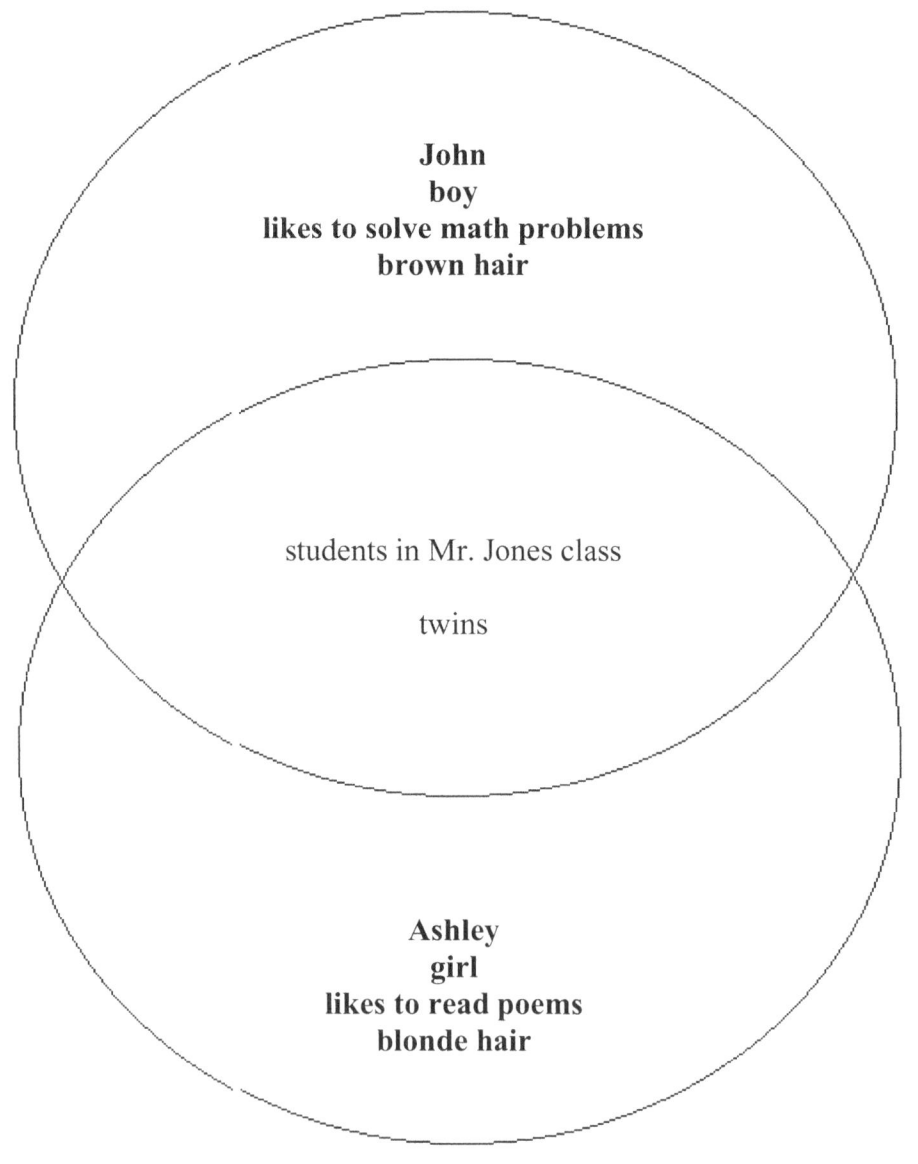

Note Taking

Older children take notes in their reading journals, while younger children and those more in need of explicit teacher support contribute their ideas and responses as part of the discussion in class. Their responses are recorded on the experiential chart.

Connecting Texts

The concept of readiness is generally regarded as a developmentally based phenomenon. Various abilities, whether cognitive, affective, or psychomotor, are perceived to be dependent upon the mastery or development of certain prerequisite skills or abilities.

Readiness for subject area learning is dependent not only on prior knowledge, but also on affective factors such as interest, motivation, and attitude. These factors are often more influential on student learning than the pre-existing cognitive base.

When texts relate to a student's life or other reading materials or areas of study, they become more meaningful and relevant to the student's learning. Students enjoy seeing reading material connect to their lives, other subject areas and other reading material.

Discussing the Text

Discussion is an activity in which the children consider a particular text. Among the prompts, the teacher-coach might suggest that the children focus on words of interest they encountered in the text. These can also be words that they heard if the text was read aloud. Children can be asked to share something funny or upsetting or unusual about the words they have read. Through this focus on children's response to words as the center of the discussion circle, peers become more interested in word study.

Furthermore, in the current teaching of literacy; reading, writing, thinking, listening, viewing, and discussing, are not viewed as separate activities or components of instruction, but rather as developing and being nurtured simultaneously and interactively.

Competency 008 Understand writing processes and how to create effective learning opportunities for promoting young children's writing skills

Skill 8.1 Recognizing the characteristics, processes, and progressions of writing development

Young children develop writing in stages just as they do reading. As with reading, writing development is not a linear progression, but rather an overlapping one. Though many label the scribbling that children start out with as prewriting, it is actually one of the stages of writing development.

Each writing stage has unique characteristics involving the areas of spelling, penmanship, print/mechanics concepts, and content. The following table explains the requisite skill for each stage and area.

	Spelling	Penmanship	Print/mechanics Concepts	Content
Role Play Writer	Scribbles and uses writing-like behavior; scribbles to represent word; no phonetic association.	Develops pencil position and traces words and letters	Develops awareness of environmental print	Uses pictures and scribble writing
Emergent Writer	Writes initial consonants; correlates some letter/sounds; each syllable has a letter	Can write on line; incorrectly mixes upper and lower case letters	Makes some letters and words; attempts to write name	Copies word and uses pattern sentences
Developing Writer	Left/right correspondence; invented spelling with initial/final consonants; few vowels	Correctly uses upper and lowercase letters	Directional writing and one-to-one writing/reading words; writes word patterns	Uses invented spelling and simple sentences
Beginning Writer	Correct spelling for most words; uses resources and decoding for spelling	Sentence structure; only focuses on one writing component at a time, i.e. spelling or punctuation	Chooses personally significant topics for writing assignments	Organizes paragraphs using complete sentences
Expanding Writer	Edits for mechanics during and after writing	Varies writing components based on writing task	Uses organization and variety of word choices	Writes in a variety of formats: poetry, stories, reports, etc.

Stages of writing development are:
- **Role Play Writer**
- **Emergent Writer**
- **Developing Writer**
- **Beginning Writer**
- **Expanding Writer**

> **See samples of the stages of writing development:**
>
> http://cfbstaff.cfbisd.edu/chienv/stages_of_writing_development.htm

The Writing Process

Learning to write is generally a sequential process. Research confirms that children develop spelling strategies in predictable stages. There is a continuous growth in writing, but the children vary in the development of these stages. A child's writing may show evidence of more than one stage. Children may even skip levels on their way to developing writing competency.

Children progress as writers from one phase to the next, with one set of skills building on the skills acquired earlier. Writing, however, combines many skills, and relies on development in many areas not specific to writing. A child's fine motor control and vocabulary, for example, must improve in order for writing to progress normally.

Cognitive theories of understanding state that learning only takes place when the new learning is based upon previous learning. Struggling students may often lack essential background knowledge necessary to successfully complete a task or use a strategy.

The best way to identify the basic terms and skills necessary for the strategy is to do a task analysis. The task analysis will help teachers to determine if students possess the prerequisite skills necessary to advance to the next stage of writing. After the task analysis is complete, there are many ways that teachers can check students' skills. These include observing student performance, using curriculum-based measures, or simply asking students.

Writing is a process that flows gradually. As you give your students time to explore and experiment with writing, you will begin to see evidence of growth. Since writing is a process and stages are connected. Students may show evidence of more than one stage in a single piece of writing.

Writing is a recursive process. As students engage in the various stages of writing, they develop and improve not only their writing skills, but their thinking skills as well. Students must understand that writing is a process and typically involves many steps when writing quality work. No matter the level of writer, students should be experienced in the following stages of the writing process.

Prewriting

Students gather ideas before writing. Prewriting may include clustering, listing, brainstorming, mapping, free writing, and charting. Providing many ways for a student to develop ideas on a topic will increase his/her chances for success. Remind students that as they prewrite, they need to consider their audience.

Prewriting strategies assist students in a variety of ways. Listed below are the most common prewriting strategies students can use to explore, plan and write on a topic. It is important to remember when teaching these strategies that not all prewriting must eventually produce a finished piece of writing. In fact, in the initial lesson of teaching prewriting strategies, it might be more effective to have students practice prewriting strategies without the pressure of having to write a finished product.

- Keep an idea book so that they can jot down ideas that come to mind.
- Write in a daily journal.
- Write down whatever comes to mind; this is called free writing. Students do not stop to make corrections or interrupt the flow of ideas.

A variation of this technique is focused free writing - writing on a specific topic - to prepare for an essay.

- Make a list of all ideas connected with their topic; this is called brainstorming
- Make sure students know that this technique works best when they let their minds work freely. After completing the list, students should analyze the list to see if a pattern or way to group the ideas emerges.
- Ask the questions Who? What? When? Where? When? and How? Help the writer approach a topic from several perspectives.
- Create a visual map on paper to gather ideas. Cluster circles and lines to show connections between ideas. Students should try to identify the relationship that exists between their ideas. If they cannot see the relationships, have them pair up, exchange papers and have their partners look for some related ideas.
- Observe details of sight, hearing, taste, touch, and taste.
- Visualize by making mental images of something and write down the details in a list.

After students have practiced each of these prewriting strategies, ask them to pick out the ones they prefer and ask them to discuss how they might use the techniques to help them with future writing assignments. It is important to remember that they can use more than one prewriting strategy at a time. Also they may find that different writing situations may suggest certain techniques.

Drafting
Students compose the first draft. Students should follow their notes/writing plan from the prewriting stage.

Revision and Editing
Revise comes from the Latin word *revidere*, meaning, "to see again." Revision is probably the most important step for the writer in the writing process. Here, students examine their work and make changes in wording, details and ideas. So many times, students write a draft and then feel they're done. On the contrary, students must be encouraged to develop, change, and enhance their writing as they go, as well as once they've completed a draft.

As you discuss revision, you begin with discussing the definition of revise. Also, state that all writing must be revised to improve it. After students have revised their writing, it is time for the final editing and proofreading.

Both teachers and students should be aware of the difference between these two writing processes. Revising typically entails making substantial changes to a written draft, and it is during this process that the look, idea and feel of a draft may be altered, sometimes significantly. Like revising, editing continues to make changes to a draft. However the chances made during the editing process do more to enhance the ideas in the draft, rather than change or alter them. Finally, proofreading is the stage where grammatical and technical errors are addressed.

Effective teachers realize that revision and editing go hand-in-hand and students often move back and forth between these stages during the course of one written work. Also, these stages must be practiced in small groups, pairs and/or individually. Students must learn to analyze and improve their own work as well as the works of their peers. Some methods to use include:

1. Students, working in pairs, analyze sentences for variety.
2. Students work in pairs or groups to ask questions about unclear areas in the writing or to help students add details, information, etc.
3. Students perform final edit.

Many teachers introduce Writer's Workshop to their students to maximize learning about the writing process. Writer's Workshops vary across classrooms, but the main idea is for students to become comfortable with the writing process to produce written work. A basic Writer's Workshop will include a block of classroom time committed to writing various projects (i.e., narratives, memoirs, book summaries, fiction, book reports, etc). Students use this time to write, meet with others to review/edit writing, make comments on writing, revise their own work, proofread, meet with the teacher, and publish their work.
Teachers who facilitate effective Writer's Workshops are able to meet with students one at a time and can guide that student in their individual writing needs. This approach allows the teacher to differentiate instruction for each student's writing level.

Students need to be trained to become effective at proofreading, revising and editing strategies. Begin by training them using both desk-side and scheduled conferences. Listed below are some strategies to use to guide students through the final stages of the writing process (and these can easily be incorporated into Writer's Workshop).

- Provide some guide sheets or forms for students to use during peer responses.
- Allow students to work in pairs and limit the agenda.
- Model the use of the guide sheet or form for the entire class.
- Give students a time limit or number of written pieces to be completed in a specific amount of time.
- Have the students read their partners' papers and ask at least three who, what, when, why, how questions. The students answer the questions and use them as a place to begin discussing the piece.
- At this point in the writing process, a mini-lesson that focuses on some of the problems your students are having would be appropriate.

To help students revise, provide students with a series of questions that will assist them in revising their writing

- Do the details give a clear picture? Add details that appeal to more than just the sense of sight.
- How effectively are the details organized? Reorder the details if it is needed.
- Are the thoughts and feelings of the writer included? Add personal thoughts and feelings about the subject.

Gone are the days when students engage in skill practice with grammar worksheets. Grammar needs to be taught in the context of the students' own work. Listed below is a series of classroom practices that encourage meaningful context-based grammar instruction, combined with occasional mini-lessons and other language strategies that can be used on a daily basis.

* Connect grammar with the student's own writing while emphasizing grammar as a significant aspect of effective writing.

* Emphasize the importance of editing and proofreading as an essential part of classroom activities.

* Provide students with an opportunity to practice editing and proofreading cooperatively.

* Give instruction in the form of 15-20 minute mini-lessons.

* Emphasize the sound of punctuation by connecting it to pitch, stress, and pause.

* Involve students in all facets of language learning including reading, writing, listening, speaking and thinking. Good use of language comes from exploring all forms of it on a regular basis.

There are a number of approaches that involve grammar instruction in the context of the writing.

1. Sentence Combining—try to use the student's own writing as much as possible. The theory behind combining ideas and the correct punctuation should be emphasized.

2. Sentence and paragraph modeling—provide students with the opportunity to practice imitating the style and syntax of professional writers.

3. Sentence transforming—give students an opportunity to change sentences from one form to another, i.e. from passive to active, inverting the sentence order, change forms of the words used.

4. Daily Language Practice—introduce or clarify common errors using daily language activities. Use actual student examples whenever possible. Correct and discuss the problems with grammar and usage.

Proofreading

Students proofread the draft for punctuation and mechanical errors. There are a few key points to remember when helping students learn to edit and proofread their work.

- It is crucial that students are not taught grammar in isolation, but in context of the writing process
- Ask students to read their writing and check for specific errors such as whether or not every sentence starts with a capital letter and has the correct punctuation at the end.
- Provide students with a proofreading checklist to guide them as they edit their work

Publishing

Students may have their work displayed on a bulletin board, read aloud in class, or printed in a literary magazine or school anthology.

It is important to realize that these steps are recursive; as a student engages in each aspect of the writing process. The students may begin with prewriting, write, revise, write, revise, edit, and publish. They do not engage in this process in a lockstep manner; it is more circular.

Developing Emergent Writing Skills

- **Assessment**
  The first step in developing young writers skills is to know where they are in developmental writing stages. Though skill are overlapping, at any one time a child will fall predominately into one or more skill areas. While the child may be an emergent writer in content, the same child may be a role player writer in penmanship. Teachers need to be aware of where each student falls at any one time in each area of writing. The best means of assessment are writing samples and/or portfolios and journals. Assessment should be ongoing, as a child's writing stage is not static.

- **Teaching strategies**
  Invented spelling is an early writing skill. Teachers should encourage and teach the child invented spelling. The child's name is usually the first meaningful writing the child does. The teacher should focus intensely on teaching the child to write her name. Teachers can develop an interest in writing in a young child by providing and guiding the student through meaningful writing tasks such as letters home to parents, thank you notes, and journal writing to share experiences.

- **Environment**
  Teachers should set up their classroom environment to encourage meaningful writing, such as having a sign-in sheet, providing pencils and pads for play, for writing traffic tickets, menus, taking restaurant orders, etc. Meaningful writing opportunities should also be provided such as journaling and writing centers, observation journals in science centers, and providing reference charts for alphabet and pattern sentences. Outside writing opportunities should be encouraged with sidewalk chalk, nature journals, and signing library books in and out.

- **Materials**
  Teachers should provide a variety of writing materials to inspire all students. Markers and construction paper provide inspiration to some students, while others prefer paints. Sponges cut into letter shapes, stamps, stencils, and hole punchers are some writing materials that can be made available. Shaving cream, sand, jello, rice, and other manipulative materials should be available for those students who need or enjoy the tactile stimulation for writing.

Skill 8.2 Analyzing factors that affect young children's development of writing skills (e.g., access to writing materials, opportunities to write, fine-motor development)

In order for children to write correctly, they must first develop their fine motor skills. Before being required to manipulate a pencil, children should have dexterity and strength in their fingers, which helps them to gain more control of small muscles.

These hands-on activities are excellent activities for practicing fine motor skills.

Tearing
Tear newspaper into strips and then crumple them into balls. Use the balls to stuff a Halloween pumpkin or other art creation.

Cutting
Cut pictures from magazines
Cut a fringe on the edge of a piece of construction paper.

Puzzles
Have children put together a puzzle with large puzzles pieces. This will help to develop proper eye-hand coordination.

Clay
Manipulating play dough into balls strengthens a child's grasp. Let the children explain to what they created from their play dough objects.

Finger Painting
Many times when a child has not developed fine motor skills yet, it helps to trace the pattern with his finger before he tries it with a pencil. Have the child trace a pattern in sand, cornmeal, finger paint, etc.

Drawing
Draw at an easel with a large crayon. Encourage children to practice their name or letters of the alphabet

The above activities will build strength in their fingers and hands, which will aid in the development of a child's writing skills.

The most important factors of learning to write are the grip on the writing instrument, the position of the arm and wrist, and the position of the writing paper.

Instructional Strategies

The Primary Grip
Beginning writers with undeveloped fine motor skills should be taught the primary grip. First, have the child join the tips of the thumb and middle finger. Then place the pen in the space between them. Finally, have the child lay the index finger on top of the pen. This way, the index finger pushes against the thumb and middle finger. As children grow, the proportions of their hands change. This allows them to hold the pen differently and write faster.

Paper Position
Right-handed children should place the paper directly in front of them and hold it in place with the left hand. The light should come from the left. Otherwise, the child's' hand will cast a shadow just where they need to see what they are writing. With the paper slightly to the right of the writer, their line of vision is clear. Teachers should check to see if the students are the children sitting upright. Make sure they are not gripping the pen too hard, and the paper in the right position.

For a left-handed child, the paper should be positioned at the left of the child's midline so that the top right hand corner of the paper is closer to the child than the top left hand corner. The child's hand should be at the left of the paper. Although the tilt of the paper varies with children, the arm should be perpendicular to the bottom of the page and the wrist should be straight, rather than bent,

Beginning Strokes

A teacher may need to teach a student the direction of the pencil strokes. A good word to practice with is the child's first name. Identify one letter at a time. Show the beginning point right on the top line and the ending point on the bottom line. Slowly write the name on one line, one letter at a time, so the child can clearly see it. Have the child write directly under your sample, not to the side. Write your sample in straight, easy to copy letters.

Problems to look for:

Gripping the pencil too tightly

A common problem for all young children learning to write is gripping the pencil too tightly, which makes writing tiresome. Usually the student learns to relax the grip as writing skill develops, but teachers can remind students to hold the instrument gently.

Holding the pencil incorrectly

If the child tends to hold the pencil too close to the point, make a mark on the pencil at the correct spot, to remind the student where to grip the pencil.

Left-handed writers

In languages that are written left-to-right; like the English language, it is more difficult to write with the left hand. A right-hander writes away from their body and pulls the pencil, while a left-hander must write toward their body and push the pencil.

Skill 8.3 **Demonstrating knowledge of strategies for helping children develop and apply writing skills and for promoting children's interest and engagement in writing for different purposes and audiences**

In the past, teachers have assigned reports, paragraphs and essays that focused on the teacher as the audience with the purpose of explaining information. However, for students to be meaningfully engaged in their writing, they must write for a variety of reasons. Writing for different audiences and purposes allows students to be more involved in their writing. If they write for the same audience and purpose, they will continue to see writing as just another assignment. Listed below are suggestions that give students an opportunity to write in more creative and critical ways.

- Write letters to the editor, to a college, to a friend, to another student that would be sent to the intended audience.
- Write stories that would be read aloud to a group (the class, another group of students, to a group of elementary school students) or published in a literary magazine or class anthology.
- Write plays that would be performed.
- Discuss the parallels between the different speech styles we use and writing styles for different readers or audiences.
- Write a particular piece for different audiences.
- Expose students to pieces of writing that are on the same topic, but for different audiences and have them identify the variations in sentence structure and style.
- As part of the prewriting have students identify the audience. Make sure students consider the following when analyzing the needs of their audience.
    1. Why is the audience reading my writing? Do they expect to be informed, amused or persuaded?
    2. What does my audience already know about my topic?
    3. What does the audience want or need to know? What will interest them?
    4. What type of language suits my readers?

Remind your students that it is not necessary to identify all the specifics of the audience in the initial stage of the writing process, but that at some point they must make some determinations about audience.

While the teaching of writing undoubtedly involves an enormous amount of work on the composition of text, it also involves the general concept of ideas conveyed in the best possible manner. In other words, the results of a survey could be explained in words, but it might be easier to understand in a graph or chart. If that is the case, why would we want to present it in words? The important point is for the information to be conveyed effectively.

So, as students write reports and respond to ideas in writing, they can learn how to incorporate multiple representations of information, including various graphic representations, into written text. While this is seemingly fairly easy to do considering the word processing technology we have available to us, students struggle with knowing how to appropriately and successfully do this. They can learn to do this in three primary ways: explanation, observation/modeling, and practice.

First, students need to have clear explanations from teachers on appropriate forms of graphical representations in text, as well as the methods to use for including those representations. They need to see plenty of examples of how it is done.

Second, they need to be able to see teacher-modeled examples where text has been replaced or enhanced by graphical representations. The more they see of examples, the clearer the concepts will be to them.

Finally, students need to get a chance to practice incorporating graphical representations in their writing. This, of course, will require technology and plenty of feedback.

Students will most likely appreciate the ability to utilize graphical representations in place of text, but they will soon realize that deciding which type of representation to use and how to actually use it will be very challenging. Generally, graphical representations should be used only if they can convey information better than written text can. This is an important principal that students will need to learn through constant practice.

> **For more strategies for teaching the writing process:**
>
> http://www.intercom.net/local/school/sdms/mspap/writ_sugg2.html

Skill 8.4   Recognizing the reciprocal relationships between children's writing and reading experiences

A student's developmental writing skills parallel their reading development stages of reading. Print awareness develops in young children as a result of listening to a story read to them by adults, and recognizing that words on a page symbolize meaning. Print awareness is the realization that writing is created with instruments such as pens, pencils, crayons and markers. Children begin to imitate the shapes, and letters they see in a book or in text. Children soon learn that the power of writing is expressing one's own ideas in print form and can be understood by others.

Due to the social nature of children's learning, early instruction must provide rich demonstrations, interactions, and models of literacy. Children learn about the relation between oral and written language and the relation between letters, sounds, and words. Classrooms should include a wide variety of print and writing activities that involve talking, reading, writing, playing, and listening to one another. Books, papers, writing tools, and functional signs should be visible everywhere in the classroom so that children can see and use literacy for multiple purposes.

Sitting down with a child and discussing the writing ideas helps the child to organize the thoughts. This also gives students the opportunity to state their ideas out loud before writing them out on paper. Allow students who have difficulty with writing to respond by art (drawing their favorite part or character) or drama (rehearsing the story). This extra time allows writers to rehearse their ideas before putting them on paper.

Most importantly, respect a student's writing. All students need to feel that their work is valued.

Skill 8.5 Understanding factors affecting spelling development (e.g., visual processing, recognizing patterns of speech sounds, word knowledge)

Spelling is of utmost importance in the writing process. At first young children will use invented spelling, in which they write the words according to letter sounds. There are several factors that influence the development of spelling, such as:

- Surrounding students with an environment rich in print
- Understanding the developmental stages of spelling
- Understanding that learning to spell is problem solving
- Teaching the rules of spelling
- Promoting an awareness about spelling

Spelling should be taught within the context of meaningful language experiences. Giving a child a list of words to learn to spell and then testing the child on the words every Friday will not aid in the development of spelling. The child must be able to use the words in context and the words must have some meaning for the child. The assessment of how well a child can spell or where there are problems also has to be done within a meaningful environment.
The main reasons for assessing spelling are:

- To find out what the child knows about spelling patterns and strategies
- To determine what the teacher needs to teach
- To develop spelling growth over a period of time

In order for spelling assessment to be authentic, it must have meaning for the child. Taking a list of words that a child misspells from a piece of writing is one example of a spelling list that the teacher can use. If the teacher keeps a list of words the children ask to spell, this can also be the basis for a word list.

Since spelling words correctly is something that does happen over time, teachers may notice that the child keeps spelling the same words incorrectly again and again. Through explicit teaching of strategies and even tricks to help spell the words, eventually they will see success in spelling. Assessment is something that has to happen over the course of a grade. Correct spelling is not something that children learn and retain automatically.

When assessing spelling, there are behaviors that teachers should look for:

- Knowledge of sounds and symbols
- Development of visual memory
- Development of morphemic knowledge
- Mastery of high frequency words at specific grade levels
- Location and knowledge of how to use spelling resources
- Attempts at spelling unknown words
- Risk taking attempts in using invented spelling

The process of learning to spell

There are five developmental stages in learning to spell:

1) **Pre-phonemic spelling**—Children know that letters stand for a message, but they do not know the relationship between spelling and pronunciation.

2) **Early phonemic spelling**—Children are beginning to understand spelling. They usually write the beginning letter correctly, with the rest consonants or long vowels.

3) **Letter-name spelling**—Some words are consistently spelled correctly. The student is developing a sight vocabulary and a stable understanding of letters as representing sounds. Long vowels are usually used accurately, but silent vowels are omitted. The child spells unknown words by attempting to match the name of the letter to the sound.

4) **Transitional spelling**—This phase is typically entered in late elementary school. Short vowel sounds are mastered and some spelling rules known. The students are developing a sense of which spellings are correct and which are not.

5) **Derivational spelling**—This is usually reached from high school to adulthood. This is the stage at which spelling rules are mastered.

Effective spelling strategies should emphasize these principles:
- knowledge of patterns, sounds, letter-sound association, syllables
- memorizing sight words
- writing those words correctly many times
- writing the words in personal writing

Spelling development, from invented to conventional spelling

There are basically four approaches for teaching spelling. These are the traditional spelling instruction, whole language, developmental, and the structured language approaches.

The **traditional approach** adheres strictly to a phonics-based approach to spelling. The student uses invented spelling, using known sounds and skipping others. The teacher sequentially teaches phonics rules and their application to spelling, including those words that don't adhere to the rules. In the traditional approach, the student learns to spell by phonemes and word families,. Spelling instruction is direct, systematic, and intensive and is believed to be the best way to insure student success. This approach utilizes the traditional basal speller, rote drill, repeated copying, especially of missed words, and weekly spelling tests.

The **whole language approach** for teaching spelling supports the idea that the student learns to spell by remembering what the word looks like rather than by remembering how it sounds. Rebecca Sitton, who has developed a whole spelling series, spearheads this group. Proponents of this group believe student success lies in learning to spell words as they need them for their personal writing. Students are directed in word wall study, both seeing, chanting, writing, and then using the words in their own personal writing. They are then taught to analyze the structure of words and learn what the base words, prefixes, and suffixes look like and mean. Classrooms are print-rich, exposing the student to the sight of many utilitarian words. It is believed that the student learns spelling best by using the words in their own reading/writing tasks. Though a few words and word structures are taught, children mainly learn as they use the word.

The **developmental approach** suggests several stages of development that students go through in their development from invented spelling to conventional spelling. This approach holds that students should be allowed to just develop without overt instruction, as they will eventually develop to traditional spelling. Different studies have suggested different numbers of stages, but benchmark stages through the continuum are:

- Precommunicative – Random letters – may match beginning sound
- Semiphonetic - One or more letters representing sounds heard, usually without medial vowels
- Phonetic – More letters are included, as are more vowels. They are usually spelled exactly as the child perceives the sounds, i.e. the letter /u might be represented as 'you'
- Transitional- Letters are included for all sounds, words contain the correct number of syllables although some vowels may be misrepresented, i.e. '-er' might be represented as '-ur'
- Conventional- Mostly correct spelling with only errors in difficult spelling patterns

The **structured language approach**, which is considered to have been developed by Samual Orton, involves an in-depth focus on letter/sound relationships and progresses through letters, phonemes, blended syllables, to whole words. There are only 40-plus phonemes used to represent every speech sound made and these are spelled with only 26 letters, so variations have to be learned (as secondary sounds). Orton also identified spelling difficulties with reading difficulties and reasoned that a focus on spelling the 40-plus phonemes would also improve the reading ability of the student.

Each method of teaching spelling has shown documented success. It appears that the clue to success is to actively address spelling issues, either in a structured format or based on words needed by individual students.

Spelling Pattern Word Wall

One of the understandings emergent readers come to about a word is that if they know how to read, write, and spell one word, they can write, read, and spell many other words as well.

Create in your classroom a spelling pattern word wall. Wylie and Durrell have identified spelling patterns that are in their classic thirty-seven "dependable" rimes. The spelling word wall can be created by stapling a piece of 3" x 5" butcher block paper to the bulletin board. Then attach spelling pattern cards around the border with thumbtacks, so that the cards can be easily removed to use at the meeting area.

Once you decide on a spelling pattern for instruction, remove the corresponding card from the word wall. Then take a 1"x 3" piece of a contrasting color of butcher block paper and tape the card to the top end of a sheet the children will use for their investigation. Next, read one of Wylie and Durrell's short rimes with the children and have them identify the pattern.

After the pattern is identified, the children can try to come up with other words that have the same spelling pattern. The teacher can write these on the spelling pattern sheet, using a different color marker to highlight the spelling pattern within the word. The children have to add to the list until the sheet is full, which might take two days or more.

After the sheet is full, the completed spelling pattern is attached to the wall.

Some of the techniques teachers use to determine the words students need to spell include:

- Lists of misspelled words from student writing
- Lists of theme words
- Lists of words from the content areas
- Word banks

It is important for beginning writers to know that spelling is an important part of the writing process. However, insisting on correct spelling right from the beginning may actually hamper the efforts of beginning writers. In early spelling development, children should be allowed to experiment with words and use invented spelling. Spelling development is something that occurs over time as a developmental process. It does develop in clearly defined stages, which the teacher should take into consideration when planning lessons. Teachers should assess students' spelling knowledge and then plan mini-lessons to whole class and small groups as they are necessary.

Some of the ways teachers can provide spelling instruction in the context of meaningful reading and writing activities include:
- Shared reading
- Guided reading
- Shared writing
- Shared reading
- Poetry reading using rhyming words with the same spelling patterns
- Reading chants
- Writing lists
- Writing daily news in the classroom
- Writing letters
- Writing invitations

By planning spelling instruction, teachers will help children recognize word patterns, help them discern spelling rules and help them develop their own tricks for remembering how to spell words. Direct instruction is necessary for students to develop the knowledge they need regarding the morphological structure of words and thus the relationships between words. Students also need to be taught graphophonic relationships to know the relationship between letters and sounds, the probability of letter sequences and the different letter patterns. Developing visual methods of recognizing correct spelling is also an aid to helping students learn to spell when they can trace around the shape of a word. This helps them develop a visual memory as to whether or not the word looks as if it is spelled correctly. Memory aids (mnemonics) also aid in spelling development, such as in the word PAINT – Pat Added Ink Not Tar.

For more strategies for teaching spelling:	See Wylie and Durrell's 37 phonemes:
http://www.readingrockets.org/article/80	http://www.mrs.norris.net/Language/Language/phonograms.htm

Along with direct teaching of spelling, teachers should model the process at all times. By talking about spelling and having students assist in class writing, they will help students develop the awareness that spelling is important. Some activities where teachers can use this approach include:

- Experience charts
- Writing notes to parents
- Writing class poems and stories
- Editing writing with students

Students also need to be encouraged to take risks with spelling. Rather than have students constantly asking how words are spelled, the teacher can use "Have a Go" Sheets. These sheets consist of three columns in which the students write the word as they think it is spelled. Then the student asks the teacher or another student if it spelled correctly. If it is incorrect, the student will tell the student which letters are in the correct place and the student will try again. After the third try, the teacher can either tell the student how to spell the word and add this to the list of words the student has to learn or work on the necessary spelling strategy

Other Spelling Activities

Spelling Bee
Have students practice their spelling words before having the actual test.

Newspaper Spelling
Have students find their spelling word in an article in the newspaper. Circle the spelling and then make a list.

Weekly Spelling Story
Post a picture or illustration on the board. Have the students write a short paragraph or several sentences (depending on the level of ability) to narrate the picture.

Spelling Poems
Have students write a short poem that includes their weekly spelling words

Students often vary in their learning styles. A visual child will be more able to learn from textbooks and worksheets. Some are auditory, learning best from hearing the rules and words. A kinesthetic child will want to feel and move, retaining information through hands on experiences. Having a broad range of learning materials will enable each student to learn at their own optimum learning level.

Skill 8.6 Demonstrating knowledge of methods for supporting children at each stage of writing development

Children develop writing skills through a series of steps. The steps and their characteristics are:

- Role Play Writing

In this stage, the child writes in scribbles and assigns a message to the symbols. Even though an adult would not be able to read the writing, the child can read what is written although it may not be the same each time the child reads it. The child will be able to read back the writing because of prior knowledge that print carries a meaning. The child will also dictate to adults who can write a message or story.

- Experimental Writing

In this stage the child writes in simple forms of language. The words usually contain letters according to the way they sound, such as the word "are" may be written as "r". However, the child does display a sense of sentence formation and writes in groups of words with a period at the end. The child is also aware of a correspondence between written words and oral language.

- Early Writing

Children start to use a small range of familiar text forms and sight words in their writing. The topics they choose for writing are ones that have some importance for them, such as their family, friends or pets. Because they are used to hearing stories, they do have a sense of how a story sounds and begin to write simple narratives. They learn that they do have to correct their writing so that others can easily read it.

- Conventional Writing

By the time students reach this stage of writing, they have a sense of audience and purpose for writing. They are able to proofread their writing and edit it for mistakes. They have gained the ability to transfer between reading and writing so that they can get ideas for writing from what they read. By this time, students also have a sense of what correct spelling and grammar look like and they can change the order of events in the writing so that it makes sense for the reader.

- Proficient Writing

This is the final stage of writing in which the students have developed through the stages of the writing process and can easily work through the drafting, revising and editing stages. They are able to look for precise words to express meaning and use a variety of sentence structures. They are able to adopt different points of view and are able to fully develop a topic.

However all children do not progress through these steps at the same pace. Some are able to progress faster than others, which is why there is always a discrepancy in the level of writing competence in any one class. Some students need more instruction than others and may even need one-on-one intervention to help them make very little progress.

It is generally accepted that early writers are found in the primary grades with some students progressing to the conventional writing stage. However, it is quite possible to find students in late elementary still in the conventional stage as proficient writing is usually found in high school. No matter how much instruction a teacher provides in any one year, it seems that the teacher will have to go over the stages of the writing process at the beginning of every year and keep re-teaching it throughout the school year.

There is no one specific method for teaching the writing process. Beginning teachers need to understand that this is a process that takes students a long time to master and that they need to continually model the steps in the writing process for the students. The prewriting stage is one that students prefer to skip and therefore is one that teachers need to constantly remind the students about. At first, this part of the process will be teacher-guided using such methodologies as helping the students discover what they want to say about a specific topic. Some of the ways students can become used to using this step before they start their actual draft include:

- Brainstorming
- Discussing
- Webbing
- Interviewing
- Surveying
- Listening
- Reading
- Writing jot notes
- Charting
- Mapping
- Outlining

Free writing is another way students can get their ideas down on paper before they start to refine their thoughts.

When teaching the drafting process, teachers should encourage the students to skip lines. This allows them space for revising and editing when they get to this stage. Quite often, students will ask how to spell words when they are writing their first draft. In this process, since spelling is not as important as it is in later stages, teachers often tell them to write the words the way they think they are spelled. There will be plenty of time to make corrections later.

Revising and editing are the hardest stages of the writing process to teach. Exemplars provide the students with examples of what good and poor writing looks like. When students have a chance to study the exemplars and discuss the merits of each, they have an idea of the improvements they need to make in their writing. In revising, students should read the writing out loud, either to themselves or to another student to pick up on what parts make sense and what parts need additions or deletions. Author's chair is a way of encouraging students to provide comments on writing, but they do need to be encouraged not to make disparaging remarks and to only provide constructive criticism.

Editing is a time-consuming task and it would be unreasonable to expect students of this age group to pick up on all the mistakes in a piece of writing. Therefore, teachers should ask students to edit for specific purposes at one time, such as correct spelling, capitalization or punctuation. The easiest way to pick up on incorrect spelling is to read the writing backwards. This way the students are focusing on each word rather than the meaning of the piece. The use of a word processor helps students in finding words that are not spelled correctly.

Publication means getting the writing ready for others to read. For many students, it means illustrating the work, creating an attractive cover or even using a word processor to produce the final draft.

DOMAIN III. LEARNING IN THE CONTENT AREAS

Competency 009 UNDERSTAND MATHEMATICS CONCEPTS AND SKILLS

Skill 9.1 Recognizing, interpreting, and using mathematical terminology, symbols, and representations (e.g., cardinal and ordinal numbers; properties of real numbers; base number systems; fractions, decimals, and percents)

Place Value

Place value is the basis of our entire number system. A place value system is one in which the position of a digit in a number determines its value. In the standard system, called base ten, each place represents ten times the value of the place to its right. You can think of this as making groups of ten of the smaller unit and combining them to make a new unit.

Ten ones make up one of the next larger unit- tens. Ten of those units make up one of the next larger unit- hundreds. This pattern continues for greater values (ten hundreds = one thousand, ten thousands = one ten thousand, etc.), and lesser, decimal values (ten tenths =1, ten hundredths = one tenth, etc.).

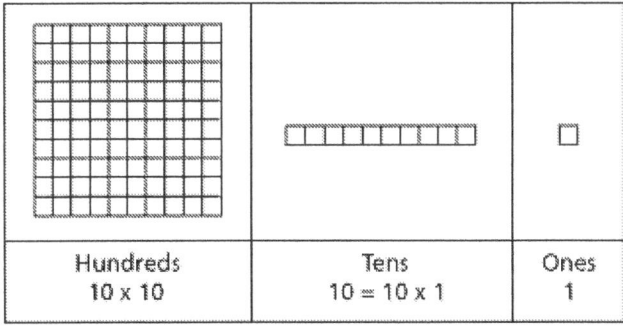

A popular activity for illustrating the base ten number system in many elementary classrooms is to count the days towards the 100th day of school. Students use straws (or small sticks) to represent each day. The students add a straw to their collection each day, and when they have ten, they bundle them with a rubber band. By the time they reach the 100th day, they have 9 bundles of 10, and when they add the last straw, they will have 10 bundles of 10. The students then bundle the 10 bundles of 10 into 1 bundle of 100.

Unifix Cubes are another excellent manipulative for teaching the base ten number system. They can be easily used as base ten blocks for exploring ones and tens. Each color can act as a group of ten when connected.

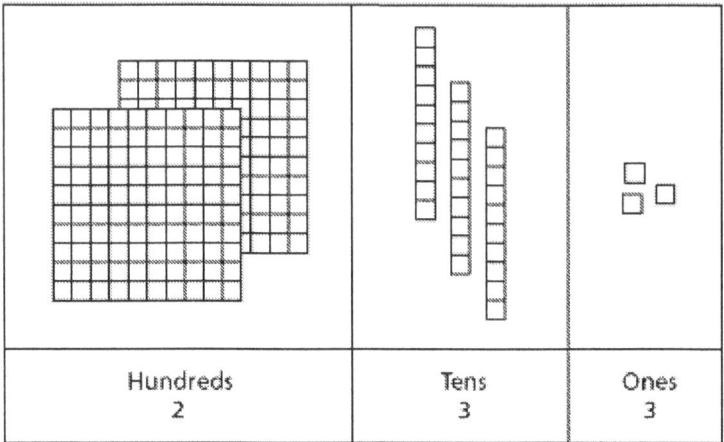

In standard form, the number modeled above is 233.

A place-value chart is a way to make sure digits are in the correct places. The value of each digit depends on its position or "place".. A great way to see the place-value relationships in a number is to model the number with actual objects (place-value blocks, bundles of craft sticks, etc.), write the digits in the chart, and then write the number in the usual, or standard form.

Place value is vitally important to all later mathematics. Without it, keeping track of greater numbers rapidly becomes impossible. (Can you imagine trying to write 999 with only ones?) A thorough mastery of place value is essential to learning the operations with greater numbers. It is the foundation for regrouping ("borrowing" and "carrying") in addition, subtraction, multiplication, and division.

Number sense is the foundation upon which all future math topics will be built. Providing young children with the opportunity to interact with objects across multiple contexts will help children begin to develop these concepts of number sense. Within this beginning area of mathematics, students will progress at different levels at different times. For example, one student may be able to count and identify a group of five, but not recognize the pattern of five on a die. Another student may count the group, recognize the pattern, and understand the concept of grouping things into piles of five and counting by the groups.

While in this beginning stage, children will be able to identify how many objects are in a group. Typically, students will have some beginning oral counting system (1-10 or 1-20). These preschool children will also begin to identify the relationships between groups of objects (size, quantity, more, less, bigger, smaller, etc.)

Preschool children should develop an understanding of one-to-one correspondence, being able to link a single number name with one object, and only one, at a time. This concept is needed in order for children to formalize the meaning of a whole number. An example would be for a child to count four blocks in a row, saying the number as each block is touched. Another example would be for a child to get a carton of milk for each of the other children at a table.

Preschool children should also be able to use one-to-one correspondence to compare the size of a group of objects. For example, students should be able to compare the number of cars they have with the number another child has and say, "I have more...or less."

Number sense develops into the further understanding of place value and how numbers are related. This involves identifying and explaining how numbers can be grouped into tens, ones and eventually hundreds or more. Using trading games, place value mats and base ten blocks students can develop these skills. These activities will progress until the student understands that the one in sixteen represents ten, not simply one.

Children first learn to count using the counting numbers (1, 2, 3 . . .). Preschool children should be able to recite the names of the numerals in order or sequence (rote counting). This might be accomplished by singing a counting song. This should progress to being able to attach a number name to a series of objects. A preschool child should understand that the last number spoken when counting a group of objects represents the total number of objects.

In kindergarten, children should learn to read the numbers 0 through 10, and in 1st grade, they should be able to read through the number 20. At first, this could involve connecting a pictorial representation of the number with a corresponding number of items. This exercise may or may not involve assistive technology. As students advance, they should be able to read the numbers as sight words.

Students should be taught that there is a naming procedure for our number system. The numbers 0, 1 . . . 12 all have unique names. The numbers 13, 14 . . . 19 are the "teens." These names are a combination of earlier names, with the ones place named first. For example, fourteen is short for "four ten" which means "ten plus four." The numbers 20, 21 . . . 99 are also combinations of earlier names, but the tens place is named first. For example, 48 is "forty-eight," which means "four tens plus eight." The numbers 100, 101 . . . 999 are combinations of hundreds and previous names. Once a number has more than three digits, groups of three digits are usually set off by commas.

Eventually, children will develop the necessary skills to extrapolate these beginning concepts to more difficult situations and problems. They will be able to make generalizations about number situations presented, even when they are unable to utilize traditionally computational methods to solve problems. For example, young children may be able to solve a multiplication problem (four rows of three chairs, how many chairs) and provide an answer using manipulatives and their number sense; however, they would still be unable to solve the more traditional problem of 4X3.

Concepts of numeracy, as well as other math concepts, should be presented to children across situations, using a variety of materials and until levels of proficiency are reached. As concepts of math build upon another, it is imperative the appropriate foundation is in place for future learning to progress. Presenting concepts and ideas early will allow students the opportunity to experience and construct their own competencies.

A number line may be introduced to help students understand addition and subtraction. Suppose we want to show 6 + 3 on a number line.

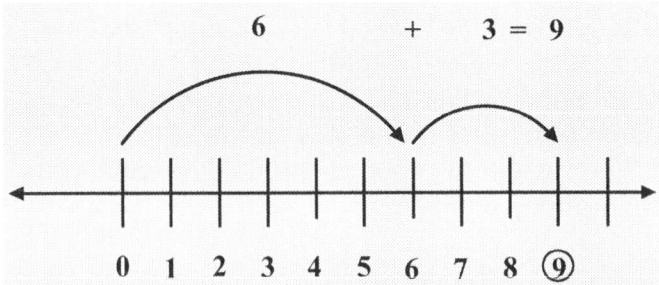

Addition can be thought of as starting from zero and counting 6 units to the right on the line (in the positive direction) and then counting 3 more units to the right. The number line shows that this is the same as counting 9 units to the right.

In the same way, a number line may be used to represent subtraction. Suppose we have 6 − 3 or rather 6 + (−3).

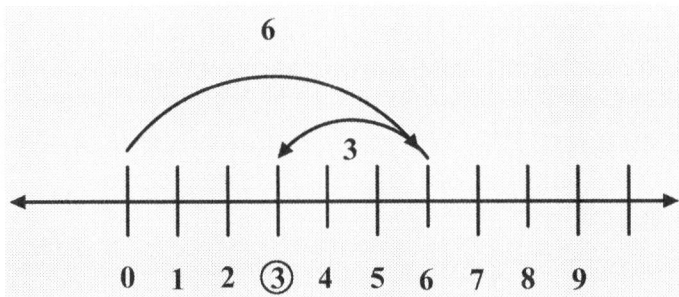

If 3 is shown by counting 3 positions to the right, then −3 can be shown as 3 positions to the left. We start from zero and count 6 positions to the right and then count 3 positions to the left. This illustrates how 6 + (−3) = 3.

As students gain an understanding of numbers and are able to read them, they should be taught to apply these concepts to everyday life applications. For example, once children can read the numbers 1 through 12, they can begin to learn how to tell time. At the very basic level, if shown a clock or a diagram of a clock, a child needs to understand that the big hand represents minutes and the little hand represents hours. The child begins to recognize that when the big hand is on the twelve and the little hand is on the two, it is 2 o'clock. As the child learns to count by fives, the concept may be expanded so that the child understands that the distance between two consecutive numbers is an interval of five minutes. The child then begins to recognize by counting by fives that when the big hand is on the 4 and the little hand is on the 2, it is twenty minutes after the hour of 2 o'clock.

Another real–life application is money. In kindergarten, students learn to recognize a penny, nickel, dime, quarter, and one-dollar bill. In 1st grade, they learn how different combinations of coins have equivalent values, for example, that 10 pennies are the same as 1 dime and 10 dimes are the same as 1 dollar. Teaching children that money has value can start with a simple exercise of counting pennies to understand their monetary value. From here, students can advance to counting nickels, dimes, and so on. The next step might be to have students combine different coins and compute the value of the combination. As students advance in their understanding of the value of money, shopping math can be introduced where students see that money has value in exchange for goods. They can also learn to make change and count change.

TEACHER CERTIFICATION STUDY GUIDE

Number Systems

The real number system includes all rational and irrational numbers.

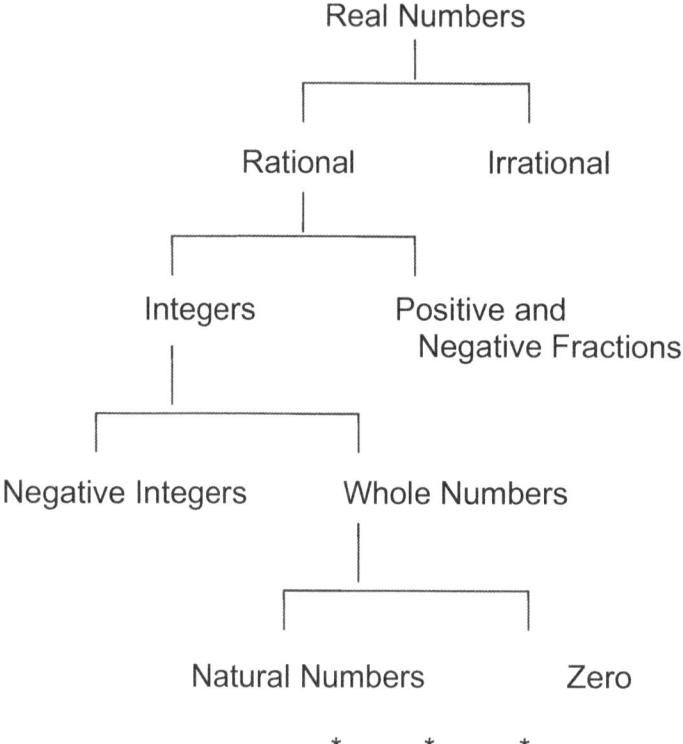

* * *

Rational numbers can be expressed as the ratio of two integers, $\frac{a}{b}$, where b = 0. For example: $\frac{2}{3}$, $-\frac{4}{5}$, $\frac{5}{1}$ = 5.

The rational numbers include integers, fractions and mixed numbers, and terminating and repeating decimals. Every rational number can be expressed as a repeating or terminating decimal and can be shown on a number line.

Integers are positive and negative whole numbers and zero.
...-6, -5, -4, -3, -2, -1, 0, 1, 2, 3, 4, 5, 6, ...

Whole numbers are natural numbers and zero.
0, 1, 2, 3, 4, 5, 6 ...

Natural numbers are the counting numbers.
1, 2, 3, 4, 5, 6, ...

Irrational numbers are real numbers that cannot be written as the ratio of two integers. These are infinite non-repeating decimals.

Examples: $\sqrt{5} = 2.2360..$, pi $= \Pi = 3.1415927...$

Percent = per 100 (written with the symbol %). Thus $10\% = \dfrac{10}{100} = \dfrac{1}{10}$.

Decimals = deci = part of ten. To find the decimal equivalent of a fraction, use the denominator to divide the numerator as shown in the following examples.

Example: Find the decimal equivalent of $\dfrac{7}{10}$.

$$\begin{array}{r} .7 \\ 10\overline{)7.0} \\ \underline{70} \\ 00 \end{array}$$

Since 10 cannot divide into 7 evenly, put a decimal point in the answer row on top; put a 0 behind 7 to make it 70. Continue the division process. If a remainder occurs, put a 0 by the last digit of the remainder and continue the division.

Thus $\dfrac{7}{10} = 0.7$

It is a good idea to write a 0 before the decimal point so that the decimal point is emphasized.

Example: Find the decimal equivalent of $\dfrac{7}{125}$.

$$\begin{array}{r} .056 \\ 125\overline{)7.000} \\ \underline{625} \\ 750 \\ \underline{750} \\ 0 \end{array}$$

Example: Convert 0.056 to a fraction.

Multiplying 0.056 by $\frac{1000}{1000}$ to get rid of the decimal point:

$$0.056 \times \frac{1000}{1000} = \frac{56}{1000} = \frac{7}{125}$$

Example: Find 23% of 1000.

$$= \frac{23}{100} \times \frac{1000}{1} = 23 \times 10 = 230$$

Example: Convert 6.25% to a fraction and to a mixed number.

$$6.25\% = 0.0625 = 0.0625 \times \frac{10000}{10000} = \frac{625}{10000} = \frac{1}{16}$$

A **decimal** can be converted to a **percent** by multiplying by 100, or merely moving the decimal point two places to the right. A **percent** can be converted to a **decimal** by dividing by 100, or moving the decimal point two places to the left.

Examples: 0.375 = 37.5%
0.7 = 70%
0.04 = 4%
3.15 = 315%

84% = 0.84
3% = 0.03
60% = 0.6
110% = 1.1
$\frac{1}{2}$% = 0.5% = 0.005

A **percent** can be converted to a **fraction** by placing it over 100 and reducing to simplest terms.

Examples: 32% = $\frac{32}{100}$ = $\frac{8}{25}$
6% = $\frac{6}{100}$ = $\frac{3}{50}$
111% = $\frac{111}{100}$ = $1\frac{11}{100}$

Common Equivalents

$$\frac{1}{2} = 0.5 = 50\%$$
$$\frac{1}{3} = 0.33\frac{1}{3} = 33\frac{1}{3}\%$$
$$\frac{1}{4} = 0.25 = 25\%$$
$$\frac{1}{5} = 0.2 = 20\%$$
$$\frac{1}{6} = 0.16\frac{2}{3} = 16\frac{2}{3}\%$$
$$\frac{1}{8} = 0.12\frac{1}{2} = 12\frac{1}{2}\%$$
$$\frac{1}{10} = 0.1 = 10\%$$
$$\frac{2}{3} = 0.66\frac{2}{3} = 66\frac{2}{3}\%$$
$$\frac{5}{6} = 0.83\frac{1}{3} = 83\frac{1}{3}\%$$
$$\frac{3}{8} = 0.37\frac{1}{2} = 37\frac{1}{2}\%$$
$$\frac{5}{8} = 0.62\frac{1}{2} = 62\frac{1}{2}\%$$
$$\frac{7}{8} = 0.87\frac{1}{2} = 87\frac{1}{2}\%$$
$$1 = 1.0 = 100\%$$

Cardinal numbers are also known as "counting" numbers because they indicate quantity. Examples of cardinal numbers are 1, 2, and 10.

Ordinal numbers indicate the order of things in a set; for ex. 1st, 2nd, 10th. They do not show quantity, only position.

	Word Name	Standard Numeral	Pictorial Model
Decimal	Three-tenths	0.3	
Fraction	One-half	$\frac{1}{2}$	
Integer or Whole Number	Three	3	

Skill 9.2 **Demonstrating knowledge of number sense and numerical operations**

Mathematical operations include addition, subtraction, multiplication, and division. Addition can be indicated by the expressions: sum, greater than, and, more than, increased by, added to. Subtraction can be expressed by: difference, fewer than, minus, less than, decreased by. Multiplication is shown by: product, times, multiplied by, twice. Division is used for: quotient, divided by, ratio.

Recognition and understanding of the relationships between concepts and topics is of great value in mathematical problem solving and the explanation of more complex processes.

For instance, multiplication is simply repeated addition. This relationship explains the concept of variable addition. We can show that the expression $4x + 3x = 7x$ is true by rewriting 4 times x and 3 times x as repeated addition, yielding the expression $(x + x + x + x) + (x + x + x)$. Thus, because of the relationship between multiplication and addition, variable addition is accomplished by coefficient addition.

Numerical Operations

Properties are rules that apply for addition, subtraction, multiplication, or division of real numbers. These properties are:

Commutative: You can change the order of the terms or factors as follows.

>   For addition: $a + b = b + a$
>   For multiplication: $ab = ba$

>   Since addition is the inverse operation of subtraction and multiplication is the inverse operation of division, no separate laws are needed for subtraction and division.

>   Example: $5 + 8 = 8 + 5 = 13$

>   Example: $2 \times 6 = 6 \times 2 = 12$

Associative: You can regroup the terms as you like.

> For addition: $a + (b + c) = (a + b) + c$
> For multiplication: $a(bc) = (ab)c$

This rule does not apply for division and subtraction.

Example: $(2 + 7) + 5 = 2 + (7 + 5)$
$9 + 5 = 2 + 12 = 14$

Example: $(3 \times 7) \times 5 = 3 \times (7 \times 5)$
$21 \times 5 = 3 \times 35 = 105$

Identity: Finding a number so that when added to a term results in that number (additive identity); finding a number such that when multiplied by a term results in that number (multiplicative identity).

> For addition: $a + 0 = a$ (zero is additive identity)
> For multiplication: $a \cdot 1 = a$ (one is multiplicative)

Example: $17 + 0 = 17$

Example: $34 \times 1 = 34$
The product of any number and one is that number.

Inverse: Finding a number such that when added to the number it results in zero; or when multiplied by the number results in 1.

> For addition: $a - a = 0$
> For multiplication: $a \cdot (1/a) = 1$

($-a$) is the additive inverse of a; ($1/a$), also called the reciprocal, is the multiplicative inverse of a.

Example: $25 - 25 = 0$

Example: $5 \times \frac{1}{5} = 1$ The product of any number and its reciprocal is one.

Distributive: This technique allows us to operate on terms within parentheses without first performing operations within the parentheses. This is especially helpful when terms within the parentheses cannot be combined.

$$a(b + c) = ab + ac$$

Example: $6 \times (4 + 9) = (6 \times 4) + (6 \times 9)$
$6 \times 13 = 24 + 54 = 78$

To multiply a sum by a number, multiply each addend by the number, then add the products.

Addition of whole numbers

Example: At the end of a day of shopping, a shopper had $24 remaining in his wallet. He spent $45 on various goods. How much money did the shopper have at the beginning of the day?

The total amount of money the shopper started with is the sum of the amount spent and the amount remaining at the end of the day.

$24
+ 45
$69   The original total was $69.

Example: A race took the winner 1 hr. 58 min. 12 sec. on the first half of the race and 2 hr. 9 min. 57 sec. on the second half of the race. How much time did the entire race take?

```
  1 hr. 58 min. 12 sec.
+ 2 hr.  9 min. 57 sec.      Add these numbers
  3 hr. 67 min. 69 sec.
       + 1 min -60 sec.      Change 60 seconds to 1 min.
  3 hr. 68 min.  9 sec.
+ 1 hr.-60 min.         .    Change 60 minutes to 1 hr.
  4 hr.  8 min.  9 sec.      ←final answer
```

Subtraction of whole numbers

Example: At the end of his shift, a cashier has $96 in the cash register. At the beginning of his shift, he had $15. How much money did the cashier collect during his shift?

The total collected is the difference of the ending amount and the starting amount.

$$\begin{array}{r}\$96\\-15\\\hline\$81\end{array}$$ The total collected was $81.

Multiplication of whole numbers

Multiplication is one of the four basic number operations. In simple terms, multiplication is the addition of a number to itself a certain number of times. For example, 4 multiplied by 3 is the equal to 4 + 4 + 4 or 3 + 3 + 3 +3. Another way of conceptualizing multiplication is to think in terms of groups. For example, if we have 4 groups of 3 students, the total number of students is 4 multiplied by 3. We call the solution to a multiplication problem the product.

The basic algorithm for whole number multiplication begins with aligning the numbers by place value with the number containing more places on top.

$$\begin{array}{r}172\\\times43\end{array}\longrightarrow$$ Note that we placed 122 on top because it has more places than 43 does.

Next, we multiply the ones' place of the second number by each place value of the top number sequentially.

$$\begin{array}{r}(2)\\172\\\times43\\\hline 516\end{array}\longrightarrow \{3\times 2=6,\ 3\times 7=21,\ 3\times 1=3\}$$

Note that we had to carry a 2 to the hundreds' column because 3 x 7 = 21. Note also that we add, not multiply, carried numbers to the product.

Next, we multiply the number in the tens' place of the second number by each place value of the top number sequentially. Because we are multiplying by a number in the tens' place, we place a zero at the end of this product.

```
    (2)
    172
  x  43         →     {4 x 2 = 8, 4 x 7 = 28, 4 x 1 = 4}
    516
   6880
```

Finally, to determine the final product we add the two partial products.

```
    172
  x  43
    516
  +6880
   7396    →   The product of 172 and 43 is 7396.
```

Example: A student buys 4 boxes of crayons. Each box contains 16 crayons. How many total crayons does the student have?

The total number of crayons is 16 x 4.

```
    16
   x 4
    64        Total number of crayons equals 64 crayons.
```

Division of whole numbers

Division, the inverse of multiplication, is another of the four basic number operations. When we divide one number by another, we determine how many times we can multiply the divisor (number divided by) before we exceed the number we are dividing (dividend). For example, 8 divided by 2 equals 4 because we can multiply 2 four times to reach 8 (2 x 4 = 8 or 2 + 2 + 2 + 2 = 8). Using the grouping conceptualization we used with multiplication, we can divide 8 into 4 groups of 2 or 2 groups of 4. We call the answer to a division problem the quotient.

If the divisor does not divide evenly into the dividend, we express the leftover amount either as a remainder or as a fraction with the divisor as the denominator. For example, 9 divided by 2 equals 4 with a remainder of 1 or 4 ½.

The basic algorithm for division is long division. We start by representing the quotient as follows.

$14\overline{)293}$ ⟶ 14 is the divisor and 293 is the dividend.
This represents 293 ÷ 14.

Next, we divide the divisor into the dividend starting from the left.

$14\overline{)293}$ with 2 on top ⟶ 14 divides into 29 two times with a remainder.

Next, we multiply the partial quotient by the divisor, subtract this value from the first digits of the dividend, and bring down the remaining dividend digits to complete the number.

```
    2
14)293
   -28↓
    13
```
⟶ 2 × 14 = 28, 29 − 28 = 1, and bringing down the 3 yields 13.

Finally, we divide again (the divisor into the remaining value) and repeat the preceding process. The number left after the subtraction represents the remainder.

```
    20
14)293
   -28
    13
    - 0
    13
```
⟶ The final quotient is 20 with a remainder of 13. We can also represent this quotient as 20 13/14.

Example: Each box of apples contains 24 apples. How many boxes must a grocer purchase to supply a group of 252 people with one apple each?

The grocer needs 252 apples. Because he must buy apples in groups of 24, we divide 252 by 24 to determine how many boxes he needs to buy.

```
    10
24)252
   -24
    12
    - 0
    12
```
⟶ The quotient is 10 with a remainder of 12.

Thus, the grocer needs 10 boxes plus 12 more apples. Therefore, the minimum number of boxes the grocer can purchase is 11 boxes.

Example: At his job, John gets paid $20 for every hour he works. If John made $940 in a week, how many hours did he work?

This is a division problem. To determine the number of hours John worked, we divide the total amount made ($940) by the hourly rate of pay ($20). Thus, the number of hours worked equals 940 divided by 20.

$$\begin{array}{r} 47 \\ 20\overline{)940} \\ \underline{-80} \\ 140 \\ \underline{-140} \\ 0 \end{array}$$

→ 20 divides into 940, 47 times with no remainder.

John worked 47 hours.

Addition and Subtraction of Decimals

When adding and subtracting decimals, we align the numbers by place value as we do with whole numbers. After adding or subtracting each column, we bring the decimal down, placing it in the same location as in the numbers added or subtracted.

Example: Find the sum of 152.3 and 36.342.

$$\begin{array}{r} 152.300 \\ +36.342 \\ \hline 188.642 \end{array}$$

Note that we placed two zeroes after the final place value in 152.3 to clarify the column addition.

Example: Find the difference of 152.3 and 36.342.

$$\begin{array}{r} 2\;9\;10 \\ 152.\cancel{300} \\ -36.342 \\ \hline 58 \end{array} \qquad \begin{array}{r} (4)11(12) \\ \cancel{152.300} \\ -36.342 \\ \hline 115.958 \end{array}$$

Note how we borrowed to subtract from the zeroes in the hundredths' and thousandths' place of 152.300.

Skill 9.3   Demonstrating understanding of fundamental concepts of algebra and geometry

Fundamental Algebra

In the very primary grades, the concept of algebra is significantly different than what an adult remembers as algebra class. As adults, we typically recall the letters being used to hold the place of a number and solving various equations to find the answer for a variable. However, for young children the basis for this concept is developed through learning about patterns, the attributes of objects and how to describe objects in detail. These ideas help students to develop the fundamental thinking and concepts behind algebraic reasoning. These patterns may begin through concrete objects, but will be further developed into counting patterns and other recognition of the patterns of numbers.

Beginning with the basic understanding of the symbols used throughout math (numerical representations) students can investigate things around them. They can gather this information and begin to report it in a way that means something to others who look at it. These facts related to their own thinking can be expanded. As students look at a variety of situations and manipulate the objects to draw new conclusions, their problem solving skills are advanced. These skills will allow students to begin to solve missing number problems or solve for unknown pieces to a situation. This can be done with the youngest students as well. An example of a preschool missing object problem might be:

Red   yellow   red   _____   red   yellow   red   yellow   red

In this case, the students would be shown real objects of two colors set in a pattern and need to determine which one is missing from the center of the pattern. This type of thinking is more complex than what comes next types of questions.

As children begin to compare, sort, order and demonstrate seriating of objects using various characteristics their thinking changes. These changes are the beginning of algebraic thought. As they add on to patterns, make changes to patterns, build their own patterns, or convert patterns into new formats, they are thinking in more complex ways. Connecting this new thinking with the understanding of the number system is the beginning of using variables to define the relationships between mathematical concepts. This method of problem solving is then defined further into the expression of these relationships in a more traditional mathematical manner. Primary students may solve problems for the number that goes in the box. For example:

$3 + \square = 5$

Pre-K children should be able to recognize and extend simple repeating patterns using objects and pictures. By patterns, we mean a sequence of symbols, sounds, movements, or objects that follow a simple rule, such as ABBABBABB. Students should be presented with a simple pattern that they try to understand. Once they have an understanding of the pattern, they should copy and extend it. Students at this age are capable of assigning letters to their patterns to verbalize how the pattern repeats. These are the very early fundamental stages of algebra.

Fundamental Geometry

Two Dimensional Geometrical Shapes

A **triangle** is a polygon with three sides.

Triangles can be classified by the types of angles or the lengths of their sides.

Classifying by angles:

An **acute** triangle has exactly three *acute* angles.
A **right** triangle has one *right* angle.
An **obtuse** triangle has one *obtuse* angle.

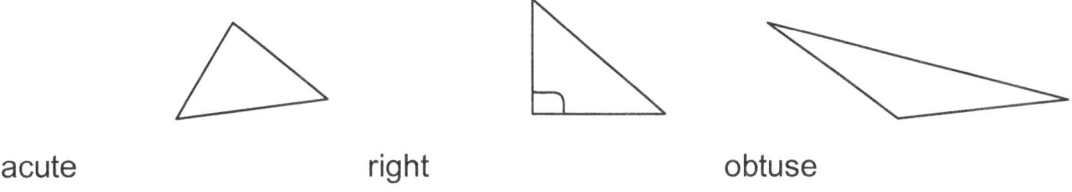

acute   right   obtuse

Classifying by sides:

All *three* sides of an **equilateral** triangle are the same length.
Two sides of an **isosceles** triangle are the same length.
None of the sides of a **scalene** triangle are the same length.

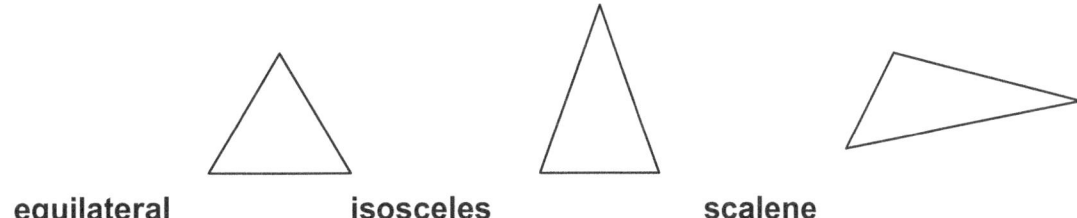

equilateral   isosceles   scalene

Three Dimensional Geometric Shapes

A **polygon** is a simple closed figure composed of line segments. In a **regular polygon** all sides are the same length and all angles are the same measure.

The union of all points on a simple closed surface and all points in its interior form a space figure called a **solid**. The five regular solids, or **polyhedra**, are the cube, tetrahedron, octahedron, icosahedron, and dodecahedron. A **net** is a two-dimensional figure that can be cut out and folded up to make a three-dimensional solid. Below are models of the five regular solids with their corresponding face polygons and nets.

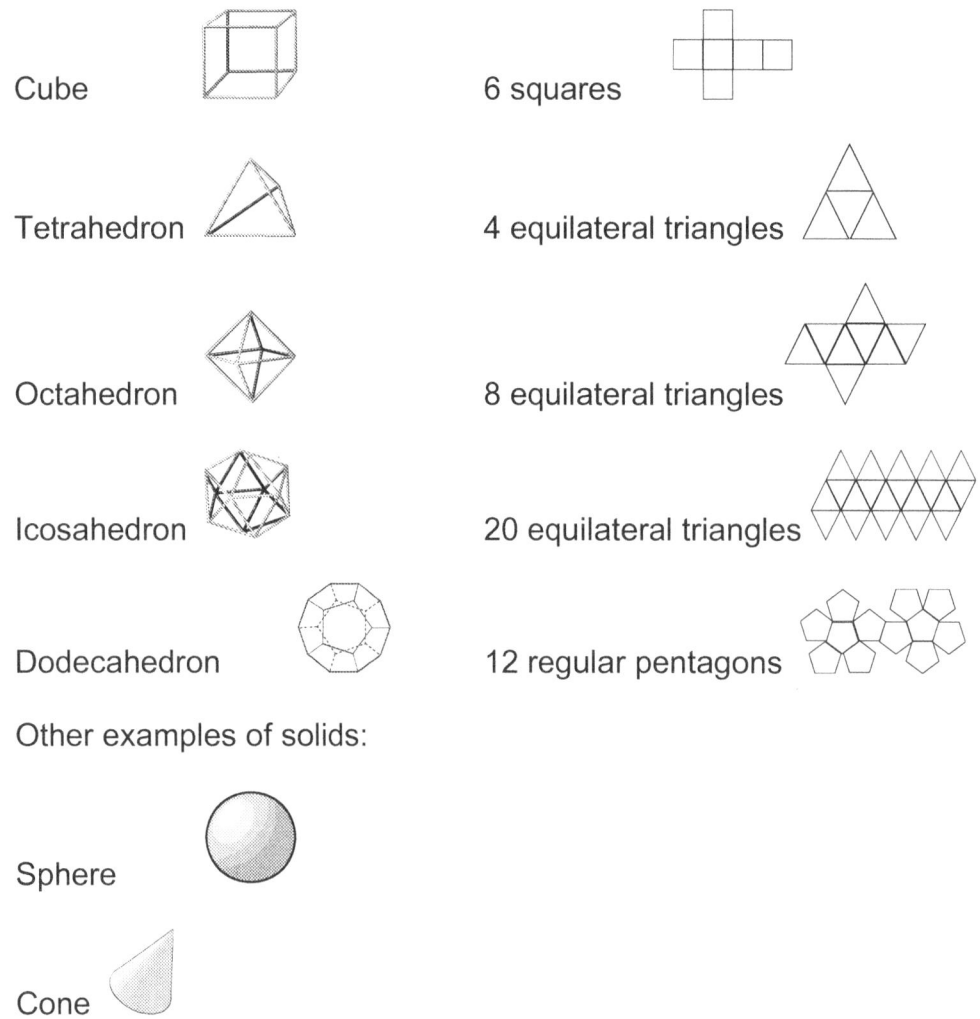

Cube   6 squares

Tetrahedron   4 equilateral triangles

Octahedron   8 equilateral triangles

Icosahedron   20 equilateral triangles

Dodecahedron   12 regular pentagons

Other examples of solids:

Sphere

Cone

A **Tessellation** is an arrangement of closed shapes that completely covers the plane without overlapping or leaving gaps. Unlike **tilings**, tessellations do not require the use of regular polygons. In art the term is used to refer to pictures or tiles mostly in the form of animals and other life forms, which cover the surface of a plane in a symmetrical way without overlapping or leaving gaps. M. C. Escher is known as the "father" of modern tessellations. Tessellations are used for tiling, mosaics, quilts, and art.

If you look at a completed tessellation, you will see the original motif repeats in a pattern. There are 17 possible ways that a pattern can be used to tile a flat surface, or "wallpaper."

There are four basic transformational symmetries that can be used in tessellations: **translation, rotation, reflection,** and **glide reflection**. The transformation of an object is called its image. If the original object was labeled with letters, such as $ABCD$, the image may be labeled with the same letters followed by a prime symbol, $A'B'C'D'$.

The tessellation below is a combination of the four types of transformational symmetry we have discussed:

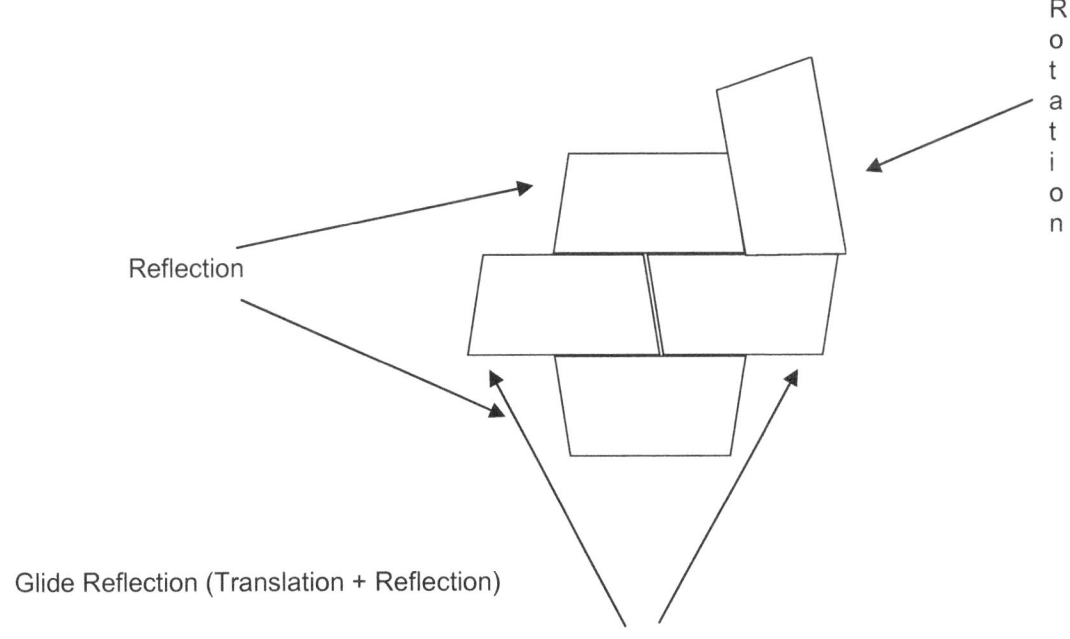

Rotation

Reflection

Glide Reflection (Translation + Reflection)

A **transformation** is a change in the position, shape, or size of a geometric figure. **Transformational geometry** is the study of manipulating objects by flipping, twisting, turning, and scaling. **Symmetry** is exact similarity between two parts or halves, as if one were a mirror image of the other.

A **translation** is a transformation that "slides" an object a fixed distance in a given direction. The original object and its translation have the same shape and size, and they face in the same direction.

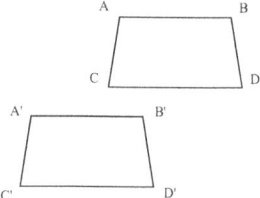

An example of a translation in architecture would be stadium seating. The seats are the same size and the same shape and face in the same direction.

A **rotation** is a transformation that turns a figure about a fixed point called the center of rotation. An object and its rotation are the same shape and size, but the figures may be turned in different directions. Rotations can occur in either a clockwise or a counterclockwise direction.

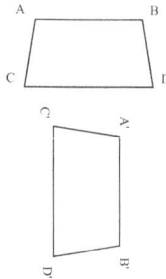

Rotations can be seen in wallpaper and art, and a Ferris wheel is an example of rotation.

An object and its **reflection** have the same shape and size, but the figures face in opposite directions.

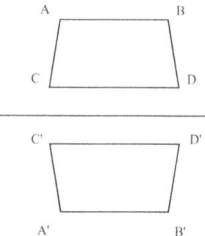

The line (where a mirror may be placed) is called the **line of reflection**. The distance from a point to the line of reflection is the same as the distance from the point's image to the line of reflection.

Skill 9.4 **Demonstrating understanding of patterns, relations, and functions (e.g., recognizing and analyzing patterns in numbers, shapes, and data; the translation of problem-solving situations into expressions and equations involving variables and unknowns)**

This is a place where we are trying to introduce some of the ideas of algebra into the lower grades. Many of the traditional ways of talking about this in algebra would certainly not be appropriate for early childhood classes. For example, we would not want to introduce the technical definition of the word "function." However, there are many types of patterns and relationships that we could address.

In arithmetic, first do the traditional counting by 2's, 5's and 10's. Then have the students start counting at a different number. For example, tell them to count by 5's beginning with 3. As they get better with their addition skills, use larger numbers for the starting number. Then give them the first few numbers of a sequence, and ask them to tell you the pattern. Finally, let them make up some sequences themselves and give them to the other students to guess what the pattern is. The possibilities are endless here.

There are also many patterns that can be devised using geometric shapes. A great deal of material is readily available on the Internet or in workbooks or in software for the computer. Make some up yourself, and also have the students make up some. Children love to make up problems for other people to solve. It makes them feel that they can become part of the world of adults this way.

Try some patterns in statistics. At this level this means presenting data to them, or having them collect the data themselves. Then ask them if they see patterns here. Again much material is available on this topic, too.

As the children progress in their mathematical education, teachers can begin to edge into the idea of relationships. For example, given that you were looking at a group of bicycles parked in front of the school, how could we calculate how many wheels there were? How could we express the relationship of the number of wheels to the number of bicycles? What if they were tricycles instead of bicycles? Try to think of other situations that your students encounter where relationships like this might enter in.

Measurement exercises lend themselves well to learning about relationships. If you have a measurement for an object expressed in centimeters, how can you use that number to figure out how many millimeters that would be? Also, if they are beginning to learn about fractions and/or decimals, you could reverse it: how can we get from millimeters to centimeters?

Of course there is always money. Children are quick to realize the importance of money in our society, and relevant problems about money will usually find an interesting audience. Using coins of different denominations as examples, you can make up many questions and exercises to illustrate patterns and relationships.

Look for ways to link mathematics to other subjects. This is very easy in science. It is also possible in geography and history (many numbers occur in reading about these subjects). Music has an important mathematical component. Art can also be related to mathematics, particularly geometry. Try to help your students make as many connections as possible between mathematics and other subjects, and between all the things they are studying in school and the real world they live in.

For more strategies for teaching problem solving:

http://www.k8accesscenter.org/training_resources/mathprimaryproblemsolving.asp

TEACHER CERTIFICATION STUDY GUIDE

Skill 9.5 **Recognizing standard and nonstandard measurement instruments and units**

Students should be able to determine what unit of measurement is appropriate for a particular problem, as indicated by the following table:

Problem Type	Unit (Customary System)	Unit (Metric System)
Length	Inch	Millimeter
	Foot	Centimeter
	Yard	Meter
Distance	Mile	Kilometer
Area	Square inches	Square millimeters
	Square feet	Square centimeters
	Square yards	Square meters
	Square miles	Square kilometers
Volume	Cubic inches	Cubic millimeters
	Cubic feet	Cubic centimeters
	Cubic yards	Cubic meters
Liquid volume	Fluid ounces	Milliliters
	Cups	Liters
	Pints	
	Quarts	
	Gallons	
Mass		Milligrams
		Centigrams
		Grams
		Kilograms
Weight	Ounces	Milligrams
	Pounds	Centigrams
	Tons	Grams
		Kilograms
Temperature	Degrees Fahrenheit	Degrees Celsius or Kelvin

We humans like to reduce everything in the real world to numbers, and the only way to do this with some things is to measure them. The most common things we measure are time, temperature, distance, weight and angles. Children have been exposed to some or all of these concepts before they start school.

EARLY CHILDHOOD EDUCATION 179

One of the most important things that must be emphasized when beginning measurement activities is that now we are entering the world of approximations. No measurement can ever be exact, and teachers should refrain from using the word "exact" in connection with measurements. Many adults are confused about this concept, so we should try to set the children straight from the outset.

The stages of measuring something are: (1) determine what to measure, (2) decide on an appropriate tool, (3) select a reasonable unit of measure, (4) estimate how much or how long the measurement will be, (5) measure and finally (6) check the reasonableness of the results.

Start with time. Most people measure time with clocks or watches. What are the units? Most children are familiar with hours and minutes. Practice this with them. With older children you can talk about timed athletic events like running, swimming, horse races, etc. At this point they would probably see the need for a smaller unit, so we could talk about seconds and even tenths of seconds. Constantly point out that 10.3 seconds only means that the time in question is closer to 10.3 than it is to 10.2 or 10.4.

Next could be temperature. Most children are aware of temperature as it is given on TV, in Fahrenheit degrees in the United States. Introduce them to the thermometer with an actual thermometer and then with a large reproduction on paper showing the degree marks. Talk about how air temperature is physically measured. For example, would we want to put the thermometer in direct sunlight? What would be a comfortable temperature? What would be very hot? Very cold? Have them estimate air temperature each day and then measure it with the thermometer. Again point out that to say the temperature is 75 degrees only means that it is closer to 75 than to 74 or 76. Point this out on the paper diagram of a thermometer scale. With older students here is a good chance to briefly introduce the idea of negative numbers. Also work with the Celsius (or centigrade) scale.

Next could be length. A great deal of time needs to be spent here. First the students need to be convinced that we need a standard unit. Does foot mean the length of just anybody's foot? Get some objects for them to measure that are very close to 3 feet or 5 feet, etc. Then introduce something smaller so that they will see the need for a smaller unit.

Prior to introducing measurement with standard tools such as a ruler, it is appropriate to teach children how to measure with non-standard units such as paper clips. Students are taught to use the paper clip as a unit and by laying the paper clips end to end. They measure an object longer than the paper clip (repetition of a single unit to measure something larger than the unit).

Students should practice measuring objects to the nearest inch. After they have been measuring for a few weeks, introduce the millimeter as a still smaller unit. Most rulers nowadays have metric on one side and standard English units on the other.

Teachers should get students used to the metric system as soon as possible, sticking with millimeter and centimeter. Use these interchangeably with inches and feet. Older children can then proceed to yards and meters. Still older ones can work on paper (or the computer) with miles and kilometers. Many, many activities must be constantly presented to get children familiar with all these units.

Some work can be done occasionally with weights. Pounds would be the obvious starting unit, then ounces for a smaller unit and tons for a larger one. Fairly early on in this work introduce the kilogram and the gram. Guess the weights of objects before actually weighing them.

Another thing students should learn to measure is liquids. Introduce the idea of gallons and quarts, but fairly soon also work with liters and milliliters. Bring in soda bottles and notice that both metric and English units are given. Briefly talk about pints and cups, as used in recipes.

The concept of area is a difficult one for them. Try to get some hint that they are ready to tackle that one. Somewhere about the end of grade 2 or beginning of grade 3 would be an appropriate time to introduce this idea. Work with squares and rectangles first, then right triangles.

Finally teachers can approach the concept of an angle, particularly a right angle because it can be associated with turns. There are many exercises available, both paper-and-pencil and computer software, for working with angles. It is probably not appropriate to introduce the protractor until about grade 3.

For all of these measurement activities, bring examples from newspapers and TV to class and discuss them. Have the children be on the lookout for such examples. What would they like to measure? What would be easy to measure? Hard to measure? Keep harping on the idea that no measurement is ever exact.

After students decide that there is some object hey want to measure, the first question to answer is "what attribute can be measured on this object?". Most physical objects would have a length, although even here there are choices to be made. Since the world is three-dimensional, students have to choose which dimension will be the length, which the width, and which the height. We use those words to distinguish the three dimensions from each other, but of course all three would be measured in length units. Other measureable attributes of common physical objects are their weight, surface area, volume and temperature.

In PreK-3 volume is not an appropriate topic, except as it might enter into a discussion of liquid measure. Also the time spent on area concepts will probably be short. Measurement of temperature will normally be confined to air temperature for this age group.

With the advent of good and inexpensive digital cameras, math teachers have wonderful opportunities to show students how pervasive mathematics and measuring are in their lives. The teacher can go around the immediate area of the school taking pictures of physical objects that illustrate various things they are studying. For example, if you are working on length measures and also geometric figures, before having them measure the length and width of a bunch of rectangles on paper, show them pictures (a powerpoint demonstration would be ideal here) of different rectangles around the neighborhood. For example, some things they can measure include the walls of the classroom, tiles on the floor or ceiling, sidewalks, exteriors of buildings, etc.

Do the same for other geometric figures. Bridges are good examples of triangles. Church windows are often circular. Children are usually quite familiar with circles, but circles introduce some very real problems. With younger students the perimeter can be approximated (remember that all measurements are approximate anyway). Using a piece of string and fitting it around a circle on a piece of paper, then measuring the length of the string that seems to fit, makes a nice little exercise.

Every math classroom should be equipped with various measuring devices-- a set of rulers, a few meter sticks, some thermometers, a few different scales for weighing objects, clocks and perhaps a stopwatch and protractors. Hands-on exercises are definitely the way to go when measuring. When showing pictures of objects we want to measure in the immediate environment, ask the students how could we measure these objects and what would be an appropriate instrument to use. What units would be best to express the measurement? Have them guess the result of measuring the object. Where could they go to find out if their guess was a good approximation to the reported measurement of this object?

Angles are difficult to teach to young children. They can be introduced by having them stand up, face front, then turn to face sideways right. What if we turned only part way to the right? How could we measure this? Don't be too fast to tell them how we adults talk about and measure angles for this. You might have some interesting ideas presented for solving this problem. Eventually, you will tell them about angles and how they are measured. Draw some angles and talk about what exactly is being measured here. Point out that the angle is no bigger if you extend the sides indefinitely. Actual measuring with protractors could be introduced if you feel the children are ready, but getting the idea of what we mean by the concept of angle is more important at first.

Skill 9.6 **Demonstrating knowledge of procedures for solving problems involving length, area, angles, volume, mass, and temperature**

The units of **length** in the customary system are inches, feet, yards and miles.

> 12 inches (in.) = 1 foot (ft.)
> 36 in. = 1 yard (yd.)
> 3 ft. = 1 yd.
> 5280 ft. = 1 mile (mi.)
> 760 yd. = 1 mi.

To change from a **larger unit to a smaller unit, multiply**.
To change from a **smaller unit to a larger unit, divide**.

Example:

$$4 \text{ mi.} = \underline{} \text{ yd.}$$
Since 1760 yd. = 1 mile, multiply $4 \times 1760 = 7040$ yd.

Example:

$$21 \text{ in.} = \underline{} \text{ ft.}$$
$21 \div 12 = 1\frac{3}{4}$ ft.

The units of **weight** are ounces, pounds and tons.

> 16 ounces (oz.) = 1 pound (lb.)
> 2,000 lb. = 1 ton (T.)

Example: $2\frac{3}{4}$ T. = _____ lb.
$2\frac{3}{4} \times 2,000 = 5,500$ lb.

The units of **capacity** are fluid ounces, cups, pints, quarts, and gallons.

> 8 fluid ounces (fl. oz.) = 1 cup (c.)
>
> 2 c. = 1 pint (pt.)
> 4 c. = 1 quart (qt.)
> 2 pt. = 1 qt.
> 4 qt. = 1 gallon (gal.)

Example1: 3 gal. = _____ qt.
$3 \times 4 = 12$ qt.

Example: $1\frac{1}{4}$ cups = _____ oz.
$1\frac{1}{4} \times 8 = 10$ oz.

Example: 7 c. = _____ pt.
$7 \div 2 = 3\frac{1}{2}$ pt.

Square units can be derived with knowledge of basic units of length by squaring the equivalent measurements.

> 1 square foot (sq. ft.) = 144 sq. in.
>
> 1 sq. yd. = 9 sq. ft.
> 1 sq. yd. = 1296 sq. in.

Example: 14 sq. yd. = _____ sq. ft.
$14 \times 9 = 126$ sq. ft.

Metric Units

The metric system is based on multiples of <u>ten</u>. Conversions are made by simply moving the decimal point to the left or right.

    kilo-   1000 thousands
    hecto- 100   hundreds
    deca-   10   tens
    nit
    deci-   .1   tenths
    centi-   .01   hundredths
    milli-   .001 thousandths

The basic unit for **length** is the meter. One meter is approximately one yard.

The basic unit for **weight** or mass is the gram. A paper clip weighs about one gram.

The basic unit for **volume** is the liter. One liter is approximately a quart.

These are the most commonly used units.

1 m = 100 cm	1000 mL = 1 L	1000 mg = 1 g
1 m = 1000 mm	1 kL = 1000 L	1 kg = 1000 g
1 cm = 10 mm		
1000 m = 1 km		

The prefixes are commonly listed from left to right for ease in conversion.

            K H D U D C M

    <u>Example:</u>   63 km = _____ m
Since there are 3 steps from <u>K</u>ilo to <u>U</u>nit, move the decimal point 3 places to the right.
            63 km = 63,000 m

    <u>Example:</u>   14 mL = _____ L
Since there are 3 steps from <u>M</u>illi to <u>U</u>nit, move the decimal point 3 places to the left.
            14 mL = 0.014 L

    <u>Example:</u>   56.4 cm = _____ mm
            56.4 cm = 564 mm

    <u>Example:</u>   9.1 m = _____ km
            9.1 m = 0.0091 km

Example 5:   75 kg = _____ m
             75 kg = 75,000,000 m

The units of **length** in the customary system are inches, feet, yards and miles.

> 12 inches (in.) = 1 foot (ft.)
> 36 in. = 1 yard (yd.)
> 3 ft. = 1 yd.
> 5280 ft. = 1 mile (mi.)
> 760 yd. = 1 mi.

To change from a **larger unit to a smaller unit, multiply**.

To change from a **smaller unit to a larger unit, divide.**

Example:

4 mi. = _____ yd.
Since 1760 yd. = 1 mile, multiply 4 × 1760 = 7040 yd.

Example:

21 in. = _____ ft.
$21 \div 12 = 1\frac{3}{4}$ ft.

The units of **weight** are ounces, pounds and tons.

> 16 ounces (oz.) = 1 pound (lb.)
> 2,000 lb. = 1 ton (T.)

Example: $2\frac{3}{4}$ T. = _____ lb.
$2\frac{3}{4} \times 2,000 = 5,500$ lb.

The units of **capacity** are fluid ounces, cups, pints, quarts, and gallons.

> 8 fluid ounces (fl. oz.) = 1 cup (c.)
>
> 2 c. = 1 pint (pt.)
> 4 c. = 1 quart (qt.)
> 2 pt. = 1 qt.
> 4 qt. = 1 gallon (gal.)

Example1: 3 gal. = _____ qt.
$3 \times 4 = 12$ qt.

Example: $1\frac{1}{4}$ cups = _____ oz.
$1\frac{1}{4} \times 8 = 10$ oz.

Example: 7 c. = _____ pt.
$7 \div 2 = 3\frac{1}{2}$ pt.

Square units can be derived with knowledge of basic units of length by squaring the equivalent measurements.

> 1 square foot (sq. ft.) = 144 sq. in.
>
> 1 sq. yd. = 9 sq. ft.
> 1 sq. yd. = 1296 sq. in.

Example: 14 sq. yd. = _____ sq. ft.
$14 \times 9 = 126$ sq. ft.

Skill 9.7 Identifying methods for collection, organization, and analysis of data

Collecting, describing, and analyzing data are fun activities in the early childhood classroom. There are numerous exciting and playful methods for collecting data to be used in various classroom lessons. Some fun ways to collect data include:

- Have students drop a piece of cereal into a bowl that is their favorite color.
- Have students draw a tally mark under their lunch choice on a bulletin board.
- Utilize a thumbs up or thumbs down approach for students' response when asking whole group questions.
- Use wipe boards
- Have the students themselves stand in lines to form a human graph to show a particular set of data

Ideas for collecting data to organize describe and analyze:

- Favorite colors
- Birthdays
- Hair/eye/clothing colors
- Favorite foods
- Favorite books
- Ending to a story (like/don't like)
- Shoe size (type/color/style)
- Favorite songs

Once the data has been collected, it needs to be organized into a format easily analyzed by the students. This can involve: tables, tally charts, and graphs. Using the real objects to form the bars of the graphs can provide the students with immediate results. This can be very important to young children. It also provides a concrete representation; whereas, transferring the data to paper to create the graph/table or chart is more abstract of a concept.

Once the graph, table or chart is completed it is important to utilize mathematical language to describe and analyze the information. Comparing two different bars on the graph, finding the greatest, finding the smallest/least or other types of analysis help students to develop their critical thinking skills. The students need to be exposed to vocabulary terms that mean the same thing (such as smallest and least).

TEACHER CERTIFICATION STUDY GUIDE

Gathering, organizing and analyzing data is an easy to incorporate daily routine into the early childhood classroom. An entire activity can be completed in five to ten minutes of the math class on a regular basis and provide students with a fun, real-life, critical thinking activity which increases not only mathematical understanding and skills, but builds vocabulary skills as well. It is also an area of math, which can help to tie together many other subject areas in an easy way.

BAR, LINE, PICTO-, AND CIRCLE GRAPHS

	Test 1	Test 2	Test 3	Test 4	Test 5
Evans, Tim	75	66	80	85	97
Miller, Julie	94	93	88	97	98
Thomas, Randy	81	86	88	87	90

Bar graphs are used to compare various quantities.

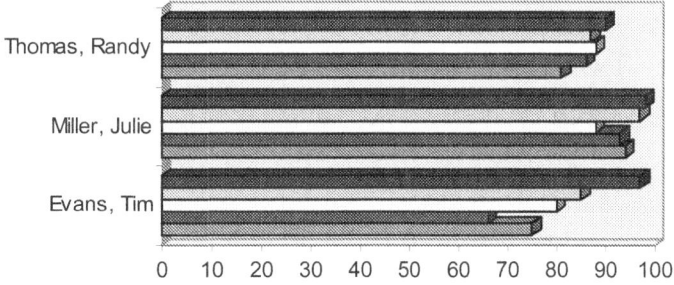

EARLY CHILDHOOD EDUCATION 189

Line graphs are used to show trends, often over a period of time.

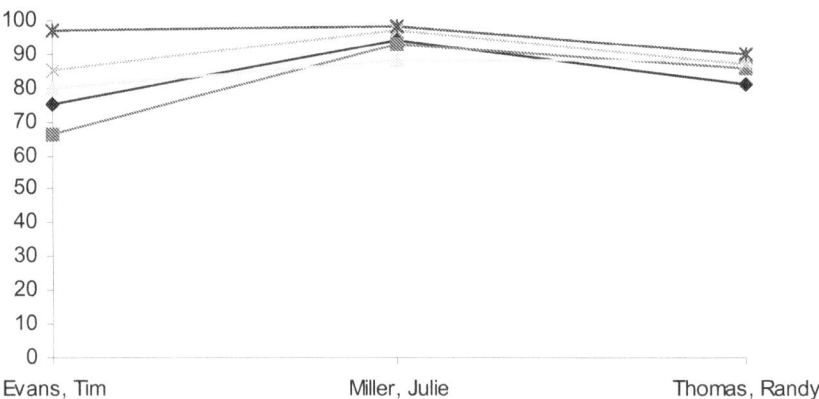

A **pictograph** shows comparison of quantities using symbols. Each symbol represents a number of items.

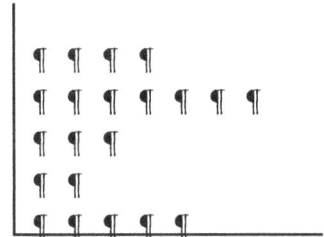

To read a bar graph or a pictograph, read the explanation of the scale that was used in the legend. Compare the length of each bar with the dimensions on the axes and calculate the value each bar represents. On a pictograph count the number of pictures used in the chart and calculate the value of all the pictures.

Skill 9.8 Applying mathematical logic and reasoning to analyze and solve problems in real-world contexts

For very young children, almost any mathematical question posed is a problem to be solved. Too often, the term problem solving is misrepresented as word problems. In fact, any problem presented to a child where they are unaware of the answer, is a problem to be solved. From the very beginning, children need to experience a variety of mathematical situations across all subject areas. Exposing children to a variety of contexts in which to solve problems allows the child to develop their own constructs upon which they can build new learning.

Problem solving is not about one strategy or right way, but rather is about allowing students of varying mathematical skills and abilities to look at the same situation presented and find a way to solve it. In a group of five, it may be reasonable to expect five different methods to reach the solution. Providing students with the means to investigate a problem allows them to be flexible in their approach. Often times, teachers limit the abilities of their students to solve problems by restricting them to one mode of reaching a solution. Parents can also be guilty of this as well. For example, the kindergartener who is presented with a problem where there are three pies and twelve people to feed may easily use pieces of real pie to work out an appropriate solution. However, the parent or teacher who indicates you must use the division algorithm to solve the problem may automatically set this same student up for failure.

Problem solving needs to be incorporated in a real way for students to understand appreciate and value the process. Using daily activities or problems can help make problem solving a regular part of a child's day. As situations arise, in any subject area, it is important for the teacher to incorporate problem-solving activities. Having the students help with lunch count, attendance, counting the number of days left in the school year, calculating the time left until recess, or other daily types of activities are examples of ways to include realistic problem solving in the classroom.

Additionally, problem-solving activities should be incorporated into all subject areas. In science, children can graph the daily temperatures and make predictions for the future temperatures. In social studies, they can gather, tabulate and calculate the data related to the topic presented (how many classmates agree that drugs are bad for your body). In language arts, children can solve problems find in all types of children's literature. Charting favorite books, calculating ages of characters in stories, and drawing maps of the setting(s) of books are some beginning examples of ways to connect the two subjects. There are also numerous exciting books written with a mathematical basis that can be used to cover both subjects in a fun manner.

It is important for the teacher to be a role model. Thinking aloud as you come across a problem in the course of the day will help the students begin to realize the necessity and real-world implications of solving problems. Encouraging students to be reflective will also help in building the necessary mathematical language. Also, students can begin to share their ideas and methods with each other, which is an excellent strategy for learning about problem solving.

Typically, there are four steps to problem solving. Teachers will need to teach each of the steps explicitly and model them regularly. The steps are:

1. Understand the problem

    This involves, among other things, understanding all the words in the problem, understanding what you are being asked to find, possibly being able to draw a picture or diagram, knowing if there is enough information, and knowing if there is too much information.

2. Devise a plan

    This involves being able to choose an appropriate strategy to solve the problem. These strategies include, but are not limited to, guessing and checking, looking for a pattern, using a model, and working backward.

3. Carry out the plan

    This is the actual solving of the problem using whatever strategy you have chosen.

4. Look back

    Included in this step is checking the answer, if possible, to make sure it is correct. This step may be extended to include determining if there might have been an easier way to find the solution.

When assessing problem solving, the most effective method is direct observation. Teachers need to observe students to determine what strategies are being implemented. Watching students solve problems presented can provide teachers with insight into future teaching opportunities and skills mastered already by the students. Problem solving alone is difficult to assign a grade, but the information gained from the process is critical to future teaching.

> **For additional math activities:**
>
> http://ofcn.org/cyber.serv/academy/ace/math/elem.html

Competency 010   **UNDERSTAND HOW TO FACILITATE LEARNING FOR YOUNG CHILDREN IN THE AREA OF MATHEMATICS**

Skill 10.1   Recognizing characteristics, processes, and progressions in children's mathematical development, including intuitive and emergent numeracy

Children are born with an innate curiosity about the world surrounding them. You can watch toddlers group their toys and explore the early mathematical concepts through their play as they complete their shape sorters or manipulate their building blocks into piles or towers. Some of the most up-to-date research in the area of mathematics indicates children may have an inborn number sense, which can help them solve some complex problems before they understand the number and symbol system used in later mathematics. This intuitive ability to understand numbers and problems is typically referred to as a child's number sense.

As with the phonemic awareness skills in reading, number sense is the foundation upon which all future math topics will be built. Providing young children with the opportunity to interact with objects across multiple contexts will help children begin to develop these concepts of number sense. Within this beginning area of mathematics, students will progress at different levels at different times. For example, one student may be able to count and identify a group of five, but not recognize the pattern of five on a die. Another student may count the group, recognize the pattern, and understand the concept of grouping things into piles of five and counting by the groups.

While in this beginning stage, children will be able to identify how many objects are in a group. Typically, students will have some beginning oral counting system (1-10 or 1-20). These preschool children will also begin to identify the relationships between groups of objects (size, quantity, more, less, bigger, smaller, etc.)

Number sense develops into the further understanding of place value and how numbers are related. This involves identifying and explaining how numbers can be grouped into tens, ones and eventually hundreds or more. Using trading games, place value mats and base ten blocks students can develop these skills. These activities will progress until the student understands that the one in sixteen represents ten, not simply one.

Eventually, children will develop the necessary skills to extrapolate these beginning concepts to more difficult situations and problems. They will be able to make generalizations about number situations presented, even when they are unable to utilize traditionally computational methods to solve problems. For example, young children may be able to solve a multiplication problem (four rows of three chairs, how many chairs) and provide an answer using manipulatives and their number sense; however, they would still be unable to solve the more traditional problem of 4X3.

Concepts of numeracy, as well as other math concepts, should be presented to children across situations, using a variety of materials and until levels of proficiency are reached. As concepts of math build upon another, it is imperative the appropriate foundation is in place for future learning to progress. Presenting concepts and ideas early will allow students the opportunity to experience and construct their own competencies.

Skill 10.2 Demonstrating knowledge of factors that affect young children's mathematical development

As with all areas of learning, there are many factors that can influence the mathematical development of children. Young children from deprived backgrounds who may have had limited play experiences may have difficulty applying concepts introduced. Prior knowledge and experiences provide a basis for students to attach new learning. Thinking of the brain as a complex filing system, students who already have a file folder full of information with which they can connect new learning are steps ahead of the child who must create the file folder from scratch. Additionally, second language students or those with disabilities may have difficulties creating the necessary framework upon which mathematical concepts can be built.

Developmentally, children all progress at their own rate. Some children, due to other impeding factors (e.g. cognitive disabilities), may not achieve the same level of understanding as others. It is important to consider developmentally appropriate activities and the natural cognitive development of students when planning mathematical instruction. However, developmental appropriateness is not a reason alone to not expose all children to more complex math concepts. There is growing evidence that children can complete complex problem solving activities using alternate means than what is considered standard mathematical procedures.

Typical mathematical development progresses through three main stages. These stages include:

1. Use of Manipulatives – During this stage, children need to work with real objects to help them solve mathematical problems. It is generally accepted practice and helpful to incorporated the use of real objects of some sort when introducing new concepts to students.
2. Use of Mental Imagery – During this stage, children begin to use pictures or mental images of the objects to solve the problems.
3. Use of Abstract Imagery – During this stage, children are able to use their understanding of number sense to complete problems. Children in this stage are no longer thinking of real objects, but are using their understanding of mathematical concepts to make broader generalizations and solve problems.

Skill 10.3 Understanding the importance of collaborating with families to promote children's mathematical development

Some of the most influential people in a child's life are their family. Ideas, values and concepts about math will be transferred from family to child. Therefore, it is important to connect with families and provide instruction, as necessary, to ensure that mathematics is seen under a positive light within the homes. Even the youngest students can experience meaningful hands-on math.

Having family math nights at school is an excellent strategy to bring math and parents together. Activity sheets can be sent home to involve the family. The activities should be highly engaging, hands on, and provide everyone with a fun and complete understanding of the math concepts being taught to the child in school. For example, have children tally how many cans/how many boxes of food are on one shelf at home, or how many spoons/how many forks are in a drawer.

Another strategy is to provide the families with newsletters, explanations, formulas or even a spare text so they can feel a part of their child's educational process. In this way, they can help the child who may be struggling and provide additional repetitions to ensure mastery.

A reasonable amount of math homework is a good way to reinforce a skill or concept that was introduced and understood at school. It is also a good way for parents to monitor the progress their children are making in math.

Families may also be encouraged to help their students practice math facts with flashcards. Prior to a test, students can take home a study packet to be signed by the parent after they have reviewed together. Perhaps the teacher will offer some incentive to do this (candy, bonus points, etc.)

Skill 10.4   Recognizing the roles of exploration, active engagement, inquiry, and questioning in building knowledge, language, and concepts related to mathematics

Teaching young children mathematics requires a progression from the tangible to the abstract. As new concepts are introduced it is important for the teacher to utilize concrete objects. This allows students to manipulate, touch and explore the learning in a real way. This exploration provides the students the opportunity to be actively engaged in the learning. In this way, students can construct their own foundations, questions, and concepts related to numbers.

Providing the students with concrete and meaningful learning experiences is more involved than simply passing out blocks or beans to help introduce a concept. It involves utilizing and developing the language of subject. Inquiry based learning provides the students with the opportunity to not only explore the materials and concepts, but to begin to organize the information in order to be able to communicate their ideas of mathematics.

Without this concrete level of exploration, students may be able to memorize rote processes for solving problems (algorithms), but they may lack the foundational understanding necessary to make mathematical connections to everyday situations and experiences. Some students will be unable to see the broader generalizations found throughout math unless they have the time and exposure to the concepts through concrete learning experiences.

Mathematics has its own language, which requires practice and development. Often students who are struggling with the concepts presented lack the appropriate vocabulary and exposure to mathematical language to be successful. It is important to promote the development of this vocabulary, just as you would do with reading vocabulary or in other subjects.

Successful math teachers introduce their students to multiple problem-solving strategies and create a classroom environment where free thought and experimentation are encouraged. Teachers can promote problem solving by allowing multiple attempts at problems, giving credit for reworking test or homework problems, and encouraging the sharing of ideas through class discussion. Once the students are successful at completing problem solving activities at the concrete level, students should be exposed to the semi concrete (use of pictures and symbols) level and finally to the abstract level (use of symbols or letters to represent numbers or concepts). There are several specific problem-solving skills with which teachers should be familiar.

The **guess-and-check** strategy calls for students to make an initial guess at the solution, check the answer, and use the outcome to guide the next guess. With each successive guess, the student should get closer to the correct answer. Constructing a table from the guesses can help organize the data.

Example: There are 100 coins in a jar, and 10 are dimes. The rest are pennies and nickels. There are twice as many pennies as nickels. How many pennies and nickels are in the jar?

There are 90 total nickels and pennies in the jar (100 coins − 10 dimes).

There are twice as many pennies as nickels. Make guesses that fulfill the criteria and adjust based on the answer found. Continue until you find the correct answer: 60 pennies and 30 nickels.

Number of Pennies	Number of Nickels	Total Number of Pennies and Nickels
40	20	60
80	40	120
70	35	105
60	30	90

When solving a problem where the final result and the steps to reach the result are given, students must **work backwards** to determine what the starting point must have been.

Example:
John subtracted 7 from his age, and divided the result by 3. The final result was 4. What is John's age?

Work backward by reversing the operations:
$4 \times 3 = 12$
$12 + 7 = 19$
John is 19 years old.

Estimation and testing for **reasonableness** are related skills students should employ prior to and after solving a problem. These skills are particularly important when students use calculators to find answers.

Example:
Find the sum of 4387 + 7226 + 5893.

    4300 + 7200 + 5800 = 17300   Estimation.
    4387 + 7226 + 5893 = 17506   Actual sum.

By comparing the estimate to the actual sum, students can determine that their answer is reasonable.

Throughout the process, students should be encouraged to develop methods for recording their information through the use of pictures, symbols, numbers or other more appropriate ideas. Venn diagrams are excellent for comparing mathematical concepts.

Learning to use pictures and numbers together to represent an idea provide students with a means to communicate to each other the concepts they are learning. Teachers can build the vocabulary and thinking skills of their students by using these pictures or student created models and providing the students with the correct mathematical name or label for the idea. Together these student-created and teacher-labeled representations can provide students with not only a communication tool, but a concrete method for explaining conjectures to each other.

In the home living area, provide muffin tins and play food muffins to match one-to-one. Have placemats, plates, plastic forks, etc. so that students can set the table – again one-to-one. In the Science area, provide a simple balance to compare the weight of groups of blocks, etc. Provide number word/concept math books in the reading area. Have number puzzles and shape sorters.

Children at this age should be able to begin to use simple quantity words such as *more, fewer, same, enough, some, many,* and *lots of* and apply these words to daily situations. "May I have one more cookie?" "She has fewer blocks than I do." "I have some toys."

Students will learn the language associated with operations:

Addition:
: How many are there in all?
How many are there all together?
What does that add up to?
If we put this together with that, how many will there be?
What is the total?

Subtraction:
: How many fewer?
How many less?
How many more than …?
How many less than …?
How many more are needed?
How many are left over?

Multiplication:
: How many in all?
How many all together?
What is the total?

Division:
: How many in each set?
How many sets?
How many times does this number go into this number?

Skill 10.5 Demonstrating knowledge of learning experiences for promoting understanding of mathematics concepts and acquisition of mathematics skills

In past times the sequence of mathematics courses in the curriculum was usually (1) arithmetic for the first eight grades, (2) then algebra in ninth grade, (3) geometry in tenth grade, (4) more algebra in eleventh grade and finally (5) trigonometry and analytic geometry in the senior year. Now we generally move things around a bit, introducing pieces of higher-level courses into the lower grades as appropriate. This means that teachers have to be constantly aware of which pieces will work for the children that they are teaching.

Most children learn about the world by observing specific things and then making generalizations about the things they have observed. This is called inductive reasoning. In the historical development of mathematics over hundreds of years, the subject has become more and more about abstract generalizations. As students proceed through the curriculum, they will eventually be able to learn these abstractions _first_ as a time-saver to acquiring additional mathematical information. Then they will be able to reason deductively. However, abstractions are not appropriate for most PreK-3 children.

We want children to see that mathematics is relevant and useful to them. Therefore, we must tie their learning to things they already know or have observed. Whenever you introduce new topics, they should be linked to things the children already are familiar with. For example, ask students to listen to the weather report on TV giving the expected temperature for the next day. In class the next day, ask them what does this number given for the temperature mean and why do we want to know it. Then you can gradually introduce a thermometer and the unit it is using to measure the temperature.

Psychologists have known for a long time that there are three ways to learn: (1) visual, (2) auditory and (3) kinesthetic. Recently it has become the practice to divide visual learners into visual/nonverbal and visual/verbal, so that we commonly speak of four learning styles today. This is a topic that all teachers should become very familiar with. First find out what style you are, and what methods of learning work best for you. Don't assume that these same methods will necessarily work best for all of your students. Many of them may be natural learners of a different type than you are. Find out what methods work well for these other learning styles and remember to include some of these activities in each lesson you teach.

Many times you may be asked to teach something you are not familiar with. Don't skip it because of that. Get on the computer, go to the library, or ask another teacher where to find out about this subject. Keep an open mind. You may find out that you really enjoy learning about things you have previously been avoiding. One of the great things about being a teacher is that you can constantly learn new things along with your students.

Finally, remember that educational theorists tend to espouse extremes, sometimes just to make a point, but other times because they really believe their way is the only right way. In mathematics we have, for example, calculators versus no calculators or hands-on learning versus drill in the basics. Avoid extremes and include a good mix of all these things in every lesson you teach.

> **For further information about Math activities for early childhood:**
>
> http://www.teach-nology.com/teachers/early_education/subject_matter/math/

Skill 10.6 Demonstrating knowledge of strategies for encouraging children to develop positive attitudes toward mathematics

No matter how challenging the activity provided, students who have been encouraged and face it with a positive attitude will be more likely to overcome the challenge presented. It is for this reason teachers need to take time to build positive interests and attitudes related to math for all of their students. Research has proven that setting high expectations with appropriate teaching and encouragement is one of the best strategies for developing higher-level thinking and math skills.

In order for this to occur, the teacher must provide an appropriate learning environment where children feel safe to take risks and are encouraged to do so. Helping students to feel welcome within the classroom and providing a comfortable, orderly classroom will go a long way in providing the most appropriate learning environment for students. These classroom management issues may seem redundant, but set the foundation for all learning experiences, not simply math.

Within the math program, it is necessary for children to understand the value and purpose in a clear and explicit manner of tasks presented. Considering student interests, how the tasks are relevant to their lives and providing open-ended learning activities help students to connect in a meaningful manner to the subject. Tapping into the natural curiosity of the students and expanding it to include interests and needs encourages students to develop a better sense of their surroundings.

Throughout all of these processes, the teacher must display a positive attitude about math. Statements that might be derogatory about the subject should be eliminated. The cliché of enthusiasm being catching is very true. The more excited and positive a teacher is about the subject, the more likely the students will be to view math as a positive part of their lives. As students struggle, it can be important for the teacher to provide the necessary scaffolding to limit frustrations or negative feelings related to the subject.

In the end, connecting math to real-life events that are of interest and meaning to the students is the key to developing this positive attitude. The students who play Little League may complete some activities based on baseball cards. Pokemon games or other high interest activities can be incorporated into the math class periodically to boost learning and interest. Cooking with students near holidays or as a special event can help students to better understand the value of the more difficult concepts of fractions. Using play and games are excellent motivators for students and can also be used to build math skills in a positive manner.

Skill 10.7 Demonstrating knowledge of strategies for encouraging the use of mathematical concepts and skills in everyday life

One of the most important concepts of any teaching is to help the students realize the importance of the skills being learned to their everyday lives outside of the school setting. This is equally true within the field of math. As students identify and realize the importance of the skills being learned to their lives at home, they will become more involved in the learning, as it has new and better value for them. For very young children, this may require specific and explicit explanations or connections.

One of the easiest ways to incorporate real life mathematical activities is to bring real life activities into the classroom. Working as a class to prepare food, where the students need to measure different ingredients before/after completing lessons on fractions, is an excellent way for the students to understand the importance of the learning, especially if you make a food the children enjoy. Other mixing activities that involve measuring math skills involve: making play dough, making slime, and creating the perfect bubble blowing mixture. Cooking and mixture activities also have a direct connection to the sciences and allow the teacher to combine subject areas into one lesson.

Other methods to incorporate math activities into more regular parts of students' lives and other subject areas include:

- Charting/graphing the weather on a regular basis
- Predicting temperatures based on a pattern or other information
- Helping students keep track of the score of a sporting event using tally marks
- Finding the age of other family members or characters in stories
- Building race cars or straw structures to represent buildings from stories or having your own race, similar to a NASCAR event
- Redesigning the layout of the classroom/cafeteria
- Playing card, dice, and board games with the students (the popular games like Pokemon involve a lot of math if played correctly)
- Timing activities or determining how long until a special event will occur

In the end, the activity does not really matter. Rather the students need to understand the importance of math in their daily lives. Also, they need to know how the learning in school directly supports their personal interests, ideas, and needs which will make the information most meaningful to the students.

> **For more information on connecting math to everyday life:**
>
> http://www.homeschooloasis.com/art_real-life_math.htm

COMPETENCY 0011 UNDERSTAND SCIENCE CONTENT AND INQUIRY PROCESSES AND HOW TO FACILITATE SCIENCE LEARNING FOR YOUNG CHILDREN

Skill 11.1   Demonstrating knowledge of basic concepts in physical, life, and Earth science

Physical Science

Everything in our world is made up of **matter**, whether it is a rock, a building, an animal, or a person. Matter is defined by its characteristics: It takes up space and it has mass.

Mass is a measure of the amount of matter in an object. Two objects of equal mass will balance each other on a simple balance scale no matter where the scale is located. For instance, two rocks with the same amount of mass that are in balance on Earth will also be in balance on the Moon. They will feel heavier on Earth than on the Moon because of the gravitational pull of the Earth. So, although the two rocks have the same mass, they will have different weights.

Weight is the measure of the Earth's pull of gravity on an object. It can also be defined as the pull of gravity between other bodies. The units of weight measurement commonly used are the pound (English measure) and the kilogram (metric measure).

Physical properties and chemical properties of matter describe the appearance or behavior of a substance. A **physical property** can be observed without changing the identity of a substance. For instance, you can describe the color, mass, shape, and volume of a book. **Chemical properties** describe the ability of a substance to be changed into new substances. Baking powder goes through a chemical change as it changes into carbon dioxide gas during the baking process.

Matter constantly changes. A **physical change** is a change that does not produce a new substance. The freezing and melting of water is an example of physical change. A **chemical change** (or chemical reaction) is any change of a substance into one or more other substances. Burning materials turn into smoke; a seltzer tablet fizzes into gas bubbles.

The **phase of matter** (solid, liquid, or gas) is identified by its shape and volume. A **solid** has a definite shape and volume. A **liquid** has a definite volume, but no shape. A **gas** has no shape or volume because it will spread out to occupy the entire space of whatever container it is in.

Energy is the ability to cause change in matter. Applying heat to a frozen liquid changes it from solid back to liquid. Continue heating it and it will boil and give off steam, a gas. **Evaporation** is the change in phase from liquid to gas. **Condensation** is the change in phase from gas to liquid.

A **magnet** is a material or object that attracts certain metals, such as cobalt, nickel, and iron and can also repel or attract another magnet. All magnets have poles: a North-seeking (N) and a South-seeking (S). In a compass, the side marked N will point toward the Earth's North magnetic pole, which is different from the North Pole (they are actually several hundred miles apart). If you cut a magnet into parts, each part will have both North and South poles. If you place magnets near each other, the opposite poles will attract and the like poles will repel each other. Therefore, a North pole will repel a North pole and attract a South pole.

The first true application of a magnet was the compass, which not only helps in navigation but also can help in detecting small magnetic fields. Magnets are also found in loudspeakers, electrical generators, and electrical motors. A very common use of magnets is to stick things to the refrigerator.

A **magnetic field** is made up of imaginary lines of flux resulting from moving or spinning electrically charged particles. These lines of magnetic flux move from one end of a magnetic object to the other, or rather, from the North-seeking pole to the South-seeking pole.

Magnetic and electric fields are similar in that in electricity, like charges repel, and in magnetism, like poles repel. They are different in that a magnet must have two poles, but an electrical charge, positive or negative, can stand alone.

Heat and temperature are different physical quantities. **Heat** is a measure of energy. **Temperature** is the measure of how hot (or cold) a body is with respect to a standard object.

We cannot rely on our sense of touch to determine temperature because the heat from a hand may be conducted more efficiently by certain objects, making them feel colder. **Thermometers** are used to measure temperature. A small amount of mercury in a capillary tube will expand when heated. The thermometer and the object whose temperature it is measuring are put in contact long enough for them to reach thermal equilibrium. Then the temperature can be read from the thermometer scale. Three temperature scales are used. These are Celsius, Fahrenheit, and Kelvin.

Life Science

All organisms are adapted to life in their unique habitat. The habitat includes all the components of their physical environment and is a necessity for the species' survival. Below are several key components of a complete habitat that all organisms require.

Food and water
Because all biochemical reactions take place in aqueous environments, all organisms must have access to clean water, even if only infrequently. Organisms also require two types of food: a source of energy (fixed carbon) and a source of nutrients. Autotrophs can fix carbon for themselves, but must have access to certain inorganic precursors. These organisms must also be able to obtain other nutrients, such as nitrogen, from their environment. Hetertrophs, on the other hand, must consume other organisms for both energy and nutrients. The species these organisms use as a food source must be present in their habitat.

Sunlight and air
This need is closely related to that for food and water because almost all species derive some needed nutrients from the sun and atmosphere. Plants require carbon dioxide to photosynthesize and oxygen is required for cellular respiration. Sunlight is also necessary for photosynthesis and is used by many animals to synthesize essential nutrients (i.e. vitamin D).

Shelter and space
The need for shelter and space vary greatly between species. Many plants do not need shelter, per se, but must have adequate soil to spread their roots and acquire nutrients. Certain invasive species can threaten native plants by out-competing them for space. Other types of plants and many animals also require protection from environmental hazards. These locations may facilitate reproduction (for instance, nesting sites) or provide seasonal shelter (for examples, dens and caves used by hibernating species).

Life Cycles

A diagram of an organism's life cycle simply reveals the various stages through which it progresses from the time it is conceived until it reaches sexual maturity and reproduces, starting the cycle over again. However, the various types of animals pass through very different phases of life. The different species may either lay eggs or give live birth, pass through metamorphosis or be born in a form similar to that of an adult, and have aquatic and terrestrial phases or spend their entire lives on land. Some classic examples are outlined here.

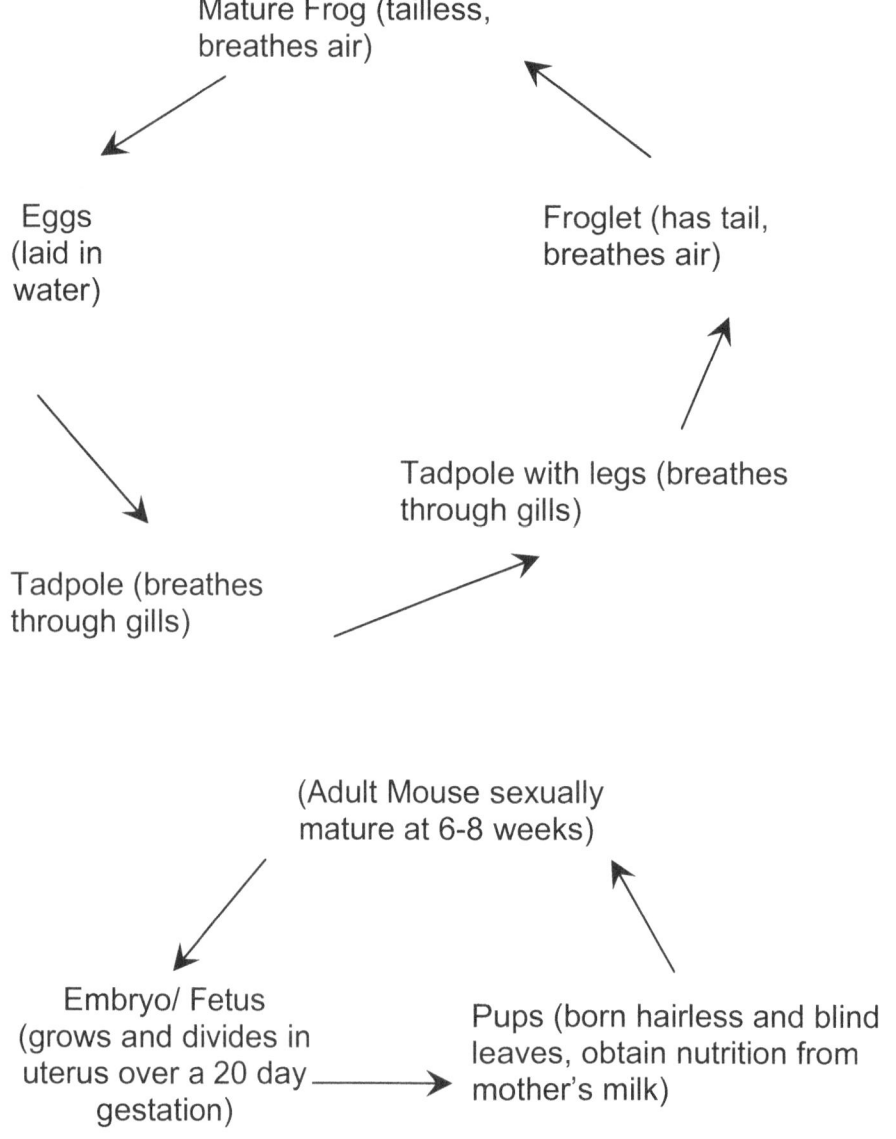

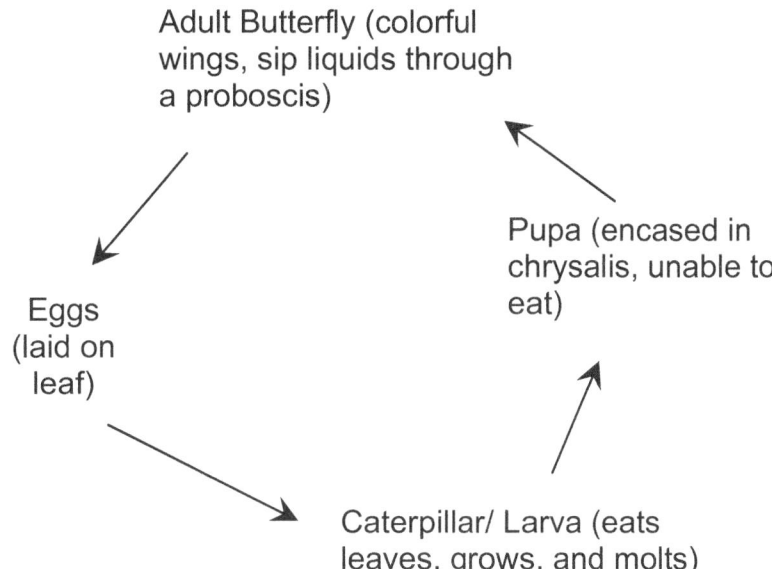

Trophic levels are based on the feeding relationships that determine energy flow and chemical cycling.

Autotrophs are the primary producers of the ecosystem. **Producers** mainly consist of plants. **Primary consumers** are the next trophic level. The primary consumers are the herbivores that eat plants or algae. **Secondary consumers** are the carnivores that eat the primary consumers. **Tertiary consumers** eat the secondary consumer. These trophic levels may go higher depending on the ecosystem. **Decomposers** are consumers that feed off animal waste and dead organisms. This pathway of food transfer is known as the food chain.

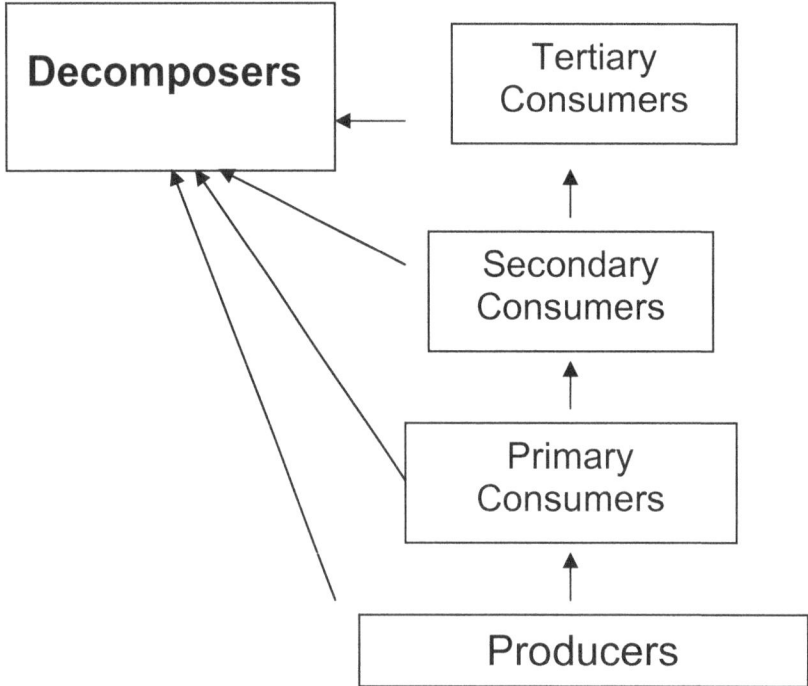

Earth Science

Space Satellites

An artificial satellite is any object placed into orbit by human endeavor. A satellite revolves around a planet in a circular or elliptical path. Most man-made satellites are useful objects placed in orbit purposely to perform some specific mission or task. Such satellites may include weather satellites, communication satellites, navigational satellites, reconnaissance satellites and scientific study satellites. Satellites are placed into orbit by first riding on a rocket or in the cargo bay of a space shuttle that is launched into space. Once the vessel has reached the satellite's destination, the satellite is released into space and remains in orbit due to the Earth's gravitational pull. The largest artificial satellite currently orbiting the Earth is the International Space Station. Currently, there are approximately 23,000 items of space junk - objects large enough to track with radar that were inadvertently placed in orbit or have outlived their usefulness - floating above Earth.

Airplanes

Airplanes or fixed-wing aircraft are heavier than aircraft that utilize the laws of physics to achieve flight. Airplanes achieve flight using the concepts of lift, weight, thrust and drag. Lift pushes the plane upward, and is created by the design of aircraft wings, which have flat bottoms and slightly rounded tops. As the aircraft is propelled forward by thrust from the engines, air moves faster over the top of the wings, and slower under the bottom. The slower airflow beneath the wing generates more pressure, while the faster airflow above generates less. This difference in pressure results in upward lift. Weight is Earth's gravity pulling down on a plane. Planes are designed to remain level, with equal weight in the front and back of the plane. Drag is the opposite force that slows a plane. Planes minimize drag with aerodynamic design.

Humankind's interest in flight is documented as far back as Greek mythology. The first real study of flight, however, is attributed to Leonardo da Vinci, who designed a craft called the orthinopter, on which the modern day helicopter is based. The Wright Brothers achieved the first successful flight off the outer banks of North Carolina. They developed their craft by first studying many early attempts at flight, and then testing their own theories using balloons and kites. The brothers designed gliders to understand craft control and wind effects. Using a wind tunnel, the Wright Brothers tested many different wing and tail shapes. After determining a glider shape that consistently passed flight tests, they began to develop a propulsion system capable of creating lift. Eventually, the brothers constructed an engine capable of generating almost 12 horsepower. On December 17, 1903, the Wright Brother's craft known as the "Flyer" lifted from ground level piloted by brother Orville, and traveled one hundred and twenty feet.

Natural Objects in the Sky

There are eight established planets in our solar system. These are Mercury, Venus, Earth, Mars, Jupiter, Saturn, Uranus, and Neptune. Pluto was known as an established planet in our solar system, but as of Summer 2006, its status is being reconsidered. The planets are divided into two groups based on their distance from the Sun. The inner planets include: Mercury, Venus, Earth, and Mars. The outer planets include: Jupiter, Saturn, Uranus, and Neptune.

Mercury - the closest planet to the Sun. Its surface has craters and rocks. The atmosphere is composed of hydrogen, helium and sodium. Mercury was named after the Roman messenger god.

Venus - has a slow rotation when compared to Earth. Venus and Uranus rotate in opposite directions from the other planets. This opposite rotation is called retrograde rotation. The surface of Venus is not visible due to the extensive cloud cover. The atmosphere is composed mostly of carbon dioxide. Sulfuric acid droplets in the dense cloud cover give Venus a yellow appearance. Venus has a greater greenhouse effect than observed on Earth. The dense clouds combined with carbon dioxide trap heat. Venus was named after the Roman goddess of love.

Earth - considered a water planet with 70% of its surface covered by water. Gravity holds the masses of water in place. The different temperatures observed on earth allow for the different states (solid, liquid, gas) of water to exist. The atmosphere is composed mainly of oxygen and nitrogen. Earth is the only planet that is known to support life.

Mars - surface contains numerous craters, active and extinct volcanoes, ridges, and valleys with extremely deep fractures. Iron oxide found in the dusty soil makes the surface seem rust colored and the skies seem pink in color. The atmosphere is composed of carbon dioxide, nitrogen, argon, oxygen and water vapor. Mars has polar regions with ice caps composed of water. Mars has two satellites and was named after the Roman war god.

Jupiter – the largest planet in the solar system. Jupiter has 16 moons. The atmosphere is composed of hydrogen, helium, methane and ammonia. There are white colored bands of clouds indicating rising gas and dark colored bands of clouds indicating descending gases. The gas movement is caused by heat resulting from the energy of Jupiter's core. Jupiter has a Great Red Spot that is thought to be a hurricane type cloud. Jupiter has a strong magnetic field.

Saturn - the second largest planet in the solar system. Saturn has rings of ice, rock, and dust particles circling it. Saturn's atmosphere is composed of hydrogen, helium, methane, and ammonia. Saturn has 20 plus satellites and was named for the Roman god of agriculture.

Uranus - the second largest planet in the solar system with retrograde revolution. Uranus is a gaseous planet. It has 10 dark rings and 15 satellites. Its atmosphere is composed of hydrogen, helium, and methane. Uranus was named after the Greek god of the heavens.

Neptune - another gaseous planet with an atmosphere consisting of hydrogen, helium, and methane. Neptune has 3 rings and 2 satellites. Neptune was named after the Roman sea god because its atmosphere is the same color as the seas.

Pluto - once considered the smallest planet in the solar system; its status as a planet is being reconsidered. Pluto's atmosphere probably contains methane, ammonia, and frozen water. Pluto has 1 satellite. Pluto revolves around the Sun every 250 years. Pluto was named after the Roman god of the underworld.

Astronomers believe that rocky fragments may have been the remains of the birth of the solar system that never formed into a planet. **Asteroids** are found in the region between Mars and Jupiter.

Comets are masses of frozen gases, cosmic dust, and small rocky particles. Astronomers think that most comets originate in a dense comet cloud beyond Pluto. Comet consists of a nucleus, a coma, and a tail. A comet's tail always points away from the sun. The most famous comet, **Halley's Comet,** is named after the person whom first discovered it in 240 B.C. It returns to the skies near earth every 75 to 76 years.

Meteoroids are composed of particles of rock and metal of various sizes. When a meteoroid travels through the earth's atmosphere, friction causes its surface to heat up and it begins to burn. The burning meteoroid falling through the earth's atmosphere is called a **meteor** (also known as a "shooting star").

Meteorites are meteors that strike the earth's surface. A physical example of a meteorite's impact on the earth's surface can be seen in Arizona. The Barringer Crater is a huge meteor crater. There are many other meteor craters throughout the world.

Astronomers use groups or patterns of stars called **constellations** as reference points to locate other stars in the sky. Familiar constellations include Ursa Major (also known as the big bear) and Ursa Minor (known as the little bear). Within the Ursa Major, the smaller constellation, The Big Dipper is found. Within the Ursa Minor, the smaller constellation, The Little Dipper is found.

Different constellations appear as the earth continues its revolution around the sun with the seasonal changes. Magnitude stars are 21 of the brightest stars that can be seen from earth. These are the first stars noticed at night. There are 15 commonly observed first magnitude stars in the Northern Hemisphere.

A vast collection of stars is defined as a **galaxy**. Galaxies are classified as irregular, elliptical, and spiral. An irregular galaxy has no real structured appearance; most are in their early stages of life. An elliptical galaxy consists of smooth ellipses, containing little dust and gas, but composed of millions or trillion stars. Spiral galaxies are disk-shaped and have extending arms that rotate around its dense center. Earth's galaxy is found in the Milky Way and it is a spiral galaxy.

Weather

Seasonal change on Earth is caused by the orbit and axial tilt of the planet in relation to the Sun's Ecliptic: the rotational path of the Sun. These factors combine to vary the degree of insolation (distribution of solar energy) at a particular location and thereby change the seasons.

World weather patterns are greatly influenced by ocean surface currents in the upper layer of the ocean. These currents continuously move along the ocean surface in specific directions. Surface currents are caused by winds and classified by temperature. Cold currents originate in the Polar regions and flow through surrounding water that is measurably warmer. Those currents with a higher temperature than the surrounding water are called warm currents and can be found near the **equator**. These currents follow swirling routes around the ocean basins and the equator. The Gulf Stream and the California Current are the two main surface currents that flow along the coastlines of the United States. The California Current is a cold current that originates in the Arctic regions and flows southward along the western coast of the United States.

A **thunderstorm** is a brief, local storm produced by the rapid upward movement of warm, moist air within a cumulonimbus cloud. Thunderstorms always produce lightning and thunder, and are accompanied by strong wind gusts and heavy rain or hail.

A severe storm with swirling winds that may reach speeds of hundreds of km per hour is called a **tornado**. Such a storm is also referred to as a "twister". Large cumulonimbus clouds cover the sky and violent thunderstorms occur. A funnel-shaped swirling cloud may extend downward from a cumulonimbus cloud and reach the ground. Tornadoes are storms that leave a narrow path of destruction on the ground.

Hurricanes are storms that develop when warm, moist air carried by trade winds rotates around a low-pressure "eye". A large, rotating, low-pressure system accompanied by heavy precipitation and strong winds is called a tropical cyclone (better known as a hurricane). In the Pacific region, a hurricane is called a typhoon.

Storms that occur only in the winter are known as blizzards or ice storms. A **blizzard** is a storm with strong winds, blowing snow and frigid temperatures. An **ice storm** consists of falling rain that freezes when it strikes the ground, covering everything with a layer of ice.

Minerals

Minerals are natural, non-living solids with a definite chemical composition and a crystalline structure. **Ores** are minerals or rock deposits that can be mined for a profit. **Rocks** are earth materials made of one or more minerals. A **Rock Facies** is a rock group that differs from comparable rocks (as in composition, age, or fossil content).

There are over 3000 minerals in Earth's crust. Minerals are classified by composition. The major groups of minerals are silicates, carbonates, oxides, sulfides, sulfates, and halides. The largest group of minerals is the silicates. Silicates are made of silicon, oxygen, and one or more other elements. This is the most abundant class of minerals on Earth and includes quartz, garnets, micas, and feldspars.

Rocks

Rocks are simply aggregates of minerals. Rocks are classified by their differences in chemical composition and mode of formation. Generally, three classes are recognized: igneous, sedimentary, and metamorphic. However, it is common that one type of rock is transformed into another and this is known as the rock cycle.

Igneous rocks are formed from molten magma. There are two types of igneous rock: volcanic and plutonic. As the name suggests, volcanic rock is formed when magma reaches the Earth's surface as lava. Plutonic rock is also derived from magma, but it is formed when magma cools and crystallizes beneath surface of the Earth. Thus, both types of igneous rock are magma that has cooled either above (volcanic) or below (plutonic) the Earth's crust. Examples of this type of rock include granite and obsidian glass.

Sedimentary rocks are formed by the layered deposition of inorganic and/or organic matter. Layers, or strata, of rock are laid down horizontally to form sedimentary rocks. Sedimentary rocks that form as mineral solutions (i.e., sea water) evaporate are called precipitate. Those that contain the remains of living organisms are termed biogenic. Finally, those that form from the freed fragments of other rocks are called clastic. Because the layers of sedimentary rocks reveal chronology and often contain fossils, these types of rock have been key in helping scientists understand the history of the earth. Chalk, limestone, sandstone, and shale are all examples of sedimentary rock.

Metamorphic rocks are created when rocks are subjected to high temperatures and pressures. The original rock, or protolith, may have been igneous, sedimentary or even an older metamorphic rock. The temperatures and pressures necessary to achieve transformation are higher than those observed on the Earth's surface and are high enough to alter the minerals in the protolith. Because these rocks are formed within the Earth's crust, studying metamorphic rocks gives us clues to conditions in the Earth's mantle. In some metamorphic rocks, different colored bands are apparent. These result from strong pressures being applied from specific directions and is termed foliation. Examples of metamorphic rock include slate and marble.

Fossil

A fossil is the trace or remains of any once living organism. The preservation of fossils in the environment is not all that common an occurrence. Although there is no formally set time limit to be considered a fossil, the term is not usually applied to remains less than 100 years old. Although soft tissues can be fossilized, they are very rare. If preserved, the fossil is usually found as hard points. Bones and shells are the most fossilized parts of the organism. Rapid burial is a major factor in fossilization. It helps to keep scavengers at bay and bacterial decay at a minimum. 99% of all fossils are found in sedimentary rock. The heat present in forming Igneous and Metamorphic rock generally obliterates organic remains.

Water

The unique properties of water are partially responsible for the development of life on Earth. Many of the unique qualities of water stem from the hydrogen bonds that form between the molecules. Hydrogen bonds are particularly strong dipole-dipole interactions that form between the H-atom of one molecule and an F, O, or N atom of an adjacent molecule. The partial positive charge on the hydrogen atom is attracted to the partial negative charge on the electron pair of the other atom. The hydrogen bond between two water molecules is shown as the dashed line below:

Erosion is the inclusion and transportation of surface materials by another moveable material, usually water, wind, or ice. The most important cause of erosion is running water. Streams, rivers, and tides are constantly at work removing weathered fragments of bedrock and carrying them away from their original location.

A stream erodes bedrock by the grinding action of the sand, pebbles and other rock fragments. This grinding against each other is called abrasion. Streams also erode rocks by dissolving or absorbing their minerals. Limestone and marble are readily dissolved by streams.

The breaking down of rocks at or near to the Earth's surface is known as **weathering**. Weathering breaks down these rocks into smaller and smaller pieces. There are two types of weathering: physical weathering and chemical weathering.

Physical weathering is the process by which rocks are broken down into smaller fragments without undergoing any change in chemical composition. Physical weathering is mainly caused by the freezing of water, the expansion of rock, and the activities of plants and animals.

Frost wedging is the cycle of daytime thawing and refreezing at night. This cycle causes large rock masses, especially the rocks exposed on mountain tops, to be broken into smaller pieces.

Chemical weathering is the breaking down of rocks through changes in their chemical composition. An example would be the change of feldspar in granite to clay. Water, oxygen, and carbon dioxide are the main agents of chemical weathering. When water and carbon dioxide combine chemically, they produce a weak acid that breaks down rocks.

Deposition, also known as sedimentation, is the term for the process by which material from one area is slowly deposited into another area. This is usually due to the movement of wind, water, or ice containing particles of matter. When the rate of movement slows down, particles filter out and remain behind, causing a build up of matter. Note that this is a result of matter being eroded and removed from another site.

Skill 11.2 Applying knowledge of scientific processes (e.g., observing, hypothesizing, experimenting)

Science may be defined as a body of knowledge that is systematically derived from study, observations and experimentation. Its goal is to identify and establish principles and theories that may be applied to solve problems.

Scientific inquiry begins with observation. Observation is a very important skill by itself, since it leads to experimentation and finally communicating the experimental findings to the society / public. After observing, a question is formed, which starts with "why" or "how." To answer these questions, experimentation is necessary. Between observation and experimentation, there are three more important steps. These are gathering information (or researching about the problem), developing a hypothesis, and designing the experiment.

As much information as possible is collected from various sources including the internet, books, journals, knowledgeable people, newspapers, etc. This lays a solid foundation for formulating a hypothesis. The third step is hypothesizing. This is making a statement about the problem with the knowledge acquired and using the two important words 'if' and 'when'. This is an educated guess about the answer to the problem or question. The 'best guess' is your hypothesis.

Designing an experiment is involves identifying a control, constants, independent variables and dependent variables. A control or standard is something we compare our results with at the end of the experiment. It is a reference. Constants are the factors we have to keep constant in an experiment to get reliable results. Independent variables are factors we change in an experiment. It is very important to bear in mind that there should be more constants than variables to obtain reproducible results in an experiment.

TEACHER CERTIFICATION STUDY GUIDE

Classifying is grouping items according to their similarities. It is important for students to realize relationships and similarity as well as differences to reach a reasonable conclusion in a lab experience. After the experiment is done, it is repeated and results are graphically presented. The results are then analyzed and conclusions drawn. It is the responsibility of the scientists to share the knowledge they obtain through their research.

After the conclusion is drawn, the final step is communication. In this age, lot of emphasis is put on the way and the method of communication. The conclusions must be communicated by clearly describing the information using accurate data, visual presentation like graphs (bar/line/pie), tables/charts, diagrams, artwork, and other appropriate media like power point presentation. Modern technology must be used whenever it is necessary. The method of communication must be suitable to the audience. Written communication is as important as oral communication.

Skill 11.3   Recognizing the roles of exploration, active engagement, inquiry, and questioning in building knowledge, language, and concepts related to science

In the Classroom

Learning can be broadly divided into two kinds - active and passive. Active learning involves, as the name indicates, a learning atmosphere full of action whereas in passive learning students are taught in a non-stimulating and inactive atmosphere. Active learning involves and draws students into it, thereby interesting them to the point of participating and purposely engaging in learning.

It is crucial that students are actively engaged, not entertained. They should be taught the answers for "How" and "Why" questions and encouraged to be inquisitive and interested.

Active learning is conceptualized as follows:

A Model of Active Learning

Experience of	Dialogue with
Doing	Self
Observing	Others

This model suggests that all learning activities involve some kind of experience or some kind of dialogue. The two main kinds of dialogue are "Dialogue with self" and "Dialogue with others". The two main kinds of experience are "Observing" and "Doing".

Dialogue with self: This is what happens when a learner thinks reflectively about a topic. They ask themselves a number of things about the topic.

Dialogue with others: When the students are listening to a book being read by another student or when the teacher is teaching, a partial dialogue takes place because the dialogue is only one sided. When they are listening to an adult and when there is an exchange of ideas back and forth, it is said to be a dialogue with others.

Observing: This is a most important skill in science. This occurs when a learner is carefully watching or observing someone else doing an activity or experiment. This is a good experience, although it is not quite like doing it for themselves.

Doing: This refers to any activity where a learner actually does something, giving the learner a firsthand experience that is very valuable.

The scientific attitude is to be curious, open to new ideas, and skeptical. In science, there is always new research, new discoveries, and new theories proposed. Sometimes, old theories are disproved. To view these changes rationally, one must have such openness, curiosity, and skepticism. (Skepticism is a Greek word, meaning a method of obtaining knowledge through systematic doubt and continual testing. A scientific skeptic is one who refuses to accept certain types of claims without subjecting them to a systematic investigation.)

The students may not have these attitudes inherently, but it is the responsibility of the teacher to encourage, nurture, and practice these attitudes so that students will have a good role model.

In the Laboratory

Observations, however general they may seem, lead scientists to create a viable question and an educated guess (hypothesis) about what to expect. While scientists often have laboratories set up to study a specific thing, it is likely that along the way they will find an unexpected result. It is always important to be open-minded and to look at all of the information. An open-minded approach to science provides room for more questioning, and, hence, more learning. A central concept in science is that all evidence is empirical. This means that all evidence must be is observed by the five senses. The phenomenon must be both observable and measurable, with reproducible results.

The question stage of scientific inquiry involves repetition. By repeating the experiment you can discover whether or not you have reproducibility. If results are reproducible, the hypothesis is valid. If the results are not reproducible, one has more questions to ask. It is also important to recognize that one experiment is often a stepping-stone for another. It is possible that data will be re-tested (by the same scientist or by another), and that a different conclusion may be found. In this way, scientific competition acts as a system of checks and balances.

Scientific theory and experimentation can be disproved and is capable of change. Science depends on communication, agreement, and disagreement among scientists. It is composed of hypotheses, theories, and laws.

hypothesis - an unproved theory or educated guess followed by research to best explain a phenomena. A theory is a proven hypothesis.

theory - the formation of principles or relationships which have been verified and accepted.

law - an explanation of events that occur with uniformity under the same conditions (laws of nature, law of gravitation).

Science is limited by the available technology. An example of this would be the relationship of the discovery of the cell and the invention of the microscope. As our technology improves, more hypotheses will become theories and possibly laws. Science is also limited by the data that is able to be collected. Data may be interpreted differently on different occasions. Science limitations cause explanations to be changeable as new technologies emerge.

Skill 11.4 Demonstrating knowledge of learning experiences for promoting understanding of science concepts and acquisition of science skills

There are two important things in teaching science. The first is theory- explaining the lesson and answering why, how, when, what and which (out of these five, why and how are the most important and useful to gain knowledge). The second is practical exploration, which implies doing an activity and gaining knowledge by experimentation. Both need to be balanced. Only then will a student fully understand science properly.

Linking of ideas is important because the students' prior knowledge is taken into consideration. Based on the prior knowledge of the students, the next step of instruction is planned. When students do not have the expected grade level knowledge, action must be taken to remedy the situation. Otherwise, the students will not be able to benefit. In science each lesson builds upon the next and previous comprehension is critical. For example, students studying life science can not understand organ systems if they do not understand that cells make up tissue, tissue makes up organs, and organs work together in systems.

Inquiry based instruction is becoming popular because the students have questions which must be answered. They need to be encouraged to ask questions and create opportunities to find answers for those questions. The best way to find answers for some of their questions is to let them investigate, experiment and discover for themselves the answers to their questions.

> **For further information on inquiry-based instruction:**
>
> http://www.neiu.edu/~middle/Modules/science%20mods/amazon%20components/AmazonComponents2.html

Skill 11.5 Demonstrating knowledge of strategies for encouraging children to develop positive attitudes toward science

Science should be exciting. Teacher behaviors that motivate students include:

- Maintain Success Expectations through teaching, goal setting, establishing connections between effort and outcome, and self-appraisal and reinforcement.
- Have a supply of intrinsic incentives such as rewards, appropriate competition between students, and the value of the academic activities.
- Focus on students' intrinsic motivation through adapting the tasks to students' interests, providing opportunities for active response, including a variety of tasks, providing rapid feedback, incorporating games into the lesson, allowing students the opportunity to make choices, create, and interact with peers.
- Stimulate students' learning by modeling positive expectations and attributions. Project enthusiasm and personalize abstract concepts. Students will be better motivated if they know what they will be learning about. The teacher should also model problem-solving and task-related thinking so students can see how the process is done.

Motivation strategies are usually aimed at getting the student actively involved in the learning process. Motivation may be achieved through extrinsic reinforcers or intrinsic reinforcers. This is accomplished by allowing the student a degree of choice in what is being taught or how it will be taught. The teacher will, if possible, obtain a commitment either through a verbal or written contract between the student and the teacher. Students also respond to regular feedback, especially when that feedback shows that they are making progress. Motivation = learning.

Skill 11.6 Demonstrating knowledge of strategies for encouraging the use of science concepts and skills in everyday life

The science subject being taught should have some practical relevance to their lives. Science has to be contextualized.

For example, students are engaged in an experiment to evaluate which fertilizer is best for their yard. It can be an investigation that leads them to discovering which one is best and also teaches them a bit of economics (cost versus effectiveness). The student is learning two things at the same time. Choosing the reasonably priced product will help him in the long run when he grows up and does budgeting for his family.

Because biology is the study of living things, we can easily apply the knowledge of biology to daily life and personal decision-making. For example, biology greatly influences the health decisions humans make everyday. What foods to eat, when and how to exercise, and how often to bathe are just three of the many decisions we make everyday that are based on our knowledge of biology. Other areas of daily life where biology affects decision-making are parenting, interpersonal relationships, family planning, and consumer spending.

If learning is connected to everyday life, students are motivated because they can easily see its relevance. If they are taught about something remote, they will not be able to relate, and the result is decreased interest, decreased motivation to study, and a general decrease in learning.

> **For more activities for teaching Science to young children:**
>
> http://www-heb.pac.dfo-mpo.gc.ca/community/education/primary/primary_e.htm

DOMAIN III. LEARNING IN THE CONTENT AREAS

Competency 0012   **UNDERSTAND SOCIAL STUDIES CONTENT AND SKILLS AND HOW TO FACILITATE SOCIAL STUDIES LEARNING**

Skill 12.1   **Demonstrating knowledge of basic concepts in geography, history, civics and economics**

Geography involves studying location and how living things and earth's features are distributed throughout the earth. The term geography is defined as the study of earth's features and living things as to their location, relationship with each other, how they came to be there, and why so important. It includes where animals, people, and plants live and the effects of their relationship with earth's physical features. Geographers also explore the locations of earth's features, how they got there, and why it is so important. Another way to describe where people live is by the **geography** and **topography** around them. The vast majority of people on the planet live in areas that are very hospitable. Yes, people live in the Himalayas and in the Sahara, but the populations in those areas are small indeed when compared to the plains of China, India, Europe, and the United States. People naturally want to live where they will not have to work really hard just to survive, and world population patterns reflect this. The six themes of geography are:

Location - including relative and absolute location. A relative location refers to the surrounding geography, e.g., "on the banks of the Mississippi River." Absolute location refers to a specific point, such as 41 degrees North latitude, 90 degrees West longitude, or 123 Main Street.

Every point on Earth has a specific **location** that is determined by an imaginary grid of lines denoting latitude and longitude. Parallels of latitude measure distances north and south of the line called the Equator. Meridians of longitude measure distances east and west of the line called the Prime Meridian. Geographers use latitude and longitude to pinpoint a place's absolute, or exact, location.

To know the absolute location of a place is only part of the story. It is also important to know how that place is related to other places—in other words, to know that place's relative location. Relative location deals with the interaction that occurs between and among places. It refers to the many ways—by land, by water, even by technology—that places are connected.

All places have characteristics that give them meaning and character and distinguish them from other places on earth. Geographers describe places by their physical and human characteristics. Physical characteristics include such elements as animal life. Human characteristics of the landscape can be noted in architecture, patterns of livelihood, land use and ownership, town planning, and communication and transportation networks.

Languages, as well as religious and political ideologies, help shape the character of a place. Studied together, the physical and human characteristics of places provide clues to help students understand the nature of places on the earth.

A basic unit of geographic study is the region, an area on the earth's surface that is defined by certain unifying characteristics. The unifying characteristics may be physical, human, or cultural. In addition to studying the unifying characteristics of a region, geographers study how a region changes over times. Using the theme of regions, geographers divide the world into manageable units for study.

Spatial organization is a description of how things are grouped in a given space. In geographical terms, this can describe people, places, and environments anywhere and everywhere on Earth. The most basic form of spatial organization for people is where they live. The vast majority of people live near other people, in villages and towns and cities and settlements. These people live near others in order to take advantage of the goods and services that naturally arise from cooperation. These villages and towns and cities and settlements are, to varying degrees, near bodies of water.

Place - A place has both human and physical characteristics. Physical characteristics include features such as mountains, rivers, deserts, etc. Human characteristics are the features created by human interaction with their environment such as canals and roads.

Human-Environmental Interaction - The theme of human-environmental interaction has three main concepts: humans adapt to the environment (wearing warm clothing in a cold climate, for instance,) humans modify the environment (planting trees to block a prevailing wind, for example,) and humans depend on the environment (for food, water and raw materials.)

Movement - The theme of movement covers how humans interact with one another through trade, communications, emigration and other forms of interaction.

Regions - A region is an area that has some kind of unifying characteristic, such as a common language, a common government, etc. There are three main types of regions. Formal regions are areas defined by actual political boundaries, such as a city, county, or state. Functional regions are defined by a common function, such as the area covered by a telephone service. Vernacular regions are less formally defined areas that are formed by people's perception, e.g. "the Middle East," and "the South."

Absolute location is the exact whereabouts of a person, place, or thing, according to any kind of geographical indicators you want to name. For example, Paris is at 48 degrees north longitude and 2 degrees east latitude.

Relative location, on the other hand, is *always* a description that involves more than one thing. When you describe a relative location, you tell where something is by describing what is around it. The same description of where the nearest post office is in terms of absolute location might be this: "It's down the street from the supermarket, on the right side of the street, next to the dentist's office

Physical locations of the earth's surface features include the four major hemispheres and the parts of the earth's continents in them. Political locations are the political divisions, if any, within each continent. Both physical and political locations are precisely determined in two *ways:* (1) Surveying is done to determine boundary lines and distance from other features. (2) Exact locations are precisely determined by imaginary lines of latitude (parallels) and longitude (meridians). The intersection of these lines at right angles forms a grid, making it impossible to pinpoint an exact location of any place using any two grip coordinates.

The Eastern Hemisphere, located between the North and South Poles and between the Prime Meridian (0 degrees longitude) east to the International Date Line at 180 degrees longitude, consists of most of Europe, all of Australia, most of Africa, and all of Asia, except for a tiny piece of the easternmost part of Russia that extends east of 180 degrees longitude.

The Western Hemisphere, located between the North and South Poles and between the Prime Meridian (0 degrees longitude) west to the International Date Line at 180 degrees longitude, consists of all of North and South America, a tiny part of the easternmost part of Russia that extends east of 180 degrees longitude, and a part of Europe that extends west of the Prime Meridian (0 degrees longitude).

The Northern Hemisphere, located between the North Pole and the Equator, contains all of the continents of Europe and North America and parts of South America, Africa, and most of Asia.

The Southern Hemisphere, located between the South Pole and the Equator, contains all of Australia, a small part of Asia, about one-third of Africa, most of South America, and all of Antarctica.

Of the seven continents, only one contains just one entire country and is the only island continent, Australia. Its political divisions consist of six states and one territory: Western Australia, South Australia, Tasmania, Victoria, New South Wales, Queensland, and Northern Territory.

Africa is made up of 54 separate countries, the major ones being Egypt, Nigeria, South Africa, Zaire, Kenya, Algeria, Morocco, and the large island of Madagascar.

Asia consists of 49 separate countries, some of which include China, Japan, India, Turkey, Israel, Iraq, Iran, Indonesia, Jordan, Vietnam, Thailand, and the Philippines.

Europe's 43 separate nations include France, Russia, Malta, Denmark, Hungary, Greece, Bosnia and Herzegovina.

North America consists of Canada and the United States of America and the island nations of the West Indies and the "land bridge" of Middle America, including Cuba, Jamaica, Mexico, Panama, and others.

Thirteen separate nations together occupy the continent of South America, among them such nations as Brazil, Paraguay, Ecuador, and Suriname.

The continent of Antarctica has no political boundaries or divisions but is the location of a number of science and research stations managed by nations, such as Russia, Japan, France, Australia, and India.

Physical geography is concerned with the locations of such earth features as climate, water, and land; how these relate to and affect each other and human activities; and what forces shaped and changed them. All three of these earth features affect the lives of all humans having a direct influence on what is made and produced, where it occurs, how it occurs, and what makes it possible. The combination of the different climate conditions and types of landforms and other surface features work together all around the earth to give the many varied cultures their unique characteristics and distinctions.

Cultural geography studies the location, characteristics, and influence of the physical environment on different cultures around the earth. Also included in these studies are comparisons and influences of the many varied cultures. Ease of travel and up-to-the-minute, state-of-the-art communication techniques ease the difficulties of understanding cultural differences making it easier to come in contact with them.

The earth's surface is made up of 70% water and 30% land. Physical features of the land surface include mountains, hills, plateaus, valleys, and plains. Other minor landforms include deserts, deltas, canyons, mesas, basins, foothills, marshes and swamps. Earth's water features include oceans, seas, lakes, rivers, and canals.

Mountains are landforms with rather steep slopes at least 2,000 feet or more above sea level. Mountains are found in groups called mountain chains or mountain ranges. At least one range can be found on six of the earth's seven continents. North America has the Appalachian and Rocky Mountains; South America the Andes; Asia the Himalayas; Australia the Great Dividing Range; Europe the Alps; and Africa the Atlas, Ahaggar, and Drakensburg Mountains.

Hills are elevated landforms rising to an elevation of about 500 to 2000 feet. They are found everywhere on earth including Antarctica where they are covered by ice.

Plateaus are elevated landforms usually level on top. Depending on location, they range from being an area that is very cold to one that is cool and healthful. Some plateaus are dry because they are surrounded by mountains that keep out any moisture. Some examples include the Kenya Plateau in East Africa, which is very cool. The plateau extending north from the Himalayas is extremely dry while those in Antarctica and Greenland are covered with ice and snow.

Plains are described as areas of flat or slightly rolling land, usually lower than the landforms next to them. Sometimes called lowlands (and sometimes located along **seacoasts**) they support the majority of the world's people. Some are found inland and many have been formed by large rivers. This resulted in extremely fertile soil for successful cultivation of crops and numerous large settlements of people. In North America, the vast plains areas extend from the Gulf of Mexico north to the Arctic Ocean and between the Appalachian and Rocky Mountains. In Europe, rich plains extend east from Great Britain into central Europe on into the Siberian region of Russia. Plains in river valleys are found in China (the Yangtze River valley), India (the Ganges River valley), and Southeast Asia (the Mekong River valley).

Valleys are land areas found between hills and mountains. Some have gentle slopes containing trees and plants; others have steep walls and are referred to as canyons. One example is Arizona's Grand Canyon of the Colorado River.

Deserts are large dry areas of land receiving ten inches or less of rainfall each year. Among the better-known deserts are Africa's large Sahara Desert, the Arabian Desert on the Arabian Peninsula, and the desert outback covering roughly one third of Australia.

Deltas are areas of lowlands formed by soil and sediment deposited at the mouths of rivers. The soil is generally very fertile and most fertile river deltas are important crop-growing areas. One well-known example is the delta of Egypt's Nile River, known for its production of cotton.

Mesas are the flat tops of hills or mountains usually with steep sides. Sometimes plateaus are also called mesas. Basins are considered to be low areas drained by rivers or low spots in mountains. Foothills are generally considered a low series of hills found between a plain and a mountain range. Marshes and swamps are wet lowlands providing growth of such plants as rushes and reeds.

Oceans are the largest bodies of water on the planet. The four oceans of the earth are the **Atlantic Ocean**, one-half the size of the Pacific and separating North and South America from Africa and Europe; the **Pacific Ocean**, covering almost one-third of the entire surface of the earth and separating North and South America from Asia and Australia; the **Indian Ocean**, touching Africa, Asia, and Australia; and the ice-filled **Arctic Ocean,** extending from North America and Europe to the North Pole. The waters of the Atlantic, Pacific, and Indian Oceans also touch the shores of Antarctica.

Seas are smaller than oceans and are surrounded by land. Some examples include the Mediterranean Sea found between Europe, Asia, and Africa; and the Caribbean Sea, touching the West Indies, South and Central America. A lake is a body of water surrounded by land. The Great Lakes in North America are a good example.

Rivers, considered a nation's lifeblood, usually begin as very small streams, formed by melting snow and rainfall, flowing from higher to lower land, emptying into a larger body of water, usually a sea or an ocean. Examples of important rivers for the people and countries affected by and/or dependent on them include the Nile, Niger, and Zaire Rivers of Africa; the Rhine, Danube, and Thames Rivers of Europe; the Yangtze, Ganges, Mekong, Hwang He, and Irrawaddy Rivers of Asia; the Murray-Darling in Australia; and the Orinoco in South America. River systems are made up of large rivers and numerous smaller rivers or tributaries flowing into them. Examples include the vast Amazon Rivers system in South America and the Mississippi River system in the United States.

Canals are man-made water passages constructed to connect two larger bodies of water. Famous examples include the **Panama Canal** across Panama's isthmus connecting the Atlantic and Pacific Oceans and the **Suez Canal** in the Middle East between Africa and the Arabian Peninsula connecting the Red and Mediterranean Seas.

Weather is the condition of the air, which surrounds the day-to-day atmospheric conditions including temperature, air pressure, wind and moisture or precipitation, which includes rain, snow, hail, or sleet.

Climate is average weather or daily weather conditions for a specific region or location over a long or extended period of time. Studying the climate of an area includes information gathered on the area's monthly and yearly temperatures and its monthly and yearly amounts of precipitation. In addition, a characteristic of an area's climate is the length of its growing season. Four reasons for the different climate regions on the earth are differences in:

- Latitude,
- The amount of moisture,
- Temperatures in land and water, and
- The earth's land surface.

There are many different climates throughout the earth. It is most unusual if a country contains just one kind of climate. Regions of climates are divided according to latitudes:

0 - 23 1/2 degrees are the "low latitudes"
23 1/2 - 66 1/2 degrees are the "middle latitudes"
66 1/2 degrees to the Poles are the "high latitudes"

The **low latitudes** are comprised of the rainforest, savanna, and desert climates. The tropical rainforest climate is found in equatorial lowlands and is hot and wet. There is sun, extreme heat and rain--everyday. Although daily temperatures rarely rise above 90 degrees F, the daily humidity is always high, leaving everything sticky and damp. North and south of the tropical rainforests are the tropical grasslands called "savannas," the "lands of two seasons"--a winter dry season and a summer wet season. Further north and south of the tropical grasslands or savannas are the deserts. These areas are the hottest and driest parts of the earth receiving less than 10 inches of rain a year. These areas have extreme temperatures between night and day. After the sun sets, the land cools quickly dropping the temperature as much as 50 degrees F.

The **middle latitudes** contain the Mediterranean, humid-subtropical, humid-continental, marine, steppe, and desert climates. Lands containing the Mediterranean climate are considered "sunny" lands found in six areas of the world: lands bordering the Mediterranean Sea, a small portion of southwestern Africa, areas in southern and southwestern Australia, a small part of the Ukraine near the Black Sea, central Chile, and Southern California. Summers are hot and dry with mild winters. The growing season usually lasts all year and what little rain falls are during the winter months. What is rather unusual is that the Mediterranean climate is located between 30 and 40 degrees north and south latitude on the western coasts of countries.

The humid **subtropical climate** is found north and south of the tropics and is moist indeed. The areas having this type of climate are found on the eastern side of their continents and include Japan, mainland China, Australia, Africa, South America, and the United States--the southeastern coasts of these areas. An interesting feature of their locations is that warm ocean currents are found there. The winds that blow across these currents bring in warm moist air all year round. Long, warm summers; short, mild winters; a long growing season allow for different crops to be grown several times a year. All contribute to the productivity of this climate type, which supports more people than any of the other climates.

Most places in the world are in some manner close to agricultural land as well. Food makes the world go round and some cities are more agriculturally inclined than others. Rare is the city, however, that grows absolutely no crops. The kind of food grown is almost entirely dependent on the kind of land available and the climate surrounding that land. Rice doesn't grow well in the desert, for instance, nor do bananas grow well in snowy lands. Certain crops are easier to transport than others and the ones that aren't are usually grown near ports or other areas of export.

Settlements begin in areas that offer the natural resources to support life – food and water. With the ability to manage the environment one finds a concentration of populations. With the ability to transport raw materials and finished products, comes mobility. With increasing technology and the rise of industrial centers, comes a migration of the workforce.

Cities are the major hubs of human settlement. Almost half of the population of the world now lives in cities. These percentages are much higher in developed regions. Established cities continue to grow. The fastest growth, however, is occurring in developing areas. In some regions there are "metropolitan areas" made up of urban and sub-urban areas. In some places cities and urban areas have become interconnected into "megalopoli" (e.g., Tokyo-Kawasaki-Yokohama).

The concentrations of populations and the divisions of these areas among various groups that constitute the cities can differ significantly. North American cities are different from European cities in terms of shape, size, population density, and modes of transportation. While in North America, the wealthiest economic groups tend to live outside the cities, the opposite is true in Latin American cities.

There are significant differences among the cities of the world in terms of connectedness to other cities. While European and North American cities tend to be well linked both by transportation and communication connections, there are other places in the world in which communication between the cities of the country may be inferior to communication with the rest of the world.

Rural areas tend to be less densely populated due to the needs of agriculture. More land is needed to produce crops or for animal husbandry than for manufacturing, especially in a city in which the buildings tend to be taller. Rural areas, however, must be connected via communication and transportation in order to provide food and raw materials to urban areas.

Civics

Citizenship in a democracy bestows on an individual certain rights, foremost being the right to participate in one's own government. Along with these rights come responsibilities, including the responsibility of a citizen to participate.

The most basic form of participation is the vote. Those who have reached the age of 18 in the US are eligible to vote in public elections. With this right comes the responsibility to be informed before voting, and not to sell or otherwise give away one's vote. Citizens are also eligible to run for public office. Along with the right to run for office comes the responsibility to represent the electors as fairly as possible and to perform the duties expected of a government representative.

In the United States, citizens are guaranteed the right to free speech; the right to express an opinion on public issues. In turn, citizens have the responsibility to allow others to speak freely. At the community level, this might mean speaking at a city council hearing while allowing others with different or opposing viewpoints to have their say without interruption or comment.

The US Constitution also guarantees freedom of religion. This means that the government may not impose an official religion on its citizens, and that people are free to practice their religion. Citizens are also responsible for allowing those of other religions to practice freely without obstruction. Occasionally, religious issues will be put before the public at the state level in the form of ballot measures or initiatives. To what extent it should be acceptable for religious beliefs to be expressed in a public setting, such as a public school, is an issue that has been debated recently.

In making decisions on matters like these, the citizen is expected to take responsibility to become informed of the issues involved and to make his vote based on his own opinion. Being informed of how one's government works and what the effects of new legislation will be is an essential part of being a good citizen.

The US Constitution also guarantees that all citizens be treated equally by the law. In addition, federal and state laws make it a crime to discriminate against citizens based on their sex, race, religion and other factors. To ensure that all people are treated equally, citizens have the responsibility to follow these laws.

These rights and responsibilities are essentially the same whether one is voting in a local school board race, for the passage of a new state law, or for the President of the United States. Being a good citizen means exercising one's own rights while allowing others to do the same.

A person who lives in a democratic society theoretically has an entire laundry list guaranteed to him or her by the government. In the United States, this is the Constitution and its Amendments. Among these very important rights are:

- the right to speak out in public;
- the right to pursue any religion;
- the right for a group of people to gather in public for *any* reason that doesn't fall under a national security cloud;
- the right *not* to have soldiers stationed in your home;
- the right *not* to be forced to testify against yourself in a court of law;
- the right to a speedy and public trial by a jury of your peers;
- the right *not* to the victim of cruel and unusual punishment;
- and the right to avoid unreasonable search and seizure of your person, your house, and your vehicle.

The terms "civil liberties" and "civil rights" are often used interchangeably, but there are some fine distinctions between the two terms. The term civil liberties is used to imply that the state has a positive role to play in assuring that all its' citizens will have equal protection and justice under the law. The term implies equal opportunities to exercise their privileges of citizenship and to participate fully in the life of the nation, regardless of race, religion, sex, color or creed. The term civil rights is used more often to refer to rights that may be described as guarantees that are specified as against the state authority implying limitations on the actions of the state to interfere with citizens' liberties. Although the term "civil rights" has thus been identified with the ideal of equality and the term "civil liberties" with the idea of freedom, the two concepts are really inseparable and interacting. Equality implies the proper ordering of liberty in a society so that one individual's freedom does not infringe on the rights of others.

The beginnings of civil liberties and the idea of civil rights in the United States go back to the ideas of the Greeks. The early British struggle for civil rights and to the very philosophies that led people to come to the New World in the first place. Religious freedom, political freedom, and the right to live one's life as one sees fit are basic to the American ideal. These were embodied in the ideas expressed in the Declaration of Independence and the Constitution.

All these ideas found their final expression in the United States Constitution's first ten amendments, known as the Bill of Rights. In 1789, the first Congress passed these first amendments and by December 1791, three-fourths of the states at that time had ratified them. The Bill of Rights protects certain liberties and basic rights. James Madison who wrote the amendments said that the Bill of Rights does not give Americans these rights. People, Madison said, already have these rights. They are natural rights that belong to all human beings. The Bill of Rights simply prevents the governments from taking away these rights.

Federal laws are passed by the Congress, and can originate in either the House of Representatives or the Senate.

The first step in the passing of a law is for the proposed law to be introduced in one of the houses of Congress. When a proposed law is under consideration by Congress, it is called a **bill**. A bill can be introduced, or sponsored, by a member of Congress by giving a copy to the clerk or by placing a copy in a special box called a hopper.

Once a bill is introduced, copies are printed and it is assigned to one of several standing committees of the house in which it was introduced. The committee studies the bill and performs research on the issues it would cover. Committees may call experts to testify on the bill and gather public comments. The committee may revise the bill. Finally, the committee votes on whether to release the bill to be voted on by the full body. A committee may also lay aside a bill so that it cannot be voted on. Once a bill is released, it can be debated and amended by the full body before being voted on. If it passes by a simple majority vote, the bill is sent to the other house of Congress, where the process begins again.

Once a bill has passed both the House of Representatives and the Senate, it is assigned to a conference committee that is made up of members of both houses. The conference committee resolves differences between the House and Senate versions of a bill, if any, and then sends it back to both houses for final approval. Once a bill receives final approval, it is signed by the Speaker of the House and the Vice President, who is also the President of the Senate, and sent to the President for consideration. The President may either sign the bill or **veto** it. If he vetoes the bill, his veto may be overruled if two-thirds of both the Senate and the House vote to do so. Once the President signs it the bill becomes a law.

The executive branch and its departments enforce federal laws. The Department of Justice, led by the United States Attorney General is the primary law enforcement department of the federal government. Other investigative and enforcement departments such as the Federal Bureau of Investigation (FBI) and the U.S. Postal Inspectors aid the Justice Department.

The U.S. Constitution and Congressional laws provide basic as well as additional rights to American citizens. These civil rights include freedom of religion, assembly, speech, voting, holding public office, and traveling throughout the country. U.S. citizens have the right to live in America and cannot be forced to leave. American citizenship is guaranteed and will not be taken away for any reason, unless one commits certain serious actions. Civil rights have limitations such as minimum age for voting and limited free speech, forbidding the damage to someone's reputation by slander and lying.

Popular sovereignty grants citizens the ability to directly participate in their own government by voting and running for public office. This ideal is based on a belief of equality that holds that all citizens have an equal right to engage in their own governance, and is established in the United States Constitution. The Constitution also contains a list of specific rights that citizens have, and which the government cannot infringe upon. Popular sovereignty also allows for citizens to change their government if they feel it is necessary. This was the driving ideal behind the Declaration of Independence and is embodied in the governmental structure laid out in the Constitution.

The **rule of law** is the ideal that the law applies not only to the governed, but to the government as well. This core value gives authority to the justice system, which grants citizens protection from the government by requiring that any accusation of a crime be proved by the government before a person is punished. This is called due process and ensures that any accused person will have an opportunity to confront his accusers and provide a defense. Due process follows from the core value of a right to liberty. The government cannot take away a citizen's liberty without reason or without proof. The correlating ideal is also a core value - that someone who does harm another or break a law will receive justice under the democratic system. The ideal of justice holds that a punishment will fit the crime, and that any citizen can appeal to the judicial system if he feels he has been wronged.

Citizens' duties also vary from nation to nation. Duties demanded by law (also considered civic responsibilities) include paying taxes, obeying laws, and defending the country. Although some governments require jury duty, in the United States this would be a duty not required by law along with voting, doing volunteer work to help others, and becoming aware of public problems.

Citizenship is granted one of two ways: either by birth or by naturalization. Some Americans hold dual citizenship.

Historical concepts are movements, belief systems or other phenomena that can be identified and examined individually or as part of a historical theme. Capitalism, communism, democracy, racism and globalization are all examples of historical concepts. Historical concepts can be interpreted as part of larger historical themes and provide insight into historical events by placing them in a larger historical context.

Almost all representative democracies in the world guarantee similar rights to their citizens, and expect them to take similar responsibilities to respect the rights of others. As a citizen of the world one is expected to respect the rights of other nations, and the people of those nations, in the same way.

Social studies provide an opportunity for students to broaden their general academic skills in many areas. By encouraging students to ask and investigate questions, they gain skill in making meaningful inquiries into social issues. Providing them with a range of sources requires students to make judgments about the best sources for investigating a line of inquiry and develops the ability to determine authenticity among those sources. Collaboration develops the ability to work as part of a team and to respect the viewpoints of others.

Historic events and social issues cannot be considered only in isolation. People and their actions are connected in many ways, and events are linked through cause and effect over time. Identifying and analyzing these social and historic links is a primary goal of the social sciences. The methods used to analyze social phenomena borrow from several of the social sciences. Interviews, statistical evaluation, observation and experimentation are just some of the ways that people's opinions and motivations can be measured. From these opinions, larger social beliefs and movements can be interpreted, and events, issues and social problems can be placed in context to provide a fuller view of their importance.

Economics

Economics is the study of how a society allocates its scarce resources to satisfy what are basically unlimited and competing wants. A fundamental fact of economics is that resources are scarce and that wants are infinite. The fact that scarce resources have to satisfy unlimited wants means that choices have to be made. If society uses its resources to produce good A then it doesn't have those resources to produce good B. More of good A means less of good B. This trade-off is referred to as the opportunity cost, or the value of the sacrificed alternative.

Economic systems refer to the arrangements a society has devised to answer what are known as the Three Questions: What goods to produce, How to produce the goods, and For Whom are the goods being produced, or how is the allocation of the output determined. Different economic systems answer these questions in different ways. These are the different "isms" that exist that define the method of resource and output allocation. A **market economy** answers these questions in terms of demand and supply and the use of markets. **Demand** is based on consumer preferences and satisfaction and refers to the quantities of a good or service that buyers are willing and able to buy at different prices during a given period of time. **Supply** is based on costs of production and refers to the quantities that sellers are willing and able to sell at different prices during a given period of time. The determination of market equilibrium price is where the buying decisions of buyers coincide with the selling decision of sellers

Consumers vote for the products they want with their dollar spending. Goods acquiring enough dollar votes are profitable, signaling to the producers that society wants their scarce resources used in this way. This is how the "What" question is answered. The producer then hires inputs in accordance with the goods consumers want, looking for the most efficient or lowest cost method of production. The lower the firm's costs for any given level of revenue, the higher the firm's profits. This is the way in which the "How" question is answered in a market economy. The "For Whom" question is answered in the marketplace by the determination of the equilibrium price. Price serves to ration the good to those who can and will transact at the market price of better. Those who can't or won't are excluded from the market. This mechanism results in market efficiency or obtaining the most output from the available inputs that are consistent with the preferences of consumers. Society's scarce resources are being used the way society wants them to be used.

Skill 12.2 Demonstrating knowledge of social studies skills (e.g., mapping, research)

We use **illustrations** of various sorts because it is often easier to demonstrate a given idea visually instead of orally. Sometimes it is even easier to do so with an illustration than a description. This is especially true in the areas of education and research because humans are visually stimulated. It is a fact that any idea presented visually in some manner is always easier to understand and to comprehend than simply getting an idea across verbally, by hearing it or reading it. Among the more common illustrations used are various types of **maps, graphs and charts**.

Photographs and globes are useful as well, but as they are limited in what kind of information that they can show, they are rarely used. Unless, as in the case of a photograph, it is of a particular political figure or a time that one wishes to visualize.

Although maps have advantages over globes and photographs, they do have a major disadvantage. This problem must be considered as well. The major problem of all maps comes about because most maps are flat and the Earth is a sphere. It is impossible to reproduce exactly on a flat surface an object shaped like a sphere. In order to put the earth's features onto a map they must be stretched in some way. This stretching is called **distortion.**

Distortion does not mean that maps are wrong it simply means that they are not perfect representations of the Earth or its parts. **Cartographers,** or mapmakers, understand the problems of distortion. They try to design them so that there is as little distortion as possible in the maps.

The process of putting the features of the Earth onto a flat surface is called **projection**. All maps are really map projections. There are many different types. Each one deals in a different way with the problem of distortion. Map projections are made in a number of ways. Some are done using complicated mathematics. However, the basic ideas behind map projections can be understood by looking at the three most common types:

(1) **Cylindrical Projections** - These are done by taking a cylinder of paper and wrapping it around a globe. A light is used to project the globe's features onto the paper. Distortion is least where the paper touches the globe. For example, suppose that the paper was wrapped so that it touched the globe at the equator, the map from this projection would have just a little distortion near the equator. However, in moving north or south of the equator, the distortion would increase as you moved further away from the equator. The best-known and most widely used cylindrical projection is the **Mercator Projection**, which was first developed in 1569 by Gerardus Mercator, a Flemish mapmaker.

(2) **Conical Projections** - The name for these maps come from the fact that the projection is made onto a cone of paper. The cone is made so that it touches a globe at the base of the cone only. It can also be made so that it cuts through part of the globe in two different places. Again, there is the least distortion where the paper touches the globe. If the cone touches at two different points, there is some distortion at both of them. Conical projections are most often used to map areas in the **middle latitudes**. Maps of the United States are most often conical projections. This is because most of the country lies within these latitudes.

(3) **Flat-Plane Projections** - These are made with a flat piece of paper. It touches the globe at one point only. Areas near this point show little distortion. Flat-plane projections are often used to show the areas of the north and south poles. One such flat projection is called a **Gnomonic Projection**. On this kind of map all meridians appear as straight lines, Gnomonic projections are useful because any straight line drawn between points on it forms a **Great-Circle Route**.

Great-Circle Routes can best be described by thinking of a globe and when using the globe the shortest route between two points on it can be found by simply stretching a string from one point to the other. However, if the string was extended in reality, so that it took into effect the globe's curvature, it would then make a great-circle. A Great-Circle is any circle that cuts a sphere, such as the globe, into two equal parts. Because of distortion, most maps do not show great-circle routes as straight lines, Gnomonic projections, however, do show the shortest distance between the two places as a straight line, because of this they are valuable for navigation. They are called Great-Circle Sailing Maps.

To properly analyze a given map one must be familiar with the various parts and symbols that most modern maps use. For the most part, this is standardized, with different maps using similar parts and symbols, these can include:

The Title - All maps should have a title, just like all books should. The title tells you what information is to be found on the map.

The Legend - Most maps have a legend. A legend tells the reader about the various symbols that are used on that particular map and what the symbols represent, (also called a *map key*).

The Grid - A grid is a series of lines that are used to find exact places and locations on the map. There are several different kinds of grid systems in use, however, most maps do use the longitude and latitude system, known as the **Geographic Grid System**.

Directions - Most maps have some directional system to show which way the map is being presented. Often on a map, a small compass will be present, with arrows showing the four basic directions, north, south, east, and west.

The Scale - This is used to show the relationship between a unit of measurement on the map versus the real world measure on the Earth. Maps are drawn to many different scales. Some maps show a lot of detail for a small area. Others show a greater span of distance, whichever is being used one should always be aware of just what scale is being used. For instance the scale might be something like 1 inch = 10 miles for a small area or for a map showing the whole world it might have a scale in which 1 inch = 1,000 miles. The point is that one must look at the map key in order to see what units of measurements the map is using.

Maps have four main properties. They are (1) the size of the areas shown on the map. (2) The shapes of the areas, (3) Consistent scales, and (4) Straight line directions. A map can be drawn so that it is correct in one or more of these properties. No map can be correct in all of them.

Equal areas - One property that maps can have is that of equal areas, In an equal area map, the meridians and parallels are drawn so that the areas shown have the same proportions as they do on the Earth. For example, Greenland is about 1eighteenth the size of South America, thus it will be show as 1eighteenth the size on an equal area map. The **Mercator projection** is an example of a map that does not have equal areas. In it, Greenland appears to be about the same size of South America. This is because the distortion is very bad at the poles and Greenland lies near the North Pole.

Conformality - A second map property is conformality, or correct shapes. There are no maps hat can show very large areas of the earth in their exact shapes. Only globes can really do that, however Conformal Maps are as close as possible to true shapes. A Lambert Conformal Conic Projection Map is often used to show the United States.

Consistent Scales - Many maps attempt to use the same scale on all parts of the map. Generally, this is easier when maps show a relatively small part of the earth's surface. For example, a map of Florida might be a Consistent Scale Map. Generally maps showing large areas are not consistent-scale maps. This is so because of distortion. Often such maps will have two scales noted in the key. One scale, for example, might be accurate to measure distances between points along the Equator. Another might be then used to measure distances between the North Pole and the South Pole.

Maps showing physical features often try to show information about the elevation or *relief* of the land. *Elevation* is the distance above or below the sea level. The elevation is usually shown with colors, for instance, all areas on a map which are at a certain level will be shown in the same color.

Relief Maps - Show the shape of the land surface, flat, rugged, or steep. Relief maps usually give more detail than simply showing the overall elevation of the land's surface. Relief is also sometimes shown with colors, but another way to show relief is by using **contour lines**. These lines connect all points of a land surface which are the same height surrounding the particular area of land.
Thematic Maps - These are used to show more specific information, often on a single *theme,* or topic. Thematic maps show the distribution or amount of something over a certain given area. Things such as population density, climate, economic information, cultural, political information, etc ...

Information can be gained looking at a map that might take hundreds of words to explain otherwise. Maps reflect the great variety of knowledge covered by political science. To show such a variety of information maps are made in many different ways. Because of this variety, maps must be understood in order to make the best sense of them.

Spatial organization is a description of how things are grouped in a given space. In geographical terms, this can describe people, places, and environments anywhere and everywhere on Earth.

The most basic form of spatial organization for people is where they live. The vast majority of people live near other people, in villages and towns and cities and settlements. These people live near others in order to take advantage of the goods and services that naturally arise from cooperation. These villages and towns and cities and settlements are, to varying degrees, near bodies of water. Water is a staple of survival for every person on the planet and is also a good source of energy for factories and other industries, as well as a form of transportation for people and goods.

Another way to describe where people live is by the **geography** and **topography** around them. The vast majority of people on the planet live in areas that are very hospitable. Yes, people live in the Himalayas and in the Sahara, but the populations in those areas are small indeed when compared to the plains of China, India, Europe, and the United States. People naturally want to live where they won't have to work really hard just to survive, and world population patterns reflect this.

We can examine the spatial organization of the places where people live. For example, in a city, where are the factories and heavy industry buildings? Are they near airports or train stations? Are they on the edge of town, near major roads? What about housing developments? Are they near these industries, or are they far away? Where are the other industry buildings? Where are the schools and hospitals and parks? What about the police and fire stations? How close are homes to each of these things? Towns and especially cities are routinely organized into neighborhoods, so that each house or home is near to most things that its residents might need on a regular basis. This means that large cities have multiple schools, hospitals, grocery stores, fire stations, etc.

Demography is the branch of science of statistics most concerned with the social well being of people. **Demographic tables** may include: (1) Analysis of the population on the basis of age, parentage, physical condition, race, occupation and civil position, giving the actual size and the density of each separate area. (2) Changes in the population as a result of birth, marriage, and death. (3) Statistics on population movements and their effects and their relations to given economic, social and political conditions. (4) Statistics of crime, illegitimacy and suicide. (5) Levels of education and economic and social statistics.

Such information is also similar to that area of science known as **vital statistics** and as such is indispensable in studying social trends and making important legislative, economic, and social decisions. Such demographic information is gathered from census, and registrar reports and the like, and by state laws such information, especially the vital kind, is kept by physicians, attorneys, funeral directors, member of the clergy, and similar professional people. In the United States such demographic information is compiled, kept and published by the Public Health Service of the United States Department of Health, Education, and Welfare.

The most important element of this information is the so-called **rate**, which customarily represents the average of births and deaths for a unit of 1000 population over a given calendar year. These general rates are called **crude rates**, which are then sub-divided into *sex, color, age, occupation, locality, etc.* They are then known as **refined rates**.

In examining **statistics** and the sources of statistical data one must also be aware of the methods of statistical information gathering. For instance, there are many good sources of raw statistical data. Books such as *The Statistical Abstract of the United States,* published by the United States Chamber of Commerce, *The World Fact Book,* published by the Central Intelligence Agency or *The Monthly Labor Review* published by the United States Department of Labor are excellent examples that contain much raw data. Many such yearbooks and the like on various topics are readily available from any library, or from the government itself. However, knowing how that data and information was gathered is at least equally as important as the figures themselves.

By having knowledge of statistical language and methodology, can one really be able to gauge the usefulness of any given piece of data presented. Thus we must first understand just what statistics are and what they can and cannot, tell us. The social sciences are built upon the philosophy that human movements and interactions can be measured, studied, and ultimately predicted using a variety of methods and research techniques. By studying how humans act individually and within their societies, the social sciences seek to discover and explain common motivations and reactions among humans.

The body of knowledge generated by the social sciences has great influence on both the individual and societal levels. Methods of individual psychological treatment, for instance, are based on ongoing research in the social science of psychology. In the larger scheme, a country bases its foreign policy largely on the analysis of political scientists and other social research.

There are many different ways to find ideas for **research problems**. One of the most common ways is through experiencing and assessing relevant problems in a specific field. Researchers are often involved in the fields in which they choose to study, and thus encounter practical problems related to their areas of expertise on a daily basis. The can use their knowledge, expertise and research ability to examine their selected research problem. For students, all that this entails is being curious about the world around them. Research ideas can come from one's background, culture, education, experiences etc. Another way to get research ideas is by exploring literature in a specific field and coming up with a question that extends or refines previous research.

Once a **topic** is decided, a research question must be formulated. A research question is a relevant, researchable, feasible statement that identifies the information to be studied. Once this initial question is formulated, it is a good idea to think of specific issues related to the topic. This will help to create a hypothesis. A research **hypothesis** is a statement of the researcher's expectations for the outcome of the research problem. It is a summary statement of the problem to be addressed in any research document. A good hypothesis states, clearly and concisely, the researchers expected relationship between the variables that they are investigating. Once a hypothesis is decided, the rest of the research paper should focus on analyzing a set of information or arguing a specific point. Thus, there are two types of research papers: analytical and argumentative.

The scientific method is the process by which researchers over time endeavor to construct an accurate (that is, reliable, consistent and non-arbitrary) representation of the world. Recognizing that personal and cultural beliefs influence both our perceptions and our interpretations of natural phenomena, standard procedures and criteria minimize those influences when developing a theory.

The scientific method has four steps:
1. Observation and description of a phenomenon or group of phenomena.
2. Formulation of a hypothesis to explain the phenomena.
3. Use of the hypothesis to predict the existence of other phenomena or to predict quantitatively the results of new observations.
4. Performance of experimental tests of the predictions by several independent experimenters and properly performed experiments.

While the researcher may bring certain biases to the study, it's important that bias not be permitted to enter into the interpretation. It's also important that data that doesn't fit the hypothesis not be ruled out. This is unlikely to happen if the researcher is open to the possibility that the hypothesis might turn out to be null. Another important caution is to be certain that the methods for analyzing and interpreting are flawless. Abiding by these mandates is important if the discovery is to make a contribution to human understanding.

The Internet and other research resources provide a wealth of information on thousands of interesting topics for students preparing presentations or projects. Using search engines like Google, Microsoft and Infotrac allow students to search multiple Internet resources or databases on one subject search. Students should have an outline of the purpose of a project or research presentation that includes:

- Purpose - identity the reason for the research information
- Objective - having a clear thesis for a project will allow the students opportunities to be specific on Internet searches
- Preparation - when using resources or collecting data, students should create folders for sorting through the information. Providing labels for the folders will create a system of organization that will make construction of the final project or presentation easier and less time consuming
- Procedure - organized folders and a procedural list of what the project or presentation needs to include will create A+ work for students and A+ grading for teachers
- Visuals or artifacts - choose data or visuals that are specific to the subject content or presentation. Make sure that poster boards or Power Point presentations can be visually seen from all areas of the classroom. Teachers can provide laptop computers for Power Point presentations.

> **For tutorials on Social Studies Skills:**
>
> http://volweb.utk.edu/school/bedford/harrisms/ssskills.htm

Skill 12.3 **Recognizing the roles of exploration, active engagement, inquiry and questioning in building knowledge, language, and concepts related to social studies**

The teacher has a broad knowledge and thorough understanding of the development that typically occurs during the students' current period of life. More importantly, the teacher understands how children learn best during each period of development. The most important premise of child development is that all domains of development (physical, social, and academic) are integrated. Development in each dimension is influenced by the other dimensions. Moreover, today's educator must also have knowledge of exceptionalities and how these exceptionalities affect all domains of a child's development.

Social and behavioral theories look at the social interactions of students in the classroom that instruct or impact learning opportunities in the classroom. The psychological approaches behind both theories are subject to individual variables that are learned and applied either proactively or negatively in the classroom. The stimulus of the classroom can promote learning or evoke behavior that is counterproductive for both students and teachers. Students are social beings that normally gravitate to action in the classroom, so teachers must be cognizant in planning classroom environments that are provide both focus and engagement in maximizing learning opportunities.

Physical Development

It is important for the teacher to be aware of the physical stage of development and how the child's physical growth and development affect the child's learning. Factors determined by the physical stage of development include: ability to sit and attend, the need for activity, the relationship between physical skills and self-esteem, and the degree to which physical involvement in an activity (as opposed to being able to understand an abstract concept) affects learning.

Cognitive (Academic) Development

Children go through patterns of learning beginning with pre-operational thought processes and move to concrete operational thoughts. Eventually they begin to acquire the mental ability to think about and solve problems in their head because they can manipulate objects symbolically. Children of most ages can use symbols such as words and numbers to represent objects and relations, but they need concrete reference points. It is essential children be encouraged to use and develop the thinking skills that they possess in solving problems that interest them. The content of the curriculum must be relevant, engaging, and meaningful to the students.

Social Development

Children progress through a variety of social stages beginning with an awareness of peers, but a lack of concern for their presence. Young children engage in "parallel" activities playing alongside their peers without directly interacting with one another. During the primary years, children develop an intense interest in peers. They establish productive, positive social and working relationships with one another. This stage of social growth continues to increase in importance throughout the child's school years including intermediate, middle school, and high school years. It is necessary for the teacher to recognize the importance of developing positive peer group relationships and to provide opportunities and support for cooperative small group projects that not only develop cognitive ability but also promote peer interaction. The ability to work and relate effectively with peers is of major importance and contributes greatly to the child's sense of competence.

In order to develop this sense of competence, children need to be successful in acquiring the knowledge and skills recognized by our culture as important, especially those skills which promote academic achievement. Elementary age children face many changes during their early school years, and these changes may positively and/or negatively impact how learning occurs. Some cognitive developments (i.e., learning to read) may broaden their areas of interest as students realize the amount of information (i.e., novels, magazines, non-fiction books) that is out there. On the other hand, a young student's limited comprehension may inhibit some of their confidence (emotional) or conflict with values taught at home (moral). Joke telling (linguistic) becomes popular with children age six or seven and children may use this newly discovered "talent" to gain friends or social "stature" in their class (social). Learning within one domain often spills over into other areas for young students.

When we say that development takes place within domains, what we mean is simply that different aspects of a human change. So, for example, physical changes take place (e.g., body growth, sexuality); cognitive changes take place (e.g., better ability to reason); linguistic changes take place (e.g., a child's vocabulary develops further); social changes take place (e.g., figuring out identity); emotional changes take place (e.g., changes in ability to be concerned about other people); and moral changes take place (e.g., testing limits).

The importance of a quality early childhood educational experience in shaping a child's development in future years has long been recognized. Approaches to achieve the desired level of quality vary greatly. Recent research has focused on alternative models of childhood education including project focus and greater emphasis on individual needs and development.

A quality preschool experience prepares the child for Kindergarten and elementary school. The early grades prepare the students for more advanced forms of learning. The research recognizes that the sooner a learning disability is recognized, the greater likelihood a successful intervention can occur. Earlier screening tools are being developed. Efforts are underway to focus greater attention in the early years on assisting young students who fall behind.

States are now required to document results of the educational system. This is an improvement over past data tracking. This has allowed greater scrutiny and examination of educational approaches and the ability to track specific intervention strategies. Thus evidence based approaches are receiving much attention.

Increasingly more States are adopting strategies to encourage improved quality or the preschool system. Greater emphasis is focused on outside evaluation of quality and standard achievements. More and more the success of preschool programs is being measured by the success of children as they enter the public school system.

Alternative learning strategies, creating quality learning environments, intervention strategies for slower learners, helping children to transition and succeed in the education system are among some of the common areas of research. Research indicates that active learning strategies are effective in helping students to comprehend social studies skills. The early years are essential in shaping socializations, reducing prejudices and accepting diversity.

Skill 12.4   Demonstrating knowledge of learning experiences for promoting understanding of social studies concepts and acquisition of social studies skills

The early years of childhood education is important in shaping the values of a democracy and preparing students for citizenship in later life. Social studies begin the exploration of the processes, rights and freedoms of a democracy. Early in a child's education they begin to learn cooperation, tolerance, and sharing.

A country's education system is an important partner in the socialization of new citizens to the practices of a democracy. Helping children to begin to learn the rights, freedoms and responsibilities is an essential component. Additionally the critical thinking skill brought through interaction and discussion will help develop the skill necessary to evaluate political policies in future years. During the early years the recalling of factual information is not as important as encouraging discussion and exploration of different perspectives.

TEACHER CERTIFICATION STUDY GUIDE

The education system helps citizens to recognize values and responsibilities. Building a loyalty to the country and its values begins in the early years. Young students enjoy learning about the world around them, the meaning of holidays, government, and the events of the world. Different perspectives are learned from the home environment, which needs to be explained and developed. Major events in the news such as elections provide an opportunity to explore democratic principles. Building the ability of children during the early grade to discuss social topics will prepare them for discussion in later years.

Students during early years can begin to understand the basic operations of citizenship and political affairs. Values of diversity, freedoms and openness to ideas and expression are shaped during the early years.

SEE also Skills 12.5 and 12.6

Skill 12.5 Demonstrating knowledge of strategies for encouraging children to develop positive attitudes toward social studies

Teachers should have a toolkit of instructional strategies, materials and technologies to encourage and teach students how to problem solve and think critically about subject content. With each curriculum chosen by a district for school implementation, comes an expectation that students must master benchmarks and standards of learning skills. There is an established level of academic performance and proficiency in public schools that students are required to master in today's classrooms. Research of national and state standards indicate that there additional benchmarks and learning objectives in the subject areas of science, foreign language, English language arts, history, art, health, civics, economics, geography, physical education, mathematics, and social studies that students are required to master in state assessments (Marzano & Kendall, 1996).

A critical thinking skill is a skill target that teachers help students develop to sustain learning in specific subject areas that can be applied within other subject areas. For example, when learning to understand algebraic concepts in solving a math word problem on how much fencing material is needed to build a fence around a backyard area that has a 8' x 12," a math student must understand the order of numerical expression in how to simplify algebraic expressions. Teachers can provide instructional strategies that show students how to group the fencing measurements into an algebraic word problem that with minor addition, subtraction and multiplication can produce a simple number equal to the amount of fencing materials needed to build the fence.

Students use basic skills to understand things that are read such as a reading passage or a math word problem or directions for a project. However, students apply additional thinking skills to fully comprehend how what was read could be applied to their own life or how to make comparatives or choices based on the factual information given. These higher-order thinking skills are called critical thinking skills as students think about thinking and teachers are instrumental in helping students use these skills in everyday activities.

There are many resources available for the teaching of social science concepts. The resources used should be appropriate to the learning objectives specified. The teacher wants to use different kinds of resources in order to make the subject matter more interesting to the student and to appeal to different learning styles. First of all a good textbook is required. This gives the student something that they can refer to and something to study from. Students generally like to have a text to refer to. The use of audio-video aides is also beneficial in the classroom environment. Most people are visual learners and will retain information better when it is in visual form. Audio-visual presentations, like movies, give them concepts in pictures that they will easily retain.

Library projects are good for students also. The library has an abundance of resources that students should become familiar with at an early age, so they learn to use the library. There are books and magazines that they can look through and read to expand their knowledge beyond the textbooks. Younger children, particularly, like to look at pictures. The computer also offers abundant opportunities as a teaching tool and resource. The Internet provides a wealth of information on all topics and something can be found that is suitable for any age group. Children like to play game, so presenting the material in a game-like format is also a good teaching tool. Making little puzzles for vocabulary or letting them present the information in the form of a story or even a play helps them learn and retain various concepts. Field trips, if possible, are also a good way to expose children to various aspects of social science. Today's world of technology makes a myriad of resources available to the teacher. The teacher should make use of as many of them as possible to keep the material more interesting for the student and to aide in their retention of the material.

Historically, previous centuries of educational research have shown a strong correlation between the need for interdisciplinary instruction and cognitive learning application. Understanding how students process information and create learning was the goal of earlier educators. Earlier researchers looked at how the brain connected information pieces into meaning and found that learning takes place along intricate neural pathways that formulate processing and meaning from data input into the brain. The implications for student learning are vast in that teachers can work with students to break down subject content area into bits of information that can be memorized and applied to a former learning experience and then processed into integral resources of information.

Skill 12.6 Identifying strategies for using everyday and current events to promote understanding of social studies concepts

Early childhood education prepares the students for a lifetime of learning, functioning and succeeding in a diverse global environment. Young learners are building a base of understanding of the world around them. Concepts like location and community are important in building not only a geographic base for future learning but also an understanding of the basic community institutions that shape our world and how they interrelate. A community involves much more than a location. It involves social systems, economics, politics, services, government providing a means of examining the various elements of social science in an integrated way.

The students are curious about the world in which they live. A complex topic such as the functioning of a community provides an opportunity to explore the complexity of the world in a helpful manner and to provide the child answers to common questions, building on real life experiences,

Location and community offer wonderful topics to help children explore the world in which we live and to begin to integrate knowledge from various disciplines. Community involves all aspects of living from employment to family to institutions. Recognizing location offers an opportunity to explore a variety to topics including countries, addresses, people, as well as community aspects. The location theme becomes one of the building blocks to geographic awareness.

The National Council for Social Studies identifies 10 themes essential to social science instruction including (www.socialstudies.org/standards/strands/):

1. Culture
2. Time, Continuity and Change
3. People, Places and Environments
4. Individual development and identity
5. Individuals, Groups and Institutions
6. Power, Authority and Governance
7. Production, Distribution and Consumption
8. Science, Technology and Society
9. Global Connections
10. Civic Ideals and Practices

Additionally national and State organizations establish standards for early childhood instruction. History standards include organizing events, knowledge of historic inquiry, understanding societal change and diversity, knowledge of science, technology, religion and philosophies, and political institutions.

Geography standards include knowledge of maps and other geographic tools, recognition of physical processes, regions, and human characteristics, people, places and environment, as well as interdependence of societies.

Economic standards include understanding of scarcity, use of resources and how different economic systems allocate resources, as well as basic economic principles including trade, exchange, business and individual behavior.

Civics standards for early childhood include describing purpose of government, understanding law and order, and the constitution framework.

Various national organizations such as the Center for Civic Education, the National Council for the Social Studies, National Geographic Society, and the National Council on Economic Education have developed national standard for the education of students

Alternative learning strategies, creating quality learning environments, intervention strategies for slower learners, helping children to transition and succeed in the education system are among some of the common areas of research. Research indicates that active learning strategies are effective in helping students to comprehend social studies skills. The early years are essential in shaping socializations, reducing prejudices and accepting diversity.

The integration of social science knowledge and the interdisciplinary nature of the topics require an interactive approach to teaching, which exposes the students to a variety of tools, documents and the contrasts that exist globally.

The National Council for the Social Sciences identifies 5 elements of successful social science education:

"A. Social Studies Teaching and Learning are powerful when they are meaningful;
B. Social Science Teaching and Learning are powerful when they are integrated;
C. Social Science Teaching and Learning are powerful when they are value-based;
D. Social Science Teaching and Learning are powerful when they are challenging;
E. Social Science Teaching and Learning are powerful when they are active;" (*A Vision of Powerful Teaching and Learning in the Social Studies. National Council for the Social Studies.*)

The complexity of the ideas of social studies is best taught through an active interaction between teacher and students, requiring preparation and reflection. The integrative nature of social studies through interaction can help students to grasp the focus of the various disciplines of the area. Values form the basis of many of the ideas of the disciplines and require an objective exploration to help students to comprehend. Challenging the minds of students through interactions aids the understanding of the material and concepts. Social studies provide opportunities for active learning both individually and in groups. The various topics of social studies offer tremendous opportunities to expose students to a variety of documents to aid the learning process.

Using themes in lesson plans which build on themes of every day life provides the student with useful information and exposure to important social awareness. Unlike other disciplines, social studies is evolving and changing daily with events around the world, new discoveries and the constant debate and reevaluation of issues. For the young learner, the relating of the various themes to events in the world developing around the school helps the student to associate the relevance of social studies to everyday life.

Much of the skills of the social studies are preparing the student for their future responsibilities as a citizen. Aiding in the analysis and understanding relative to daily events, is helpful to the student in developing and practicing the skills needed for future success in the world.

The use of everyday events helps to make the social studies relevant to the student, helping to understand the events of the world.

Integrating disciplines provides an opportunity for the student to learn broader perspectives and also utilizes available educational time more efficiently. Particularly during the early years as students learn basic reading, mathematics and writing skills, time available for development of social studies proficiencies is limited. Integrating social studies with the learning of other skills allows students to gain a greater understanding of the world in which we live.

Integrating educational curriculum is a common strategy incorporated with various learning approaches including projects and learning centers. Young learners have the opportunity to witness how various aspects or themes of everyday life are viewed from multiple disciplines.

Within the social sciences an integrated approach allows a theme to be explored across the social sciences including anthropology, geography, economics and history among others, while learning math, reading, or other important skills. As a result greater mastery of the topic occurs.

Skill 12.7 Demonstrating knowledge of how to promote children's use of social studies skills (e.g., conflict resolution, community building) in a variety of settings

Conflict has occurred throughout history in society. Conflict can be as simple as a difference of opinion or as complex as a divorce or a custody battle. Conflict resolved poorly can lead to violence or one side simply giving up. Much of the work of the legal system deals with resolving conflicts through civil action filed in a Court of Law. Legal action is usually the most costly resolution option.

Two parties can choose to negotiate the conflict either between parties or with the assistance of a third party. Negotiation provides the opportunity for issues to be debated and both sides to attempt to persuade the other side to their position. Often the best solutions are win-win solutions where the solution leaves both parties better off, as opposed to the traditional win-lose solution common to legal procedures. Often in a dispute a compromise is reached where at least one party agrees to a settlement that does not meet all of the criteria but is adequate to resolve the conflict.

Mediation provides a third party who acts as the mediator, listening to both sides and attempting to negotiate a settlement of the dispute. When both parties agree to **arbitrate** a dispute, a third party hears the positions and issues an opinion, which may be binding on the parties.

In order to develop this sense of competence, children need to be successful in acquiring the knowledge and skills recognized by our culture as important, especially those skills which promote academic achievement. Elementary age children face many changes during their early school years, and these changes may positively and/or negatively impact how learning occurs. Some cognitive developments (i.e., learning to read) may broaden their areas of interest as students realize the amount of information (i.e., novels, magazines, non-fiction books) that is out there. On the other hand, a young student's limited comprehension may inhibit some of their confidence (emotional) or conflict with values taught at home (moral). Joke telling (linguistic) becomes popular with children age six or seven and children may use this newly discovered "talent" to gain friends or social "stature" in their class (social). Learning within one domain often spills over into other areas for young students.

Competition for control of areas of the earth's surface is a common trait of human interaction throughout history. This competition has resulted in both destructive conflict and peaceful and productive cooperation. Societies and groups have sought control of regions of the earth's surface for a wide variety of reasons including religion, economics, politics and administration. Numerous wars have been fought through the centuries for the control of territory for each of these reasons.

In measuring the social significance of an event or issue, one of the first questions to ask is how many people are affected. Wide sweeping events such as wars, natural disasters, revolutions, etc., are significant partly because they can change the way of life for many people in a short time. By involving parents, caregivers, colleagues and the community in the education of students in the social studies, we are all benefiting by learning about what is going on in our world and how we interact with each other.

> **For more information and activities for teaching Social Studies:**
>
> http://www.socialstudiesforkids.com/
>
> http://www.usask.ca/education/ideas/tplan/sslp/sslp.htm

Competency 013 Understand the visual and performing arts and how to facilitate young children's learning in and appreciation of the arts

Skill 13.1 Demonstrating knowledge of basic concepts and skills (e.g., creating, appreciating) in visual arts, music, movement, and drama

It is vital that students learn to identify characteristics of visual arts that include materials, techniques and processes necessary to establish a connection between art and daily life. Early ages should begin to experience art in a variety of forms. It is important to reach many areas at an early age to establish a strong artistic foundation for young students. Students should be introduced to the simple recognition of simple patterns found in the art environment. They must also identify art materials such as clay, paint and crayons. Each of these types of material should be introduced and explained for use in daily lessons with young children.

Young students may need to be introduced to items that are developmentally appropriate for their age and for their fine motor skills. Many Pre-Kindergarten and Kindergarten students use oversized pencils and crayons for the first semester. Typically, after this first semester, development occurs to enable children to gradually develop into using smaller sized materials.

Students should begin to explore artistic expression at this age using colors and mixing. The color wheel is a vital lesson for young children and students begin to learn the uses of primary colors and secondary colors. By the middle of the school year students should be able to explain this process. For example, a student needs orange paint, but only has a few colors. Students should be able to determine that by mixing red and yellow that orange is created.

Teachers should begin to plan and use variation using line, shape, texture and many different principles of design. By using common environmental figures such as people, animals and buildings teachers can base many art lessons on characteristics of readily available examples. Students should be introduced to as many techniques as possible to ensure that all strands of the visual arts and materials are experienced at a variety of levels.

By using original works of arts students should be able to identify visual and actual textures of art and based their judgments of objects found in everyday scenes. Other examples that can be described as subjects could include landscapes, portraits and still life.

The major areas that young students should experience should include the following:

1. Painting-using tempra or watercolors.
2. Sculpture-typically using clay or play-dough.
3. Architecture-building or structuring design using 3D materials such as cardboard and poster board to create a desired effect.
4. Ceramics- another term for pottery using a hollow clay sculpture and pots made from clay and fired in a kiln using high temperature to strengthen them.
5. Metalworking-another term for engraving or cutting design or letters into metal with a sharp tool printmaking.
6. Lithography is an example of planographics, where a design is drawn on a surface and then the print is lifted from the surface.

Music

Music education is important throughout a child's elementary education. A comprehensive music curriculum not only teaches elements and appreciation of music, but also skills such as concentration, counting, listening, and cooperation. In addition, music has been connected with creating an effective educational environment that is more conducive to learning in other academic areas.

Basic Music Techniques

Some of the most basic music techniques include learning about rhythm, tempo, melody, and harmony. **Rhythm** refers to the pattern of regular or irregular pulses in music that result from the melodic beats of the music. When rhythm is measured and divided into parts of equal time value, it is called **meter**. Simple techniques to teach and practice rhythm include clapping hands and tapping feet to the beat of the music. Teachers can also incorporate the use of percussion instruments to examine rhythmic patters, which also increases students' awareness of rhythm. As a result of exercises such as these, students learn the basics of conducting music, and through conducting, students learn to appreciate and develop musical awareness. Understanding rhythm also introduces students to the concept of **tempo**, or the speed of a given musical piece. Practicing with well-known songs with a strong musical beat such as "Happy Birthday" helps students become aware of patterns and speed.

The **melody** of a musical piece refers to the pattern of single tones in a composition that is distinguished from rhythm and harmony. The melody of a musical piece is often considered the "horizontal" aspect of the piece that flows from start to finish. **Harmony** refers to the combination of single tones at one time in a musical piece, or the full sound of different notes at the same time. To practice these concepts, students can compose their own ascending and descending melodies on staff paper. Students should be able to sing the melodies by reading the notation.

Movement

Begin with primitive patterns of **rhythm**. Rhythm is the basis of dance. A child can sit in a chair and clap or tap their hands on their legs to express thoughts of rhythm. With older children, imagery enables a dancer to visualize and internalize the particular qualities of a specific movement.

Because the younger child is more unsteady the initial level emphasis is not on gracefulness but rather to develop **body awareness**. The uniqueness of dance is that it is self-expression that can be guided through instruction. The student is taught the elements that are available such as **time and space.** Therefore, the student is incorporating **listening skills** to develop a sense of tempo.

Creative dance is the one that is most natural to a young child. Creative dance depicts feelings through movement. It is the initial reaction to sound and movement. The older elementary student will incorporate mood and expressiveness. Stories can be told to release the dancer into imagination.

Isadora Duncan is credited with being the mother of modern dance. **Modern dance** today refers to a concept of dance where the expressions of opposites are developed such as fast-slow, contract- release, vary height and level to fall and recover. Modern dance is based on four principles, which are substance, dynamism, metakinesis, and form.

Students should be able to judge the effectiveness of a dance composition based on the intent, structure, meaning and purpose. Dance is a way of expressing everything from feelings of mood to appreciation of cultures and historical time periods. Students express empathy for others as they take on various roles within the dance. The application and participation in dances helps students develop self confidence, body awareness, and communication skills and provide experiences in areas otherwise left undiscovered. School settings for dance have a feel of community. Therefore, a good way to evaluate dance in a school setting is as a group experience rather than a technical skill level of individuals which is best left to dance schools. Dance is a way of expressing the connections and relationships between the dancers and appreciation of dance as creative expression.

Drama

It is vital that teachers be trained in critical areas that focus on important principles of theatre education. The basic course of study should include state mandated topics in arts education, instructional materials, products in arts, both affective and cognitive processes of art, world and traditional cultures, and the most recent teaching tools, media and technology.

Areas that should be included are as follows:

Acting - Acting requires the student to demonstrate the ability to effectively communicate using skillful speaking, movement, rhythm, and sensory awareness.

Directing - Direction requires the management skills to produce and perform an onstage activity. This requires guiding and inspiring students as well as script and stage supervision.

Designing - Designing involves creating and initiating the onsite management of the art of acting.

Scriptwriting - Scriptwriting demands that a leader be able to produce original material and staging an entire production through the writing and designing a story that has performance value.

Each of the above mentioned skills should be incorporated in daily activities with young children. It is important that children are exposed to character development through stories, role-play, and modeling through various teacher guided experiences. Some of the experiences that are age appropriate for early childhood level include puppet theatre, paper dolls, character sketches, storytelling, and re-telling of stories in a student's own words.

> For more information on teaching art to young children:
>
> http://www.cln.org/subjects/art_inst.html

Skill 13.2 Recognizing the roles of exploration, active engagement, inquiry, and questioning in building knowledge, language, and concepts related to the arts

The process of creating art is a discovery process. As soon as early childhood students are exposed to the basic elements of the arts, the process of discovery begins. As students increase their knowledge base, they question their basic assumptions, and the creative process evolves with each new creation. Fingers and toes are added to stick figures; what once was a melody, now also includes harmony; basic movements are coordinated into a dance combination; pretending to be an old woman evolves to a storytelling piece about an old woman who lives in a house by the sea and makes dolls for little children. Students begin to use the arts as a language to reflect on the world as they see it.

Visual Art

Students should have an early introduction to the principles of visual art and should become familiar with the basic level of the following terms:

abstract
an image that reduces a subject to its essential visual elements, such as lines, shapes, and colors.

background
portions or areas of composition that are behind the primary or dominant subject matter or design areas

balance
the arrangement of one or more elements in a work of art so that they appear symmetrical or asymmetrical in design and proportion

contrast
> juxtaposing one or more elements in opposition, to show their differences

emphasis
> making one or more elements in a work of art stand out in such a way as to appear more important or significant

sketch
> an image-development strategy; a preliminary drawing

texture
> the way something feels by representation of the tactile character of surfaces

unity
> the arrangement of one or more of the elements used to create a coherence of parts and a feeling of completeness or wholeness

After learning the above terms and how they relate to the use of line, color, value, space, texture and shape, an excellent opportunity is to have students create an "art sample book." Such books could include a variety of materials that would serve as examples, such as sandpaper and cotton balls to represent texture elements. Samples of square pieces of construction paper designed into various shapes could represent shape. String samples could represent the element of lines.

The sampling of art should also focus clearly on colors necessary for the early childhood student. Color can be introduced more in-depth when discussing **intensity**, the strength of the color, and **value**, the lightness or darkness of the colors. Another valuable tool regarding color is the use of a color wheel, and allowing students to experiment with the mixing of colors to create their own art experience.

> **For further reading about the benefits of teaching art to young children:**
>
> http://www.newhorizons.org/strategies/arts/front_arts.htm

Dance

Begin with primitive patterns of **rhythm**. Rhythm is the basis of dance. A child can sit in a chair and clap or tap their hands on their legs to express thoughts of rhythm. With older children, imagery enables a dancer to visualize and internalize the particular qualities of a specific movement.

Because the younger child is less steady, the initial level emphasis is not on gracefulness, but rather to develop **body awareness**. The uniqueness of dance is that it is self-expression that can be guided through instruction. The student learns the elements that are available, such as **time and space**. Therefore, the student is incorporating **listening skills** to develop a sense of tempo.

Practice, dedication and focus are essential in training for serious participation in dance. Each practice should begin with a warm-up consisting of stretches and movements to prevent muscular injury and to prepare the muscles for strenuous activity. The rehearsal period of individual movements, gestures and phrases of dance would comprise the major portion of the practice period ending with relaxation exercises enabling the individual to return gradually to normal metabolic levels. The rehearsal period stresses the individual characteristics of the steps and dances being performed. Each genre of dance has its own unique techniques. Fitness is important in developing a body that is flexible, strong, and fluid in movement. Dedication and commitment to dance as a profession iare paramount where long hours on a daily basis develop expertise.

The various styles of dance can be explained as follows:
- Creative dance
- Modern dance
- Social dance
- Dance of other cultures
- Structured dance
- Ritual Dance
- Ballet

Creative dance is the one that is most natural to a young child. Creative dance depicts feelings through movement. It is the initial reaction to sound and movement. The older elementary student will incorporate mood and expressiveness. Stories can be told to release the dancer into imagination.

Isadora Duncan is credited with being the mother of modern dance. **Modern dance** today refers to a concept of dance where the expressions of opposites are developed such as fast-slow, contract- release, vary height and level to fall and recover. Modern dance is based on four principles, which are substance, dynamism, metakinesis, and form.

Skill 13.3　Demonstrating knowledge of learning experiences for promoting arts concepts and skills

Visual Arts

The components and strands of visual art encompass many areas. Students are expected to fine tune observation skills and be able to identify and recreate the experiences that teachers provide for them as learning tools. For example, students may walk as a group on a nature hike taking in the surrounding elements and then begin to discuss the repetition found in the leaves of trees, or the bricks of the sidewalk, or the size and shapes of the buildings and how they may relate. They may also use such an experience to describe lines, colors, shapes, forms and textures. Beginning elements of perspective are noticed at an early age. The questions of why buildings look smaller when they are at a far distance and bigger when they are closer are sure to spark the imagination of early childhood students. Students can then take their inquiry to higher level of learning with some hands-on activities such as building three-dimensional buildings and construction using paper and geometric shapes. Eventually students should acquire higher level thinking skills such as analysis, in which they will begin to question artists, artwork, and analyze many different aspects of visual art.

An excellent opportunity is to have students create an "art sample book." Such books could include a variety of materials that would serve as examples, such as sandpaper and cotton balls to represent texture elements. Samples of square pieces of construction paper designed into various shapes could represent shape. String samples could represent the element of lines.

The sampling of art should also focus clearly on colors necessary for the early childhood student. Color can be introduced more in-depth when discussing **intensity**,-the strength of the color, and **value**- the lightness or darkness of the colors. Another valuable tool regarding color is the use of a color wheel, and allowing students to experiment with the mixing of colors to create their own art experience.

Works of art should most often be interpreted through a wide variety of rich art and literature experience. Students will be able to react to art experiences by understanding the definitions of the basic principles such as line, color, value, space, texture, and shape and form in art. Early Childhood students are most greatly affected by these experiences. One resource is the author Eric Carle. His books are age appropriate for young children and include a wide variety of shape, color, line, and media for young students to explore. Once students have been introduced to a wide range of materials, they are able to better relate and explain the elements they have observed through artwork and generously illustrated literature. Literature is the most common form of exposure for young students, but video and other types of media also provided rich art experiences as well.

> **For further reading on the principles of visual art:**
>
> http://www.ket.org/artonair/teachers/perception.htm

Music

Students can explore creating moods with music, analyzing stories and creating musical compositions that reflect or enhance it. Their daily routines can include exploration, interpretation, and understanding of musical sound. Immersing them in musical conversations as they sing, speak rhythmically, and walk in-step stimulates their awareness of the beauty and structure of musical sound.

In some schools, computer-assisted programs provide students with opportunities to evaluate music. Programs are designed to present two performances of one or more musical pieces so the students can work with the teacher to compare and contrast the pieces. The Internet allows students to collect musical information for evaluation and provide information about studied or performed compositions. Knowledge of these resources and tools enable teachers to provide the richest education in music.

Drama

In theatre, students should learn to use all of their five senses to observe their environment and recreate experiences through drama and other theatre skills. Using role play and prior knowledge of experiences, students should develop the ability to react to a feeling or a situation to expand their ability to develop character. Using sight, smell, taste, touch, hearing and memory recall, students should be able to retell stories, myths, and fables. Opportunities to perform using costumes and props for performances should be provided. Students can relate to familiar jobs that are relevant to their everyday experiences and should be provided with opportunities to "act out" some of the following: firefighters, police officers, teachers, doctors, nurses, postal employees, clerks, and other service related professions that students may have witnessed.

Skill 13.4 Demonstrating knowledge of strategies for supporting children's creativity and for encouraging children to develop positive attitudes toward the arts

Education experts agree that the arts curriculum content for early childhood students should emphasize the experimental and discovery aspects of the arts, rather than a perfect result. Early childhood students are developing their sense of self and how they fit into society, and their curriculum should allow for an open creative process with little judgment. Students should feel safe as they use dance, drama, music or visual arts in expressing themselves, without the threat of criticism. Countless research projects provide anecdotal evidence of young students blossoming through the arts and becoming more social or increasing their cognitive skills or motor skills.

Some of the areas that can be modeled by the teacher include the following:
- Experimentation through works of art using a variety of mediums, drawing, painting, sculpture, ceramics, printmaking and video
- Producing a collection of art works (portfolio) and using a variety of mediums, topics, themes and subject matter
- Conveying meaning through choosing specific art works
- Creating and evaluating different art works and mediums
- Reflection on various works

Some examples include:
- Mixing paint in ranges of shades and tints
- Including in the portfolio works that display at least two mediums
- Trying to include at least ten works of art in each portfolio
- Including early sketches, research and development of each project with each entry
- Painting a picture using tempra or watercolor recalling a specific experience or memory

Music

The ability to repeat melodies and rhythms of varying lengths and read musical notation are early signs of creative development. Older students expand their skills by learning to play an instrument or singing. The motor skills and listening techniques required to play an instrument or to learn a vocal piece of music are important indicators of creative development.

The use of music vocabulary taught in the classroom and the ability to describe music using this vocabulary is another barometer of creative development in music. Students show musical development by using words such as legato, staccato, forte and piano to describe music. They can also classify a musical work, such as a symphony, and name typical instruments used in performing that work, such as the violin, viola, cello, and bass. These are all signs that students are developing their knowledge and skills in the arts.

Movement

Students should be able to judge the effectiveness of a dance composition based on the intent, structure, meaning and purpose. Dance is a way of expressing everything from feelings of mood to appreciation of cultures and historical time periods. Students express empathy for others as they take on various roles within the dance. The application and participation in dances helps students develop self-confidence, body awareness, and communication skills and provide experiences in areas otherwise left undiscovered. School settings for dance have a feel of community. Therefore, a good way to evaluate dance in a school setting is as a group experience rather than a technical skill level of individuals, which is best left to dance schools. Dance is a way of expressing the connections and relationships between the dancers and appreciation of dance as creative expression.

Drama

In drama, creative development is gauged by the degree to which a student is able to apply the ten elements of acting. A teacher can monitor a student's use of the five senses in improvisation exercises and dramatic performances, as well as their ability to answer the five essential questions of Who, What, Where, When, and Why.

Students' abilities to demonstrate various aspects of a dramatic production, such as acting, directing, set design, scriptwriting, and audience participation are additional indicators of creative development. It is important for the student to understand that drama is not only a game of make-believe, but that there are many pieces that go into a theatrical production.

SEE Skill 13.5 or details of resources for promoting positive attitudes toward the arts through exposure to hands on activities in visual arts, dance, theatre and music.

Skill 13.5 Demonstrating knowledge of activities and resources for promoting aesthetic appreciation

A live performance or first hand view of the arts is invaluable when it comes to promoting children's aesthetic appreciation of the arts. The best resources for teachers are local performing arts venues, art museums, symphonies, operas and dance companies. All of these venues have outreach programs geared toward elementary school students. In fact, many of the venues provide programs where artists visit the school and offer hands on lessons for kids, as well as a live performance. Kindling an appreciation of the arts in students is a priority for most arts organizations, as these students will become their future patrons.

> **Two excellent online resources for arts appreciation are:**
>
> http://www.metmuseum.org/

The **Explore and Learn** section of the Metropolitan Museum of Art online has a vast collection of images, video and printed material. The **Timeline of Art History** allows students to explore history through images at the Museum of Art.

Arts Edge on the Kennedy Center website provides a wealth of information for teachers. The **Look.Listen.Learn** section highlights various arts forms through audio, video, images, printed material and interactive exercises.

> **Links to websites for both of these programs:**
>
> http://artsedge.kennedy-center.org/

Skill 13.6   Recognizing the role of the arts in promoting self expression, creative thinking, and a healthy self-concept

Visual Arts

At any age, students should be asked to compile a variety of their best works of art using different types of media. This is typically referred to as a portfolio, which is beneficial for all students from early childhood through the high school grades. Teachers are then able to explain choices of media and how it was chosen and used in a variety of ways using many different topics. The portfolio should begin with an early sample of the student's work, which is called a rough draft or a sketch. It can then be tracked to see the progress of each individual throughout the course of building the portfolio. By the end of the portfolio experience, the growth in uses of medium and techniques should be clear and progress can be tracked through a use of a rubric or by observation.

SEE also Skill 13.3

Skill 13.7   Recognizing the role of the arts as a way for children to express and understand knowledge and ideas in other curricular areas

The arts provide essential opportunities to explore connections among all disciplines. Content areas are unique, but they share common themes and terms and ideas. Skills developed in the arts enhance learning across content areas. Conversely, increased knowledge in curriculum content areas enhance the depth of knowledge and experience in the arts.

Charles Fowler effectively argues in his book, Strong Arts, Strong Schools: the Promising Potential and Shortsighted Disregard of the Arts in American Schooling, that the best schools have the best arts programs. He explains that we need to utilize every possible way to represent and interpret our world, and that means combining content areas, not isolating them. Science, Math, Literature, History or the Arts by themselves only convey a part of the subject. Charles Fowler believes that integrating these programs to provide students with a more complete picture is crucial. He uses the Grand Canyon as an example. A teacher can discuss mathematically the dimensions of the Grand Canyon or the science behind how it was formed, but this lesson is taken a step further by providing examples of artistic renderings of the Grand Canyon or asking students to write a poem describing the canyon. This integration provides a more three dimensional understanding of the subject.

Using African cultural history as another example, a teacher begins with a short history lesson on select African cultures. Geography may also come into play in the lesson, as the teacher chooses a specific region, such as Senegal-Gambia in West Africa, to describe to the children what an area of Africa looks like. This may be expanded to a music lesson on African musical styles and how they influenced Western music, such as gospel, jazz, spirituals, hip hop and rap. The teacher can introduce various African instruments, and discuss what the instruments are made of and how they are played. Students will learn several drum techniques and experiment with creating their own unique drum beats. Again, at the end of this lesson students have experienced Africa through an integrated teaching approach, and they come away with a more complete understanding.

Lynn Hallie Najem provides further evidence of the importance of integrating the arts into standard curriculum in her research article, "Sure It's Fun, But Why Bother With It During the School Day? The Benefits of Using Drama with Primary Students". In her research, she found that integrating the arts into primary school curriculum had a very positive effect on the self-esteem of students and opened them up to learning in all subject areas.

> **Read the text of this article:**
>
> http://www.madison.k12.wi.us/

AEPA Pre Test

Subarea I. Child Development and Learning

1. What developmental patterns should a professional teacher assess to meet the needs of each student? (Skill 1.1; Average rigor)

    A. Academic, regional, and family background

    B. Social, physical, and academic

    C. Academic, physical, and family background

    D. Physical, family, and ethnic background

2. The various domains of development are best described as: (Skill 1.1; Average rigor)

    A. Integrated

    B. Independent

    C. Simultaneous

    D. Parallel

3. Which of the following best describes how different areas of development impact each other? (Skill 1.2; Average rigor)

    A. Development in other areas cannot occur until cognitive development is complete.

    B. Areas of development are inter-related and impact each other.

    C. Development in each area is independent of development in other areas.

    D. Development in one area leads to a decline in other areas.

4. A student has developed and improved in vocabulary. However, the student is not confident enough to use the improved vocabulary, and the teacher is not aware of the improvement. What is this an example of? (Skill 1.2; Rigorous)

    A. Latent development

    B. Dormant development

    C. Random development

    D. Delayed development

5. Which of the following has been shown to have the greatest impact on a student's academic performance? (Skill 1.3; Easy)

   A. The teacher's expectations

   B. Strict discipline

   C. The student's social skills

   D. Measurable objectives

6. According to Piaget, when does the development of symbolic functioning and language first take place? (Skill 1.4; Average rigor)

   A. Concrete operations stage

   B. Formal operations stage

   C. Sensory-motor stage

   D. Pre-operational stage

7. Playing team sports at young ages should be done for the following purpose: (Skill 1.5; Rigorous)

   A. To develop the child's motor skills

   B. To prepare children for competition in high school

   C. To develop the child's interests

   D. Both A and C

8. The stages of play development from infancy stages to early childhood includes a move from: (Skill 1.5; Rigorous)

   A. Cooperative to solitary

   B. Solitary to cooperative

   C. Competitive to collaborative

   D. Collaborative to competitive

9. Which of the following is NOT an economic factor that may influence the health of a child? (Skill 1.7; Easy)

   A. Pollution

   B. Malnutrition

   C. Neglect

   D. Poor medical care

10. Which of the following is the main source of energy in the diet? (Skill 1.8; Easy)

    A. Vitamins

    B. Minerals

    C. Water

    D. Carbohydrates

11. Which of the following would be likely to influence a student's learning and academic progress? (Skill 2.1; Easy)

    A. Relocation

    B. Emotional abuse

    C. Bullying

    D. All of the above

12. Which of the following best explains why emotional upset and emotional abuse can reduce a child's classroom performance? (Skill 2.1; Rigorous)

    A. They reduce the energy that students put towards schoolwork.

    B. They lead to a reduction in cognitive ability.

    C. They contribute to learning disorders such as dyslexia.

    D. They result in the development of behavioral problems.

13. A teacher has a class with several students from low income families in it. What would it be most important for a teacher to consider when planning homework assignments to ensure that all students have equal opportunity for academic success? (Skill 2.2; Rigorous)

    A. Access to technology

    B. Ethnicity

    C. Language difficulties

    D. Gender

14. Family members with high levels of education often have high expectations for student success. This shows how students are influenced by their family's: (Skill 2.2; Easy)

    A. Attitude

    B. Resources

    C. Income

    D. Culture

15. **Why is it most important for teachers to ensure that students from different economic backgrounds have access to the resources they need to acquire the academic skills being taught? (Skill 2.4; Rigorous)**

    A. All students must work together on set tasks.

    B. All students must achieve the same results in performance tasks.

    C. All students must have equal opportunity for academic success.

    D. All students must be fully included in classroom activities.

16. **A teacher attempting to create a differentiated classroom should focus on incorporating activities that: (Skill 2.4; Rigorous)**

    A. Favor academically advanced students

    B. Challenge special education students to achieve more

    C. Are suitable for whichever group of students is the majority

    D. Meet the needs of all the students in the class

17. **When developing lessons, it is important that teachers provide equity in pedagogy so that: (Skill 2.4; Rigorous)**

    A. Unfair labeling of students will not occur

    B. Student experiences will be positive

    C. Students will achieve academic success

    D. All of the above

18. **Which of the following is NOT a communication issue related to diversity within the classroom? (Skill 2.4; Average rigor)**

    A. Learning disorders

    B. Sensitive terminology

    C. Body language

    D. Discussing differing viewpoints and opinions

19. **One common factor for students with all types of disabilities is that they are also likely to demonstrate difficulty with: (Skill 2.5; Average rigor)**

    A. Social skills

    B. Cognitive skills

    C. Problem-solving skills

    D. Decision-making skills

20. A student does not respond to any signs of affection and responds to other children by repeating back what they have said. What condition is the student most likely to have? (Skill 2.5; Average rigor)

    A. Mental retardation

    B. Autism

    C. Giftedness

    D. Hyperactivity

21. Which of the following conditions is more common for girls than boys? (Skill 2.5; Average rigor)

    A. Attention deficit disorder

    B. Aggression

    C. Phobias

    D. Autism

22. In successful inclusion of students with disabilities: (Skill 2.5; Average rigor)

    A. A variety of instructional arrangements are available

    B. School personnel shift the responsibility for learning outcomes to the student

    C. The physical facilities are used as they are

    D. Regular classroom teachers have sole responsibility for evaluating student progress

23. Mr. Gorman has taught a concept to his class. All of the students have grasped the concept except for Sam. Mr. Gorman should: (Skill 3.2; Rigorous)

    A. Reteach the concept to the whole class in exactly the same way

    B. Reteach the concept to Sam in exactly the same way

    C. Reteach the concept to Sam in a different way

    D. Reteach the concept to the whole class in a different way

24. Mrs. Gomez has a fully integrated early childhood curriculum. This is beneficial to students because it: (Skill 3.2; Rigorous)

    A. Is easier to plan for and maintain

    B. Allows students to apply their unique skills

    C. Helps the students see the relationships between subjects and concepts

    D. Provides opportunities for social interaction

Subarea II. Communication, Language and Literacy Development

25. The relationship between oral language and reading skills is best described as: (Skill 4.1; Average rigor)

    A. Reciprocal

    B. Inverse

    C. Opposite

    D. There is no relationship.

26. A teacher is showing students how to construct grammatically correct sentences. What is the teacher focusing on? (Skill 4.1; Average rigor)

    A. Morphology

    B. Syntax

    C. Semantics

    D. Pragmatics

27. A teacher writes the following words on the board: cot, cotton, and cottage. What is the teacher most likely teaching the students about? (Skill 4.1; Rigorous)

    A. Morphology

    B. Syntax

    C. Semantics

    D. Pragmatics

28. While standing in line at the grocery store, three-year-old Megan says to her mother in a regular tone of voice, "Mom, why is that woman so fat?" What does this indicate a lack of understanding of? (Skill 4.2; Easy)

   A. Syntax

   B. Semantics

   C. Morphology

   D. Pragmatics

29. Which of the following is the first component of the constructivist model? (Skill 4.2; Rigorous)

   A. There are at least seven different types of learning.

   B. Learning depends on the social environment.

   C. Learner creates knowledge

   D. Learning progresses through set stages.

30. Students are about to read a text that contains words that will need to be understood for the students to understand the text. When should the vocabulary be introduced to students? (Skill 4.5; Rigorous)

   A. Before reading

   B. During reading

   C. After reading

   D. It should not be introduced.

31. Which of the following are examples of temporal words? (Skill 4.6; Easy)

   A. Beside and behind

   B. Hotter and colder

   C. In and on

   D. Before and after

32. Which principle of Stephen Krashen's research suggests that the learning of grammatical structures is predictable? (Skill 5.1; Average rigor)

   A. The affective filter hypothesis

   B. The input hypothesis

   C. The natural order hypothesis

   D. The monitor hypothesis

33. Above what age does learning a language become increasingly difficult? (Skill 5.2; Average rigor)

   A. 3

   B. 5

   C. 7

   D. 10

34. Ms. Chomski is presenting a new story to her class of first graders. In the story, a family visits their grandparents where they all gather around a record player and listen to music. Many students do not understand what a record player is, especially some children for whom English is not their first language. Which of the following would Ms. Chomski be best to do? (Skill 5.2; Rigorous)

   A. Discuss what a record player is with her students

   B. Compare a record player with a CD player

   C. Have students look up record player in a dictionary

   D. Show the students a picture of a record player

35. Jose moved to the United States last month. He speaks little to no English at this time. His teacher is teaching the class about habitats in science and has chosen to read a story about various habitats to the class. The vocabulary is difficult. What should Jose's teacher do with Jose? (Skill 5.3; Average rigor)

   A. Provide Jose with additional opportunities to learn about habitats

   B. Read the story to Jose multiple times

   C. Show Jose pictures of habitats from his native country

   D. Excuse Jose from the assignment

36. In the early childhood classroom, it is important to limit teacher talk. What is the main problem with teacher talk? (Skill 5.5; Rigorous)

    A. It is often one sided and limited.

    B. The vocabulary is too difficult for children.

    C. It promotes misbehavior.

    D. It only creates gains in receptive language.

37. Which of the following is a convention of print that children learn during reading activities? (Skill 6.3; Average rigor)

    A. The meaning of words

    B. The left to right motion

    C. The purpose of print

    D. The identification of letters

38. In her kindergarten class, Mrs. Thomas has been watching the students in the drama center. She has watched the children pretend to complete a variety of magic tricks. Mrs. Thomas decides to use stories about magic to share with her class. Her decision to incorporate their interests into the reading shows that Mrs. Thomas understands that: (Skill 6.7; Rigorous)

    A. Including student interests is important at all times

    B. Teaching by themes is crucial for young children

    C. Young children respond to literature that reflects their lives

    D. Science fiction and fantasy are the most popular genres

39. Which of the following is NOT a characteristic of a fable? (Skill 6.8; Easy)

    A. Have animal characters that act like humans

    B. Considered to be true

    C. Teaches a moral

    D. Reveals human foibles

40. **Alphabet books are classified as:** (Skill 6.8; Average rigor)

    A. Concept books

    B. Easy-to-read books

    C. Board books

    D. Pictures books

41. **The works of Paul Bunyan, John Henry, and Pecos Bill are all exaggerated accounts of individuals with superhuman strength. What type of literature are these works?** (Skill 6.8; Easy)

    A. Fables

    B. Fairytales

    C. Tall tales

    D. Myths

42. **Which of the following is NOT a motivation behind providing reading activities, including reading aloud, to young children?** (Skill 7.1; Rigorous)

    A. Developing word consciousness skills

    B. Developing functions of print skills

    C. Developing phonics skills

    D. Developing language skills

43. **Which of the following is an appropriate way for students to respond to literature?** (Skill 7.1; Easy)

    A. Art

    B. Drama

    C. Writing

    D. All of the above

44. **John is having difficulty reading the word reach. In isolation, he pronounces each sound as /r/ /ee/ /sh/. Which of the following is a possible instructional technique which could help solve John's reading difficulty?** (Skill 7.2; Rigorous)

    A. Additional phonemic awareness instruction

    B. Additional phonics instruction

    C. Additional skill and drill practice

    D. Additional minimal pair practice

45. According to Marilyn Jager Adams, which skill would a student demonstrate by identifying that cat does not belong in the group of words containing dog, deer, and dress? (Skill 7.2; Average rigor)

   A. Recognize the odd member in a group

   B. Replace sounds in words

   C. Count the sounds in a word

   D. Count syllables in a word

46. Which of the following is NOT true about phonological awareness? (Skill 7.2; Average rigor)

   A. It may involve print.

   B. It is a prerequisite for spelling and phonics.

   C. Activities can be done by the children with their eyes closed.

   D. It starts before letter recognition is taught.

47. Which of the following explains a significant difference between phonics and phonemic awareness? (Skill 7.3; Average rigor)

   A. Phonics involves print, while phonemic awareness involves language.

   B. Phonics is harder than phonemic awareness.

   C. Phonics involves sounds, while phonemic awareness involves letters.

   D. Phonics is the application of sounds to print, while phonemic awareness is oral.

48. To decode is to: (Skill 7.3; Easy)

   A. Construct meaning

   B. Sound out a printed sequence of letters

   C. Use a special code to decipher a message

   D. Revise for errors in grammar

49. Ms. Walker's lesson objective is to teach her first graders the concept of morphology in order to improve their reading skills. Which group of words would be most appropriate for her to use in this lesson? (Skill 7.3; Rigorous)

   A. Far, farm, farmer

   B. Far, feather, fever

   C. Far, fear, fare

   D. Far, fare, farce

50. Which stage of reading skill development occurs first? (Skill 7.3; Average rigor)

   A. Schema stage

   B. Early semantic stage

   C. Orthographic stage

   D. Simultaneous stage

51. Which of the following is an important feature of vocabulary instruction according to the National Reading Panel? (Skill 7.4; Rigorous)

   A. Repetition of vocabulary items

   B. Keeping a consistent task structure at all times

   C. Teaching vocabulary in more than one language

   D. Isolation vocabulary instruction from other subjects

52. The attitude an author takes toward his or her subject is the: (Skill 7.6; Easy)

   A. Style

   B. Tone

   C. Point of view

   D. Theme

53. George has read his second graders three formats of the story "The Three Little Pigs." One is the traditional version, one is written from the wolf's point of view, and the third is written from the first pig's point of view. As George leads a discussion on the three texts with his students, he is trying to help his students develop their ability to: (Skill 7.7; Rigorous)

   A. Compare and contrast texts

   B. Understand point of view

   C. Recognize metaphors

   D. Rewrite fictional stories

54. What is the first step in developing writing skills? (Skill 8.1; Easy)

   A. Early writing

   B. Experimental writing

   C. Role play writing

   D. Conventional writing

55. Which of the following is NOT a prewriting strategy? (Skill 8.1; Rigorous)

   A. Analyzing sentences for variety

   B. Keeping an idea book

   C. Writing in a daily journal

   D. Writing down whatever comes to mind

56. Which of the following is probably the most important step for the writer in the writing process? (Skill 8.1; Average rigor)

   A. Revision

   B. Discovery

   C. Conclusion

   D. Organization

57. The students in Tina's classroom are working together in pairs. Each student is reading another student's paper and asking who, what, when, where, why, and who questions. What is this activity helping the students to do? (Skill 8.1; Rigorous)

    A. Draft their writing

    B. Paraphrase their writing

    C. Revise their writing

    D. Outline their writing

58. Young children learning to write commonly grip the pencil: (Skill 8.2; Average rigor)

    A. Too far from the point

    B. With the wrong hand

    C. With too many fingers

    D. Too tightly

59. Which of the following approaches to student writing assignments is most likely to lead to students becoming disinterested? (Skill 8.3; Average rigor)

    A. Designing assignments where students write for a variety of audiences.

    B. Designing assignments where the teacher is the audience.

    C. Designing assignments where students write to friends and family.

    D. Designing assignments where students write to real people such as mayors, the principle, or companies.

60. As a part of prewriting, students should identify their audience. Which of the following questions will help students to identify their audience? (Skill 8.3; Average rigor)

    A. Why is the audience reading my writing?

    B. What does my audience already know about my topic?

    C. Both A and B

    D. None of the above

61. **Which of these describes the best way to teach spelling? (Skill 8.5; Rigorous)**

   A. At the same time that grammar and sentence structure is taught.

   B. Within the context of meaningful language experiences.

   C. Independently so that students can concentrate on spelling.

   D. In short lessons as students pick up spelling almost immediately.

62. **When editing, teachers should direct students to: (Skill 8.6; Rigorous)**

   A. Edit for general understanding, while ignoring grammar and spelling.

   B. Edit for one specific purpose at a time.

   C. Identify all spelling, capitalization, and punctuation errors.

   D. Be critical of their work and that of others.

Subarea III. Learning in the Content Areas

63. **Kindergarten students are participating in a calendar time activity. One student adds a straw to the "ones can" to represent that day of school. What math principle is being reinforced? (Skill 9.1; Rigorous)**

   A. Properties of a base ten number system

   B. Sorting

   C. Counting by twos

   D. Even and odd numbers

64. **First grade students are arranging four small squares of identical size to form a larger square. Each small square represents what part of the larger square? (Skill 9.1; Average rigor)**

   A. One half

   B. One whole

   C. One fourth

   D. One fifth

65. What is the answer to this problem? (Skill 9.2; Easy)

    25 ÷ 5 =

    A. 5

    B. 30

    C. 125

    D. 20

66. Third grade students are studying percents. When looking at a circle graph divided into three sections, they see that one section is worth 80% and one section is worth 5%. What will the remaining section be worth? (Skill 9.2; Rigorous)

    A. 100%

    B. 85%

    C. 75%

    D. 15%

67. Which of the following letters does NOT have a line of symmetry? (Skill 9.3; Rigorous)

    A. O

    B. D

    C. M

    D. J

68. Kindergarten students are doing a butterfly art project. They fold paper in half. On one half, they paint a design. Then they fold the paper closed and reopen. The resulting picture is a butterfly with matching sides. What math principle does this demonstrate? (Skill 9.3; Rigorous)

    A. Slide

    B. Rotate

    C. Symmetry

    D. Transformation

69. What number comes next in this pattern? (Skill 9.3; Average rigor)

    3, 8, 13, 18, ____

    A. 21

    B. 26

    C. 23

    D. 5

70. What is the main purpose of having kindergarten students count by twos? (Skill 9.4; Rigorous)

    A. To hear a rhythm

    B. To recognize patterns in numbers

    C. To practice addition

    D. To become familiar with equations

71. The term *millimeters* indicates which kind of measurement? (Skill 9.5; Easy)

    A. Volume

    B. Weight

    C. Length

    D. Temperature

72. What type of graph would be best to use to show changes in the height of a plant over the course of a month? (Skill 9.7; Average rigor)

    A. Circle graph

    B. Bar graph

    C. Line graph

    D. Pictograph

73. A teacher completes a survey of student eye color. The teacher then creates a graph so students can compare how many students have each eye color. What type of graph should be used? (Skill 9.7; Rigorous)

    A. Bar graph

    B. Pictograph

    C. Circle graph

    D. Line graph

74. Which of the following skills would a student develop first? (Skill 10.1; Average rigor)

    A. Understanding place value

    B. Recognizing number patterns

    C. Counting objects

    D. Solving number problems

75. Maddie is a first grade teacher who understands the importance of including the family when providing instruction. She wants to take several steps to provide families with a connection to what the students are doing in her math class. Which of the following is NOT a strategy she could incorporate? (Skill 10.3; Rigorous)

   A. Including a math portion in her regular newsletter

   B. Incorporating manipulatives into her math lessons

   C. Translating math homework into the native language of the students in her classroom

   D. Having a family math night at school

76. George has successfully mastered his basic addition facts. However, as his teacher presents more complex addition problems, it is obvious to him that George is lacking a basic understanding of the concept of addition. What would George's teacher be best to do to increase his basic understanding? (Skill 10.4; Average rigor)

   A. Provide additional instruction with hands on materials

   B. Have George practice his addition facts more frequently

   C. Have George complete more challenging addition problems

   D. Provide George with remediation

77. Carrie approaches her teacher after class and expresses her personal frustration with math and her feeling that she will never get it. Which of the following is NOT a suitable method Carrie's teacher can utilize to improve Carrie's feelings about math? (Skill 10.6; Average rigor)

   A. Incorporating some of Carrie's specific interests into math lessons

   B. Holding Carrie to high expectations

   C. Sharing with Carrie her own struggles and dislike for math

   D. Providing Carrie with extra positive reinforcement and encouragement

78. The principal walks into your classroom during math class. He sees your students making cake mixtures. Later, the principal questions your lesson. What would be the best explanation for your lesson? (Skill 10.7; Rigorous)

   A. The students earned a reward time and it was free choice.

   B. You were teaching the students how math is used in real-life situations.

   C. You had paperwork to complete and needed the time to complete it.

   D. It kept the students interested in math and prevented boredom.

79. What is a large, rotating, low-pressure system accompanied by heavy precipitation and strong winds known as? (Skill 11.1; Average rigor)

   A. A hurricane

   B. A tornado

   C. A thunderstorm

   D. A tsunami

80. What does a primary consumer most commonly refer to? (Skill 11.1; Average rigor)

    A. Herbivore

    B. Autotroph

    C. Carnivore

    D. Decomposer

81. Airplanes generate pressure and remain balanced by: (Skill 11.1; Rigorous)

    A. Fast air movement over wings and slow movement under wings

    B. Slow air movement over wings and fast movement under wings

    C. Air movement that is equal above and below wings

    D. Air movement that only occurs over the wings

82. The breakdown of rock due to acid rain is an example of: (Skill 11.1; Rigorous)

    A. Physical weathering

    B. Frost wedging

    C. Chemical weathering

    D. Deposition

83. What is the last step in the scientific method? (Skill 11.2; Average rigor)

    A. Pose a question

    B. Draw a conclusion

    C. Conduct a test

    D. Record data

84. Which term best describes Newton's universal gravitation? (Skill 11.3; Rigorous)

    A. Theory

    B. Hypothesis

    C. Inference

    D. Law

85. When teaching science, which of the following is a method of focusing on students' intrinsic motivation? (Skill 11.5; Average rigor)

   A. Adapting the lessons to students' interests

   B. Providing regular feedback

   C. Supplying rewards for the highest achievers

   D. Having regular science tests

86. What does geography include the study of? (Skill 12.1; Easy)

   A. Location

   B. Distribution of living things

   C. Distribution of the earth's features

   D. All of the above

87. Economics is the study of how a society allocates its scarce resources to satisfy: (Skill 12.1; Average rigor)

   A. Unlimited and competing wants

   B. Limited and competing wants

   C. Unlimited and cooperative wants

   D. Limited and cooperative wants

88. The two elements of a market economy are: (Skill 12.1; Rigorous)

   A. Inflation and deflation

   B. Supply and demand

   C. Cost and price

   D. Wants and needs

89. Who has the power to veto a bill that has passed the House of Representatives and the Senate? (Skill 12.1; Rigorous)

   A. The President

   B. The Vice President

   C. The Speaker of the House

   D. Any member of Congress

90. Which part of a map shows the relationship between a unit of measurement on the map versus the real world measure on the Earth? (Skill 12.2; Easy)

    A. Scale

    B. Title

    C. Legend

    D. Grid

91. What is the most important focus in developing social studies skills during the early years? (Skill 12.4; Average rigor)

    A. Recalling facts

    B. Understanding statistics

    C. Discussing ideas

    D. Memorizing rights and responsibilities

92. What is one of the ten essential themes identified by the National Council for Social Studies? (Skill 12.6; Average rigor)

    A. Culture

    B. Lifestyle

    C. Population

    D. Democracy

93. Which subject would a color wheel most likely be used for? (Skill 13.1; Easy)

    A. Visual arts

    B. Music

    C. Movement

    D. Drama

94. A student art sample book would include cotton balls and sand paper to represent: (Skill 13.2; Easy)

    A. Color

    B. Lines

    C. Texture

    D. Shape

95. Which terms refers to the arrangement of one or more items so that they appear symmetrical or asymmetrical? (Skill 13.2; Average rigor)

    A. Balance

    B. Contrast

    C. Emphasis

    D. Unity

96. The four principles of modern dance are substance, form, metakinesis, and: (Skill 13.3; Rigorous)

    A. Dynamism

    B. Function

    C. Space

    D. Performance

97. What should the arts curriculum for early childhood avoid? (Skill 13.4; Average rigor)

    A. Judgment

    B. Open expression

    C. Experimentation

    D. Discovery

98. What would the viewing of a dance company performance be most likely to promote? (Skill 13.5; Average rigor)

    A. Critical-thinking skills

    B. Appreciation of the arts

    C. Improvisation skills

    D. Music vocabulary

99. In which subject is it most important for students to work with costumes and props? (Skill 13.6; Easy)

    A. Visual arts

    B. Music

    C. Movement

    D. Drama

100. According to Charles Fowler, why is it important for arts to be incorporated into the teaching of other subject areas? (Skill 13.7; Rigorous)

    A. It reduces loss of interest in the subject.

    B. It enhances the likelihood that students will retain the information.

    C. It provides a three dimensional view of the subject.

    D. It encourages the development of personal connections with the subject.

TEACHER CERTIFICATION STUDY GUIDE

Pre Test Answer Key

1.	B	35.	A	69.	C
2.	A	36.	A	70.	B
3.	B	37.	B	71.	C
4.	A	38.	C	72.	C
5.	A	39.	B	73.	A
6.	D	40.	A	74.	C
7.	D	41.	C	75.	B
8.	B	42.	C	76.	A
9.	A	43.	D	77.	C
10.	D	44.	A	78.	B
11.	D	45.	A	79.	A
12.	A	46.	A	80.	A
13.	A	47.	D	81.	A
14.	A	48.	B	82.	C
15.	C	49.	A	83.	B
16.	D	50.	A	84.	D
17.	D	51.	A	85.	A
18.	A	52.	B	86.	D
19.	A	53.	A	87.	A
20.	B	54.	C	88.	B
21.	C	55.	A	89.	A
22.	A	56.	A	90.	A
23.	C	57.	C	91.	C
24.	C	58.	D	92.	A
25.	A	59.	A	93.	A
26.	B	60.	C	94.	C
27.	A	61.	B	95.	A
28.	D	62.	B	96.	A
29.	C	63.	A	97.	A
30.	A	64.	C	98.	B
31.	D	65.	A	99.	D
32.	C	66.	D	100.	C
33.	C	67.	D		
34.	D	68.	C		

Pre Test Rigor Table

	Easy %20	Average rigor %40	Rigorous %40
Question #	5, 9, 10, 11, 14, 28, 31, 39, 41, 43, 48, 52, 54, 65, 71, 86, 90, 93, 94, 99	1, 2, 3, 6, 18, 19, 20, 21, 22, 25, 26, 32, 33, 35, 37, 40, 45, 46, 47, 50, 56, 58, 59, 60, 64, 69, 72, 74, 76, 77, 79, 80, 83, 85, 87, 91, 92, 95, 97, 98,	4, 7, 8, 12, 13, 15, 16, 17, 23, 24, 27, 29, 30, 34, 36, 38, 42, 44, 49, 51, 53, 55, 57, 61, 62, 63, 66, 67, 68, 70, 73, 75, 78, 81, 82, 84, 88, 89, 96, 100

TEACHER CERTIFICATION STUDY GUIDE

Pre Test Answer Key Rationale

Subarea I. Child Development and Learning

1. What developmental patterns should a professional teacher assess to meet the needs of each student? (Skill 1.1; Average rigor)

    A. Academic, regional, and family background
    B. Social, physical, and academic
    C. Academic, physical, and family background
    D. Physical, family, and ethnic background

Answer B: Social, physical, and academic

The effective teacher applies knowledge of physical, social, and academic developmental patterns and of individual differences, to meet the instructional needs of all students in the classroom.

2. The various domains of development are best described as: (Skill 1.1; Average rigor)

    A. Integrated
    B. Independent
    C. Simultaneous
    D. Parallel

Answer A: Integrated

The most important premise of child development is that all domains of development (physical, social, and academic) are integrated.

3. Which of the following best describes how different areas of development impact each other? (Skill 1.2; Average rigor)

   A. Development in other areas cannot occur until cognitive development is complete.
   B. Areas of development are inter-related and impact each other.
   C. Development in each area is independent of development in other areas.
   D. Development in one area leads to a decline in other areas.

Answer B: Areas of development are inter-related and impact each other.

Child development does not occur in a vacuum. Each element of development impacts other elements of development. For example, as cognitive development progresses, social development often follows. The reason for this is that all areas of development are fairly inter-related.

4. A student has developed and improved in vocabulary. However, the student is not confident enough to use the improved vocabulary, and the teacher is not aware of the improvement. What is this an example of? (Skill 1.2; Rigorous)

   A. Latent development
   B. Dormant development
   C. Random development
   D. Delayed development

Answer A: Latent development

Latent development refers to the way that development in students may not always be observable. A student that has developed and improved in the area of vocabulary, but lacks the confidence to use the vocabulary would not show any outward signs of the development, and so the change may remain hidden. Teachers should be aware of this in order to identify a child's future or near-future capabilities.

TEACHER CERTIFICATION STUDY GUIDE

5. **Which of the following has been shown to have the greatest impact on a student's academic performance? (Skill 1.3; Easy)**

    A. The teacher's expectations
    B. Strict discipline
    C. The student's social skills
    D. Measurable objectives

Answer A: The teacher's expectations

Considerable research has been done, over several decades, regarding student performance. Time and again, a direct correlation has been demonstrated between the teacher's expectations for a particular student and that student's academic performance. This may be unintended and subtle, but the effects are manifest and measurable.

6. **According to Piaget, when does the development of symbolic functioning and language first take place? (Skill 1.4; Average rigor)**

    A. Concrete operations stage
    B. Formal operations stage
    C. Sensory-motor stage
    D. Pre-operational stage

Answer D: Pre-operational stage

The pre-operational stage is where children begin to understand symbols. For example, as they learn language, they begin to realize that words are symbols of thoughts, actions, items, and other elements in the world. This stage lasts into early elementary school.

7. **Playing team sports at young ages should be done for the following purpose: (Skill 1.5; Rigorous)**

    A. To develop the child's motor skills
    B. To prepare children for competition in high school
    C. To develop the child's interests
    D. Both A and C

Answer D: Both A and C

Sports, for both boys and girls, can be very valuable. Parents and teachers, though, need to remember that sports at young ages should only be for the purpose of development of interests and motor skills—not competition. Many children will learn that they do not enjoy sports, and parents and teachers should be respectful of these decisions.

8. The stages of play development from infancy stages to early childhood includes a move from: (Skill 1.5; Rigorous)

   A. Cooperative to solitary
   B. Solitary to cooperative
   C. Competitive to collaborative
   D. Collaborative to competitive

Answer B: Solitary to cooperative

The stages of play development move from mainly solitary in the infancy stages to cooperative in early childhood. However, even in early childhood, children should be able to play on their own and entertain themselves from time to time.

9. Which of the following is NOT an economic factor that may influence the health of a child? (Skill 1.7; Easy)

   A. Pollution
   B. Malnutrition
   C. Neglect
   D. Poor medical care

Answer A: Pollution

Malnutrition, neglect, and poor medical care are economic factors that may influence the health of a child. Pollution could influence the health of a child, but it is not an economic factor.

10. Which of the following is the main source of energy in the diet? (Skill 1.8; Easy)

    A. Vitamins
    B. Minerals
    C. Water
    D. Carbohydrates

Answer D: Carbohydrates

The components of nutrition are carbohydrates, proteins, fats, vitamins, minerals, and water. Carbohydrates are the main source of energy (glucose) in the human diet. Common sources of carbohydrates are fruits, vegetables, grains, dairy products, and legumes.

11. Which of the following would be likely to influence a student's learning and academic progress? (Skill 2.1; Easy)

    A. Relocation
    B. Emotional abuse
    C. Bullying
    D. All of the above

Answer D: All of the above

Children can be influenced by social and emotional factors. Relocation, emotional, abuse, and bullying can all have a negative impact on a student's learning and academic progress.

12. Which of the following best explains why emotional upset and emotional abuse can reduce a child's classroom performance? (Skill 2.1; Rigorous)

    A. They reduce the energy that students put towards schoolwork.
    B. They lead to a reduction in cognitive ability.
    C. They contribute to learning disorders such as dyslexia.
    D. They result in the development of behavioral problems.

Answer A: They reduce the energy that students put towards schoolwork.

Although cognitive ability is not lost due to abuse, neglect, emotional upset, or lack of verbal interaction, the child will most likely not be able to provide as much intellectual energy as the child would if none of these things were present. This explains why classroom performance is often negatively impacted.

TEACHER CERTIFICATION STUDY GUIDE

13. A teacher has a class containing several students from low income families. What would be the most important factor for a teacher to consider when planning homework assignments to ensure that all students have equal opportunity for academic success? (Skill 2.2; Rigorous)

    A. Access to technology
    B. Ethnicity
    C. Language difficulties
    D. Gender

Answer A: Access to technology

Families with higher incomes are able to provide increased opportunities for students. Students from lower income families will need to depend on the resources available from the school system and the community. To ensure that all students have equal opportunity for academic success, teachers should plan assessments so that not having access to technology does not disadvantage students from low income families.

14. Family members with high levels of education often have high expectations for student success. This shows how students are influenced by their family's: (Skill 2.2; Easy)

    A. Attitude
    B. Resources
    C. Income
    D. Culture

Answer A: Attitude

Parental/family influences on students include the influence of attitude. Family members with high levels of education often have high expectations for student success and this can have a positive impact on the student. The opposite can occur for some students from families with low levels of education. However, some families have high expectations for student success based on aspirations for their children regardless of their own status.

EARLY CHILDHOOD EDUCATION

15. **Why is it most important for teachers to ensure that students from different economic backgrounds have access to the resources they need to acquire the academic skills being taught? (Skill 2.4; Rigorous)**

    A. All students must work together on set tasks.
    B. All students must achieve the same results in performance tasks.
    C. All students must have equal opportunity for academic success.
    D. All students must be fully included in classroom activities.

Answer C: All students must have equal opportunity for academic success.

The economic backgrounds of students can impact the resources they have. Regardless of the positive or negative impacts on the students' education from outside sources, it is the teacher's responsibility to ensure that all students in the classroom have an equal opportunity for academic success. This includes ensuring that all students have equal access to the resources needed to acquire the skills being taught.

16. **A teacher attempting to create a differentiated classroom should focus on incorporating activities that: (Skill 2.4; Rigorous)**

    A. Favor academically advanced students
    B. Challenge special education students to achieve more
    C. Are suitable for whichever group of students is the majority
    D. Meet the needs of all the students in the class

Answer D: Meet the needs of all the students in the class

A differentiated classroom is one that meets the needs of special education students, the regular mainstream students, and those that are academically advanced. The purpose of the differentiated classroom is to provide appropriate activities for students at all levels.

17. When developing lessons, it is important that teachers provide equity in pedagogy so that: (Skill 2.4; Rigorous)

   A. Unfair labeling of students will not occur
   B. Student experiences will be positive
   C. Students will achieve academic success
   D. All of the above

Answer D: All of the above

When there is equity pedagogy, teachers can use a variety of instructional styles to facilitate diversity in cooperative learning and individualized instruction that will provide more opportunities for positive student experiences and academic success. Empowering the school culture and climate by establishing an anti-bias learning environment and promoting multicultural learning inclusion will also discourage unfair labeling of certain students.

18. Which of the following is NOT a communication issue related to diversity within the classroom? (Skill 2.4; Average rigor)

   A. Learning disorders
   B. Sensitive terminology
   C. Body language
   D. Discussing differing viewpoints and opinions

Answer A: Learning disorders

There are several communication issues that the teacher in a diverse classroom should be aware of. These include being sensitive to terminology, being aware of body language, and emphasizing the discussion of differing viewpoints and opinions.

19. One common factor for students with all types of disabilities is that they are also likely to demonstrate difficulty with: (Skill 2.5; Average rigor)

   A. Social skills
   B. Cognitive skills
   C. Problem-solving skills
   D. Decision-making skills

Answer A: Social skills

Students with disabilities (in all areas) may demonstrate difficulty in social skills. For a student with a hearing impairment, social skills may be difficult because of not hearing social language. However, the emotionally disturbed student may have difficulty because of a special type of psychological disturbance. An autistic student, as a third example, would be unaware of the social cues given with voice, facial expression, and body language. Each of these students would need social skill instruction but in a different way.

20. A student does not respond to any signs of affection and responds to other children by repeating back what they have said. What condition is the student most likely to have? (Skill 2.5; Average rigor)

   A. Mental retardation
   B. Autism
   C. Giftedness
   D. Hyperactivity

Answer B: Autism

There are six common features of autism. They are:

Apparent sensory deficit – lack of reaction to or overreaction to a stimulus.

Severe affect isolation – lack of response to affection, such as smiles and hugs.

Self-stimulation – repeated or ritualistic actions that make no sense to others.

Tantrums and self-injurious behavior (SIB) – throwing tantrums, injuring oneself, or aggression.

Echolalia (also known as "parrot talk") – repetition of sounds or responding to others by repeating what was said to him.

Severe deficits in behavior and self-care skills – behaving like children much younger than themselves.

21. **Which of the following conditions is more common for girls than boys? (Skill 2.5; Average rigor)**

    A. Attention deficit disorder
    B. Aggression
    C. Phobias
    D. Autism

Answer C: Phobias

Many more boys than girls are identified as having emotional and behavioral problems, especially hyperactivity and attention deficit disorder, autism, childhood psychosis, and problems with undercontrol such as aggression and socialized aggression. Girls have more problems with overcontrol, such as withdrawal and phobias.

22. **In successful inclusion of students with disabilities: (Skill 2.5; Average rigor)**

    A. A variety of instructional arrangements are available
    B. School personnel shift the responsibility for learning outcomes to the student
    C. The physical facilities are used as they are
    D. Regular classroom teachers have sole responsibility for evaluating student progress

Answer A: A variety of instructional arrangements are available

All students have the right to an education, but there cannot be a singular path to that education. A teacher must acknowledge the variety of learning styles and abilities among students within a class apply multiple instructional and assessment processes to ensure that every child has appropriate opportunities to master the subject matter, demonstrate such mastery, and improve and enhance learning skills with each lesson.

23. Mr. Gorman has taught a concept to his class. All of the students have grasped the concept except for Sam. Mr. Gorman should: (Skill 3.2; Rigorous)

   A. Reteach the concept to the whole class in exactly the same way
   B. Reteach the concept to Sam in exactly the same way
   C. Reteach the concept to Sam in a different way
   D. Reteach the concept to the whole class in a different way

Answer C: Reteach the concept to Sam in a different way

There is always more than one way to approach a problem, an example, a process, fact or event, or any learning situation. Varying approaches for instruction helps to maintain the students' interest in the material and enables the teacher to address the diverse needs of individuals to comprehend the material.

24. Mrs. Gomez has a fully integrated early childhood curriculum. This is beneficial to students because it: (Skill 3.2; Rigorous)

   A. Is easier to plan for and maintain
   B. Allows students to apply their unique skills
   C. Helps the students see the relationships between subjects and concepts
   D. Provides opportunities for social interaction

Answer C: Helps the students see the relationships between subjects and concepts

An integrated curriculum is a curriculum in which lessons are taught in several different subject areas according to the outcomes that deal with the same concepts. It may also be known as thematic teaching or interdisciplinary teaching.

TEACHER CERTIFICATION STUDY GUIDE

Subarea II. Communication, Language and Literacy Development

25. The relationship between oral language and reading skills is best described as: (Skill 4.1; Average rigor)

    A. Reciprocal
    B. Inverse
    C. Opposite
    D. There is no relationship.

Answer A: Reciprocal

A highly developed oral language vocabulary helps to build reading skills comprehension. The inverse is true as well, with highly developed reading and comprehension skills helping to develop oral language skills.

26. A teacher is showing students how to construct grammatically correct sentences. What is the teacher focusing on? (Skill 4.1; Average rigor)

    A. Morphology
    B. Syntax
    C. Semantics
    D. Pragmatics

Answer B: Syntax

Syntax refers to the rules or patterned relationships that correctly create phrases and sentences from words. When readers develop an understanding of syntax, they begin to understand the structure of how sentences are built, and eventually the beginning of grammar.

27. A teacher writes the following words on the board: cot, cotton, and cottage. What is the teacher most likely teaching the students about? (Skill 4.1; Rigorous)

    A. Morphology
    B. Syntax
    C. Semantics
    D. Pragmatics

Answer A: Morphology

Morphology is the study of word structure. When readers develop morphemic skills, they are developing an understanding of patterns they see in words. For example, English speakers realize that cat, cats, and caterpillar share some similarities in structure. This understanding helps readers to recognize words at a faster and easier rate, since each word doesn't need individual decoding.

28. While standing in line at the grocery store, three-year-old Megan says to her mother in a regular tone of voice, "Mom, why is that woman so fat?" What does this indicate a lack of understanding of? (Skill 4.2; Easy)

    A. Syntax
    B. Semantics
    C. Morphology
    D. Pragmatics

Answer D: Pragmatics

Pragmatics is the development and understanding of social relevance to conversations and topics. It develops as children age. In this situation, Megan simply does not understand to the same level of an adult how that question could be viewed as offensive to certain members of society.

29. **Which of the following is the first component of the constructivist model? (Skill 4.2; Rigorous)**

    A. There are at least seven different types of learning.
    B. Learning depends on the social environment.
    C. Learner creates knowledge
    D. Learning progresses through set stages.

Answer C: Learner creates knowledge

Researchers have shown that the constructivist model is comprised of the four components:
1. Learner creates knowledge
2. Learner constructs and makes meaningful new knowledge from existing knowledge
3. Learner shapes and constructs knowledge by life experiences and social interactions
4. In constructivist learning communities, the student, teacher and classmates establish knowledge cooperatively on a daily basis.

30. **Students are about to read a text that contains words that will need to be understood for the students to understand the text. When should the vocabulary be introduced to students? (Skill 4.5; Rigorous)**

    A. Before reading
    B. During reading
    C. After reading
    D. It should not be introduced.

Answer A: Before reading

Vocabulary should be introduced before reading if there are words within the text that are definitely keys necessary for reading comprehension.

31. Which of the following are examples of temporal words? (Skill 4.6; Easy)

    A. Beside and behind
    B. Hotter and colder
    C. In and on
    D. Before and after

Answer D: Before and after

Temporal words are words that indicate time. Before and after are two examples of temporal words.

32. Which principle of Stephen Krashen's research suggests that the learning of grammatical structures is predictable? (Skill 5.1; Average rigor)

    A. The affective filter hypothesis
    B. The input hypothesis
    C. The natural order hypothesis
    D. The monitor hypothesis

Answer C: The natural order hypothesis

Stephen Krashen's natural order hypothesis suggests that the learning of grammatical structures is predictable and follows a natural order.

33. Above what age does learning a language become increasingly difficult? (Skill 5.2; Average rigor)

    A. 3
    B. 5
    C. 7
    D. 10

Answer C: 7

The most important concept to remember regarding the difference between learning a first language and a second one is that if the learner is approximately age seven or older, learning a second language will occur very differently in the learner's brain than it would had the learner been younger. The reason for this is that there is a language-learning function that exists in young children that appears to go away as they mature. Learning a language prior to age seven is almost guaranteed, with relatively little effort.

TEACHER CERTIFICATION STUDY GUIDE

34. Ms. Chomski is presenting a new story to her class of first graders. In the story, a family visits their grandparents where they all gather around a record player and listen to music. Many students do not understand what a record player is, especially some children for whom English is not their first language. Which of the following would Ms. Chomski be best to do? (Skill 5.2; Rigorous)

    A. Discuss what a record player is with her students
    B. Compare a record player with a CD player
    C. Have students look up record player in a dictionary
    D. Show the students a picture of a record player

Answer D: Show the students a picture of a record player

The most effective method for ensuring adequate comprehension is through direct experience. Sometimes this cannot be completed and therefore it is necessary to utilize pictures or other visual aids to provide the students with experience in another mode besides oral language.

35. Jose moved to the United States last month. He speaks little or no English at this time. His teacher is teaching the class about habitats in science and has chosen to read a story about various habitats to the class. The vocabulary is difficult. What should Jose's teacher do with Jose? (Skill 5.3; Average rigor)

    A. Provide Jose with additional opportunities to learn about habitats
    B. Read the story to Jose multiple times
    C. Show Jose pictures of habitats from his native country
    D. Excuse Jose from the assignment

Answer A: Provide Jose with additional opportunities to learn about habitats

Students who are learning English should be exposed to a variety of opportunities to learn the same concepts as native speakers. Content should not be changed, but the manner in which it is presented and reinforced should be changed.

36. **In the early childhood classroom, it is important to limit teacher talk. What is the main problem with teacher talk? (Skill 5.5; Rigorous)**

   A.   It is often one sided and limited.
   B.   The vocabulary is too difficult for children.
   C.   It promotes misbehavior.
   D.   It only creates gains in receptive language.

Answer A: It is often one sided and limited.

While it is important to expose children to numerous opportunities throughout the day to read and interact with print, it is equally important for students to have the opportunity to express themselves and communicate with each other. Teacher-talk, is often one sided and limited. Instead, teachers should provide opportunities for students to develop and expand their vocabularies.

37. **Which of the following is a convention of print that children learn during reading activities? (Skill 6.3; Average rigor)**

   A.   The meaning of words
   B.   The left to right motion
   C.   The purpose of print
   D.   The identification of letters

Answer B: The left to right motion

During reading activities, children learn conventions of print. Children learn the way to hold a book, where to begin to read, the left to right motion, and how to continue from one line to another.

38. In her kindergarten class, Mrs. Thomas has been watching the students in the drama center. She has watched the children pretend to complete a variety of magic tricks. Mrs. Thomas decides to use stories about magic to share with her class. Her decision to incorporate their interests into the reading shows that Mrs. Thomas understands that: (Skill 6.7; Rigorous)

   A. Including student interests is important at all times
   B. Teaching by themes is crucial for young children
   C. Young children respond to literature that reflects their lives
   D. Science fiction and fantasy are the most popular genres

Answer C: Young children respond to literature that reflects their lives

Children's literature is intended to instruct students through entertaining stories, while also promoting an interest in the very act of reading, itself. Young readers respond best to themes that reflect their lives.

39. Which of the following is NOT a characteristic of a fable? (Skill 6.8; Easy)

   A. Have animal characters that act like humans
   B. Considered to be true
   C. Teaches a moral
   D. Reveals human foibles

Answer B: Considered to be true

The common characteristics of fables are animals that act like humans, a focus on revealing human foibles, and teaching a moral or lesson. Fables are not considered to be true.

40. Alphabet books are classified as: (Skill 6.8; Average rigor)

   A. Concept books
   B. Easy-to-read books
   C. Board books
   D. Pictures books

Answer A: Concept books

Concept books are books that combine language and pictures to show concrete examples of concepts. One category of concept books is alphabet books, which are popular with children from preschool through to grade 2.

41. The stories of Paul Bunyan, John Henry, and Pecos Bill are all exaggerated accounts of individuals with superhuman strength. What type of literature are these works? (Skill 6.8; Easy)

    A. Fables
    B. Fairytales
    C. Tall tales
    D. Myths

Answer C: Tall tales

Tall tales are purposely exaggerated accounts of individuals with superhuman strength. The stories of Paul Bunyan, John Henry, and Pecos Bill are all examples of tall tales. Fables are usually stories about animals with human features that often teach a lesson. Fairytales usually focus on good versus evil, reward and punishment. Myths are stories about events from the earliest times.

42. Which of the following is NOT a motivation behind providing reading activities, including reading aloud, to young children? (Skill 7.1; Rigorous)

    A. Developing word consciousness skills
    B. Developing functions of print skills
    C. Developing phonics skills
    D. Developing language skills

Answer C: Developing phonics skills

There are almost unlimited positive reasons for encouraging adults to provide reading activities for young children. While it can be true that reading aloud may improve the phonics skills for some students, it is not a motivation for providing such activities to students.

TEACHER CERTIFICATION STUDY GUIDE

43. **Which of the following is an appropriate way for students to respond to literature? (Skill 7.1; Easy)**

    A. Art
    B. Drama
    C. Writing
    D. All of the above

Answer D: All of the above

Responding to literature through art, writing, and drama helps children to reflect on the books they have read and make them a part of their lives.

44. **John is having difficulty reading the word reach. In isolation, he pronounces each sound as /r/ /ee/ /sh/. Which of the following is a possible instructional technique which could help solve John's reading difficulty? (Skill 7.2; Rigorous)**

    A. Additional phonemic awareness instruction
    B. Additional phonics instruction
    C. Additional skill and drill practice
    D. Additional minimal pair practice

Answer A: Additional phonemic awareness instruction

John is having difficulty with the sound symbol relationship between the /ch/ and /sh/. While it may appear at first that this is a phonics problem, in fact, it is important to begin with the earlier skill of phonemic awareness to ensure the student has a solid foundational understanding of the oral portions before moving totally into the sound symbol arena. If John is able to distinguish between the two sounds orally, it is obvious more phonics instruction is needed. However, proceeding directly to phonics instruction may be pointless and frustrating for John if he is unable to hear the distinctions.

TEACHER CERTIFICATION STUDY GUIDE

45. According to Marilyn Jager Adams, which skill would a student demonstrate by identifying that cat does not belong in the group of words containing dog, deer, and dress? (Skill 7.2; Average rigor)

    A. Recognize the odd member in a group
    B. Replace sounds in words
    C. Count the sounds in a word
    D. Count syllables in a word

Answer A: Recognize the odd member in a group

One of Marilyn Jager Adams' basic types of phonemic awareness tasks involves the ability to do oddity tasks, which involves recognizing the member of a set that is different among the group. In this example, the word cat is the odd member because it starts with a different sound.

46. Which of the following is NOT true about phonological awareness? (Skill 7.2; Average rigor)

    A. It may involve print.
    B. It is a prerequisite for spelling and phonics.
    C. Activities can be done by the children with their eyes closed.
    D. It starts before letter recognition is taught.

Answer A: It may involve print.

All of the options are correct aspects of phonological awareness except the first one, because phonological awareness does not involve print.

47. Which of the following explains a significant difference between phonics and phonemic awareness? (Skill 7.3; Average rigor)

    A. Phonics involves print, while phonemic awareness involves language.
    B. Phonics is harder than phonemic awareness.
    C. Phonics involves sounds, while phonemic awareness involves letters.
    D. Phonics is the application of sounds to print, while phonemic awareness is oral.

Answer D: Phonics is the application of sounds to print, while phonemic awareness is oral.

Both phonics and phonemic awareness activities involve sounds, but it is with phonics that the application of these sounds is applied to print. Phonemic awareness is an oral activity.

48. To decode is to: (Skill 7.3; Easy)

    A. Construct meaning
    B. Sound out a printed sequence of letters
    C. Use a special code to decipher a message
    D. Revise for errors in grammar

Answer B: Sound out a printed sequence of letters

Decoding is the process students use to figure out unknown words when reading.

49. Ms. Walker's lesson objective is to teach her first graders the concept of morphology in order to improve their reading skills. Which group of words would be most appropriate for her to use in this lesson? (Skill 7.3; Rigorous)

    A. Far, farm, farmer
    B. Far, feather, fever
    C. Far, fear, fare
    D. Far, fare, farce

Answer A: Far, farm, farmer

The concept of morphology is to understand how words relate to each other and can be built upon to increase reading skills. In the correct answer, the student can utilize the information they learned from learning to read far to help them decode the other words.

50. Which stage of reading skill development occurs first? (Skill 7.3; Average rigor)

    A. Schema stage
    B. Early semantic stage
    C. Orthographic stage
    D. Simultaneous stage

Answer A: Schema stage

Reading develops in sequential skills levels. The first stage is the schema stage. This stage is a pre-reading level involving page turning and telling story from memory.

51. Which of the following is an important feature of vocabulary instruction according to the National Reading Panel? (Skill 7.4; Rigorous)

    A. Repetition of vocabulary items
    B. Keeping a consistent task structure at all times
    C. Teaching vocabulary in more than one language
    D. Isolation vocabulary instruction from other subjects

Answer A: Repetition of vocabulary items

According to the National Reading Panel, repetition and multiple exposures to vocabulary items are important. Students should be given items that will be likely to appear in many contexts.

52. The attitude an author takes toward his or her subject is the: (Skill 7.6; Easy)

    A. Style
    B. Tone
    C. Point of view
    D. Theme

Answer B: Tone

Tone is the attitude an author takes toward his or her subject. That tone is exemplified in the language of the text.

53. George has read his second graders three formats of the story "The Three Little Pigs." One is the traditional version, one is written from the wolf's point of view, and the third is written from the first pig's point of view. As George leads a discussion on the three texts with his students, he is trying to help his students develop their ability to: (Skill 7.7; Rigorous)

    A. Compare and contrast texts
    B. Understand point of view
    C. Recognize metaphors
    D. Rewrite fictional stories

Answer A: Compare and contrast texts

George understands the importance of developing critical thinking skills in young children. He has read three different formats of the same story in order to help his students develop their ability to compare texts.

54. What is the first step in developing writing skills? (Skill 8.1; Easy)

    A. Early writing
    B. Experimental writing
    C   Role play writing
    D. Conventional writing

Answer C: Role play writing

Children develop writing skills through a series of steps. These steps are: role play writing, experimental writing, early writing, and then conventional writing. In the role play writing stage, the child writes in scribbles and assigns a message to the symbols. Even though an adult would not be able to read the writing, the child can read what is written although it may not be the same each time the child reads it. S/he will be able to read back the writing because of prior knowledge that print carries a meaning.

55. Which of the following is NOT a prewriting strategy? (Skill 8.1; Rigorous)

    A. Analyzing sentences for variety
    B. Keeping an idea book
    C. Writing in a daily journal
    D. Writing down whatever comes to mind

Answer A: Analyzing sentences for variety

Prewriting strategies assist students in a variety of ways. Common prewriting strategies include keeping an idea book for jotting down ideas, writing in a daily journal, and writing down whatever comes to mind, which is also called "free writing." Analyzing sentences for variety is a revising strategy.

56. Which of the following is probably the most important step for the writer in the writing process? (Skill 8.1; Average rigor)

    A. Revision
    B. Discovery
    C. Conclusion
    D. Organization

Answer A: Revision

Revision is probably the most important step for the writer in the writing process. Here, students examine their work and make changes in wording, details, and ideas. So many times, students write a draft and then feel they're done. Students must be encouraged to develop, change, and enhance their writing as they go, as well as once they've completed a draft.

57. The students in Tina's classroom are working together in pairs. Each student is reading another student's paper and asking who, what, when, where, why, and who questions. What is this activity helping the students to do? (Skill 8.1; Rigorous)

    A. Draft their writing
    B. Paraphrase their writing
    C. Revise their writing
    D. Outline their writing

Answer C: Revise their writing

Students need to be trained to become effective at proofreading, revising and editing strategies. One way to do this is to have the students read their partners' papers and ask at least three who, what, when, why, how questions. The students answer the questions and use them as a place to begin discussing the piece.

58. **Young children learning to write commonly grip the pencil: (Skill 8.2; Average rigor)**

   A. Too far from the point
   B. With the wrong hand
   C. With too many fingers
   D. Too tightly

Answer D: Too tightly

A common problem for all young children learning to write is gripping the pencil too tightly, which makes writing tiresome. Usually the student learns to relax their grip as writing skill develops, but teachers can remind students to hold the instrument gently.

59. **Which of the following approaches to student writing assignments is most likely to lead to students becoming disinterested? (Skill 8.3; Average rigor)**

   A. Designing assignments where students write for a variety of audiences.
   B. Designing assignments where the teacher is the audience.
   C. Designing assignments where students write to friends and family.
   D. Designing assignments where students write to real people such as mayors, the principle, or companies.

Answer B: Designing assignments where the teacher is the audience

In the past, teachers have assigned reports, paragraphs and essays that focused on the teacher as the audience with the purpose of explaining information. However, for students to be meaningfully engaged in their writing, they must write for a variety of reasons. Writing for different audiences and aims allows students to be more involved in their writing. If they write for the same audience and purpose, they will continue to see writing as just another assignment

60. **As a part of prewriting, students should identify their audience. Which of the following questions will help students to identify their audience? (Skill 8.3; Average rigor)**

    A. Why is the audience reading my writing?
    B. What does my audience already know about my topic?
    C. Both A and B
    D. None of the above

Answer C: Both A and B

As part of prewriting, students should identify the audience. Make sure students consider the following when analyzing the needs of their audience: why the audience is reading the writing; what the audience already knows about the topic; what the audience needs or wants to know; what will interest the reader; and what type of language will suit the reader.

61. **Which of these describes the best way to teach spelling? (Skill 8.5; Rigorous)**

    A. At the same time that grammar and sentence structure is taught.
    B. Within the context of meaningful language experiences.
    C. Independently so that students can concentrate on spelling.
    D. In short lessons as students pick up spelling almost immediately.

Answer B: Within the context of meaningful language experiences.

Spelling should be taught within the context of meaningful language experiences. Giving a child a list of words to learn to spell and then testing the child on the words every Friday will not aid in the development of spelling. The child must be able to use the words in context and they must have some meaning for the child. The assessment of how well a child can spell or where there are problems also has to be done within a meaningful environment.

TEACHER CERTIFICATION STUDY GUIDE

62. **When editing, teachers should direct students to: (Skill 8.6; Rigorous)**

    A. Edit for general understanding, while ignoring grammar and spelling.
    B. Edit for one specific purpose at a time.
    C. Identify all spelling, capitalization, and punctuation errors.
    D. Be critical of their work and that of others.

Answer B: Edit for one specific purpose at a time.

Editing is a time-consuming task and it would be unreasonable to expect students to pick up on all the mistakes in a piece of writing. Therefore, teachers should ask students to edit for specific purposes at one time, such as correct spelling, capitalization or punctuation.

Subarea III. Learning in the Content Areas

63. **Kindergarten students are participating in a calendar time activity. One student adds a straw to the "ones can" to represent that day of school. What math principle is being reinforced? (Skill 9.1; Rigorous)**

    A. Properties of a base ten number system
    B. Sorting
    C. Counting by twos
    D. Even and odd numbers

Answer A: Properties of a base ten number system

As the students group craft sticks into groups of tens to represent the days of school, they are learning the properties of our base ten number system.

64. **First grade students are arranging four small squares of identical size to form a larger square. Each small square represents what part of the larger square? (Skill 9.1; Average rigor)**

    A. One half
    B. One whole
    C. One fourth
    D. One fifth

Answer C: One fourth

Four of the small squares make up the area of the large square. Each small square is one fourth of the larger square.

65. What is the answer to this problem? (Skill 9.2; Easy)

    25 ÷ 5 =

    A. 5
    B. 30
    C. 125
    D. 20

Answer A: 5

Twenty-five can be divided into five equal groups of five.

66. Third grade students are studying percents. When looking at a circle graph divided into three sections, they see that one section is worth 80% and one section is worth 5%. What will the remaining section be worth? (Skill 9.2; Rigorous)

    A. 100%
    B. 85%
    C. 75%
    D. 15%

Answer D: 15%

Percentages use the base ten number system. Percentages of a total amount will always add up to 100%. Since the two sections add to 85%, the third section must be 15%.

67. Which of the following letters does NOT have a line of symmetry? (Skill 9.3; Rigorous)

    A. O
    B. D
    C. M
    D. J

Answer D: J

For an object to show symmetry, it must be able to be divided into identical halves. The letter O has an unlimited number of lines of symmetry. The letter D has a horizontal line of symmetry. The letter M has a vertical line of symmetry. The letter J does not have a line of symmetry.

68. Kindergarten students are doing a butterfly art project. They fold paper in half. On one half, they paint a design. Then they fold the paper closed and reopen. The resulting picture is a butterfly with matching sides. What math principle does this demonstrate? (Skill 9.3; Rigorous)

   A. Slide
   B. Rotate
   C. Symmetry
   D. Transformation

Answer C: Symmetry

By folding the painted paper in half, the design is mirrored on the other side, creating symmetry and reflection. The butterfly design is symmetrical about the center.

69. What number comes next in this pattern? (Skill 9.3; Average rigor)

   3, 8, 13, 18, ____

   A. 21
   B. 26
   C. 23
   D. 5

Answer C: 23

This pattern is made by adding five to the preceding number. The next number is found by adding 5 to 18, which gives the answer 23.

70. What is the main purpose of having kindergarten students count by twos? (Skill 9.4; Rigorous)

   A. To hear a rhythm
   B. To recognize patterns in numbers
   C. To practice addition
   D. To become familiar with equations

Answer B: To recognize patterns in numbers

Recognizing patterns in numbers is an early skill for multiplication. It will also help children recognize patterns in word families such as *bit, hit, fit*.

71. The term *millimeters* indicates which kind of measurement? (Skill 9.5; Easy)

    A. Volume
    B. Weight
    C. Length
    D. Temperature

Answer C: Length

The term *millimeters* is a reference to length in the metric system.

72. What type of graph would be best to use to show changes in the height of a plant over the course of a month? (Skill 9.7; Average rigor)

    A. Circle graph
    B. Bar graph
    C. Line graph
    D. Pictograph

Answer C: Line graph

A line graph shows trends over time. A line graph would show how the plant's height changed over time.

73. A teacher completes a survey of student eye color. The teacher then creates a graph so students can compare how many students have each eye color. What type of graph should be used? (Skill 9.7; Rigorous)

    A. Bar graph
    B. Pictograph
    C. Circle graph
    D. Line Graph

Answer A: Bar graph

Bar graphs are used to compare various quantities. In this case, the bar graph would show the number of students with each eye color. By looking at the graph, students would be able to compare how many students have each eye color. While a pictograph is also possible, if there are many different eye colors in the class, it would take up a lot of space to graph it this way.

74. Which of the following skills would a student develop first? (Skill 10.1; Average rigor)

   A.   Understanding place value
   B.   Recognizing number patterns
   C.   Counting objects
   D.   Solving number problems

Answer C: Counting objects

As with the phonemic awareness skills in reading, number sense is the foundation upon which all future math topics will be built. While in this beginning stage, children will be able to identify how many objects are in a group.

75. Maddie is a first grade teacher who understands the importance of including the family when providing instruction. She wants to take several steps to provide families with a connection to what the students are doing in her math class. Which of the following is NOT a strategy she could incorporate? (Skill 10.3; Rigorous)

   A.   Including a math portion in her regular newsletter
   B.   Incorporating manipulatives into her math lessons
   C.   Translating math homework into the native language of the students in her classroom
   D.   Having a family math night at school

Answer B: Incorporating manipulatives into her math lessons

While incorporating manipulatives into her curriculum is an excellent strategy, which should take place in every math classroom, it does not promote the inclusion of family into the curriculum.

76. George has successfully mastered his basic addition facts. However, as his teacher presents more complex addition problems, it is obvious to him that George is lacking a basic understanding of the concept of addition. What would George's teacher be best to do to increase his basic understanding? (Skill 10.4; Average rigor)

    A. Provide additional instruction with hands on materials
    B. Have George practice his addition facts more frequently
    C. Have George complete more challenging addition problems
    D. Provide George with remediation

Answer A: Provide additional instruction with hands on materials

When students have the time to explore and build their own constructs using concrete objects, they are able to make more generalizations. Students may be able to memorize pieces of rote information, but without the foundational exposure to hands on materials they may not be able to demonstrate these generalizations. It is the role of the teacher to take the time to provide these opportunities.

77. Carrie approaches her teacher after class and expresses her personal frustration with math and her feeling that she will never get it. Which of the following is NOT a suitable method Carrie's teacher can utilize to improve Carrie's feelings about math? (Skill 10.6; Average rigor)

    A. Incorporating some of Carrie's specific interests into math lessons
    B. Holding Carrie to high expectations
    C. Sharing with Carrie her own struggles and dislike for math
    D. Providing Carrie with extra positive reinforcement and encouragement

Answer C: Sharing with Carrie her own struggles and dislike for math

While it may seem to be a bonding experience to share your own personal struggles and dislike for the subject with a student who feels the same way, it is important for the teacher to maintain excitement and enthusiasm for the subject. Carrie's teacher would be better to share positive aspects about how math as affected her life, than to share any negative feelings. Building a positive excitement and interest in the subject is an important part of teaching.

78. The principal walks into your classroom during math class. He sees your students making cake mixtures. Later, the principal questions your lesson. What would be the best explanation for your lesson? (Skill 10.7; Rigorous)

   A. The students earned a reward time and it was free choice.
   B. You were teaching the students how math is used in real-life situations.
   C. You had paperwork to complete and needed the time to complete it.
   D. It kept the students interested in math and prevented boredom.

Answer B: You were teaching the students how math is used in real-life situations.

Providing the students with the opportunity to explore how math is around them and how it is utilized in everyday experiences is important. As students identify and realize the importance of the skills being learned to their lives at home, they will become more involved in the learning, as it has new and better value for them.

79. What is a large, rotating, low-pressure system accompanied by heavy precipitation and strong winds known as? (Skill 11.1; Average rigor)

   A. A hurricane
   B. A tornado
   C. A thunderstorm
   D. A tsunami

Answer A: A hurricane

Hurricanes are storms that develop when warm, moist air carried by trade winds rotates around a low-pressure "eye". These form a large, rotating, low-pressure system and are accompanied by heavy precipitation and strong winds. They are also known as tropical cyclones or typhoons.

80. **What does a primary consumer most commonly refer to? (Skill 11.1; Average rigor)**

   A. Herbivore
   B. Autotroph
   C. Carnivore
   D. Decomposer

Answer A: Herbivore

Autotrophs are the primary producers of the ecosystem. Producers mainly consist of plants. Primary consumers are the next trophic level. The primary consumers are the herbivores that eat plants or algae. Secondary consumers are the carnivores that eat the primary consumers. Tertiary consumers eat the secondary consumer. These trophic levels may go higher depending on the ecosystem.

81. **Airplanes generate pressure and remain balanced by: (Skill 11.1; Rigorous)**

   A. Fast air movement over wings and slow movement under wings
   B. Slow air movement over wings and fast movement under wings
   C. Air movement that is equal above and below wings
   D. Air movement that only occurs over the wings

Answer A: Fast air movement over wings and slow movement under wings

Airplanes or fixed-wing aircraft are heavier than aircraft that utilize the laws of physics to achieve flight. As the aircraft is propelled forward by thrust from the engines, air moves faster over the top of the wings and slower under the bottom. The slower airflow beneath the wing generates more pressure, while the faster airflow above generates less. This difference in pressure results in upward lift.

82. The breakdown of rock due to acid rain is an example of: (Skill 11.1; Rigorous)

   A. Physical weathering
   B. Frost wedging
   C. Chemical weathering
   D. Deposition

Answer C: Chemical weathering

The breaking down of rocks at or near to the Earth's surface is known as weathering. Chemical weathering is the breaking down of rocks through changes in their chemical composition. The breakdown of rock due to acid rain is an example of chemical weathering.

83. What is the last step in the scientific method? (Skill 11.2; Average rigor)

   A. Pose a question
   B. Draw a conclusion
   C. Conduct a test
   D. Record data

Answer B: Draw a conclusion

The steps in the scientific method, in order, are: pose a question, form a hypothesis, conduct a test, observe and record data, and draw a conclusion.

84. Which term best describes Newton's universal gravitation? (Skill 11.3; Rigorous)

   A. Theory
   B. Hypothesis
   C. Inference
   D. Law

Answer D: Law

A hypothesis is an unproved theory or educated guess followed by research to best explain a phenomenon. A theory is the formation of principles or relationships, which have been verified and accepted. It is a proven hypothesis. A law is an explanation of events that occur with uniformity under the same conditions, such as laws of nature or laws of gravitation.

85. When teaching science, which of the following is a method of focusing on students' intrinsic motivation? (Skill 11.5; Average rigor)

   A. Adapting the lessons to students' interests
   B. Providing regular feedback
   C. Supplying rewards for the highest achievers
   D. Having regular science tests

Answer A: Adapting the lessons to students' interests

Teachers can focus on students' intrinsic motivation through adapting the tasks to students' interests, providing opportunities for active response, including a variety of tasks, providing rapid feedback, incorporating games into the lesson, and allowing students the opportunity to make choices, create, and interact with peers.

86. What does geography include the study of? (Skill 12.1; Easy)

   A. Location
   B. Distribution of living things
   C. Distribution of the earth's features
   D. All of the above

Answer D: All of the above

Geography involves studying location and how living things and earth's features are distributed throughout the earth. It includes where animals, people, and plants live and the effects of their relationship with earth's physical features.

87. **Economics is the study of how a society allocates its scarce resources to satisfy: (Skill 12.1; Average rigor)**

   A. Unlimited and competing wants
   B. Limited and competing wants
   C. Unlimited and cooperative wants
   D. Limited and cooperative wants

Answer A: Unlimited and competing wants

Economics is the study of how a society allocates its scarce resources to satisfy what are basically unlimited and competing wants. A fundamental fact of economics is that resources are scarce and that wants are infinite.

88. **The two elements of a market economy are: (Skill 12.1; Rigorous)**

   A. Inflation and deflation
   B. Supply and demand
   C. Cost and price
   D. Wants and needs

Answer B: Supply and demand

A market economy is based on supply and demand. Demand is based on consumer preferences and satisfaction and refers to the quantities of a good or service that buyers are willing and able to buy at different prices during a given period of time. Supply is based on costs of production and refers to the quantities that sellers are willing and able to sell at different prices during a given period of time.

89. **Who has the power to veto a bill that has passed the House of Representatives and the Senate? (Skill 12.1; Rigorous)**

   A. The President
   B. The Vice President
   C. The Speaker of the House
   D. Any member of Congress

Answer A: The President

Once a bill receives final approval by a conference committee, it is signed by the Speaker of the House and the Vice President, who is also the President of the Senate, and sent to the President for consideration. The President may either sign the bill or veto it. If he vetoes the bill, his veto may be overruled if two-thirds of both the Senate and the House vote to do so. Once the President signs it the bill becomes a law.

90. Which part of a map shows the relationship between a unit of measurement on the map versus the real world measure on the Earth? (Skill 12.2; Easy)

- A. Scale
- B. Title
- C. Legend
- D. Grid

Answer A: Scale

The scale of a map is used to show the relationship between a unit of measurement on the map versus the real world measure on the Earth.

91. What is the most important focus in developing social studies skills during the early years? (Skill 12.4; Average rigor)

- A. Recalling facts
- B. Understanding statistics
- C. Discussing ideas
- D. Memorizing rights and responsibilities

Answer C: Discussing ideas

The early years of childhood education is important in shaping the values of a democracy and preparing students for citizenship in later life. Social studies begin the exploration of the processes, rights and freedoms of a democracy. Early in a child's education they begin to learn cooperation, tolerance, and sharing. During the early years, the recalling of factual information is not as important as encouraging discussion and exploration of different perspectives.

TEACHER CERTIFICATION STUDY GUIDE

92. **What is one of the ten essential themes identified by the National Council for Social Studies? (Skill 12.6; Average rigor)**

    A. Culture
    B. Lifestyle
    C. Population
    D. Democracy

Answer A: Culture

The National Council for Social Studies identifies 10 themes essential to social science instruction. These are:
1. Culture
2. Time, Continuity and Change
3. People, Places and Environments
4. Individual development and identity
5. Individuals, Groups and Institutions
6. Power, Authority and Governance
7. Production, Distribution and Consumption
8. Science, Technology and Society
9. Global Connections
10. Civic Ideals and Practices

93. **Which subject would a color wheel most likely be used for? (Skill 13.1; Easy)**

    A. Visual arts
    B. Music
    C. Movement
    D. Drama

Answer A: Visual arts

A color wheel is an important tool in teaching students visual arts. It is used to teach students about primary colors and secondary colors. It is also used to help students learn about mixing colors.

EARLY CHILDHOOD EDUCATION

94. **A student art sample book would include cotton balls and sand paper to represent: (Skill 13.2; Easy)**

    A. Color
    B. Lines
    C. Texture
    D. Shape

Answer C: Texture

Texture refers to the way something feels because of the tactile quality of its surface. An art sample book can include materials such as cotton balls and sand paper as examples of different textures.

95. **Which terms refers to the arrangement of one or more items so that they appear symmetrical or asymmetrical? (Skill 13.2; Average rigor)**

    A. Balance
    B. Contrast
    C. Emphasis
    D. Unity

Answer A: Balance

The principles of visual are that students should be introduced to include abstract, background, balance, contrast, emphasis, sketch, texture, and unity. Balance refers to the arrangement of one or more elements in a work of art so that they appear symmetrical or asymmetrical in design and proportion.

96. **The four principles of modern dance are substance, form, metakinesis, and: (Skill 13.3; Rigorous)**

    A. Dynamism
    B. Function
    C. Space
    D. Performance

Answer A: Dynamism

Modern dance is a type of dance where the focus is on expressing opposites, such as fast-slow or contract-release. Modern dance is based on four principles. These are substance, form, metakinesis, and dynamism.

97. What should the arts curriculum for early childhood avoid? (Skill 13.4; Average rigor)

   A. Judgment
   B. Open expression
   C. Experimentation
   D. Discovery

Answer A: Judgment

The arts curriculum for early childhood should focus on the experimental and discovery aspects of the arts. The emphasis should be on creative processes with little judgment and criticism should be minimal.

98. What would the viewing of a dance company performance be most likely to promote? (Skill 13.5; Average rigor)

   A. Critical-thinking skills
   B. Appreciation of the arts
   C. Improvisation skills
   D. Music vocabulary

Answer B: Appreciation of the arts

Live performances are an important part of learning arts and help to develop aesthetic appreciation of the arts. A dance company performance is one example of a live performance that students could attend.

99. In which subject is it most important for students to work with costumes and props? (Skill 13.6; Easy)

   A. Visual arts
   B. Music
   C. Movement
   D. Drama

Answer D: Drama

When studying drama, students should experience working with props and performing in costume. These can both help students act out experiences and tend to increase creativity.

100. **According to Charles Fowler, why is it important for arts to be incorporated into the teaching of other subject areas? (Skill 13.7; Rigorous)**

    A. It reduces loss of interest in the subject.
    B. It enhances the likelihood that students will retain the information.
    C. It provides a three dimensional view of the subject.
    D. It encourages the development of personal connections with the subject.

Answer C: It provides a three dimensional view of the subject.

Charles Fowler has argued that the best schools also have the best arts programs. According to Fowler, integrating arts with other subject areas gives a more complete view of the subject. Students then gain a more three dimensional understanding of the subject.

AEPA Post Test

1. Which of the following is NOT one of the three domains of development? (Skill 1.1; Easy)

   A. Physical

   B. Social

   C. Emotional

   D. Academic

2. Mrs. Potts is conducting a language development task with her students. She forms students into small mixed-ability groups. She then gives each group a discussion question. Each group is asked to discuss the question, while ensuring that each person has a chance to give their opinion. What approach to language development is this activity based on? (Skill 1.1; Rigorous)

   A. Linguistic approach

   B. Cognitive approach

   C. Socio-cognitive approach

   D. Learning approach

3. Which of the following is a true statement? (Skill 1.2; Average rigor)

   A. Physical development does not influence social development.

   B. Social development does not influence physical development.

   C. Cognitive development does not influence social development.

   D. All domains of development are integrated and influence other domains.

4. Mrs. Smith writes an encouraging note to each student in her classroom every week. These notes encourage the students to improve upon their previous work and to strive to do even better in the future. Mrs. Smith is most likely trying to: (Skill 1.3; Rigorous)

   A. Maintain good discipline

   B. Hold the students to high standards

   C. Meet the needs of individual students

   D. Improve her test scores

5. According to Piaget, during what stage do children learn to manipulate symbols and objects? (Skill 1.4; Average rigor)

   A. Concrete operations

   B. Pre-operational

   C. Formal operations

   D. Conservative operational

6. How many stages of intellectual development does Piaget define? (Skill 1.4; Easy)

   A. Two

   B. Four

   C. Six

   D. Eight

7. Which of the following is a true statement? (Skill 1.5; Rigorous)

   A. Recess is not important to a child's development.

   B. Playtime is only provided in schools to help children release energy.

   C. Play has an important and positive role in child development.

   D. Solitary play is always an indication that a child has development issues.

8. A teacher is planning to get all of her students involved in sports for the purpose of helping develop hand-eye coordination and teamwork skills. What would be the most appropriate approach when planning the sports activities? (Skill 1.5; Rigorous)

   A. Encourage competition among students so they become used to the pressure of competing.

   B. Ensure that students who dislike sports continue until they enjoy sports.

   C. Choose activities that are beyond the student's current abilities so students are prompted to improve.

   D. Maintain a relaxed atmosphere and remind students that the sport is designed to be fun.

9. The principal finds Mr. Thomas's class outside on the playground. The entire class is playing in small groups and everyone is involved and seems to be enjoying the activity. However, it is not recess time on Mr. Thomas's schedule. Later, the principal questions Mr. Thomas about his time on the playground. What would Mr. Thomas be best to say to justify his time spent on the playground in a meaningful manner? (Skill 1.5; Rigorous)

   A. I was helping the students develop motor skills.

   B. I was providing the students with a break.

   C. I was providing the students with an extra recess.

   D. I was allowing the students the chance to work off their extra energy.

10. A learning activity for students below age eight should focus on: (Skill 1.6; Rigorous)

    A. Complex activities

    B. Applying the information

    C. Short time frames

    D. Challenging students

11. Maintaining body weight is best accomplished by: (Skill 1.8; Average rigor)

    A. Dieting

    B. Aerobic exercise

    C. Lifting weights

    D. Equalizing caloric intake relative to output

12. Which of the following is a sign of emotional neglect? (Skill 2.1; Average rigor)

    A. Jealousy of other children

    B. Aggression

    C. Lack of attention to schoolwork

    D. All of the above

13. Mr. De Vries observes that a student appears socially awkward, has difficulty expressing thoughts in words, and is sometimes aggressive. What is most likely to be limiting the student's development? (Skill 2.1; Rigorous)

    A. Emotional abuse

    B. The recent divorce of the student's parents

    C. Lack of verbal interaction

    D. Poor nutrition

14. Because teachers today will deal with an increasingly diverse group of cultures in their classrooms, they must: (Skill 2.4; Average rigor)

    A. Ignore the cultures represented

    B. Demonstrate sensitivity for diversity

    C. Provide a celebration for each culture represented

    D. Focusing on teaching the majority

15. Mrs. Peck wants to justify the use of personalized learning communities to her principal. Which of the following reasons would she be best to use? (Skill 2.4; Rigorous)

    A. They are likely to engage students and maintain their interest.

    B. They provide a supportive environment to address academic and emotional needs.

    C. They encourage students to work independently.

    D. They are proactive in their nature.

16. What criteria are used to assess whether a child qualifies for services under IDEA? (Skill 2.5; Rigorous)

    A. Having a disability only

    B. Having a disability and demonstrating educational need only

    C. Demonstrating educational need only

    D. Having a disability, demonstrating educational need, and having financial support

17. Which of the following is an example of content that has been differentiated to meet the needs of individual learners? (Skill 2.5; Rigorous)

    A. Flexible group activities on various levels

    B. Accepting different final projects from various students

    C. Research projects based on student's interests

    D. Individual tutoring by the teacher to address student weaknesses

18. A child exhibits the following symptoms: inability to appreciate humor, indifference to physical contact, abnormal social play, and abnormal speech. What is the likely diagnosis for this child? (Skill 2.5; Average rigor)

    A. Separation anxiety

    B. Mental retardation

    C. Autism

    D. Hypochondria

19. What actions are observed in aggressive children? (Skill 2.5; Easy)

    A. Vandalism

    B. Destruction of property

    C. Verbal abuse

    D. All of the above

20. What area of differentiated instruction is a teacher focusing on when planning how to teach the material? (Skill 2.5; Average rigor)

    A. Content

    B. Process

    C. Product

    D. Assessment

21. Which is the best approach to the holistic teaching of a concept? (Skill 3.1; Rigorous)

    A. Start with the whole concept and then move on to the parts.

    B. Teach only the parts and avoid focusing on the whole.

    C. Focus only on the whole to avoid students becoming confused by the parts.

    D. Begin with parts until students have developed their own understanding of the whole.

22. Providing instruction from various points of view, not only helps students academically, but it also allows them to: (Skill 3.2; Rigorous)

    A. Work cooperatively and contribute to a team

    B. Develop the personal skill of being able to view situations from multiple viewpoints

    C. Become problem solvers with the ability to apply creative thinking to common problems

    D. Develop tolerance and patience

23. When teaching in a diverse classroom, teachers should: (Skill 3.2; Rigorous)

    A. Plan, devise, and present material in a multicultural manner

    B. Research all possible cultures and expose the children to those

    C. Focus on the curriculum and whatever multicultural opportunities are built into it already

    D. Utilize single format instruction to present material in a multicultural manner

24. Which of the following is the most important reason for integrating the curriculum? (Skill 3.4; Average rigor)

    A. It increases ease of lesson planning.

    B. It meets the needs of diverse students.

    C. It breaks down barriers between subjects.

    D. It narrows the focus of study.

25. Alex is part of a small reading group where the teacher is teaching Alex about the word families -art and -at. Which of the following is Alex's teacher working on with his reading group? (Skill 4.1; Rigorous)

    A. Syntax

    B. Morphology

    C. Semantics

    D. Phonics

26. Michael keeps using phrases such as "she go to the store." Which of the following areas should Michael's teacher work on to improve Michael's skills? (Skill 4.1; Average rigor)

    A. Morphology

    B. Syntax

    C. Phonics

    D. Semantics

27. Children who are having difficulty understanding non-literal expressions are having difficulties with which of the following areas? (Skill 4.1; Rigorous)

    A. Syntax

    B. Morphology

    C. Semantics

    D. Phonics

28. Children having difficulties with spelling, reading accuracy, and reading comprehension skills are also likely to have difficulties with: (Skill 4.1; Rigorous)

    A. Cognitive skills

    B. Development factors

    C. Math skills

    D. Speech and language skills

29. What does the Multiple Intelligence Theory developed by Howard Gardner explain? (Skill 4.2; Average rigor)

    A. How the intelligence of students depends on the environment

    B. How the intelligence of students constantly change

    C. How students have different levels of overall intelligence

    D. How students learn in at least seven different ways

30. Which of the following is an example of paralanguage? (Skill 4.3; Easy)

    A. Intonation

    B. Gesture

    C. Facial expression

    D. Clothing

31. Children typically develop oral language by listening to: (Skill 4.3; Easy)

    A. Teachers

    B. Parents

    C. Peers

    D. All of the above

32. Which form of language development occurs first? (Skill 4.3; Easy)

    A. Nonverbal

    B. Oral language

    C. Written language

    D. Interplay of oral and written language

33. A teacher reads a book to students. The students are then encouraged to ask who, what, where, when, and why questions. What is this activity designed to help develop? (Skill 4.4; Rigorous)

    A. Motor skills

    B. Social skills

    C. Higher cognitive skills

    D. Decision making skills

34. Mrs. Miller's second grade science class is beginning a new unit on magnetism. She is concerned the students will have trouble with some of the concepts due to the unfamiliar vocabulary. When is the best time for Mrs. Miller to introduce the new vocabulary? (Skill 4.5; Rigorous)

    A. During reading

    B. Before reading

    C. After reading

    D. It should not be introduced

35. Which of the following are examples of comparative words? (Skill 4.6; Easy)

    A. Beside and behind

    B. Hotter and colder

    C. In and on

    D. Before and after

36. Which principle of Stephen Krashen's research suggests that a language learner will learn best when the instruction or conversation is just above the learner's ability? (Skill 5.1; Rigorous)

   A. The affective filter hypothesis

   B. The input hypothesis

   C. The natural order hypothesis

   D. The monitor hypothesis

37. During which stage of language acquisition would it be most inappropriate to ask a student to make a long speech? (Skill 5.1; Average rigor)

   A. Intermediate fluency

   B. Emergent speech

   C. Early production

   D. Advanced fluency

38. A language-learning function exists in the brain that makes it easier for children to learn a language below age: (Skill 5.2; Average rigor)

   A. 2

   B. 7

   C. 10

   D. 14

39. What are many of the current ESOL approaches used in classrooms today based on? (Skill 5.2; Easy)

   A. Social learning methods

   B. Native tongue methods

   C. ESL learning methods

   D. Special education methods

40. Mr. Phillips has called a parent meeting with Maria's parents. Maria is struggling with acquiring the necessary comprehension skills to maintain grade level standards. Maria's parents speak Spanish in the home and are eager and willing to do anything to help Maria succeed in school. Which of the following strategies below will help Maria, while maintaining and fostering the importance of her native language? (Skill 5.3; Rigorous)

    A. Encouraging Maria's parents to enroll in an English language course

    B. Making sure Maria speaks only English during classroom activities

    C. Encouraging Maria's parents to read and discuss books written in Spanish

    D. Ensuring that Maria's parents only speak English in the home

41. Ms. Arnold has the first grade students sitting around the word wall. Which of the following activities would be inappropriate for her to use with this group of students? (Skill 5.5; Rigorous)

    A. Having the students clap out the syllables of some of the displayed words

    B. Discussing word meanings

    C. Teaching new vocabulary words in isolation

    D. Finding all the words on the wall that meet certain criteria

42. Which of the following is NOT an example of how families affect a student's education? (Skill 6.2; Easy)

    A. Culturally

    B. Socio-economically

    C. Attitudes

    D. School resources

43. Johnny loves to listen to stories and points to signs all around the room that have letters on them. This suggests that Johnny: (Skill 6.4; Average rigor)

    A. Will be a good reader

    B. Has good emergent literacy skills

    C. Has good phonemic awareness skills

    D. Understands grammar

44. Which of the following concepts of print can be taught during a read aloud? (Skill 6.4; Easy)

    A. Front and back of book

    B. Author

    C. Title location

    D. All of the above

45. Mrs. Gomez sends home book club order forms every month. Which of the following would explain why Mrs. Gomez feels this is so important? (Skill 6.7; Average rigor)

    A. To reduce the number of books the school needs to provide

    B. To earn items for her classroom at a discounted rate

    C. To increase student's enjoyment of reading

    D. To please parents who enjoy book clubs

46. Which of the following types of children's literature would you be unlikely to utilize in a kindergarten classroom? (Skill 6.8; Easy)

    A. Fable

    B. Science fiction

    C. Epic

    D. Fairy tale

47. Mr. Stine put puppet making materials in his art center after reading the children a story. The students who had chosen to make puppets were asked to use them to retell the story he read in front of the class. Mr. Stine was helping the children: (Skill 7.1; Rigorous)

A. Improve their art skills

B. Respond to literature

C. Improve their oral presentation skills

D. Increase their listening skills

48. Which of the following demonstrates the difference between phonemic awareness and phonological awareness? (Skill 7.2; Rigorous)

A. Phonemic awareness is the understanding that words are made up of sounds, while phonological awareness is the understanding that letters are the representation of sounds.

B. Phonemic awareness is the ability to rhyme and identify beginning sounds, while phonological awareness is the understanding that letters are the representation of sounds.

C. Phonemic awareness is the ability to distinguish sounds, while phonological awareness is the understanding that letters are the representation of sounds.

D. Phonemic awareness is the understanding that words are made up of sounds, while phonological awareness is the ability to distinguish sounds.

49. Which of the following early reading skills develops first? (Skill 7.2; Average rigor)

   A. Comprehension

   B. Phonics

   C. Phonemic awareness

   D. Letter identification

50. The smallest unit of sound is the: (Skill 7.2; Easy)

   A. Phoneme

   B. Morpheme

   C. Syllable

   D. Letter

51. Ms. Smith hands each child in the classroom a letter of the alphabet. Each child then has to go around the classroom and find at least five things in the classroom that begin with that letter. What is Ms. Smith teaching the students? (Skill 7.3; Rigorous)

   A. Phonemic awareness

   B. Vocabulary

   C. Meaning of print

   D. Letter identification

52. Which of the following is NOT a core part of phonics instruction? (Skill 7.3; Rigorous)

   A. Alphabetic principle

   B. Vowel Patterns

   C. Letter names

   D. Consonant Patterns

53. A student can read spontaneously the words the, there, boy, and book. These words make up the student's: (Skill 7.3; Rigorous)

   A. Personal vocabulary

   B. Recognition vocabulary

   C. Sight vocabulary

   D. Working vocabulary

54. Which of the following is NOT an important feature of vocabulary instruction according to the National Reading Panel? (Skill 7.4; Rigorous)

   A. Repetition of vocabulary items

   B. Learning vocabulary in isolation

   C. Learning vocabulary in rich contexts

   D. Restructuring vocabulary tasks when necessary

55. Which of the following correctly describes the importance of developing fluent reading skills? (Skill 7.5; Rigorous)

    A. Automacity with text is necessary to be considered a reader.

    B. Fluency directly correlates to comprehension.

    C. Prosody allows students to sound better when reading aloud.

    D. Fluency is measured on high stakes tests.

56. Which of the following areas correlate with a child's general language skills? (Skill 7.6; Average rigor)

    A. Reading comprehension

    B. Phonics

    C. Phonemic awareness

    D. All of the above

57. Making inferences from a text means that the reader: (Skill 7.6; Rigorous)

    A. Is making informed judgments based on available evidence

    B. Is determining how the author has supported their ideas

    C. Is making a guess based on what the reader would like to be true of the text

    D. All of the above

58. Mr. Lotus wants the class to compare two characters from a book. Which of the following would be a good tool for Mr. Lotus to use? (Skill 7.7; Rigorous)

    A. Venn diagram

    B. KWL Chart

    C. Outline

    D. Literature circle discussion

59. Which of the following shows the normal progression of writing skills over time? (Skill 8.1; Rigorous)

   A. Scribbles, words, sentences, sounds, phrases

   B. Sounds, words, phrases, scribbles, sentences

   C. Sounds, scribbles, words, phrases, sentences

   D. Scribbles, sounds, words, phrases, sentences

60. Which of the following is NOT a good example of fine motor practice for young students? (Skill 8.2; Easy)

   A. Throwing a ball

   B. Manipulating clay

   C. Cutting

   D. Tearing

61. Which of the following skills have a reciprocal relationship? (Skill 8.4; Average rigor)

   A. Reading and phonics

   B. Writing and phonics

   C. Reading and writing

   D. Reading and comprehension

62. Mrs. Myers has discovered numerous words that are repeatedly spelled wrong in Tina's writing. These same words seem to be used by Tina in a lot of her writing as well. What would Mrs. Myers be best to do? (Skill 8.5; Average rigor)

   A. Drill Tina on those words

   B. Add those words to Tina's regular weekly spelling test

   C. Work with Tina to make an individual spelling dictionary to help her learn these words

   D. Have Tina look the words up in the dictionary and correct them

Child Growth and Development

63. Which math principle indicates that a student should "carry" the one in the following addition problem? (Skill 9.1; Rigorous)

    ```
     54
    +29
    ---
     83
    ```

    A. Counting by tens

    B. Properties of a base ten number system

    C. Problem checking

    D. Adding numbers that are too big

64. At snack time, three friends break a cracker into three equal parts. What portion of the original cracker does each part represent? (Skill 9.1; Easy)

    A. One fourth

    B. One half

    C. One whole

    D. One third

65. What is the answer to this problem? (Skill 9.2; Easy)

    $7 \times 9 =$

    A. 36

    B. 16

    C. 63

    D. 2

66. Students are making three-dimensional figures by folding a net made up of four equilateral triangles. What three-dimensional figure are the students making? (Skill 9.3; Rigorous)

    A. Cube

    B. Tetrahedron

    C. Octahedron

    D. Cone

67. In which problem would students need an understanding of basic algebraic concepts? (Skill 9.3; Average rigor)

    A. $5 + 6 + 5 =$

    B. $3 + 3 + 3 + 3 + 3 =$

    C. $10 \times 0 =$

    D. $3 + \square = 9$

68. A teacher plans an activity that involves students calculating how many chair legs are in the classroom, given that there are 30 chairs and each chair has 4 legs. This activity is introducing the ideas of: (Skill 9.4; Average rigor)

   A. Probability

   B. Statistics

   C. Geometry

   D. Algebra

69. The term "cubic feet" indicates which kind of measurement? (Skill 9.5; Average rigor)

   A. Volume

   B. Mass

   C. Length

   D. Distance

70. Which of the following types of graphs would be best to use to record the eye color of the students in the class? (Skill 9.7; Average rigor)

   A. Bar graph or circle graph

   B. Pictograph or bar graph

   C. Line graph or pictograph

   D. Line graph or bar graph

71. Which type of graph uses symbols to represent quantities? (Skill 9.7; Average rigor)

   A. Bar graph

   B. Line graph

   C. Pictograph

   D. Circle graph

72. Students are working with a set of rulers and various small objects from the classroom. Which concept are these students exploring? (Skill 9.7; Average rigor)

   A. Volume

   B. Weight

   C. Length

   D. Temperature

73. Mr. Lacey is using problem solving to help students develop their math skills. The class receives a box of pencils and the pencils have to be divided so that each student has the same number of pencils. What step should come first in problem solving? (Skill 9.8; Rigorous)

    A. Find a strategy to solve the problem

    B. Identify the problem

    C. Count the number of pencils

    D. Make basic calculations

74. What is the foundation of math skills and topics? (Skill 10.1; Easy)

    A. Number sense

    B. Place value

    C. Addition

    D. Computation skills

75. Which stage of mathematical development do students progress through first? (Skill 10.2; Average rigor)

    A. Use of mental imagery

    B. Use of manipulatives

    C. Use of abstract imagery

    D. Use of pattern recognition

76. Which strategy involves students guessing a solution, checking the answer, and using the outcome to guide the next guess? (Skill 10.4; Average rigor)

    A. Problem-and-solution

    B. Closer-and-closer

    C. Guess-and-check

    D. Try-and-retry

77. Students typically learn through: (Skill 10.5; Average rigor)

    A. Verbal questioning

    B. Visual processing

    C. Deductive reasoning

    D. Inductive reasoning

78. Educational theorists describe three ways of learning: visual, auditory, and kinesthetic. In the classroom, it is important to: (Skill 10.5; Rigorous)

   A. Teach based on the way of learning closest to your own preference

   B. Teach based on only one of the three ways of learning

   C. Teach based on all the ways of learning in a balanced approach

   D. Teach what is in the curriculum regardless of ways of learning

79. What groups or patterns of stars do astronomers use as reference points in the sky? (Skill 11.1; Average rigor)

   A. Galaxies

   B. Nebula

   C. Constellations

   D. All of the above

80. What is a change that produces new material known as? (Skill 11.1; Average rigor)

   A. Physical change

   B. Chemical change

   C. Phase change

   D. Reversible change

81. Which of the following units is a measure of temperature? (Skill 11.1; Average rigor)

   A. Watts

   B. Joules

   C. Kelvin

   D. Ounces

82. Phase of matter is identified by: (Skill 11.1; Rigorous)

   A. Shape and mass

   B. Shape and volume

   C. Volume and mass

   D. Shape, mass, and volume

83. What should an experiment have a minimum number of to produce accurate and easily correlated results? (Skill 11.2; Average rigor)

   A. Controls
   B. Variables
   C. Samples
   D. Participants

84. Scientific inquiry begins with: (Skill 11.3; Easy)

   A. A hypothesis
   B. An observation
   C. A conclusion
   D. An experiment

85. What is the main benefit of teaching science in a context where it is relevant to the lives of students? (Skill 11.6; Average rigor)

   A. It reduces costs for the school.
   B. It allows science to be integrated with other subjects.
   C. It increases student motivation.
   D. It promotes independence.

86. Which term describes an area of lowland formed by soil and sediment deposited at the mouths of rivers? (Skill 12.1; Average rigor)

   A. Plateau
   B. Basin
   C. Mesa
   D. Delta

87. Which of the following describes how citizens are able to directly participate in their own government by voting for and running for office? (Skill 12.1; Average rigor)

   A. Popular sovereignty
   B. Due process
   C. Rule of law
   D. Democracy

88. What is the study of how a society allocates its scarce resources to satisfy what are basically unlimited and competing wants? (Skill 12.1; Average rigor)

   A. Geography
   B. Economics
   C. Geology
   D. Ecology

EARLY CHILDHOOD EDUCATION

89. What is a proposed law called while it is under consideration by Congress? (Skill 12.1; Easy)

   A.   Bill

   B.   Amendment

   C.   Veto

   D.   Hopper

90. Which of the following is NOT one of the basic themes of geography? (Skill 12.1; Rigorous)

   A.   Spatial organization

   B.   Polarity

   C.   Location

   D.   Movement

91. Which hypothesis is valid? (Skill 12.2; Rigorous)

   A.   An unknown factor causes tomato plants to produce no fruit sometimes.

   B.   A tomato plant will produce tasty fruit if it is watered.

   C.   A tomato plant will grow faster in full sunlight than partial sunlight.

   D.   A tomato plant given this fertilizer will produce better fruit than all others.

92. Which of the following is a means of dispute resolution where a third parties helps to settle the dispute? (Skill 12.7; Average rigor)

   A.   Observation

   B.   Intervention

   C.   Regulation

   D.   Mediation

93. What should be the first thing taught when introducing dance? (Skill 13.1; Easy)

   A.   Rhythm

   B.   Feelings

   C.   Empathy

   D.   Texture

94. When discussing color, the intensity of a color refers to the color's: (Skill 13.2; Average rigor)

   A.   Strength

   B.   Value

   C.   Lightness or darkness

   D.   Associated emotions

95. Which terms refers to the juxtaposition of one or more elements in opposition? (Skill 13.2; Average rigor)

   A. Balance

   B. Contrast

   C. Emphasis

   D. Unity

96. Which activity would be most suitable for beginning students of visual arts? (Skill 13.3; Rigorous)

   A. Analyzing famous works of arts

   B. Reflecting on the possible meanings of art work

   C. Observing the shapes and forms of common objects

   D. Using blocks to construct three-dimensional shapes

97. What should the arts curriculum for early childhood students focus on? (Skill 13.4; Average rigor)

   A. Judgment

   B. Criticism

   C. Interpretation

   D. Experimentation

98. What venues offer suitable opportunities for allowing students to view live performances? (Skill 13.5; Easy)

   A. Symphonies

   B. Dance companies

   C. Art museums

   D. All of the above

99. In which subject is it most important for students to be encouraged to use all five senses? (Skill 13.6; Average rigor)

   A. Visual arts

   B. Music

   C. Movement

   D. Drama

100. According to Lynn Hallie Najem's research, integrating arts into a primary school curriculum tends to increase students': (Skill 13.7; Rigorous)

   A. Self-esteem

   B. Motivation

   C. Empathy

   D. Attendance

Post Test Answer Key

1.	C	35.	B	69.	A
2.	C	36.	B	70.	B
3.	D	37.	C	71.	C
4.	B	38.	B	72.	C
5.	A	39.	A	73.	B
6.	B	40.	C	74.	A
7.	C	41.	B	75.	B
8.	D	42.	D	76.	C
9.	A	43.	B	77.	D
10.	C	44.	D	78.	C
11.	D	45.	C	79.	C
12.	D	46.	C	80.	B
13.	C	47.	B	81.	C
14.	B	48.	D	82.	B
15.	B	49.	D	83.	B
16.	B	50.	A	84.	B
17.	C	51.	C	85.	C
18.	C	52.	C	86.	D
19.	D	53.	C	87.	A
20.	B	54.	B	88.	B
21.	A	55.	B	89.	A
22.	B	56.	A	90.	B
23.	A	57.	A	91.	C
24.	C	58.	A	92.	D
25.	B	59.	D	93.	A
26.	B	60.	A	94.	A
27.	C	61.	A	95.	B
28.	D	62.	C	96.	C
29.	D	63.	B	97.	D
30.	A	64.	D	98.	D
31.	D	65.	C	99.	D
32.	A	66.	B	100.	A
33.	C	67.	D		
34.	B	68.	D		

Post Test Rigor Table

	Easy %20	Average rigor %40	Rigorous %40
Question #	1, 6, 19, 30, 31, 32, 35, 39, 42, 44, 46, 50, 60, 64, 65, 74, 84, 89, 93, 98	3, 5, 11, 12, 14, 18, 20, 24, 26, 29, 37, 38, 43, 45, 49, 56, 61, 62, 67, 68, 69, 70, 71, 72, 75, 76, 77, 79, 80, 81, 83, 85, 86, 87, 88, 92, 94, 95, 97, 99	2, 4, 7, 8, 9, 10, 13, 15, 16, 17, 21, 22, 23, 25, 27, 28, 33, 34, 36, 40, 41, 47, 48, 51, 52, 53, 54, 55, 57, 58, 59, 63, 66, 73, 78, 82, 90, 91, 96, 100

Post Test Answer Key Rationale

Subarea I. Child Development and Learning

1. Which of the following is NOT one of the three domains of development? (Skill 1.1; Easy)

    A. Physical
    B. Social
    C Emotional
    D. Academic

Answer C: Emotional

The three domains of development are physical, social, and academic.

2. Mrs. Potts is conducting a language development task with her students. She forms students into small mixed-ability groups. She then gives each group a discussion question. Each group is asked to discuss the question, while ensuring that each person has a chance to give their opinion. What approach to language development is this activity based on? (Skill 1.1; Rigorous)

    A. Linguistic approach
    B. Cognitive approach
    C. Socio-cognitive approach
    D. Learning approach

Answer C: Socio-cognitive approach

The socio-cognitive allowed that determining the appropriateness of language in given situations for specific listeners is as important as understanding semantic and syntactic structures. By engaging in conversation, children at all stages of development have opportunities to test their language skills, receive feedback, and make modifications.

TEACHER CERTIFICATION STUDY GUIDE

3. Which of the following is a true statement? (Skill 1.2; Average rigor)

   A. Physical development does not influence social development.
   B. Social development does not influence physical development.
   C. Cognitive development does not influence social development.
   D. All domains of development are integrated and influence other domains.

Answer D: All domains of development are integrated and influence other domains.

Child development does not occur in a vacuum. Each element of development impacts other elements of development. For example, as children develop physically, they develop the dexterity to demonstrate cognitive development, such as writing something on a piece of paper.

4. Mrs. Smith writes an encouraging note to each student in her classroom every week. These notes encourage the students to improve upon their previous work and to strive to do even better in the future. Mrs. Smith is most likely trying to: (Skill 1.3; Rigorous)

   A. Maintain good discipline
   B. Hold the students to high standards
   C. Meet the needs of individual students
   D. Improve her test scores

Answer B: Hold the students to high standards

Time and again, a direct correlation has been demonstrated between the teacher's expectations for a particular student and that student's academic performance. A note encouraging the students to improve and do even better in the future is one way to hold students to high standards.

TEACHER CERTIFICATION STUDY GUIDE

5. According to Piaget, during what stage do children learn to manipulate symbols and objects? (Skill 1.4; Average rigor)

   A. Concrete operations
   B. Pre-operational
   C. Formal operations
   D. Conservative operational

Answer A: Concrete operations

In the pre-operational stage, children begin to understand symbols. In the concrete operations stage, children go one step beyond this and begin to learn to manipulate symbols, objects and other elements.

6. How many stages of intellectual development does Piaget define? (Skill 1.4; Easy)

   A. Two
   B. Four
   C. Six
   D. Eight

Answer B: Four

Jean Piaget's theory describes how human minds develop through four stages. The first stage is the sensory-motor stage. This occurs up to age 2 and involves understanding the world via the senses. The second stage is the pre-operational stage. It occurs from ages 2 to 7 and involves understanding symbols. The concrete operations stage occurs from ages 7 to 11 and is where children begin to develop reason. The final stage is the formal operations stage. It involves the development of logical and abstract thinking.

TEACHER CERTIFICATION STUDY GUIDE

7. **Which of the following is a true statement? (Skill 1.5; Rigorous)**

   A. Recess is not important to a child's development.
   B. Playtime is only provided in schools to help children release energy.
   C. Play has an important and positive role in child development.
   D. Solitary play is always an indication that a child has development issues.

Answer C: Play has an important and positive role in child development.

Too often, recess and play is considered peripheral or unimportant to a child's development. It's sometimes seen as a way to allow kids to just get physical energy out or a "tradition" of childhood. The truth is, though, that play is very important to human development. Play is an activity that helps teach basic values such as sharing and cooperation. It also teaches that taking care of oneself (as opposed to constantly working) is good for human beings and further creates a more enjoyable society.

8. **A teacher is planning to get all of the students involved in sports for the purpose of helping develop hand-eye coordination and teamwork skills. What would be the most appropriate approach when planning the sports activities? (Skill 1.5; Rigorous)**

   A. Encourage competition among students so they become used to the pressure of competing.
   B. Ensure that students who dislike sports continue until they enjoy sports.
   C. Choose activities that are beyond the student's current abilities so students are prompted to improve.
   D. Maintain a relaxed atmosphere and remind students that the sport is designed to be fun.

Answer D: Maintain a relaxed atmosphere and remind students that the sport is designed to be fun.

Sports can be valuable in child development. They can develop motor skills, social skills, and help students develop personal interests. It is important that sporting activities for young children focus on the positive benefits such as the development of motor skills and personal interests, rather than focusing on competition.

9. The principal finds Mr. Thomas's class outside on the playground. The entire class is playing in small groups and everyone is involved and seems to be enjoying the activity. However, it is not recess time on Mr. Thomas's schedule. Later, the principal questions Mr. Thomas about his time on the playground. What would Mr. Thomas be best to say to justify his time spent on the playground in a meaningful manner? (Skill 1.5; Rigorous)

   A. I was helping the students develop motor skills.
   B. I was providing the students with a break.
   C. I was providing the students with an extra recess.
   D. I was allowing the students the chance to work off their extra energy.

Answer A: I was helping the students develop motor skills.

Extra movement and play time is essential for young children. It develops motor skills, builds cooperative learning skills, and provides the opportunity for social skills to develop in a more natural setting. It also provides a chance for the teacher to observe these areas in his/her students for reporting to parents.

10. A learning activity for students below age eight should focus on: (Skill 1.6; Rigorous)

    A. Complex activities
    B. Applying the information
    C. Short time frames
    D. Challenging students

Answer C: Short time frames

Younger children tend to process information at a slower rate than older children (age eight and older). Learning activities selected for younger students (below age eight) should focus on short time frames in highly simplified form.

11. Maintaining body weight is best accomplished by: (Skill 1.8; Average rigor)

    A. Dieting
    B. Aerobic exercise
    C. Lifting weights
    D. Equalizing caloric intake relative to output

Answer D: Equalizing caloric intake relative to output

The best way to maintain a body weight is by balancing caloric intake and output. Extensive dieting (caloric restriction) is not a good option as this would result in weakness. Exercise is part of the output process that helps balance caloric input and output.

12. Which of the following is a sign of emotional neglect? (Skill 2.1; Average rigor)

    A. Jealousy of other children
    B. Aggression
    C. Lack of attention to schoolwork
    D. All of the above

Answer D: All of the above

Signs of emotional neglect include jealousy of other children, aggression, lack of attention to schoolwork, and feelings of anger toward others. These can also be signs that a student has recently endured a family upset.

13. Mr. De Vries observes that a student appears socially awkward, has difficulty expressing himself in words, and is sometimes aggressive. What is most likely to be limiting the student's development? (Skill 2.1; Rigorous)

    A. Emotional abuse
    B. The recent divorce of the student's parents
    C. Lack of verbal interaction
    D. Poor nutrition

Answer C: Lack of verbal interaction

When a child has had little verbal interaction, the symptoms can be rather similar to the symptoms of abuse or neglect. The child might have a "deer in the headlights" look and maintain a very socially awkward set of behaviors. In general, such a child will have a drastically reduced ability to express him or herself in words, and often, aggression can be a better tool for the child to get his or her thoughts across.

14. Because teachers today will deal with an increasingly diverse group of cultures in their classrooms, they must: (Skill 2.4; Average rigor)

    A. Ignore the cultures represented
    B. Demonstrate sensitivity for diversity
    C. Provide a celebration for each culture represented
    D. Focusing on teaching the majority

Answer B: Demonstrate sensitivity for diversity

To deal with a diverse group of cultures in their classrooms, teachers must show respect to all parents and families and demonstrate sensitivity for diversity. They need to set the tone that suggests that their mission is to develop students into the best people they can be. They also need to realize that various cultures have different views of how children should be educated.

15. Mrs. Peck wants to justify the use of personalized learning communities to her principal. Which of the following reasons would she be best to use? (Skill 2.4; Rigorous)

   A. They are likely to engage students and maintain their interest.
   B. They provide a supportive environment to address academic and emotional needs.
   C. They encourage students to work independently.
   D. They are proactive in their nature.

Answer B: They provide a supportive environment to address academic and emotional needs.

Personalized learning communities provide supportive learning environments that address the academic and emotional needs of students. In personalized learning communities, relationships and connections between students, staff, parents and community members promote lifelong learning for all students. School communities that promote an inclusion of diversity in the classroom, community, curriculum and connections enable students to maximize their academic capabilities and educational opportunities.

16. What criteria are used to assess whether a child qualifies for services under IDEA? (Skill 2.5; Rigorous)

   A. Having a disability only
   B. Having a disability and demonstrating educational need only
   C. Demonstrating educational need only
   D. Having a disability, demonstrating educational need, and having financial support

Answer B: Having a disability and demonstrating educational need only

Based on IDEA, eligibility for special education services is based on a student having one of a listed set of disabilities (or a combination thereof) and demonstration of educational need through professional evaluation.

17. Which of the following is an example of content which has been differentiated to meet the needs of individual learners? (Skill 2.5; Rigorous)

   A. Flexible group activities on various levels
   B. Accepting different final projects from various students
   C. Research projects based on student's interests
   D. Individual tutoring by the teacher to address student weaknesses

Answer C: Research projects based on student's interests

Differentiated instruction encompasses several areas: content, process, and product. Differentiating content means that students will have access to content that piques their interest about a topic, with a complexity that provides an appropriate challenge to their intellectual development.

18. A child exhibits the following symptoms: inability to appreciate humor, indifference to physical contact, abnormal social play, and abnormal speech. What is the likely diagnosis for this child? (Skill 2.5; Average rigor)

   A. Separation anxiety
   B. Mental retardation
   C. Autism
   D. Hypochondria

Answer C: Autism

According to many psychologists who have been involved with treating autistic children, it seems that these children have built a wall between themselves and everyone else, including their families and even their parents. They are often indifferent to physical contact, engage in abnormal social play, display abnormal speech, are unable to appreciate humor, and cannot empathize with others.

19. What actions are observed in aggressive children? (Skill 2.5; Easy)

   A. Vandalism
   B. Destruction of property
   C. Verbal abuse
   D. All of the above

Answer D: All of the above

Aggressive children often fight or instigate their peers to strike back at them. Aggressiveness may also take the form of vandalism or destruction of property. Aggressive children also engage in verbal abuse.

TEACHER CERTIFICATION STUDY GUIDE

20. **What area of differentiated instruction is a teacher focusing on when planning how to teach the material? (Skill 2.5; Average rigor)**

    A. Content
    B. Process
    C. Product
    D. Assessment

Answer B: Process

The effective teacher will seek to connect all students to the subject matter through multiple techniques, with the goal that each student, through their own abilities, will relate to one or more techniques and excel in the learning process. This is known as differentiated instruction, and focuses on content (what is being taught), process (how the material will be taught), and product (the expectations placed on students to demonstrate their knowledge or understanding).

21. **Which is the best approach to the holistic teaching of a concept? (Skill 3.1; Rigorous)**

    A. Start with the whole concept and then move on to the parts.
    B. Teach only the parts and avoid focusing on the whole.
    C. Focus only on the whole to avoid students becoming confused by the parts.
    D. Begin with parts until students have developed their own understanding of the whole.

Answer A: Start with the whole concept and then move on to the parts.

Holistic teaching of a concept should begin with the whole concept and then move to the parts. Let students observe the parts carefully and give them a chance to experiment on their own. This is usually done through play or learning centers in the classroom. When children internalize the small parts of the whole they can then grasp the whole concept.

TEACHER CERTIFICATION STUDY GUIDE

22. **Providing instruction from various points of view, not only helps students academically, but it also allows them to: (Skill 3.2; Rigorous)**

    A. Work cooperatively and contribute to a team
    B. Develop the personal skill of being able to view situations from multiple viewpoints
    C. Become problem solvers with the ability to apply creative thinking to common problems
    D. Develop tolerance and patience

Answer B: Develop the personal skill of being able to view situations from multiple viewpoints

When the teacher actively and frequently models viewing from multiple perspectives as an approach to learning in the classroom, the students not only benefit through improved academic skill development, they also begin to adopt this approach for learning and contemplating as a personal skill. And the ability to consider a situation, issue, problem or event from multiple viewpoints is a skill that will serve the individual well, throughout his or her academic career and beyond.

23. **When teaching in a diverse classroom, teachers should: (Skill 3.2; Rigorous)**

    A. Plan, devise, and present material in a multicultural manner
    B. Research all possible cultures and expose the children to those
    C. Focus on the curriculum and whatever multicultural opportunities are built into it already
    D. Utilize single format instruction to present material in a multicultural manner

Answer A: Plan, devise, and present material in a multicultural manner

Curriculum objectives and instructional strategies may be inappropriate and unsuccessful when presented in a single format which relies on the student's understanding and acceptance of the values and common attributes of a specific culture which is not his or her own. Planning, devising and presenting material from a multicultural perspective can enable the teacher in a culturally diverse classroom to ensure that all the students achieve the stated, academic objective.

TEACHER CERTIFICATION STUDY GUIDE

24. Which of the following is the most important reason for integrating the curriculum? (Skill 3.4; Average rigor)

    A. It increases ease of lesson planning.
    B. It meets the needs of diverse students.
    C. It breaks down barriers between subjects.
    D. It narrows the focus of study.

Answer C: It breaks down barriers between subjects.

The integrated curriculum is a method that teaches students to break down barriers between subjects. Lessons are planned around broad themes that students can identify with, such as "The Environment." Major concepts are pulled from this broad concept, and teachers then plan activities that teach these concepts.

Subarea II. Communication, Language and Literacy Development

25. Alex is part of a small reading group where the teacher is teaching about the word families -art and -at. Which of the following is Alex's teacher working on with his reading group? (Skill 4.1; Rigorous)

    A. Syntax
    B. Morphology
    C. Semantics
    D. Phonics

Answer B: Morphology

Morphology is the study of the inside parts of words. By working with word families and providing instruction into these parts of word, Alex's teacher is developing the morphology skills of the students.

EARLY CHILDHOOD EDUCATION

26. Michael keeps using phrases such as "she go to the store." Which of the following areas should Michael's teacher work on to improve Michael's skills? (Skill 4.1; Average rigor)

   A. Morphology
   B. Syntax
   C. Phonics
   D. Semantics

Answer B: Syntax

Syntax is the understanding of the rules of the English language to put words together in a grammatically appropriate manner. Michael is having difficulty with this concept and could benefit from some more instruction in this area.

27. Children who are having difficulty understanding non-literal expressions are having difficulties with which of the following areas? (Skill 4.1; Rigorous)

   A. Syntax
   B. Morphology
   C. Semantics
   D. Phonics

Answer C: Semantics

Listening and understanding the intentions of speakers (teacher/peers) involves semantics. A student that is having difficulty understanding non-literal expressions is having difficulty with semantics.

28. Children having difficulties with spelling, reading accuracy, and reading comprehension skills are also likely to have difficulties with: (Skill 4.1; Rigorous)

   A. Cognitive skills
   B. Development factors
   C. Math skills
   D. Speech and language skills

Answer D: Speech and language skills

While students who have difficulties with speech and language skills often have difficulties with reading, the converse is also true. Students who are struggling with spelling, reading accuracy and comprehension may also have hidden difficulties with speech and language skills.

TEACHER CERTIFICATION STUDY GUIDE

29. **What does the Multiple Intelligence Theory developed by Howard Gardner explain? (Skill 4.2; Average rigor)**

    A. How the intelligence of students depends on the environment
    B. How the intelligence of students constantly change
    C. How students have different levels of overall intelligence
    D. How students learn in at least seven different ways

Answer D: How students learn in at least seven different ways

Gardner's Multiple Intelligence Theory suggests that students learn in (at least) seven different ways. These include visually/spatially, musically, verbally, logically/mathematically, interpersonally, intrapersonally, and bodily/kinesthetically.

30. **Which of the following is an example of paralanguage? (Skill 4.3; Easy)**

    A. Intonation
    B. Gesture
    C. Facial expression
    D. Clothing

Answer A: Intonation

Paralanguage is one of the components of nonverbal communication. Paralanguage includes pitch, stress, intonation, and voice quality.

31. **Children typically develop oral language by listening to: (Skill 4.3; Easy)**

    A. Teachers
    B. Parents
    C. Peers
    D. All of the above

Answer D: All of the above

Children develop oral language by listening to others. This includes listening to teachers, parents, and peers.

TEACHER CERTIFICATION STUDY GUIDE

32. Which form of language development occurs first? (Skill 4.3; Easy)

    A. Nonverbal
    B. Oral language
    C. Written language
    D. Interplay of oral and written language

Answer A: Nonverbal

The development of language progresses through several stages. These stages are: nonverbal, oral language, interplay of oral and written language, and written language.

33. A teacher reads a book to students. The students are then encouraged to ask who, what, where, when, and why questions. What is this activity designed to help develop? (Skill 4.4; Rigorous)

    A. Motor skills
    B. Social skills
    C. Higher cognitive skills
    D. Decision making skills

Answer C: Higher cognitive skills

Teaching the art of questioning is one activity that can be used to promote language development. This involves reading a book to the students and allowing them to ask curiosity questions (who, what, why, when and where). This encourages the students to develop higher cognitive skills through questions.

34. Mrs. Miller's second grade science class is beginning a new unit on magnetism. She is concerned the students will have trouble with some of the concepts due to the unfamiliar vocabulary. When is the best time for Mrs. Miller to introduce the new vocabulary? (Skill 4.5; Rigorous)

   A. During reading
   B. Before reading
   C. After reading
   D. It should not be introduced.

Answer B: Before reading

If the text, itself, in the judgment of the teacher, contains difficult concepts for the children to grasp, the vocabulary should be introduced before reading.

35. Which of the following are examples of comparative words? (Skill 4.6; Easy)

   A. Beside and behind
   B. Hotter and colder
   C. In and on
   D. Before and after

Answer B: Hotter and colder

Comparative words are words that compare. Hotter and colder are both comparative words.

36. Which principle of Stephen Krashen's research suggests that a language learner will learn best when the instruction or conversation is just above the learner's ability? (Skill 5.1; Rigorous)

   A. The affective filter hypothesis
   B. The input hypothesis
   C. The natural order hypothesis
   D. The monitor hypothesis

Answer A: The input hypothesis

The input hypothesis, sometimes referred to as "comprehensible input", states that a language learner will learn best when the instruction or conversation is just above the learner's ability. That way, the learner has the foundation to understand most of the language, but still will have to figure out, often in context, what that extra, more difficult element means.

37. **During which stage of language acquisition would it be most inappropriate to ask a student to make a long speech? (Skill 5.1; Average rigor)**

    A. Intermediate fluency
    B. Emergent speech
    C. Early production
    D. Advanced fluency

Answer C: Early production

The second phase of language acquisition is early production. This is where the student can actually start to produce the target language. It is quite limited, and teachers most likely should not expect students to produce eloquent speeches during this time.

38. **A language-learning function exists in the brain that makes it easier for children to learn a language below age: (Skill 5.2; Average rigor)**

    A. 2
    B. 7
    C. 10
    D. 14

Answer B: 7

The most important concept to remember regarding the difference between learning a first language and a second one is that if the learner is approximately age seven or older, learning a second language will occur very differently in the learner's brain than it will had the learner been younger. The reason for this is that there is a language-learning function that exists in young children that appears to go away as they mature. Learning a language prior to age seven is almost guaranteed, with relatively little effort.

39. What are many of the current ESOL approaches used in classrooms today based on? (Skill 5.2; Easy)

   A. Social learning methods
   B. Native tongue methods
   C. ESL learning methods
   D. Special education methods

Answer A: Social learning methods

Many ESOL approaches are based on social learning methods. By being placed in mixed level groups or by being paired with a student of another ability level, students will get a chance to practice English in a natural, non-threatening environment.

40. Mr. Phillips has called a parent meeting with Maria's parents. Maria is struggling with acquiring the necessary comprehension skills to maintain grade level standards. Maria's parents speak Spanish in the home and are eager and willing to do anything to help Maria succeed in school. Which of the following strategies below will help Maria, while maintaining and fostering the importance of her native language? (Skill 5.3; Rigorous)

   A. Encouraging Maria's parents to enroll in an English language course
   B. Making sure Maria speaks only English during classroom activities
   C. Encouraging Maria's parents to read and discuss books written in Spanish
   D. Ensuring that Maria's parents only speak English in the home

Answer C: Encouraging Maria's parents to read and discuss books written in Spanish

The foundations upon which comprehension skills are learned are not unique to one language. If Maria is indeed struggling with comprehension, it does not matter which language she uses to practice her skills. By encouraging Maria's parents to utilize their skills in their native language, they can feel a more active member of Maria's educational process and continue to embrace their heritage and native language.

41. Ms. Arnold has the first grade students sitting around the word wall. Which of the following activities would be inappropriate for the teacher to use with this group of students? (Skill 5.5; Rigorous)

   A. Having the students clap out the syllables of some of the displayed words
   B. Discussing word meanings
   C. Teaching new vocabulary words in isolation
   D. Finding all the words on the wall that meet certain criteria

Answer B: Discussing word meanings

While brief discussions of meanings might be used during word wall activities, it is not the purpose of a word wall. Meanings should be discussed in context rather than in the isolation of word walls. It might be appropriate to develop a vocabulary board, where words, pictures and meanings are connected instead.

42. Which of the following is NOT an example of how families affect a student's education? (Skill 6.2; Easy)

   A. Culturally
   B. Socio-economically
   C. Attitudes
   D. School resources

Answer D: School resources

School resources are not impacted by the family. Within the school setting, it is imperative that teachers level the playing field for all students. It is important for teachers to set high expectations and provide students with the necessary support to fulfill these expectations

TEACHER CERTIFICATION STUDY GUIDE

43. **Johnny loves to listen to stories and points to signs all around the room that have letters on them. This suggests that Johnny: (Skill 6.4; Average rigor)**

    A. Will be a good reader
    B. Has good emergent literacy skills
    C. Has good phonemic awareness skills
    D. Understands grammar

Answer B: Has good emergent literacy skills

Enjoying stories and being aware of environmental print are factors in emergent literacy skills, not necessarily directly attributed to phonemic awareness, phonics, or future reading abilities. However, those students with good emergent literacy skills are more likely to be more successful in all of those skills than students who have poor emergent literacy skills.

44. **Which of the following concepts of print can be taught during a read aloud? (Skill 6.4; Average rigor)**

    A. Front and back of book
    B. Author
    C. Title location
    D. All of the above

Answer D: All of the above

All concepts of print can and should be modeled to students through reading aloud activities.

45. **Mrs. Gomez sends home book club order forms every month. Which of the following would explain why Mrs. Gomez feels this is so important? (Skill 6.7; Easy)**

    A. To reduce the number of books the school needs to provide
    B. To earn items for her classroom at a discounted rate
    C. To increase student's enjoyment of reading
    D. To please parents who enjoy book clubs

Answer C: To increase student's enjoyment of reading

In the case of book clubs, students can pick books that spark their interest. Mrs. Gomez understands that it is important for students to enjoy reading and wants to provide as many opportunities as possible for this to happen within her classroom.

EARLY CHILDHOOD EDUCATION

46. Which of the following types of children's literature would you be unlikely to utilize in a kindergarten classroom? (Skill 6.8; Easy)

   A. Fable
   B. Science fiction
   C. Epic
   D. Fairy tale

Answer C: Epic

It would be unlikely that you would use a full epic in a kindergarten classroom. The complexity of a combination poem and story to the extent of an epic story would be difficult for this particular age range to understand.

47. Mr. Stine put puppet making materials in his art center after reading the children a story. The students who had chosen to make puppets were asked to use them to retell the story he read in front of the class. Mr. Stine was helping the children: (Skill 7.1; Rigorous)

   A. Improve their art skills
   B. Respond to literature
   C. Improve their oral presentation skills
   D. Increase their listening skills

Answer B: Respond to literature

The purpose of the activity was to allow students to respond to literature. There are numerous strategies which can be used to allow students the opportunity to interact with literature. Mr. Stine incorporated one that allows students an opportunity to utilize different areas of multiple intelligences as well.

TEACHER CERTIFICATION STUDY GUIDE

48. Which of the following demonstrates the difference between phonemic awareness and phonological awareness? (Skill 7.2; Rigorous)

   A. Phonemic awareness is the understanding that words are made up of sounds, while phonological awareness is the understanding that letters are the representation of sounds.
   B. Phonemic awareness is the ability to rhyme and identify beginning sounds, while phonological awareness is the understanding that letters are the representation of sounds.
   C. Phonemic awareness is the ability to distinguish sounds, while phonological awareness is the understanding that letters are the representation of sounds.
   D. Phonemic awareness is the understanding that words are made up of sounds, while phonological awareness is the ability to distinguish sounds.

Answer D: Phonemic awareness is the understanding that words are made up of sounds, while phonological awareness is the ability to distinguish sounds.

The concept of phonemic awareness and phonological awareness are often misunderstand and confused. It is important to understand clearly the difference and realize they cannot and should not be used interchangeably.

49. Which of the following early reading skills develops first? (Skill 7.2; Average rigor)

   A. Comprehension
   B. Phonics
   C. Phonemic awareness
   D. Letter identification

Answer D: Phonemic awareness

In typically developing children, phonemic awareness skills should be developed before the other reading skills listed.

50. The smallest unit of sound is the: (Skill 7.2; Easy)

    A. Phoneme
    B. Morpheme
    C. Syllable
    D. Letter

Answer A: Phoneme

A phoneme is the smallest unit of sound that has a different meaning. A morpheme is a word or word part that cannot be divided into any smaller parts of meaning.

51. Ms. Smith hands each child in the classroom a letter of the alphabet. Each child then had to go around the classroom and find at least five things in the classroom which begin with that letter. What is Ms. Smith teaching the students? (Skill 7.3; Rigorous)

    A. Phonemic awareness
    B. Vocabulary
    C. Meaning of print
    D. Letter identification

Answer C: Meaning of print

Connecting letters to objects or sounds helps the students begin to recognize that print has meaning. This is an essential foundation skill for students to develop before phonics instruction is begun.

52. Which of the following is NOT a core part of phonics instruction? (Skill 7.3; Rigorous)

    A. Alphabetic principle
    B. Vowel Patterns
    C. Letter names
    D. Consonant Patterns

Answer C: Letter names

While it is consistent and regular instruction in early childhood classrooms, the names in and of themselves are not direct phonics instruction. Tying the sound and symbol is phonics.

53. **A student can read spontaneously the words the, there, boy, and book. These words make up the student's:** (Skill 7.3; Rigorous)

    A. Personal vocabulary
    B. Recognition vocabulary
    C. Sight vocabulary
    D. Working vocabulary

Answer C: Sight vocabulary

Sight words are words that the reader learns to read spontaneously either because of frequency or lack of conformity to orthographic rules. For example, words like 'the', 'what', and 'there' because they don't conform to rules, and words like 'boy', 'girl', and 'book' because they are seen very frequently in early reading texts.

54. **Which of the following is NOT an important feature of vocabulary instruction according to the National Reading Panel?** (Skill 7.4; Rigorous)

    A. Repetition of vocabulary items
    B. Learning vocabulary in isolation
    C. Learning vocabulary in rich contexts
    D. Restructuring vocabulary tasks when necessary

Answer B: Learning vocabulary in isolation

One of the conclusions drawn by the National Reading Panel was that vocabulary can be acquired through incidental learning. This means that much of a student's vocabulary will have to be learned in the course of doing things other than explicit vocabulary learning.

55. **Which of the following correctly describes the importance of developing fluent reading skills? (Skill 7.5; Rigorous)**

 A. Automacity with text is necessary to be considered a reader.
 B. Fluency directly correlates to comprehension.
 C. Prosody allows students to sound better when reading aloud.
 D. Fluency is measured on high stakes tests.

Answer B: Fluency directly correlates to comprehension.

Research over the years has shown a correlation between adequate rates of fluency and student's comprehension. It is important to know appropriate reading rates at different grade levels and to realize that fluency has different levels: letter fluency, sound fluency, word fluency, phrase fluency, and finally oral reading fluency.

56. **Which of the following areas correlate with a child's general language skills? (Skill 7.6; Average rigor)**

 A. Reading comprehension
 B. Phonics
 C. Phonemic awareness
 D. All of the above

Answer A: Reading comprehension

It has been found that a child's overall general language skills have a direct correlation between his/her reading comprehension skills. This demonstrates the relationship between language skills and literacy skills.

57. **Making inferences from a text means that the reader: (Skill 7.6; Rigorous)**

 A. Is making informed judgments based on available evidence
 B. Is determining how the author has supported their ideas
 C. Is making a guess based on what the reader would like to be true of the text
 D. All of the above

Answer A: Is making informed judgments based on available evidence

In order to draw inferences and make conclusions, a reader must use prior knowledge and apply it to the current situation. An inference is an informed judgment based on available evidence.

58. Mr. Lotus wants the class to compare two characters from a book. Which of the following would be a good tool for Mr. Lotus to use? (Skill 7.7; Rigorous)

   A. Venn diagram
   B. KWL Chart
   C. Outline
   D. Literature circle discussion

Answer A: Venn diagram

A Venn diagram is a tool that is commonly used to compare and contrast two characters, stories, or objects.

59. Which of the following shows the normal progression of writing skills over time? (Skill 8.1; Rigorous)

   A. Scribbles, words, sentences, sounds, phrases
   B. Sounds, words, phrases, scribbles, sentences
   C. Sounds, scribbles, words, phrases, sentences
   D. Scribbles, sounds, words, phrases, sentences

Answer D: Scribbles, sounds, words, phrases, sentences

The normal progression of writing skills occurs in the following order: scribbles, sounds, words, phrases, and then sentences.

60. Which of the following is NOT a good example of fine motor practice for young students? (Skill 8.2; Easy)

   A. Throwing a ball
   B. Manipulating clay
   C. Cutting
   D. Tearing

Answer A: Throwing a ball

Manipulating clay, cutting, and tearing are all good examples of fine motor practice for young students. Throwing a ball is an activity that develops gross motor skills.

61. Which of the following skills have a reciprocal relationship? (Skill 8.4; Average rigor)

    A. Reading and phonics
    B. Writing and phonics
    C. Reading and writing
    D. Reading and comprehension

Answer A: Reading and writing

Often teachers will see a reciprocal relationship between reading and writing skills. As students are able to read sounds, they will notice these same sounds showing up in students writing. It is important for teachers to continually show students how the two relate and are connected.

62. Mrs. Myers has discovered numerous words that are repeatedly spelled wrong in Tina's writing. These same words seem to be used by Tina in a lot of her writing as well. What would Mrs. Myers be best to do? (Skill 8.5; Average rigor)

    A. Drill Tina on those words

    B. Add those words to Tina's regular weekly spelling test

    C. Work with Tina to make an individual spelling dictionary to help her learn these words

    D. Have Tina look the words up in the dictionary and correct them

Answer C: Work with Tina to make an individual spelling dictionary to help her learn these words

While there are teachers who will do any of the choices listed, it is most effective to provide individual spelling dictionaries or spelling word wall file folders to help students to improve specific and individual words, which may or may not be beneficial to other students.

Subarea III. Learning in the Content Areas

63. Which math principle indicates that a student should "carry" the one in the following addition problem? (Skill 9.1; Rigorous)

```
  54
 +29
  83
```

- A. Counting by tens
- B. Properties of a base ten number system
- C. Problem checking
- D. Adding numbers that are too big

Answer B: Properties of a base ten number system

In a base ten number system, groups of ten ones are regrouped and carried into the tens column. In the addition problem shown, four ones plus nine ones is equal to 13 ones. The ten ones are regrouped and carried into the tens column.

64. At snack time, three friends break a cracker into three equal parts. What portion of the original cracker does each part represent? (Skill 9.1; Easy)

- A. One fourth
- B. One half
- C. One whole
- D. One third

Answer D: One third

If the cracker is broken into three equal parts, each part represents one third of the whole.

TEACHER CERTIFICATION STUDY GUIDE

65. What is the answer to this problem? (Skill 9.2; Easy)

    7 x 9 =

    A. 36
    B. 16
    C. 63
    D. 2

Answer C: 63

The answer to this multiplication problem is 63. It can also be computed by adding seven nine times. 7 + 7 + 7 + 7 + 7 + 7 + 7 + 7 + 7 = 63

66. **Students are making three-dimensional figures by folding a net made up of four equilateral triangles. What three-dimensional figure are the students making? (Skill 9.3; Rigorous)**

    A. Cube
    B. Tetrahedron
    C. Octahedron
    D. Cone

Answer B: Tetrahedron

A net is a two-dimensional figure that can be cut out and folded up to make a three-dimensional solid. A tetrahedron is made by folding a net made up of four equilateral triangles.

67. In which problem would students need an understanding of basic algebraic concepts? (Skill 9.3; Average rigor)

    A. 5 + 6 + 5 =
    B. 3 + 3 + 3 + 3 + 3 =
    C. 10 x 0 =
    D. 3 + ☐ = 9

Answer D: 3 + ☐ = 9

By rearranging the numbers in this equation to calculate for the missing value, students are demonstrating basic algebraic concepts. The other choices are simple computation problems.

68. A teacher plans an activity that involves students calculating how many chair legs are in the classroom, given that there are 30 chairs and each chair has 4 legs. This activity is introducing the ideas of: (Skill 9.4; Average rigor)

   A. Probability
   B. Statistics
   C. Geometry
   D. Algebra

Answer D: Algebra

This activity involves recognizing patterns. It could also involve problem-solving by developing an expression that represents the problem. Activities such as this do not introduce the terms of algebra, but they introduce some of the ideas of algebra.

69. The term "cubic feet" indicates which kind of measurement? (Skill 9.5; Average rigor)

   A. Volume
   B. Mass
   C. Length
   D. Distance

Answer A: Volume

The word *cubic* indicates that this is a term describing volume.

70. Which of the following types of graphs would be best to use to record the eye color of the students in the class? (Skill 9.7; Average rigor)

   A. Bar graph or circle graph
   B. Pictograph or bar graph
   C. Line graph or pictograph
   D. Line graph or bar graph

Answer B: Pictograph or bar graph

A pictograph or a line graph could be used. In this activity, a line graph would not be used because it shows change over time. Although a circle graph could be used to show a percentage of students with brown eyes, blue eyes, etc. that representation would be too advanced for early childhood students.

71. Which type of graph uses symbols to represent quantities? (Skill 9.7; Average rigor)

    A. Bar graph
    B. Line graph
    C. Pictograph
    D. Circle graph

Answer C: Pictograph

A pictograph shows comparison of quantities using symbols. Each symbol represents a number of items.

72. Students are working with a set of rulers and various small objects from the classroom. Which concept are these students exploring? (Skill 9.7; Average rigor)

    A. Volume
    B. Weight
    C. Length
    D. Temperature

Answer C: Length

The use of a ruler indicates that the activity is based on exploring length.

73. Mr. Lacey is using problem solving to help students develop their math skills. The class receives a box of pencils and the pencils have to be divided so that each student has the same number of pencils. What step should come first in problem solving? (Skill 9.8; Rigorous)

    A. Find a strategy to solve the problem
    B. Identify the problem
    C. Count the number of pencils
    D. Make basic calculations

Answer B: Identify the problem

The first step in problem solving is always to identify the problem.

74. What is the foundation of math skills and topics? (Skill 10.1; Easy)

   A. Number sense
   B. Place value
   C. Addition
   D. Computation skills

Answer A: Number sense

As with the phonemic awareness skills in reading, number sense is the foundation upon which all future math topics will be built. Providing young children with the opportunity to interact with objects across multiple contexts will help children begin to develop these concepts of number sense.

75. Which stage of mathematical development do students progress through first? (Skill 10.2; Average rigor)

   A. Use of mental imagery
   B. Use of manipulatives
   C. Use of abstract imagery
   D. Use of pattern recognition

Answer B: Use of manipulatives

Typical mathematical development progresses through three main stages. These stages are: use of manipulatives, use of mental imagery, and use of abstract imagery.

76. Which strategy involves students guessing a solution, checking the answer, and using the outcome to guide the next guess? (Skill 10.4; Average rigor)

   A. Problem-and-solution
   B. Closer-and-closer
   C. Guess-and-check
   D. Try-and-retry

Answer C: Guess-and-check

The guess-and-check strategy calls for students to make an initial guess at the solution, check the answer, and use the outcome to guide the next guess. With each successive guess, the student should get closer to the correct answer. Constructing a table from the guesses can help organize the data.

77. **Students typically learn through: (Skill 10.5; Average rigor)**

    A. Verbal questioning
    B. Visual processing
    C. Deductive reasoning
    D. Inductive reasoning

Answer D: Inductive reasoning

Most children learn about the world by observing specific things and then making generalizations about the things they have observed. This is called inductive reasoning. In

78. **Educational theorists describe three ways of learning: visual, auditory, and kinesthetic. In the classroom, it is important to: (Skill 10.5; Rigorous)**

    A. Teach based on the way of learning closest to your own preference
    B. Teach based on only one of the three ways of learning
    C. Teach based on all the ways of learning in a balanced approach
    D. Teach what is in the curriculum regardless of ways of learning

Answer C: Teach based on all the ways of learning in a balanced approach

Psychologists have known for a long time that there are three ways to learn: (1) visual, (2) auditory and (3) kinesthetic. This is a topic that all teachers should become very familiar with. First find out what style you are, and what methods of learning work best for you. Don't assume that these same methods will necessarily work best for all of your students. Many of them may be natural learners of a different type than you are. Find out what methods work well for these other learning styles and remember to include some of these activities in each lesson you teach

TEACHER CERTIFICATION STUDY GUIDE

79. **What groups or patterns of stars do astronomers use as reference points in the sky? (Skill 11.1; Average rigor)**

    A. Galaxies
    B. Nebula
    C. Constellations
    D. All of the above

Answer C: Constellations

Astronomers use groups or patterns of stars called constellations as reference points to locate other stars in the sky. Familiar constellations include Ursa Major (also known as the big bear) and Ursa Minor (known as the little bear). Within the Ursa Major, the smaller constellation, The Big Dipper is found. Within the Ursa Minor, the smaller constellation, The Little Dipper is found.

80. **What is a change that produces new material known as? (Skill 11.1; Average rigor)**

    A. Physical change
    B. Chemical change
    C. Phase change
    D. Reversible change

Answer B: Chemical change

Matter constantly changes. A physical change is a change that does not produce a new substance. The freezing and melting of water is an example of physical change. A chemical change (or chemical reaction) is any change of a substance into one or more other substances.

81. **Which of the following units is a measure of temperature? (Skill 11.1; Average rigor)**

    A. Watts
    B. Joules
    C. Kelvin
    D. Ounces

Answer C: Kelvin

There are three units that measure temperature: Kelvin, Celsius, and Fahrenheit. Watts is a measure of power, joules are a measure of energy, and ounce is a unit of mass.

EARLY CHILDHOOD EDUCATION

82. **Phase of matter is identified by: (Skill 11.1; Rigorous)**

   A. Shape and mass
   B. Shape and volume
   C. Volume and mass
   D. Shape, mass, and volume

Answer B: Shape and volume

The phase of matter (solid, liquid, or gas) is identified by its shape and volume. A solid has a definite shape and volume. A liquid has a definite volume, but no shape. A gas has no shape or volume.

83. **What should an experiment have a minimum number of to produce accurate and easily correlated results? (Skill 11.2; Average rigor)**

   A. Controls
   B. Variables
   C. Samples
   D. Participants

Answer B: Variables

A variable is a factor or condition that can be changed in an experiment. A good experiment will try to manipulate as few variables as possible, so that the results of the experiment can be identified as occurring because of the change in the variable.

84. **Scientific inquiry begins with: (Skill 11.3; Easy)**

   A. A hypothesis
   B. An observation
   C. A conclusion
   D. An experiment

Answer B: An observation

Observations, however general they may seem, lead scientists to create a viable question and an educated guess (hypothesis) about what to expect. The hypothesis can be tested by an experiment, and a conclusion drawn based on the experiment.

85. What is the main benefit of teaching science in a context where it is relevant to the lives of students? (Skill 11.6; Average rigor)

   A. It reduces costs for the school.
   B. It allows science to be integrated with other subjects.
   C. It increases student motivation.
   D. It promotes independence.

Answer C: It increases student motivation.

If learning is connected to everyday life, students are motivated because they can easily see its relevance. If they are taught about something remote, they will not be able to relate, and the result is decreased interest, decreased motivation to study, and a general decrease in learning.

86. Which term describes an area of lowland formed by soil and sediment deposited at the mouths of rivers? (Skill 12.1; Average rigor)

   A. Plateau
   B. Basin
   C. Mesa
   D. Delta

Answer D: Delta

Deltas are areas of lowlands formed by soil and sediment deposited at the mouths of rivers. The soil is generally very fertile and most fertile river deltas are important crop-growing areas.

87. Which of the following describes how citizens are able to directly participate in their own government by voting for and running for office? (Skill 12.1; Average rigor)

   A. Popular sovereignty
   B. Due process
   C. Rule of law
   D. Democracy

Answer A: Popular sovereignty

Popular sovereignty grants citizens the ability to directly participate in their own government by voting and running for public office. This ideal is based on a belief of equality that holds that all citizens have an equal right to engage in their own governance, and is established in the United States Constitution.

88. What is the study of how a society allocates its scarce resources to satisfy what are basically unlimited and competing wants? (Skill 12.1; Average rigor)

   A. Geography
   B. Economics
   C. Geology
   D. Ecology

Answer B: Economics

Economics is the study of how a society allocates its scarce resources to satisfy what are basically unlimited and competing wants. A fundamental fact of economics is that resources are scarce and that wants are infinite. The fact that scarce resources have to satisfy unlimited wants means that choices have to be made.

89. What is a proposed law called while it is under consideration by Congress? (Skill 12.1; Easy)

   A. Bill
   B. Amendment
   C. Veto
   D. Hopper

Answer A: Bill

The first step in the passing of a law is for the proposed law to be introduced in one of the houses of Congress. A proposed law is called a bill while it is under consideration by Congress. A bill becomes a law once it is signed by the President.

90. Which of the following is NOT one of the basic themes of geography? (Skill 12.1; Rigorous)

   A. Spatial organization
   B. Polarity
   C. Location
   D. Movement

Answer B: Polarity

Geography can be divided into six themes. They are location, special organization, place, human-environment interaction, movement, and regions.

TEACHER CERTIFICATION STUDY GUIDE

91. **Which hypothesis is valid? (Skill 12.2; Rigorous)**

     A. An unknown factor causes tomato plants to produce no fruit sometimes.
     B. A tomato plant will produce tasty fruit if it is watered.
     C. A tomato plant will grow faster in full sunlight than partial sunlight.
     D. A tomato plant given this fertilizer will produce better fruit than all others.

Answer C: A tomato plant will grow faster in full sunlight than partial sunlight.

A valid hypothesis must be able to be proven either right or wrong. "An unknown factor causes tomato plants to produce no fruit sometimes" cannot be proven definitely right or wrong since it is too vague. "A tomato plant will produce tasty fruit if it is watered" cannot be proven either right or wrong because the measurement "tasty" is subjective. "A tomato plant given this fertilizer will produce better fruit than all others" cannot be tested because it cannot be proven that the fruit is better than all others. "A tomato plant will grow faster in full sunlight than partial sunlight" is valid because it can be proven right or wrong.

92. **Which of the following is a means of dispute resolution where a third parties helps to settle the dispute? (Skill 12.7; Average rigor)**

     A. Observation
     B. Intervention
     C. Regulation
     D. Mediation

Answer D: Mediation

Mediation provides a third party who acts as the mediator, listening to both sides and attempting to negotiate a settlement of the dispute. When both parties agree to arbitrate a dispute, a third party hears the positions and issues an opinion, which may be binding on the parties.

93. What should be the first thing taught when introducing dance? (Skill 13.1; Easy)

    A. Rhythm
    B. Feelings
    C. Empathy
    D. Texture

Answer A: Rhythm

Rhythm is the basis of dance. Teaching dance should begin by focusing on rhythm. This can be achieved through activities such as children clapping their hands or tapping their feet to express rhythm.

94. When discussing color, the intensity of a color refers to the color's: (Skill 13.2; Average rigor)

    A. Strength
    B. Value
    C. Lightness or darkness
    D. Associated emotions

Answer A: Strength

Color is an important consideration when viewing art. Color can be considered in more depth by focusing on intensity, which is the strength of the color, and value, which is the lightness or darkness of the color.

95. Which terms refers to the juxtaposition of one or more elements in opposition? (Skill 13.2; Average rigor)

    A. Balance
    B. Contrast
    C. Emphasis
    D. Unity

Answer B: Contrast

The principles of visual are that students should be introduced to include abstract, background, balance, contrast, emphasis, sketch, texture, and unity. Contrast is the juxtaposition of one or more elements in opposition, for the purpose of showing their differences.

TEACHER CERTIFICATION STUDY GUIDE

96. Which activity would be most suitable for beginning students of visual arts? (Skill 13.3; Rigorous)

   A. Analyzing famous works of arts
   B. Reflecting on the possible meanings of art work
   C. Observing the shapes and forms of common objects
   D. Using blocks to construct three dimensional shapes

Answer C: Observing the shapes and forms of common objects

Beginning students of visual arts should be learning to develop their observation skills, such as by observing objects or the environment and noting features such as shape, color, size, repeating patterns, or other aspects. Students can then progress to hands-on activities and later to analysis activities.

97. What should the arts curriculum for early childhood students focus on? (Skill 13.4; Average rigor)

   A. Judgment
   B. Criticism
   C. Interpretation
   D. Experimentation

Answer D: Experimentation

The arts curriculum for early childhood should focus on the experimental and discovery aspects of the arts. The focus should not be on perfect results, open creative processes with little judgment should be emphasized, and criticism should be minimal.

TEACHER CERTIFICATION STUDY GUIDE

98. What venues offer suitable opportunities for allowing students to view live performances? (Skill 13.5; Easy)

   A. Symphonies
   B. Dance companies
   C. Art museums
   D. All of the above

Answer D: All of the above

Live performances are an important part of learning arts and help to develop aesthetic appreciation of the arts. Local performing venues, art museums, symphonies, and dance companies can all provide opportunities for live performances.

99. In which subject is it most important for students to be encouraged to use all five senses? (Skill 13.6; Average rigor)

   A. Visual arts
   B. Music
   C. Movement
   D. Drama

Answer D: Drama

In drama, students should be encouraged to use all five senses. All five senses should be used in observing the environment. Experiences should also be recreated and stories, myths, and fables told that incorporate the use of all five senses.

100. According to Lynn Hallie Najem's research, integrating arts into a primary school curriculum tends to increase students': (Skill 13.7; Rigorous)

   A. Self-esteem
   B. Motivation
   C. Empathy
   D. Attendance

Answer A: Self-esteem

Lynn Hallie Najem's research focused on the benefits of incorporating the arts in the primary school curriculum. It was found that it can increase students' self-esteem and can also increase students' interest in all subject areas.

XAMonline, INC. 21 Orient Ave. Melrose, MA 02176

Toll Free number 800-509-4128

TO ORDER Fax 781-662-9268 OR www.XAMonline.com

ARIZONA Teacher Certification -AEPA- 2007

PO# Store/School:

Address 1:

Address 2 (Ship to other):

City, State Zip

Credit card number _____-_____-_____-_____ expiration_____

EMAIL _____

PHONE   FAX

13# ISBN 2007	TITLE	Qty	Retail	Total
978-1-58197-747-9	AEPA EARLY CHILDHOOD EDUCATION 36			
978-1-58197-738-7	AEPA ELEMENTARY EDUCATION 01			
978-1-58197-703-5	AEPA ENGLISH 02			
978-1-58197-731-8	AEPA SOCIAL STUDIES 03			
978-1-58197-732-5	AEPA BIOLOGY 07			
978-1-58197-722-6	AEPA CHEMISTRY 08			
978-1-58197-748-6	AEPA PHYSICS 09			
978-1-58197-728-8	AEPA MIDDLE SCHOOL MATHEMATICS 37			
978-1-58197-733-2	AEPA MATHEMATICS 10			
978-1-58197-746-2	AEPA HEALTH 18			
978-1-58197-734-9	AEPA LIBRARY-EDUCATIONAL MEDIA 12			
978-1-58197-729-5	AEPA ART SAMPLE TEST 13			
978-1-58197-735-6	AEPA SPANISH 15			
978-1-58197-743-1	AEPA HISTORY 05			
978-1-58197-736-3	AEPA FRENCH SAMPLE TEST 16			
978-1-58197-739-4	AEPA SPECIAL EDUCATION - EMOTIONAL DISABILTIES 24			
978-1-58197-737-0	AEPA SPECIAL EDUCATION: CROSS-CATEGORY 22			
978-1-58197-745-5	AEPA CONSTITUTION OF THE UNITED STATES AND ARIZONA 33			
978-1-58197-740-0	AEPA POLITICAL SCIENCE/AMERICAN GOVERNMENT 06			
978-1-58197-741-7	AEPA PROFESSIONAL KNOWLEDGE - ELEMENTARY & SECONDARY 91, 92			
			SUBTOTAL	
			Ship	$8.25
			TOTAL	

CPSIA information can be obtained at www.ICGtesting.com
Printed in the USA
BVOW10s0547261214

380722BV00002B/7/A